SOCIAL CHARACTER IN A MEXICAN VILLAGE
ERICH FROMM AND MICHAEL MACCOBY

SOCIAL CHARACTER

ERICH FROMM
MICHAEL MACCOBY

IN A
MEXICAN
VILLAGE

A Sociopsychoanalytic Study

Prentice-Hall, Inc., Englewood Cliffs, New Jersey

SOCIAL CHARACTER IN A MEXICAN VILLAGE
ERICH FROMM AND MICHAEL MACCOBY

P-13-815670-0
C-13-815688-3

Library of Congress Catalog Card Number 77-129337

Printed in the United States of America

Current printing (last digit):
10   9   8   7   6   5   4   3   2

PRENTICE-HALL INTERNATIONAL, INC., *London*
PRENTICE-HALL OF AUSTRALIA, PTY., LTD., *Sydney*
PRENTICE-HALL OF CANADA, LTD., *Toronto*
PRENTICE-HALL OF INDIA PRIVATE LIMITED, *New Delhi*
PRENTICE-HALL OF JAPAN, INC., *Tokyo*

Contents

Foreword

While the motivations for undertaking this research are explained in Chapter 1, this foreword is meant to give a short history of its development.

In 1957 one of the authors (Fromm) had developed a general plan for the study and chosen the particular village for two reasons: one, that it was rather representative of many villages in the fruitful valley areas south and southwest of Mexico City; it was representative, inasmuch as its inhabitants were of mixed Spanish-Indian extraction (*mestizo*), that its method of agriculture and its economic structure was essentially the same as that of hundreds of other villages in the same climate and altitude. Furthermore, it was chosen because the village was an *ejido* (made up of small plots given to the villagers as a result of the Revolution of 1910-20), and we were particularly interested to see the influence of the ejido structure on the personality of the inhabitants.[1] The other reason for choosing it was that it had a Center for Rural Welfare (*Centro de Bienestar Rural*) established by the Department of Public Health and Welfare, which facilitated our access to and acceptance by the village. The late Dr. José Zozaya, who showed a great interest in the study, was particularly helpful in creating interest in this project in the Department of Public Health. We also acknowledge gratefully the financial contribution to the study from this Department of the Mexican Government; although limited, it was nevertheless very helpful in the first steps of the investigation.

In the first phase of the study, all collaborators including the Director worked without monetary compensation. They were mainly members of the Mexican Psychoanalytic Society, specifically Dr. Aniceto Aramoni,

---

[1] See Chapter 3 for a fuller description of an ejido. The problem of how typical is the village will be discussed in Chapter 5.

Dr. José Díaz, Dr. Jorge Velasco Alzaga, Dr. Alfonso Millán, Dr. Guillermo Dávila, Dr. Francisco Garza, Dr. Jorge Silva, Dr. Armando Hinojosa, Dr. Ramón de la Fuente, Dr. Jorge Derbez, and Dr. Arturo Higareda. Dr. Millán and Dr. Aramoni were particularly helpful in the original formulation of the questionnaire. Dr. Millán also participated in the general planning and by arranging for the exhibition of educational movies for the villagers, which continued for over a few years. This presentation of movies not only was a stimulus that made the villagers more willing to cooperate with the study, but it also resulted in interesting observations, collected by Dr. Millán, about the reactions of the people to these presentations.

In 1958 Dr. G. Gilbert volunteered his services to the study for nine months; he was assisted by Dr. R. Núñez and Dr. Alicia Quiroz in administering the Rorschach test to a sample of the population consisting of 110 inhabitants. The results of some of these tests were used to compare the scoring of character from the projective interview with character scored from the Rorschach (see Appendix).

During the same period, Mr. Paul Senior, then a student of psychology, came for two summers to administer Rorschach tests to the children, the results of which gave us an important preliminary view of child character. He also administered the Andersen story test, collected dreams, and applied a shorter interview covering basic attitudes and the child's view of his parents.

The first year was mainly used to establish a closer contact with the villagers, which eventually led to their willingness to participate in answering the questionnaire. Since, as will be shown in the text, these were long and required the taking down of the individual answers, the sessions often lasted from three to six hours for one questionnaire, not counting the additional time the interviewer lost by looking for the villagers when they did not show up, misunderstood appointments, etc. Furthermore, many questions of the first preliminary questionnaire were tried out and modified in this process. By the beginning of 1958 it was clear, however, that the study could not be continued on the basis of voluntary participation, since nobody, including the director, could afford to devote the necessary time to it without some compensation. The study was put on a new footing by the willingness of the Foundations Fund for Research in Psychiatry to support the study by a grant (FFRP Grant 58-176). This first grant was later increased to make it possible for the study to add a full-time associate to the staff. Later in 1958 Dr. Theodore Schwartz, an anthropologist experienced in field research and statistical methods, accepted this position, and his wife, Dr. Lola Romanucci Schwartz, at that time a doctoral student of anthropology, volunteered her valuable cooperation for the duration of their stay with this study, from 1958 to 1961. Their work was of decisive importance for the progress of the study. They contributed in many different ways, mainly in the following: first, by their close contact with the villagers (they resided in the village for 13 months, and outside of this period visited it three or four times per week) they were able to collect a rich body of direct observations which made it possible to get a vivid picture of the villagers to complement that from the testing and other artificial devices. Their observations permitted us to know a great deal about the intimate life of the villagers, to form an idea, for instance, of which individuals were severe or mild alcoholics, which people were the most and the least successful, about their mores and their married life. All these observations permitted us to judge to what extent the answers we got to the questionnaire were ideological or corresponded to facts in the lives of the villagers. Dr. Lola Schwartz wrote her doctoral thesis on the villagers' concepts of morality, and Dr. Theodore Schwartz set forth a wealth of observations and theoretical ideas in a large manuscript, so far unpublished.

Furthermore, Theodore Schwartz conducted, and also interpreted, a number of interviews with the villagers and in this way contributed very directly to the material which is used in this study. Eventually, he organized and helped to execute an economic census which, as the reader will find in Chapter 3, is of basic importance to the study; he also developed the index of socioeconomic status, which resulted in a very satisfactory analysis of the position of each inhabitant in the socioeconomic structure.

The time required for the completion of the study turned out to be much longer than had been estimated originally. It was possible to continue the study only because of the continued help of the Foundations Fund for Research in Psychiatry, which renewed the grant for the periods 1959-1961 (FFRP Grant 58-190), 1961-1962 (FFRP Grant 60-224), and 1962-1963 (FFRP Grant 62-248). This helped to make it possible not only to pay salaries for the Director of the study and the Chief Assistant, but also to compensate a number of co-workers who helped in the testing and in other activities in the village, to be described later.

In 1960 Dr. Michael Maccoby joined the study, several months before Dr. T. Schwartz and Dr. L. Schwartz had to leave Mexico. He was supported by a research and training fellowship from the Institute of Mental Health, U. S. Public Health Service. His emphasis was similar to that of the other author. He came to be trained by Fromm in psychoanalysis, and shared Fromm's emphasis on the depth psychological aspect of the social character and on the usefulness of the interpretative questionnaire. By frequent visits to the village and numerous meetings with the adults, adolescents and children of the village (individually and in groups), Maccoby maintained the close contact established by Drs. T. and L. Schwartz, and added to our knowledge of the villagers. He was in particularly close touch with the adolescents by supervising the boys' club (see Chapter 11) and, assisted by Dr. Nancy Modiano, studied the children in the village (see Chapter 9).[2] Most important, he revised the scoring of all the interviews, of the Rorschach and TAT tests taken so far, and administered more tests. He was assisted by Dr. Isidro Galván. He also planned and carried out the statistical analysis of the quantitative data. He shares with Fromm the responsibility for the final structure of the study, the analysis of the findings and the presentation as it appears in this volume. In the continuous discussion of the two authors over eight years, a fruitful interchange of ideas occurred, which up to the time of the final revision of the manuscript led to new insights and formulations, some of which had to be omitted from this presentation for reasons of space.

Another person whose help was of great importance to the study was Dr. Felipe Sánchez, who resided in the village for many years as head of the Center for Rural Welfare, and as physician. He helped a great deal by his close contact with the villagers, and by his knowledge of their behavior. He did much of the actual interviewing with supervision from the authors and worked on the socioeconomic census together with the Schwartzes.

During the whole study a permanent seminar took place in which Fromm discussed with those who were participating in the work of the questionnaire the theoretical questions of psychoanalytic characterology and social character, and the methods of interpretation. In these discussions many of the important theoretical and clinical problems were discussed, and a certain amount of common understanding was achieved.

While the village study was carried on, Dr. Guillermo Dávila organized a study of urban (Mexico City) workers with the same methods we applied in the village. It was hoped that significant data would emerge with regard to the difference between these two social groups. Regrettably, Dr. Dávila died in 1968 before his study was sufficiently completed to allow comparisons.

In the summer of 1963, when the grant from the Foundations Fund for Research in Psychiatry expired, all the material had been collected, but the revision of the material and its analysis was not finished. In the following years both authors worked together in revising and reanalyzing the material, in clarifying many difficult problems which had arisen, and in writing the final text. Due to an illness of Fromm and professional obligations of Maccoby, this work proceeded more slowly than had been anticipated, and was completely finished only now at the writing of this foreword.

Among the many others who worked for the study, and who have not been mentioned so far, were the following: Miss Guadelupe

[2] Dr. Modiano collaborated in formulating the material on the development of the children, reported in Chapter 10.

Castro, and Miss Virginia Heras; Miss Bertha Javkin and Mrs. Italia Millán participated in the study by administering projective tests to the villagers.

Mrs. Marta Salinas did most interesting work from the middle of 1959 to 1962 by giving a course in literature, using books which attracted the villagers' attention in line with their knowledge and interests. While only a small core group attended the readings regularly, and also borrowed books to read aside from the regular sessions, there was a larger and somewhat more fluctuating attendance. Her work, in which with great understanding of the psychology of the peasant she gained their interest and cooperation, showed interesting results for the possibilities and limitations of a direct cultural influence.

Of great help for the study was the cooperation of the American Friends Service Committee through their center, the Casa de los Amigos in Mexico City. The head of this center, E. Duckles, showed great understanding and sympathy for our study, and from 1961 through 1963 made it possible for members of the group selected by the Friends for work in Mexico to participate in our study by assisting Dr. Maccoby in the work of the boys' club. These included: Thomas Fletcher, David Spinny, and Ned Filor. We also benefited from the work of Dr. Patricia Lander and Miss Edith Churchill who helped organize a library for the children.

Mrs. Mary Elmendorf showed her interest and sympathy in our work by aiding in equipping the boys' club with tools and materials. Animals from the Heifer Project were made available due to the help of Mr. Paul Stone.

Dr. Adan Graetz prepared and initiated a study of the prevalence of parasitosis in the village, which was carried out by Dr. F. Biagi and his assistants from the Medical School of the National University of Mexico. The study led also to a program of treatment under the direction of Dr. Biagi.

We also wish to thank Professor Carlos Hank Gonzáles (now Governor of the State of Mexico) and Lic. Ernesto Millán for giving us the opportunity to visit and learn about the CONASUPO program, described in Chapter 10, and Father William Wasson for the rich information given us about the institution he founded.

As far as the statistical work of the study is concerned, we owe sincere thanks to Professor Louis McQuitty, now at the University of Miami. He was most helpful and cooperative in discussing with us the statistical problems of our study, making us thoroughly acquainted with his methods of factor analysis and typal analysis, and made available to us the use of the computer and the assistance of the facilities of Michigan State University for the statistical elaboration of our data.

We are also particularly indebted to Professor Arthur Couch, then of Harvard University, now at the Tavistock Clinic, for his advice and very generous help in carrying out the factor analysis of adult character which is reported in Chapter 5.

We also wish to thank Dr. David Peizer of the Center for Advanced Study in the Behavioral Sciences for his suggestions about interpreting the factor analysis.

We are also indebted to Professor Sergio Beltrán of the Centro Electrónico de Cálculo at the National Autonomous University of Mexico for his cooperation and help and, with the assistance of the computers of the Center, for other statistical processing of our material. Mrs. G. U. de Beltrán was very helpful during that time in assisting us in this work, as was Mr. Adrian Cañedo, who served as statistical assistant to Dr. Maccoby and contributed ideas concerning ways of analyzing the data.

We are also grateful to Professor George M. Foster of the University of California and Professor Albert Hirschman of Harvard University for helpful comments on earlier drafts of the manuscript.

So many people were helpful in this study that it is difficult to express our indebtedness to each one in the proper proportion. But in concluding we want to express our gratitude not only to the Foundations Fund for Research in Psychiatry as an institution, but quite specifically to Professor Frederick Redlich who, together with Dr. David Shakow of the National Institute of Mental Health Education and Welfare, visited the study in Mexico and made valuable suggestions.

We deeply appreciate the Fund's unwavering interest and sympathetic understanding for the unforeseen difficulties which delayed the completion of the study. We are also indebted to Dr. Max M. Levin, Executive Officer of the Foundations Fund, and to Dr. Clark J. Bailey, his successor, for their interest. And we wish to thank the Medical School of the National Autonomous University of Mexico (U.N.A.M.) for administering the grant.

We also acknowledge gratefully a grant from the Albert and Mary Lasker Foundation, which enabled us to meet additional expenses at a time after the grant from the Foundations Fund had expired, a year's fellowship from the Center for Advanced Study in the Behavioral Sciences to Dr. Maccoby, which gave him the opportunity to spend more time rewriting parts of the study, and a fellowship from the Institute for Policy Studies where he worked on final revisions.

One last remark is necessary to explain why we speak in the title of "a Mexican village," rather than mention the name of the village. The reason lies in the fact that we want to do our utmost to protect the anonymity of the villagers, without whose cooperation this study would not have been possible. We made the promise that their identity would be protected, and we want to be faithful to this promise. However, the fact that we do not mention the name of the village is only of minor importance in comparison with the consequences that this respect for the villagers' anonymity has for the substance of the study. We could have added many illustrative descriptions of individuals, and particularly, we could have followed our desire to publish a short "case history" of villagers representing the various character types with which we deal. This, however, would have been possible only by revealing details which would have permitted identifying individuals in this small community of only about 162 households. (In a study of a population of several thousands the possibility of identification is reduced to a minimum.) There was often the temptation to present illustrations which would have greatly enriched this study. Confronted with the alternative of violating the privacy of the villagers and the promise we gave them and, on the other hand, omitting valuable material from this work, we chose the latter alternative.

ERICH FROMM
MICHAEL MACCOBY
February, 1970
Cuernavaca, Mexico

1

The Social Character of the Peasant and Problems of Methodology

This study deals with the social character of the Mexican peasant. Its aim is to analyze the interrelations and interactions between his emotional attitudes rooted in his character and the socioeconomic conditions under which he lives.

THE PEASANT

In this introductory chapter we need to discuss the basic concepts in our investigations: the concept of the "peasant" and of peasant character; the dynamic concept of character and of social character, and the problem of methodology in the study of the social character.

What is a peasant? In the following we call peasants such villagers whose main occupation is farming, although they may also work as potters or fishermen. The English word peasant, like the Spanish word *campesino,* means a man of the countryside, of the land. However, peasants are distinguished from both modern farmers and many indigenous tribesmen who also work the land.

Unlike that of the modern farmer, the peasant's mode of production is highly individualistic. The peasant works close to the margin of subsistence. He does not have the capital or the technology employed by the modern farmer. He works alone or with his family, with one or several hired hands, using no more complicated tools than a hoe and a plow.

The peasant differs from most indigenous tribesmen in that he is dependent on the urban society, economically, culturally, and politically. He must sell his produce in urban markets, and in exchange he needs money to buy the goods produced in the city. His religion, many of his medical

1

practices,[1] and much of his folklore (many games and songs) were developed in the city. Furthermore, the peasant is subject to the government of the city or state, which levies his taxes, makes and enforces laws, and drafts him into its armies. In contrast, many primitive tribesmen live in isolated villages which are self-controlled, and culturally and economically autonomous; compared to these tribesmen, peasants are relatively powerless in making basic decisions that affect their lives.[2]

In this definition of peasantry, one theoretical problem remains. How do we define the agricultural worker who is not an independent small farmer, but who works as a *peon,* or day laborer (*jornalero*), on a plantation or *hacienda?* Like the peasant, the peon uses rudimentary methods. Like the free peasant he depends on the city for his culture and religion,

---

[1] This definition of a peasant is essentially in accord with that of most anthropologists, such as Redfield (1956), Foster (1967), and Wolf (1955, 1966). Foster quotes Kroeber's statement that "Peasants constitute part societies with part cultures." They are "definitely rural—yet live in relation to market towns; they form a class segment of a larger population which usually contains also urban centers. . . . They lack the isolation, the political autonomy, and self-sufficiency of tribal populations, but their local units retain much of their old identity, integration, and attachment to soil and cults." See "What is a Peasant," in Potter, Diaz, and Foster (1967), p. 2ff. Foster, like a number of anthropologists, stresses a "structural and relational" definition of peasantry—the peasant's relative powerlessness and tie to the city—rather than his mode of production. Although he states that most peasants are agriculturists, he notes that some are not. While we agree that the peasant's relationship to the larger society is important for the understanding of his character, we consider the mode of production an essential element in the definition of peasantry and an essential factor in the formation of peasant character. Furthermore, we consider that the mode of production of the independent peasant is closer to that of the independent village potter or fisherman than it is to the modern farmer. Both work alone or with their families; both employ rudimentary methods; both live on the margin of subsistence without the possibility of accumulating capital.

In considering the lack of cooperation and class consciousness of the French peasant, Karl Marx pointed to the importance of the peasant mode of production in forming political attitudes. In *The 18th Brumaire of Louis Napoleon,* he wrote:

> "Throughout the country they live in almost identical conditions, but enter very little into relationships with one another. Their mode of production isolates them, instead of bringing them into mutual contact. The isolation is intensified by the inadequacy of all the means of communication . . . and poverty. Their farms are so small that there is practically no scope for division of labour . . . Among the peasantry therefore there can be no diversity of development, no differentiation of talents, no wealth of social relationship. Each family is almost self-sufficient, producing on its own plot of land the greater part of its requirements, and thus providing itself with the necessities of life through an interchange with nature rather than by means of intercourse with society."

[2] Even many practices of village curers (*curanderos*) come from the city. As Foster (1967) has shown, the principal system to which health and medical ideas and practices in many Mexican villages conform "is a folk variant of Greek humoral pathology, based on the Hippocratic doctrine of the four humors, elaborated by the Roman physician Galen, further developed in the Arab world by such men as Rhazes (c. 850-925) and Avicenna (980-1037), and transmitted to Spain when that country was dominated by the Moslems." (P. 185.)

and he is even more powerless, economically and politically. The essential difference lies in the fact that the peasant owns—legally or factually—his land and is dependent only on nature and the market; on the other hand the peon resembles a serf more than a free peasant. The peon class might be defined in S. Mintz's terms as "rural proletarians." Peasant villages, such as the one we have studied, frequently have a population made up of both peasants and peons.

Over half the population of the world still lives in peasant villages. Increasingly, peasants are being subjected to new pressures as most countries, with the exception of those that are highly industrialized, are trying to move from an agricultural to a partly or mainly industrial production. In the process of industrial development, a number of people from the countryside are swelling the population of the cities where to make a living they must adapt to work that is different from what they have known before. At the same time, new demands for greater production are being made on the farmers who are expected to feed growing populations and support the process of industrialization. The peasant is expected to change both his attitudes and techniques to satisfy new goals set by the city.

The traditional peasant agriculture produced only the surplus necessary to provide the food for a small and relatively stable population. However, in the modern world, agriculture is expected to provide for an ever-growing population. Technological advances in agriculture offer the promise of greatly increasing production. For the first time in thousands of years the human and animal driven plough, in its more or less developed forms, is being replaced by the tractor, and the work done by the human arm can be done by machines for ploughing, planting, and harvesting. New seeds requiring careful fertilization, such as the Mexican dwarf wheat, promise much greater yields to feed hungry populations. The "peasant" can become a "farmer" who uses techniques and methods entirely different from those that characterized agriculture in past history.

How does this change take place? What does it require humanly? Not only does the peasant have to use complicated machines, but optimal production also requires a change from his traditional individualistic form of work. To learn new techniques, he must cooperate with extension services, try out hybrid seeds and new methods, and work in coordination with others. He may need to cooperate with others by fitting himself into an overall plan as it exists in large farming enterprises, be they cooperative, capitalist, or communist.

From the traditional peasant's point of view, the new agricultural technology may be felt as more a threat than an opportunity. It requires that he learn new skills and change deep-rooted attitudes. Yet, if he does not adapt to the new technology, he runs the risk of being overrun. In capitalistic countries, he is unable to compete with the agricultural entrepreneurs who are the first to employ the new methods. In communist countries, peasants have been forced even more directly to adapt to the new system. In all of these countries, it is not possible for the peasant to stand still. The new technology and social forms have upset the traditional society.

It is often assumed that the new tasks and the changed ways of functioning—either for industrial work or mechanized farming—require merely schooling and some technical training. From this viewpoint "education" is all the peasant needs in order to adjust himself to the demands of industrial society. However, experiences throughout the world show that schooling and technical knowledge are not enough to transform the old-fashioned peasant into a modern farmer even when he wants to learn the new methods. Indeed, as we shall see in Chapter 3, the schooling received by villagers is not likely to be of use to them in their work. Those who have studied the problem closely conclude that a change of attitudes, or, as we would prefer to say, "character," is required before literacy and new technological knowledge will make any decisive difference.[3] It is a most interesting fact that peasants in most parts of the world (the exception seems to be Southeast Asia) share by and large the same attitudes and behavior traits. They are highly individualistic, conservative, suspicious and reluctant to spend.[4] It seems to us, as we shall try to explain later, that this attitude fits in best with the mode of production of traditional agriculture, while it does not fit in with the requirements of mechanized or industrial agriculture. The farmer in the industrial society must be open to new ideas, cooperative to a certain degree, capable of planning and investing for the future, and hence willing to spend something now, the reward for which accrues only at a future time. In all countries in the process of industrialization—both capitalistic and communistic—a lag is to be found between new technological possibilities and the peasant's ability to adapt his personality to making use of the new ways. This holds true for most countries within the Soviet bloc, for most of Asia, for countries in the Mediterranean area, as well as for a number of Latin American countries. (The same difficulty existed, of course, for the transformation of

---

3 For example, Max F. Millikan and David Hapgood in summarizing the conclusions of a six weeks conference of 44 students of agriculture in underdeveloped countries write the following: "A final generalization is that the fundamental problem confronting agriculture is not so much the adoption and spread of any particular set of research institutions; rather, it is to build into the whole agricultural process—from the farmer to the minister of agriculture—an attitude of experiment, trial and error, continued innovation, and adaptation of new ideas. Without this change in attitudes, improvements in performance, though they may occur, will be halting and transitory and thus will provide no lasting contribution to agricultural productivity." See *No Easy Harvest, The Dilemma of Agriculture in Underdeveloped Countries* (Boston: Little, Brown and Company, 1967), p. 27.

4 See Chapter 6.

the peasant in Northern Europe and the United States from the 19th to the beginning of the 20th century. This transformation, however, was a very slow one compared with the rapid pace of industrialization taking place now and expected in the future in many of the countries just mentioned.)

In discussing the future of the peasant an important issue needs to be raised. The general trend in the world is determined by the attempt to employ more advanced technology everywhere. This means that agriculture should develop in the direction of industrial society, implying optimal use of machinery and the rational organization of work. If this were all, there would be no problem, except the technical one. But together with the new techniques go new values which tend towards maximal consumption, the subordination of man under the requirements of the machine and profit, alienation, the destruction of traditional peasant culture with its trans-utilitarian value of enjoyment of life in art, dance, music, and rituals. It seems that the trend throughout the world is toward technical improvement of agriculture (even though so far very little has been done in this direction) and the destruction of life-centered values. To most people, this may present no problem; they are willing to bury the traditional culture if the new "progressive" spirit is furthered.

For some people, like the authors of this book who are concerned about the high price in human terms which is paid for industrialization, the question arises whether a new industrialized agriculture could be created which could be blended with the humanistic spirit (which found one expression in traditional culture). We shall return to this question in Chapter 10, but we raise the issue here because it is the perspective under which this whole book must be understood.

Many attempts to persuade, encourage, or force the peasant to change have failed, in part because planners have not understood or respected his character. Peasants in communist countries have preferred to kill their cattle rather than to give the government the larger part of it, or to give it to a commune. Often they have remained adamant even when it seemed that compromise might have been better from the standpoint of their long-range material advantage.[5]

---

[5] There are some programs that have succeeded because they have taken these emotional attitudes into account. In Chapter 10, we refer to the CONASUPO program in Mexico and to the Yugoslavian programs. However, it must be remembered that higher income as an incentive which is generally supposed to operate universally has this motivating force only in certain societies like the industrial feudal society of Mexico. Higher income as such was not a generally operative incentive for the medieval peasant. The striving of large parts of the population was not to fall below the traditional standard of living. Greed for profit was restricted to a relatively small group of enterprising individuals who were adventurous, rather than typically representative of the majority. Cf. the writings of Max Weber and R. H. Tawney on this point.

In many predominantly agricultural countries, however, certain changes are taking place in the attitudes of peasants due to the fact that radio sets and at least a few television sets are now to be found in many villages and furthermore to the fact that because of improved transportation many peasants visit larger cities. Their appetites are whetted for the commodities which the industrial production offers. As the material products of the industrial society appear more attractive, the peasants become less satisfied with the traditional standard of living and traditional pleasures. They want money to buy the consumer goods advertised on radio and television and to participate in the glamour of the new industrial culture. Many of the Mexican peasants used to attain this aim, although in a very modest way, by going as seasonal workers (*braceros*) to the United States and returning with wrist watches, radio sets, and secondhand cars. Frequently, those with more initiative chose this solution, and in this way the village was often drained of its most energetic and enterprising elements. But this solution of a symbiotic relationship with a foreign economy and culture was, of course, no solution for the Mexican peasant in general, even while it lasted. Unless his whole agricultural system is made more productive and leaves him with a greater surplus, he is simply not able to buy the commodities he wants, and his "rising expectations" lead to disappointment and to apathy. Very often he leaves the countryside under the illusion that just by being in the city he can participate in the brilliant life he has seen on the movie screen, only to find that his living conditions have not improved, and that he is forced into a slum existence. A much better system of schooling in the village, and industrial training courses might improve his chances in the city. But even if schooling and industrial training were greatly improved, his personal character would still be an obstacle to making a good living. Punctuality, discipline, planning, abstract thinking are necessary to make the best use of such new training possibilities even if they existed more amply.[6] Without these traits, a person cannot rise above the level of simple manual work. The result of all these circumstances is that, on the one hand, while industry needs skilled workers, the increasing numbers of unprepared peasants coming to the city do not fulfill the requirements of the industrial society; and on the other hand, not many peasants who remain in the village fulfill the conditions for a more advanced method of agricultural organization.

Once one's attention is turned to these considerations, the study of the character of the peasant, and particularly the interaction of psychological and socioeconomic factors in the formation and possible change of his character becomes relevant for all agricultural societies in transition:

---

[6] For a study of differences in the cognitive style of village and urban children, see Maccoby and Modiano (1969).

we believe that a better understanding of the Mexican peasant will further an understanding of the possibilities for the peasant in other societies.

THE DYNAMIC CONCEPT OF CHARACTER

There is, of course, a considerable literature on the peasant, written from a sociological and anthropological standpoint, although this literature is by no means as extended as one would expect, considering the importance of the problem.[7] Most of the literature on peasants is written from the standpoint of describing behavior traits, attitudes, ideas and economic systems of peasants, while this study is a sociopsychological one, focused around the dynamic concept of character and "social character." We believe that just as psychoanalysis studies the character of an individual in terms of analyzing the underlying forces which in a structuralized form make up his character and motivate him to feel and think in certain ways, the character common to a whole group, *social character,*[8] has the same dynamic function and can be studied empirically. The salient point here is our psychoanalytic conviction that the behavioristic concepts conventionally used in the study of peasants and other social groups, do not penetrate to the psychic forces which motivate and feed the attitudes and behavior traits.

This brings up the old disagreement between psychoanalytically and behavioristically oriented social scientists. The majority of social scientists criticize psychoanalysis for what they consider to be a lack of scientific method; the psychoanalysts have retorted that with the narrow (and old-fashioned) criteria of the scientific method, the behaviorists deal only with the less important problems, rather than find new methods which suit the more important ones. However this may be, we cannot hope, in presenting this study, to convince those social scientists who have no confidence in the psychoanalytic theory; on the contrary, its shortcomings may even reinforce their negative position. On the other hand, we cannot even count on the

---

[7] For an extensive bibliography on peasant studies, see J. M. Potter, M. N. Diaz and G. M. Foster (1967).

[8] The concept of social character was originally developed by E. Fromm. He spoke of the "character matrix common to all members of the group" in *Die Entwicklung des Christusdogmas,* Imago, 16, 1930. (English translation: *The Dogma of Christ* [New York: Holt, Rinehart & Winston, Inc., 1963]). In *Ueber Methode und Aufgabe einer analytischen Sozialpsychologie,* Zeitschrift fur Sozialforschung, 1, 1932, Hirschfeld Verlag, Leipzig, pp. 28-54, he used the term "the drive structure, (Triebstruktur), the libidinous and largely unconscious attitude of a group," and in *Die Psychoanalytische Charakterologie und ihre Bedeutung fur die Sozialpsychologie* (ibid. 3, 1932), he spoke of the "character" of a society. In *Escape from Freedom,* (New York: Holt, Rinehart & Winston, Inc., 1941), the English equivalent "social character" was used. The two papers of 1932 are to be published in an English translation in 1970 in E. Fromm, *The Crisis of Psychoanalysis* (New York: Holt, Rinehart and Winston, Inc.).

sympathy of many of our psychoanalytic colleagues, because the revisions of Freud's theories which we have made will appear to some of them as an abandonment of Freud's essential findings, although we ourselves, together with not a few others, believe that they constitute a needed development of his theories, and an affirmation of what is their essence.

In publishing this work we count on having the attention of those who are not dogmatically sealed off from at least being interested in a new venture: the application of psychoanalytic categories to the study of social groups, by the minute examination of the personality of each member of the group, by the simultaneous and equally minute observation of all socio-economic data and cultural patterns, and, eventually, by the attempt to use refined statistical methods for the analysis of the data.

In developing our theme and our methods, we were aware that even more than in most research, we would have to learn while we were working, and indeed had we had the knowledge we have now at the beginning, we would have improved the study considerably. But we are not too much disturbed by this, because we are interested not only in the correctness of all our conclusions and hypotheses, but equally in demonstrating a new method for the application of psychoanalysis to social science.

The behavioristic view is that behavior is the ultimately attainable and at the same time scientifically satisfactory datum in the study of man. From this standpoint behavior traits and character traits are identical and from a positivistic standpoint, even the concept "character" may not be legitimate in scientific parlance.

From the psychoanalytic standpoint, a character trait is an energy-charged part of the whole system-character, which can be understood fully only if one understands the whole system. Character traits are the roots of behavior traits, and one character trait may express itself in one or more different behavior traits; its existence may not be conscious, but it can be inferred from various phenomena (like small details of behavior, dreams, etc.).

Behavior, which is essentially an adaptation to realistic circumstances, changes relatively easily when circumstances make another kind of behavior more advisable; character traits usually persist even when they become harmful under changed circumstances (especially neurotic character traits).

The discovery of the dynamic concept of character was undoubtedly one of Freud's greatest contributions to the science of man. He had begun to develop it in his first paper on the Anal Character (1908). The essential point of that paper was that certain behavior traits, namely stubbornness, orderliness, and parsimony, were more often than not to be found together as a syndrome of traits. Furthermore, wherever that syndrome existed, one could find peculiarities in the sphere of toilet training and in the vicissitudes of sphincter control and in certain behavioral traits related to bowel movements and feces. Thus, Freud's first step was to discover a syndrome of behavioral traits and to relate them to the way the child acted (in part as a response to certain demands by those who trained him) in the sphere of bowel movements and elimination. His brilliant and creative step was to relate these two sets of behavioral complexes by a theoretical consideration based on a previous assumption about the evolution of the libido. This assumption was that during an early phase of childhood development, after the mouth has ceased to be the main organ of lust and satisfaction, the anus becomes an important erogenous zone, and most libidinal wishes are centered around the process of the retention and evacuation of the excrements. His next conclusion was to explain the syndrome of behavioral traits as sublimation of, or reaction formation against, the libidinous satisfaction or frustration of anality. Stubbornness and parsimony were supposed to be the sublimation of the original refusal to give up the pleasure of retaining the stool; orderliness the reaction formation against the original desire of the infant to evacuate whenever he pleased. In this story Freud gave an explanation for the traits which were part of the original anal syndrome, which was later enlarged to comprise a number of other traits.[9] Freud showed that the three original traits of the syndrome, which until then appeared to be quite unrelated among each other, formed part of a structure or system, because they were all rooted in the same source of anal libido which manifests itself in these traits, either directly or by reaction formation or sublimation. In this way Freud was able to explain why these traits are charged with energy and, in fact, very resistant to change. In principle the same procedure was applied to the study of the oral-receptive and the oral-sadistic character and to the concept of the genital character. The most important later addition to the concept of the anal character was the assumption that sadistic behavior was also part of the anal syndrome.

The fruitfulness of this new dynamic concept of character for the study of individual or social behavior is immediately apparent. A simple example will tend to clarify this: If a person is poor, his behavior may be a hoarding or stingy one, that is to say, he shows great reluctance to make any but the most necessary expenditures. This can, of course, be a behavioral trait responding to the necessities of the realistic situation. A poor person is forced to behave that way if he is to survive. Should his economic situation improve, he would also change his behavior accordingly and no longer insist on avoiding any expense which is not absolutely necessary. We call such a person thrifty or parsimonious. However, when parsimoniousness is

---

[9] Traits which were added later to the original syndrome are exaggerated cleanliness and punctuality; they are also to be understood as reaction formations to the original anal impulses.

a character trait it exists regardless of the economic circumstances of the person. When we speak of this type of a characterologically thrifty person we speak of a "miser," and by this we refer to his character rather than only to thrifty behavior.[10] As long as such a person is poor, one will of course be prone to explain his behavior as a reaction to his poverty. But such an explanation fails if the miser, having become rich, continues to act according to his previous pattern.

That miserliness as a character trait is not learned, nor an adaptive response, is borne out by the following considerations: (1) Miserliness is to be found among people for whom it was never adaptive and who never learned it.[11] (2) The miser acts according to the hoarding principle not only with regard to material things, where savings might be rationalized as being useful, but also to save his physical, sexual, or mental energy, because he feels any expenditure of energy as a loss. (3) When the miser acts true to his pattern he experiences a strong satisfaction, which can even sometimes be observed in his smug facial expression. (4) Any attempt to change his behavior pattern meets with great difficulties (resistance). Many a miser who lives in a milieu where miserly behavior is unpopular would love to change his behavior pattern, yet often he cannot. If this were only a matter of learned behavior this difficulty would be hard to understand. But it becomes very understandable if one thinks of it as a trait charged with energy, which is part of a character system and which could change only if the whole system changed. If the behaviorist point were right, then it would be indeed difficult to understand why individuals or classes often act against their own interests, even against their interest in survival, when rationally and realistically alternative behavior patterns are at hand. In fact, all the irrational passions of man, of which history is a sad record, are nonadaptive and even harmful. The frequent inability of societies to change their traditional character traits for the sake of adaptive ones is one of the causes of their destruction.

Courage may serve as another example for the difference between behavior trait and character trait. Courage as behavior trait might thus be described: a behavior of a person who in the pursuit of an aim is not easily deterred by danger to life, health, freedom, or property. Such a definition virtually covers all kinds of courageous behavior.

The picture, however, is different if we take into account the motivation—often unconscious—of acting courageously. A courageous person (for instance, a soldier in a war) can be motivated by dedication to his goal or

---

[10] The character of the miser has been brilliantly described in fiction by Molière and Balzac.

[11] An example we have observed is that of a millionaire who spends not a little time and energy to watch that no letter sent out by him or his office has more than the necessary stamps.

sense of duty, and we usually have this motivation in mind when we speak of courage as being a virtue. But courage can also be motivated by vanity, the wish for recognition and admiration; or by suicidal tendencies in which loss of life might be desired even though unconsciously; or by lack of imagination, which makes the individual blind to dangers; or by the fear of being considered a coward; or by liquor; [12] or by all or any of these motivations blended with each other.

Are individuals aware of their motivation? Whatever the motive of the person who behaves courageously, he will usually assume that he is motivated by dedication or duty, and so will those who witness his behavior. In cases where the motivating force is not dedication but a less noble impulse, the real motivation is more likely to remain unconscious.

Is the behavior the same, regardless of the different motivations? On the surface it seems to be the same, but a detailed analysis of the behavior will show that this is not so. Let us take as an example an army officer in charge of a company. If he is motivated by a sense of dedication to a goal or by a sense of duty, he will take risks and demand that his soldiers take risks, which are in proportion to the importance of the tactical goals. If, on the other hand, he is motivated by vanity or suicidal tendencies, he will risk the lives of his soldiers (and his own life) unnecessarily; he may even disobey orders from his superiors and thus do harm to the general tactical or strategic plans. Differences in the motivation of leading generals and politicians might spell the difference between life and death for the nations they lead.

One important difference between behavior traits and character traits needs to be stressed. The behavior trait is an adaptive response to a given social situation and is essentially the result of learning. For this reason, as we have already said, behavior traits can change relatively easily when conditions change.

Character traits, on the other hand, are part of a dynamic system, the system-character. They change only inasmuch as the whole system changes, but not independently. The system as a whole has been formed in response to the total social configuration; however, this response is not an arbitrary one but conditioned by the nature of man, which determines the ways in which human energy can be channeled. *The system-character is the relatively permanent form in which human energy is structuralized in the process of relating to others and of assimilating nature.* It is the result of dynamic interaction of the system-man and the system-society in which he lives.

---

[12] It is a well-known fact, that in the first World War large quantities of liquor were distributed before an attack, in various of the warring armies. The Italian soldiers, for instance, always knew ahead of time when an attack was to take place by the arrival of large quantities of wine.

It is precisely this systemic, structural quality which is essential in Freud's character-concept. It may be that for this very reason it has not found the full understanding and recognition it deserves. It is to be hoped that the recent interest in systems and structure will also lead to a new appreciation of the psychoanalytic concept of character.

The significance of the dynamic concept of character becomes even clearer when looked upon from a sociobiological rather than from Freud's mechanistic-physiological standpoint. The instinctive determination of actions is weaker in man than in all other animals. In fact, instinctive behavior hardly exists in man. Like other animals, man has to act and to make decisions, but unlike other animals he cannot make these decisions automatically, because his instincts do not determine his decisions. If, on the other hand, every decision were made on the basis of conscious deliberation, an individual would be overwhelmed by information and by doubt. Many vital decisions have to be made in a time range much shorter than a deliberation of what is best would require. Character in the dynamic sense *becomes a substitute for instinct.* The person with what Freud calls an "anal character" will "instinctively" hoard, shy away from expenditures, and act strongly against any menace to his possessions. He does not have to *think* about these reactions because his character-system makes him act spontaneously without having to think, in spite of the fact that his actions are not determined by instinct.[13]

A further significant function of character in the dynamic sense is that it unifies a person's action. The anal character who tends to be hoarding, punctual, over-clean, suspicious, and constantly on the defensive, has built up an integrated system which has its own logic and order. He is not stingy today and magnanimous tomorrow, or cold and closed today and warm and open tomorrow. In other words, because of the unifying nature of a system, constant friction between various tendencies is avoided. This friction would exist if a person were to make each of his choices consciously and as a result of deliberation or mood. This function of unification is important, because otherwise the friction of conflicting tendencies would result in a marked waste of energy within the whole system; in fact, living would be rather precarious.

Having pointed out the significance of Freud's discovery of the dynamic concept of character, we must add that of course this concept was by no means unknown before Freud. From Heraclitus, who said, "character is man's fate," to Greek and Shakespearean drama, to Balzac's novels,

---

[13] The contradiction between the theory of instinctively determined vs. learned-conditioned behavior could in our opinion be solved if both sides examined minutely the character-passions which are not instinctive, yet not essentially learned, but a dynamic adaption of the system of psychic energy (character) to given circumstances.

we find the same concept of character, namely that man is driven to act the way he acts, that there are several systems of character which lead to different actions, and that one can understand personality only if one understands the system underlying man's behavior. But Freud was the first scientist and psychologist who elaborated on the concept of character in a scientific way and who laid the foundations for a systematic study of character structure.

Even though the concept of character as it is used in this study is built on these foundations, it differs with respect to a number of theoretical elements which formed part of Freud's original theory.

To begin with, we do not consider that instinct mediates human relationships. For instance, the infant's bond to the mother is not primarily based on satisfaction of the sucking instinct, but has to be understood in a much wider sense. While to give sucking satisfaction is one of the mother's functions, there are other functions which are more important, as, for example, skin contact.[14, 15] But still more important is the factor of unconditional love, which has nothing to do with a specific need, but rather with the quality of the whole relationship of mother to infant. Mother is always there, always ready to help, always ready to alleviate discomfort, to respond. She mediates all of reality; she *is* reality, she is the world; she is the comforting, all-reliable goddess—at least in the first years of the child's life. The crucial question is not the mechanistic one of which instincts are satisfied, but the sociobiological one: which function the mother has in and for the total life process of the infant at a given point of its development.

Freud's clinical descriptions of the oral-receptive, oral-exploitative, and anal character seem to us essentially correct and confirmed by experiences in the analysis of individuals, as well as analytical research into the character structure of groups. The difference lies not in the *description* of

---

[14] This fact has been brilliantly illuminated by H. F. Harlow's animal experiments with artificial mothers. (Cf. H. F. Harlow, "The Nature of Love," *American Psychologist,* 13:675-685 (1958).

[15] Cf. the excellent discussion of the views of various analytic and nonanalytic authors on the question of instinctive mediation of the infant's relatedness to mother by David Schechter, "On the Emergence of Human Relatedness," and the literature cited there. (To be published.)

It is interesting to note that Freud in one passing remark toward the end of his life (1938) wrote on the irrelevance of sucking: "In these two relations (feeding and care of the child's body) lies the root of a mother's importance. Unique, without parallel, established unalterably for a whole life time as the first and strongest love object and as a prototype for all later love relations—for both sexes. In all this the phylogenic foundation has so much the upper hand over personal accidental experience that it makes no difference whether a child has really sucked at the breast or has been brought up at the bottle and never enjoyed the tenderness of a mother's care." (Standard Edition Vol. 23, p. 188.)

the character syndrome, but in its *theoretical explanation,* which has some significant consequences for the application of the character syndromes, as Freud found them in the individual, to understanding social character. As we already pointed out, Freud's guiding theoretical concepts referred to the vicissitudes in the evolution of libido. His stages of character development follow the stages of libido development in the sense that their sequence was the same, and furthermore that the energy with which the character syndrome is charged is derived from the sexual energy vested in the corresponding pregenital erogenous zones.

We, on the other hand, start out from a sociobiological question: What kind of ties to the world, persons and things, must—and can—man develop in order to survive, given his specific equipment and the nature of the world around him? Man has to fulfill two functions in order to survive. First, he has to provide for his material needs (food, shelter, etc.) and for the survival needs of the group in terms of procreation and protection of the young. Fromm has called this "the process of assimilation," and he has pointed out in his characterology that there are only certain specific ways in which man can assimilate things for his own use: either by receiving them passively (receptive character), by taking them by force (exploitative character), by hoarding whatever he has (hoarding character), or by producing through work that which he needs (productive character). However, man being endowed with self-awareness, with a need to choose, to plan, and to foresee dangers and difficulties, and being uprooted from his original home within nature by the absence of instinctive determination, could not remain sane even if he took care of all his material needs, unless he were able to establish some form of relatedness to others that allows him to feel "at home" and saves him from the experience of complete affective isolation and separateness, which is in fact the basis of severe mental sickness. (To relate oneself is also a social necessity because no social organization could exist unless the members of the organization had some feeling of relatedness among themselves.) Man, inasmuch as he is an animal, is driven to avoid death, while man *qua* man is driven to avoid madness. This he does by means of various forms of relating himself, in the "process of socialization."

He can relate himself to others in a symbiotic way (sadistically or masochistically), in purely destructive ways, in a narcissistic way, and in a loving way.[16, 17]

---

[16] The destructive and narcissistic forms of relatedness are really negative forms of relatedness, but only a lengthy discussion, for which there is no space here, could show why these negative forms of relatedness are attempts to solve the problem of socialization, although unsuccessfully.

[17] Other, less fundamental and more role-oriented attitudes will be discussed in Chapter 5.

Affinities exist between certain character structures referring to assimilation and others referring to socialization, which will be described later on in the text. Both the process of assimilation and the process of socialization have as their aim not only survival (physical and psychic) but also the expression of man's potential by the active use of his physical, affective, and intellectual powers. In this process of becoming what he potentially is, man expresses his energies in the most adequate way. When he cannot express his self actively, he suffers, is passive, and tends to become sick.[18]

To sum up: in talking about the receptive, exploitative, hoarding, and productive orientations we do not refer to a form of relatedness to the world which is mediated by certain forms of the sexual instinct, but to forms of relatedness of the human being to the world in the process of living.[19]

This conceptual change leads also to a change in the concept of energy, with which the character system is charged. For Freud this energy was the sexual energy, libido. From our theoretical standpoint it is the energy within a total living organism which tends to survive and to express itself. There is no need to speak of "desexualized energy," which is a discovery only if one started with an orthodox viewpoint. Descriptively, we use the generalized concept of energy similar to the use of "libido" by C. G. Jung.

Freud's concept of character was developed by clinical observation of individuals, not of groups. Furthermore, he saw the basis for the develop-

---

[18] This problem has been deeply understood by many philosophers. Among modern psychiatrists and psychologists, Kurt Goldstein has deepened its understanding and demonstrated its importance, and later A. Maslow and others have given special attention to it.

[19] This noninstinctive yet dynamic concept of character has been developed by Fromm (1947). Erikson (1963) has expressed a similar point of view in terms of "modes," without emphasizing so clearly the difference from Freud.

Erikson (1963) has demonstrated in regard to the Yurok Indians that character is not determined by libidinal fixations. Erikson shows that the typical Yurok has an anal-hoarding character, including stinginess, suspiciousness and obstinacy. He writes that "All 'wishful thinking' was put in the service of economic pursuits" (p. 177). The ideal of the Yurok was to be "clean," "sensible," and "restrained." Yet there is no evidence that these traits can be traced to constraints on anal eroticism. Indeed, Erikson writes that "there seems to be no specific emphasis on feces or the anal zone . . ." (p. 178). And "there is no shame concerning the surface of the human body" (p. 179). Rather, the economic demands of Yurok life as peasant fishermen appear to make what we would term a moderately productive hoarding orientation the one best suited for survival, and Yurok institutions reinforce the ideals that fit this character type. In describing Yurok character, Erikson rejects an essential part of the libido theory, and his results confirm the position earlier taken by Fromm (1941). But he has continued to speak, it seems to us somewhat inconsistently, in terms of instinct and libido theory and avoided emphasizing his sharp break with an important Freudian position concerning character formation.

ment of the individual character in another "private" phenomenon—the individual family. He did not apply his concepts of character to societies or classes.

This statement does not imply that Freud's theory lacked a social orientation. He was very aware that individual psychology can rarely neglect the relationship of one individual to another and that—as he wrote in *Group Psychology and the Analysis of the Ego* (1922)—"individual psychology is from the very beginning at the same time social psychology in the enlarged but completely legitimate sense." He went even further. He speculated upon the possibilities of collective neuroses and concluded this speculation with the following statement: "In spite of these difficulties we may expect that one day someone will venture upon this research into the pathology of civilized communities." [20] But in spite of these speculations Freud never went beyond the study of the individual character and its roots in the individual family.

THE SOCIAL CHARACTER

The concept of the *social character* is based on the premise that not only is the energy of the individual structured in terms of Freud's dynamic character concept, but that there is a character structure common to most members of groups or classes within a given society. It is this common character structure which Fromm has called "social character." The concept of social character does not refer to the complete or highly individualized, in fact, unique character structure as it exists in an individual, but to a "character matrix," *a syndrome of character traits which has developed as an adaptation to the economic, social, and cultural conditions common to that group.* There are, of course, deviants in a group whose character is entirely different from that of the majority. But the common character traits are so important because the fact that they are common to most members has the result that group behavior—action, thought, and feeling—is motivated by those traits which are shared. The leaders in any given group will often be those whose individual character is a particularly intense and complete manifestation of the social character—if not of the whole society at least of a powerful class within it.

There are examples in which the social character of a group is relatively easy to observe. In primitive societies, for instance, we find not rarely that the whole group partakes of the same social character. In some cases this social character is peaceful, friendly, cooperative, and unaggres-

---

[20] Cf. Freud's *Civilization and Its Discontents* (London: The Hogarth Press, Ltd., 1953), p. 142.

sive. In other cases it is aggressive, destructive, sadistic, suspicious.[21] In more developed societies we usually find that various classes have a different social character, depending on their different role in the social structure.[22] An example is the hoarding character of the middle class of 19th-century capitalism. The middle class was motivated to save, economize, hold on to its possessions, to be punctual and orderly, not only in their business behavior, but also in their sexual mores.[23] The European upper classes had a very different social character. They were not given to saving, but to spending and enjoying, and they were not bound by the Victorian moral restrictions in their behavior.

A more recent example is the lower middle class in Germany, after the first World War. The character matrix of this class can be described as hoarding, hating and sadistic, and Fromm (1941) has shown how their rapidly declining role in the social process led to this character formation. This was the class from which Hitler recruited his original adherents, and from it came also the most brutal and sadistic elements of the Nazi movement.

The concept of social character explains how psychic energy in *general* is transformed into the *specific* form of psychic energy which every society needs to employ for its own functioning. In order to appreciate this fact one must consider that there is no "society" in general but that there exist only specific social structures; that each society and class demands different kinds of functions from its members. The mode of production varies from society to society and from class to class. A serf, a free peasant, an industrial worker in the 19th century and one in an automated society, an independent entrepreneur of the 19th century and an industrial manager of the 20th century have different functions to fulfill. Furthermore, the different social context demands that they relate themselves in different ways to equals, superiors, and inferiors. To give specific examples: the industrial worker has to be disciplined and punctual; the 19th-century

---

[21] The Hopi Indians are a good example of the former, the Kwakiutl of the latter. Cf. Margaret Mead, *Cooperation and Competition Among Primitive Peoples* (New York: McGraw-Hill, 1937), and Ruth Benedict, *Patterns of Culture* (Boston: Houghton Mifflin, 1934). In contrast, a strictly Freudian anthropologist, D. Freeman, disagrees with this viewpoint and, following Freud's thesis of the death instinct, he finds only evidence for the ubiquity of destructiveness in the anthropological material. Cf. Derek Freeman, "Human Aggression in Anthropological Perspective," *The Natural History of Aggression,* I. D. Garthy and F. I. Ebling, eds. (London and New York: Academic Press, 1964).

[22] Our data show this to be the case also in the society we studied.

[23] This character trait is to be found in the rules for life which Benjamin Franklin laid down. Among the virtues Franklin thought to be the most important are, among others, moderation, orderliness, parsimony, cleanliness, justice, chastity, while charity, love, or compassion are not even mentioned.

bourgeois had to be parsimonious, individualistic, and self-reliant; today, members of all classes, except the poor, have to work in teams, and they must wish to spend and to consume new products. It is socially necessary that in exercising these functions, man must invest much of his psychic energy. If he were *forced* to act, only the least skilled work could be done. If, on the other hand, he exercised his functions only when he considered it necessary for his survival or well-being, he might sometime decide that he preferred to act in ways different from the socially prescribed ones. This would not be a sufficient basis for the proper functioning of a society. The demands of his social role must become "second nature," i.e., *a person must want to do what he has to do.* Society must produce not only tools and machines but also the type of personality that employs energy voluntarily for the performance of a social role. This *process of transforming general psychic energy into specific psychosocial energy* is mediated by the social character.

People, acting according to the demands of the social character, are satisfied when the social patterns enable them to act according to their character. The member of the 19th-century middle class, who liked to save, was satisfied when his social system gave him the opportunity to save. This means that society not only transforms psychic energy into socially useful energy; it also in this very process gives the premium of satisfaction to those who act as they are supposed to act. In addition, of course, those whose individual character is most fully equated with the social character receive also the social awards which proper social behavior carries with it, in terms of material success and recognition of being "good" and "virtuous." Those persons who in their individual character are most alike to the social character often become, if gifted, the leaders of their respective groups.

The formation of the social character is mediated by the influence of the "total culture": the methods of raising children, of education in terms of schooling, literature, art, religion, customs; in short, the whole cultural fabric guarantees its stability.[24] In fact, one possible definition of culture would be that culture is the totality of all those arrangements which produce and stabilize the social character. The social character often lags

---

[24] What is described here are the phenomena which Marx has subsumed under the concept of "ideological superstructure," which has often been understood as a reflex-like consequence of the socioeconomic structure. Marx and Engels themselves were much less simplistic in this respect, and viewed the question of how this superstructure is produced as one which had not found a satisfactory solution. In the concept of the social character, the connection between the economic basis and the superstructure is understood in their interaction. The practice of life, as it results from the socioeconomic structure, produces a certain social character which, in turn, produces the superstructure, which in turn reinforces the social character. The social character, in this view, is the intermediary between basic economic structure and superstructure.

behind new social and economic developments because rooted in tradition and custom it is more stable than economic and political changes. This lag is often harmful to classes and whole societies which cannot adapt themselves to the requirements of new circumstances because their traditional character makes the adaptive behavior difficult to achieve. The most striking and alarming example of this lag today lies in the conflict between traditional feelings about national sovereignty, national honor, victorious war, and the new technology, particularly in the field of nuclear armament and biological warfare. It is precisely this lag and the stubbornness with which the traditional character persists which makes it difficult to explain social behavior as exclusively or even mainly as learned, or mediated by imitation.

At this point we must refer to a difference between the classic and our own concept of character which we have not dealt with earlier—a difference which is especially relevant to the understanding of the concept of social character and social change. According to Freud, as we have pointed out, the evolution of character follows the stages of the evolution of the libido, and this evolution is supposed to be inherent in the physiological structure of man. He made the assumption that the character formation is more or less complete at the Oedipal stage around age six. This stage is followed by a period of latency, and later by puberty, adolescence and adulthood, but changes in character are exceedingly rare.[25] As a result the assumption was made that the childhood experiences are not only basic for character formation, but also fixed and not subject to later change, at least not without psychoanalytic therapy.

In contrast, while we fully recognize the fundamental importance of childhood experiences, our theoretical viewpoint concerning the essential influences in character formation are different and imply eventually a different viewpoint about the possibility of later change. As we have pointed out, man has a number of ascertainable ways to assimilate and to relate. While there is a certain sequence in the development of the child with regard to these stages, it does not seem to be a strict sequence as Freud assumed. On the contrary, from clinical and social data we are willing to hypothesize that the child starts out with all the potential modes, some stronger, others weaker constitutionally, and that he experiments with various character orientations, and that eventually those become dominant which are most suited for adaptation to his particular environment. However, adaptation to circumstances unfavorable to growth usually have important "side effects." Thus, for example, when a child submits to the demands for total obedience of a sadistic mother or father, while he adapts himself to the necessities of the situation, because he is frightened, some-

---

[25] According to the later concept of character analysis, such changes can be brought about by psychoanalytic interpretation, although only with great difficulty.

thing happens to him. He may develop an intense hostility against the parent, which he represses, since it would be too dangerous to express it or even be aware of it. This repressed hostility, while it is not manifest, is a dynamic factor in his character structure. It may create new anxiety and thus lead to more deeply rooted submission; it may lead to a vague defiance directed against no one in particular but rather toward life in general; it may even lead to unforeseen murderous impulses.[26]

It needs to be emphasized that the influence of the family, although it is extremely powerful, must always work through the child's constitution. By constitution (or endowment) we mean more than just temperament in the classic sense. Rather, we refer to the basic structure of personality. Relationships in the family either help bring out this structure to its best fruition, or they tend to distort it. Just as a pear seed cannot produce an apple tree, but only better or worse pear trees, depending on the conditions of soil and climate, so a child can only develop his given potential structure in the most harmonious vital form or in a negative form. For instance, a highly sensitive and unaggressive child may become, under favorable influences, an introspective, artistic and spiritual-minded person. Under the influence of cold and authoritarian parents, the same child is likely to become intimidated, frightened, and resentful, with the result that he wastes most of his energy by not being able to *be* what he *potentially is*. This holds true especially when parents try to force on the child a pattern of personality which is socially desirable or preferable to them but which clashes with the constitutionally given personality. The growing child may *act* in terms of the superimposed personality, but he will not be in touch with the deepest sources of his original self. To be sure, one can condition a child by rewards and punishments, by manipulating his anxiety, to become what he is not, but the result will be inner conflict, waste of energy, lack of joy, in many cases neurosis, and sometimes psychosis.

All these considerations are based on the assumption that maximal well-being is attained only if the person becomes what he potentially is, if he develops his self, his center, hence an authentic sense of identity.[27]

---

[26] However, all family influence is not pathogenic. A child with productive-loving parents will be respected and stimulated to trust his own feelings and to develop his given capabilities.

[27] Erik H. Erikson has written extensively about the sense of "identity" but his concept of identity is ambiguous. Sometimes he gives a meaning to the concept similar to ours. On the other hand, however, for him the basis of identity is the child's identifications with others.

Elsewhere he speaks of identity as if it meant the congruence between social role and the subjective experience of self. This use of the concept avoids coming to grips with the question of whether or not a society stimulates or cripples the development of the individual self and whether it offers a pseudo identity in place of the original self. For example, he writes (1963) that "ego identity is, as pointed out,

That the child's reaction to his family environment also depends on his constitution can be seen by comparing children in the same family. One child may resist adaptation because his will is stronger, while another will quickly give in. The same is true of a child's reaction to pressures outside the family. The conditions of life outside the family as well as within may allow the child to exercise his capabilities, but they often pressure him to adapt in ways which clash with his genuine wishes. How he resolves the conflict, either by resisting or adapting, will depend to a large extent on constitutional factors.

For example, although a child in an authoritarian family will usually conform to expectations, it is possible also that he may resist in terms of strengthening his original tendencies, of strengthening his integrity, and becoming sensitive to sadism. In other words, while most children probably become like, for instance, their authoritarian-sadistic parents, some become the exact opposite. This general formulation must be qualified more specifically. If the child is himself endowed with strong sadistic tendencies, his conforming to the parental pattern may be supported by this tendency toward sadism. On the other hand, an individual may conform outwardly and yet underneath preserve his original self, with the result that there is an internal conflict between two tendencies. Indeed, one of the more significant aims of psychoanalysis is to resolve such conflicts.[28]

The importance of childhood experiences by no means excludes later changes in character. This is to say, while the character under the influence of early experience (plus constitution) is formed in the first years, the structure is normally flexible enough so that changes may occur at a later period. In principle, we would not even set an age limit to the possibilities of such changes, for the better or worse. However, there is a good reason why one might conceive a completely inflexible character. The character of

---

more than the sum of childhood identifications. It is the accrued experience of the ego's ability to integrate all identifications with the vicissitudes of the libido, with the aptitudes development out of endowment, and with the opportunities offered in social roles. The sense of ego identity, then, is the accrued confidence that the inner sameness and continuity prepared in the past are matched by the sameness and continuity of one's meaning for others, as evidenced in the tangible promise of a 'career.' " (Pp. 261-262.)

[28] One finds not so rarely that people coming from an environment which seems to predetermine them to a sadistic or destructive character turn out to be unusually kind and free from the very tendencies which "influence" them in their childhood. The reason can be twofold. Either their nonsadistic endowment was so strong that no enviromental influence could touch it *or* in the very fight against destructiveness in their environment, their own nondestructive (self-affirming biophilic) tendencies are more fully developed and "steeled." The same principle holds true for conflicts within the individual. The fight against sadistic and destructive tendencies often leads to stronger nondestructive tendencies than in those cases in which such a struggle was unnecessary.

the child, as we believe with Freud, develops as a result of dynamic adaptation to the family constellation. Since the family represents the spirit of the society into which the child enters, the same influences which have been the main determining influences from the beginning continue to mold the adolescent's and adult's character structure. Institutions of schooling, work, and leisure do not differ essentially from the way of life transmitted to the child in his family. Thus the character structure acquired in childhood is constantly reinforced in later life, provided the social circumstances do not change drastically. Since this is not normally the case, the impression arises that the character is definitely formed at the age of six and not subject to any later change.

However, the fact that certain character orientations, generally those adaptive to the child's environment, become dominant does not mean that the others simply disappear or are irretrievably lost by repression. Naturally, when circumstances do not change, the most adaptive character orientation becomes more and more firm. But when circumstances do change in a significant way, the child and even later the adult has the possibility of bringing forth orientations which have been latent, and which are more suited to meeting the new circumstances. This process of change is a complicated one. The initial character system will not disappear, but it will be partly replaced by, partly blended with, a new character structure which may not be radically different from the original one, but sufficiently so to create a very different set of motivating character traits. In fact, if that were not so, no character change by psychoanalytical intervention could occur. That the early adopted character structure seems to remain dominant in most people throughout their lives is due less to the fact that it is rigid and incapable of modification than to the mutually reinforcing relationship between character and environment.

One word of caution is necessary: the character structure is a system, and like every other system it has a great power of cohesion because each part is geared to every other part, and a change in one part necessitates a change in every other part. That is why mere teaching has little influence, or why even the attempt to change one trait or a symptom by force, for instance by punishment or reward, remains ineffective. A system very soon absorbs the changes brought about in one particular trait, and either the trait returns very soon, or it is deeply repressed and waits for circumstances when it can again come forth.[29] As with any other system, a systemic change is possible only if a whole set of circumstances is changed in such a way that it applies to the system as a whole, and brings forth other latent systems which until then have remained dormant. An example may clarify this point: if an aggressive child is punished, or if on the other hand he is

---

[29] Cf. Freud's concept of the "return of the repressed."

indulged in the expression of his aggression, the aggressive behavior may change but not the aggressive character. But if a new development creates a set of new conditions, such as for instance a combination of unconditional love, stimulation, nonpunishment, occasions for active participation and responsibility, a situation of noncompetitive solidarity and unsentimental matter-of-factness, this new combination may very well bring forth a latent character system in such a way that the aggression dries up. This concept of "drying up" is important. Any environmental system either feeds certain character traits or tends to dry them up. Both are processes which occur slowly and which occur only if one has the patience to wait for the change rather than give up if it does not occur as an immediate result of the new elements one has introduced.

The possibility for change depends on the fact that all elements of the character system have retained a certain flexibility or, to put it more precisely, a certain regenerative power. When that is the case, one might speak of a basically healthy character, even though it may have unhealthy manifestations in a given situation. However, it sometimes happens that either for constitutional reasons, or for reasons of the intensity of early experiences, certain parts of the character lose their capacity for regenerative adaptation, become ossified, or "die." If this occurs in more than a minimal way, the psychic system loses its regenerative power and can be considered incapable of change. A system in which this occurs may be considered to be truly sick, and it is a question which can only be decided from case to case whether fundamental changes in the social system (or therapeutic intervention) may succeed in overcoming this inflexibility, bringing to life those elements which have been frozen.[30]

THE METHOD

The second interest that motivated this study was in a *method* that would permit the application of analytic sociopsychological categories to social investigation, in ways other than by individual or group analysis of the members of a community. The latter possibility necessarily excludes itself, not only in Mexico but practically everywhere, partly because it would require an amount of time for which the personnel and the means are not available, and partly because only a part—and perhaps a small one —of the population would be willing to undergo such a procedure.

Social research has been mainly restricted to methods which yield behavioral data, such as opinions and conscious attitudes. There have been

---

[30] Cf. Freud's (1937) paper "Analysis—Terminable and Interminable," in which he deals with the problem of the difficulty of change even with psychoanalytic therapy.

a number of attempts to analyze the unconscious trends in a social group on the basis of intuitive observation or study of the existing reports on the experience and behavior of group members, for instance, the anthropological studies of A. Kardiner, the studies of American character by David Riesman, and of national character by G. Gorer. Studies have also been carried out on the relationship between unconscious motivations and political attitudes, using both structured interviews (for instance, the work of B. Smith, J. S. Bruner and R. White and that of Robert Lane) and pre-coded projective questions (particularly *The Authoritarian Personality* by Adorno, et al. (1950), and the many studies based on it).

It is not our purpose to review these studies but rather to point to essential differences from our own.[31] The most important difference, of course, is theoretical. We have tried to discover the nuclear character of each villager and to find the relationship between character and specific need. In contrast to *The Authoritarian Personality,* we used open-ended questions which required psychoanalytic interpretation in a manner which we shall describe.[32]

The first time such a method was applied was in a study undertaken by the Institute for Social Research at the University of Frankfurt, which was begun in 1931.[33] A short description of the method used in that earlier study will explain the basic elements of the method used in the study of the Mexican village.

The immediate reason for the study was the interest in knowing how many of the German workers and employees were reliable fighters against Nazism. As to their political opinions, respondents were all anti-Nazis,

---

[31] The method of interpretative questionnaire interview has been used by Dr. Armando Hinojosa in his book *Analisis Psicológico del Estudiante Universitario* (Mexico: La Prensa Médica Mexicana, 1967). He applies the categories of character developed in *Man for Himself.* He differs from our method by not separating the productive character, but rather contrasting positive-productive and negative-unproductive aspects of the various character orientations.

[32] *The Authoritarian Personality* has been criticized for its lack of distinction between people with the authoritarian-sado-masochistic character and others with a more conventional "authoritarianism." Adorno and his collaborators combined questions having to do with traditionalism, conventionalism, and cognitive rigidity together with sado-masochism, destructiveness, and idealization of power. This criticism is reviewed in Roger Brown, *Social Psychology* (New York: The Free Press, 1965).

[33] A preliminary report of the study is to be found in *Studien über Autorität und Familie* [Studies on Authority and Family] (Paris: Felix Alcan, 1936). The victory of Hitler forced the contributors of this study to leave Germany, and it took some time until the analysis of the study could be finished at the branch of the Institute for Social Research in Geneva and eventually at Columbia University. The study was planned and directed by Fromm in collaboration with Ernest Schachtel, Anna Hartoch, and the counsel of Paul Lazarsfeld in all matters of statistical problems. Regrettably, the final results of the study were never published.

most of them either socialists or communists. It was hypothesized that those who had an authoritarian character would in the event of Hitler's victory become Nazis, that those with an anti-authoritarian democratic-revolutionary character would become fighters against Nazism, and that those with a mixed character would become neither ardent Nazis nor ardent anti-Nazis.

This hypothesis was based on the theoretical assumption that *opinions* held at a given time are relatively unreliable if circumstances change drastically. An opinion in itself is nothing but the acceptance of a thought pattern shared by the society in general or by a particular group as, in that case, the German workers and employees. The assumption was made that only those opinions constitute powerful motivations for action which are rooted in the character structure of a person—if they are, as one might say, "gut opinions." In the case of an opinion rooted in the character structure, one should speak of a conviction, rather than of an opinion. Deeply rooted convictions are, indeed, most powerful motivations for action once the possibilities for such action have arisen. (This holds true for any kind of conviction, whether it is rational or irrational, good or evil, right or wrong.) It followed from this general assumption that only if one had knowledge of the character structure of German workers and employees could one predict their probable reaction to a Nazi victory. The main interest was not the social character in its broad sense, but that aspect most relevant to the Nazi challenge: the authoritarian vs. the democratic-revolutionary character.[34] The problem, then, was to find a method which would permit applying interviews, and their statistical elaboration, to the dynamic concept of the authoritarian character.

The study was undertaken on the basis of an analogy between a social and a personal psychoanalytic interview. When a psychoanalyst interviews a person, even before he begins to use the method of free association and dream interpretation, he tries to understand the unconscious meaning of certain phrases and statements used by the patient, a meaning which the patient did not intend to express or is not aware of expressing. Psychoanalytic interviews offer ample examples for this procedure. If a man asserts an unusual number of times during the first interview how much he loves his wife, but then discusses what his plans would be in the unfortunate case of her death, it hardly requires a psychoanalyst to recognize that he "protests too much," and assurances of his love may not mean what he believes or intends them to mean. It was assumed that the same method could be used in an interview using a large number of relevant questions.

---

[34] Cf. the concept of the revolutionary character in Fromm (1963) and Chapter 4 for a further discussion of types of political character.

Technically, this demanded that the questions not require "yes" or "no" answers, nor the checking of a number of preformulated answers in terms of "very much," "somewhat," etc., but that the original answer of the interviewee be taken down verbally and immediately by the interviewer. Single answers were not tabulated in a mechanical way. Rather, by analyzing each answer and the totality of the answers to the questionnaire, the study attempted to arrive at the knowledge of the dynamic tendencies of a respondent's character most relevant to his political attitude. Furthermore, the interest of the study was to compare the character structures found in each questionnaire with all others, and with objective data such as age, income, sex, and education.

The differences between this type of questionnaire, which may be called the "interpretative questionnaire," and most other questionnaires used in social research is not primarily that which exists between open and preformulated questionnaires, but it is the different use made of the answers. In the conventional questionnaire, the answers are taken as raw material or coded according to behavioral categories, and the task is to analyze them statistically, either simply in terms of the frequency of each single answer or, in a more sophisticated way, by factor analysis, which shows clusters of answers found together with significant frequency. The main effort is directed toward the choice of an adequate sample of relevant questions and toward the most fruitful statistical elaboration. All these steps have to be taken in the interpretative questionnaire also, but they seem relatively simple in comparison with that element characteristic of the interpretative questionnaires only and that is the interpretation of the answers with regard to their unconscious or unintended meaning. The task of interpretation is, like any other psychoanalytic interpretation, difficult, and takes a great deal of time.[35] It requires knowledge of psychoanalytic theory and therapy (including the experience of one's own analysis), a clinical psychoanalytic experience, and, as in everything else, skill and talent. Psychoanalytic interpretation—of associations and dreams as well as of answers to a questionnaire—is an art like the practice of medicine, in which certain theoretical principles are applied to empirical data.

The most important factor, then, to ensure the correctness of the interpretation and hence of the results of the whole investigation which rests upon the interpretative data, depends on the qualifications of the interpreter. For those psychologists—and they are in the majority—who use as their basic data behavior which is immediately demonstrable and easily

---

[35] Indeed, Maccoby spent over a year using most of his time to analyze more than 400 questionnaires. After analyzing the first 150 questionnaires, he felt that what he had learned in the meantime made him question his scoring, and he started again from the beginning.

coded into descriptive categories, the psychoanalytic interpretation appears to be highly subjective, if not unscientific, and they will object to the "subjective" factor in the interpretation, which makes it impossible to control the correctness of the interpretation. We do not want to enter here into a discussion of scientific methodology, and the problems of "facts," "proof," etc., a discussion which involves the difference between the traditional mechanical model of scientific method and the model as it exists in theoretical physics and biochemistry. We do want to point out that the problem of an alleged subjectivity exists also in a traditional field like medicine. Take the interpretation of an X-ray picture; in the case of a typical picture, even most beginners will give the same interpretation; on the other hand in an atypical picture even the most experienced specialists may disagree among themselves. Only the further course of the illness or surgery can decide which interpretation was correct. But when the interpretation has been made and serves as the basis for further treatment, one trusts the patient's life on the assumption that the interpretation of a skilled physician is likely to be correct. There is, in fact, nothing subjective, in the usual sense, in his diagnosis. He is a highly trained observer whose judgment results from a mixture of experience, skill, intelligence, and concentration. However, he cannot *prove* the correctness of his interpretation in a way which would convince everybody (which is, incidentally, also sometimes the case in highly sophisticated scientific experiments) and least of all those physicians with less skill and talent than his own; and eventually there is, of course, the possibility that he may be wrong.

The case of the psychoanalytic interpretation is not different; here, too, future developments may "prove" the correctness of the interpretation; furthermore, as in many other fields of science, the inner consistency of the interpretation with many other data and with theoretical assumptions, tends to confirm the probability of correctness.[36] Indeed, a certain amount of uncertainty is the price the psychoanalytic researcher pays for the attempt to arrive at a deeper understanding of the most relevant data.[37] The traditional behavioral scientist often has greater certainty, but he pays the price

---

[36] See, for an easily accessible example, *The Double Helix,* by James D. Watson (New York: Atheneum Publishers, 1968) for a description of how modern biochemistry goes about finding a structure. While there are of course important differences, the way of thinking used by the psychoanalyst to discover character structure is more similar to the method used to discover the double helix than to the approach of behavioristic psychology.

[37] The device of ensuring the validity of an answer by agreement between various observers offers no solution. An interpretation is not more right because 10 people commit the same error than when the better qualified investigator remains in a minority. Majority opinion is the least dangerous method to arrive at political decisions; applied to research it is of little value. More about this will follow in Appendix B.

of having to restrict his research to problems which are hospitable to his methods.

While not all the questions used in the German study proved to be fruitful for analytical investigation, many of them did, and what is more important, one could see a certain pattern or structure running through the whole questionnaire, and often one could guess the answers to the second half of the questions after having analyzed the first half. To give a simple example for the application of the interpretative method: to the question "Which men in history do you admire most?" some answered "Alexander the Great, Nero, Marx, and Lenin," while others answered "Socrates, Pasteur, Kant, Marx, and Lenin." While in the conventional questionnaire, "Marx and Lenin" would be treated as identical in both answers, according to the interpretative method, "Marx and Lenin" have an entirely different meaning in each of these two answers. In the first they were representatives of power and/or military force, in the second, benefactors of the human race. This means that the first respondent admired powerful totalitarian leaders, and the second humanists. Regardless of the objective validity of his judgment, subjectively the first answer can be classified as an authoritarian, and the second as an anti-authoritarian.

Another example of the interpretative method is the following: to the question "What do you think about the use of makeup by women?" (this was a controversial issue at that time among German workers, many of whom thought it was a bourgeois habit), some answered "I am in favor of it because it makes a woman feel more feminine and attractive and thus makes her happier"; this answer was interpreted as indicating a non-authoritarian character, because it revealed the respondent's love of life and a nonauthoritarian attitude toward women. If someone answered: "I am against it because it is a bourgeois habit," the answer was classified as nonconclusive, and not interpreted because it reflected a cliché and revealed little about the character of the respondent. If the answer was: "I am against it because it makes women look like whores," or "because makeup is poison," the answer was interpreted as revealing an authoritarian-sadistic streak of character. The rationale of this interpretation is that words like "whore" or "poison" express a destructive-hostile attitude. However, one single answer was not considered sufficiently weighty to interpret the character structure of a respondent as authoritarian or non-authoritarian, respectively; but when a number of answers had the same quality, while no other answers showed the contrary, the character of the respondent was coded as being authoritarian or nonauthoritarian, respectively. When there was a clear contradiction between the two tendencies in one questionnaire, the respondent was classified as an ambivalent or mixed character.

The obvious difficulty in the interpretative method is that many answers correspond to the cultural patterns of thought in any given society or social class. Hence many answers do not express the emotional attitude of the individual respondent, but rather the ideology of his group, which he has accepted. How do we know what is genuine and authentic and what is an ideological and borrowed phrase? First of all by knowing the ideology and clichés current in the group. But more important than this is the principle so successfully used by psychoanalysis, that our knowledge of the unconscious motivation of a person is not derived primarily when he speaks in general or even abstract terms, but in the very small details of his expressions and formulations, the precise words he uses, or in the contradictions, unconscious to him, between various statements, or in the unwarranted over-emphasis of the one or the other feeling. It is the small detail in behavior and expression which is important in psychoanalytic investigation, not that which is embodied in general statements of opinions and beliefs. The method used in the interpretative questionnaire takes account of these small details, and they form the main basis for interpretation.

The results of the use of the interpretative questionnaire in the German study, sad as it was from a political standpoint, were very encouraging, as far as the method is concerned. A rather clear-cut picture was obtained of authoritarian, anti-authoritarian, and ambivalent characters, which were consistent within themselves; when the final statistical elaboration was finished, it turned out that, roughly speaking, about 15 percent of the respondents showed a strongly anti-authoritarian character, about 10 percent an authoritarian character, and about 75 percent an ambivalent character. Our theoretical assumption seemed to have been confirmed by these results. Although there are no data available which show exactly the political attitudes of workers and employees under Hitler,[38] there is little doubt that while the figures were not necessarily exact, they correspond to an order of magnitude which existed among the German workers and employees under Hitler; the vast majority among them were neither ardent Nazis nor ardent fighters against Nazism, a small minority became genuine converts to Nazism, and a larger one remained faithful to their anti-Nazi convictions and fought Nazism in whatever way they could. Hitler's concentration camps were full of them. This of course does not mean that all ardent fighters against Nazism had a democratic-revolutionary character. These figures represent trends, affinities, correlations and do not pretend to make statements about every individual in these groupings.

In this study, the interpretative questionnaire was further devel-

---

[38] One interesting datum is that Hitler discontinued the shop stewards' elections because, in spite of pressure and terror, the Nazis could not obtain a majority among workers.

oped to probe beyond political character to include questions that would allow us to determine the individual's mode of assimilation, mode of relatedness, and parental fixations. The questionnaire (see Appendix A) was formulated on the basis of theoretical considerations as to the kinds of questions that elicit the material which reveals an individual's character. It was modified after pretesting which showed the questions that in fact stimulated useful responses in the village. Direct and projective questions were also added after the preliminary stage because they helped to elicit material which clarified certain aspects of character.

In Appendix A we report examples of isolated responses which illustrate different character types, but this is by no means easy to do. Our method of interpretation was to determine whether a response indicated a particular character orientation only after we had read the whole questionnaire. We did this because any response—like any behavior trait—may have a different motive, depending on the total character structure.

The present volume is an attempt to apply the method of the interpretative questionnaire to the character structure of Mexican peasants in a more ample form and with more refined methods than have been used before. It is centered around the correlation between work, mode of production, family relations, and the character structures prevalent among the peasants. It is based on the thorough study of each individual over 16, and of half the children in the village.

2

A Mexican
Peasant Village

The setting of the study is a small village, of about 800 inhabitants, in the State of Morelos, about 50 miles south of Mexico City. The village is located in one of the greenest valleys of Mexico, fertilized by underground springs and mountain streams which become rivers crisscrossing the valley. It has a sub-tropical climate, with a dry winter. The average yearly temperature is 72 degrees; it is never cold and seldom uncomfortably hot. For centuries the main crops grown in the area have been sugarcane and rice, and they are also the two major crops of the village, where most of the people are occupied in agriculture. Cane is irrigated from the river and underground springs, and the rains which fall from May to October allow the villagers to flood the bordered rice fields. The climate and relative abundance of water also support the year-round planting of other crops, and the earth is hospitable to the many fruit trees, flowers, and medicinal herbs that can be found throughout the valley.

THE PAST AND THE PRESENT

The population of the village is mestizo, meaning of mixed Indian and Spanish ancestry. Before the Spanish Conquest, the area was populated by a mixture of Toltecs and Chichimecs, later joined by Nahuatlaca tribes, especially the Tlahuicas. After 1436, the Aztecs, led by Moctezuma Ilhuicamina, completed the conquest of the area, making the Province of Tlalnahuac, the present State of Morelos, a part of the Aztec Empire. When the Aztec Empire crumbled, its provinces were quickly incorporated into the new Spanish system. In April of 1521, Hernán Cortés conquered the province after nine days of fighting. In 1529, he received most of the state from the Spanish king as a feudal fief, including 23,000 vassals, and it became the Marquesado del Valle.

Today there is no longer any trace of an Indian heritage in the village. The villagers are children of the Spanish Conquest. Like 90 percent of all Mexicans, they speak Spanish exclusively. Nearby are villages where people still speak Nahuatl and maintain some of the old customs,[1] but the villagers we have studied have lost all cultural ties with the Aztec past. Only place names remain as reminders of prehispanic culture.

Most villagers do not identify themselves with the past, but see themselves as underprivileged, inferior members of modern society. They would like to escape from peasant poverty and participate in the many good things that have been invented to make life more comfortable and enjoyable. Some villagers, especially the new entrepreneurs and the better-off farmers with land, have high aspirations for their children, if not for themselves. They are the ones who see schooling as the means to enter the new industrial society. These peasants are almost completely oriented to material progress and individual profit, and less tied to tradition. They are the richest peasants, the ones who have risen above mere subsistence. For many of the others, the demands of modern industrial society are in conflict with traditional forms, with the love of leisure and fiestas, and with the suspicion of modern forms as corrupting and dangerous.

During the past 50 years, the village has been caught up in a process of rapid change. Before 1910, it was a hacienda. After 1923, it became a community of small landholders (*ejidatarios*). When we arrived in the late 1950s, it had become a society that was of two classes, a small group of landholders and a larger group of the landless.

Today, the spread of communications and new technologies has favored the rise of a new entrepreneurial class and has supported the new ideas and aspirations. In such a period of change, individuals doubt traditional beliefs, many feel hopeless about the future in the village, and the younger generation seeks models outside of the family. As the villagers increasingly see life in terms of the consumer ideals of the city, they become more and more frustrated with the village which can never satisfy these needs. The villager probably feels more dissatisfied and hopeless than the villager of pre-industrial times, who did not have the feeling that he could never manage to buy the commodities that he was told make life worthwhile. Furthermore, as the villagers are attracted increasingly to radio, television, and movies, they have lost interest in more active forms of entertainment and self-expression. One older villager stated:

---

[1] For a description of an indigenous village, Tepoztlán, which is not far from the village and where some inhabitants still speak Nahuatl, see O. Lewis (1951). It is noteworthy that even in 1910, only 9 percent of Morelos' population spoke Nahuatl. See Womack (1969), p. 71.

In the past the only diversions were musical. They sang and played instruments. If we wanted any other attractions, we had to invent them. That is why we made up and performed comedies and dramas and presented them to the public in the fiestas we used to celebrate. Because at that time there were no movies, there was no television nor radio, nor electric light. We used to try to add a little more to the fiestas by organizing theatrical works. Then, afterwards, and with great enthusiasm, the musical band was organized. After a time, it played very well. But then—the electricity came. There were radios. There were juke boxes. Television. They brought a movie to show once a week. And then no one was interested. Thus ended the enthusiasm for the band and for the theatrical works.

The result is the growing feeling that nothing offered by the village can compare with the glamour and excitement of the consumer economy in the city, and that life is hardly worth living for those who are doomed to the rural backwater.

The present-day village was formed in 1923 at the end of the Revolution, after the overthrow of the hacienda which had dominated the area for three centuries. The ruins of the hacienda and the stone aqueduct, as well as some beliefs and practices, are remnants of the past. But there are many modern influences. Although the streets are unpaved, the village has worked hard to bring electricity and piped drinking water into many of the houses. Besides radios and an increasing number of television sets, villagers have contact with the urban world through sons and daughters who work in large cities and through the score of families from Mexico City who have built weekend residences in the village, attracted by its climate and beauty. Modernization, represented by new industries nearby, paved roads, and concrete plazas to replace the picturesque tree-filled *zocalos,* signify progress for most villagers.

Most of the present inhabitants migrated to the village after the Revolution, in search of land and new opportunities. The Revolution was a time of great upheaval for the peasants of the area, whether they were fighting on one side or the other, or hiding in terror from both armies. Villagers describe the famine and disease that together with violence took the lives of 23 percent of Morelos during the revolutionary years. It was common for families to be uprooted from their villages, to flee to the mountains where they lived on herbs and grasses. Women were unprotected, as their husbands went off to fight, or were conscripted by the government to join the armies in the north. The fighting in Morelos began in 1911 and did not end until 1920. One can hardly exaggerate the extent of the destruction, especially by the government armies which in 1914 and later in 1916 burned villages and ruthlessly murdered or deported peasants suspected of following the revolutionary peasant leader, Emiliano Zapata. By 1918, with the haciendas in ruins and most of the now-broken families living on the edge of starvation, the great flu epidemic of that year claimed the lives of a quarter of the state's population which had survived the violence of the previous eight years. In 1919, displaced villagers began to return and were joined by thousands of migrants who swelled the population during the 1920s and early 1930s, attracted by the generous land policies of Emiliano Zapata's successors, who were put in charge of the state by the national government of General Álvaro Obregon.

The inhabitants of the village originated from both haciendas and from free villages. Before the Revolution, 38 haciendas in the hands of 21 different proprietors owned 56 percent of the state, including an even larger percentage of the fertile valley land. Twenty-six percent of the land was communal grazing land including mountains, while only 18 percent was held by small proprietors, and this included urban land holdings. The haciendas of Morelos were devoted exclusively to the cultivation of cane, while the small landowners planted corn, garden vegetables, and rice. The identification of cane with hacienda domination, and of rice and vegetables with independence lasts to this day, if not in the conscious minds of the villagers, then in the attitudes associated with the planting of these crops (see Chapter 6).

The peasants of the free villages owned small plots of land and in some cases shared communal land for planting or grazing. The main reason that the Revolutionary flame burned so intensely in the State of Morelos was that, in the years preceding the Revolution, many free peasants were losing their lands to the haciendas and being forced into the role of landless peons. One important factor in this development, as Domingo Diez (1967) writes in his history of Morelos, was that the haciendas developed a new method of sugar refining. This combined with the increasing ease of rail transportation made it more profitable to grow more cane and to take over more land from the free villages. Diez writes:

> In this year of 1880 the first machinery for setting up the centrifugal method was established in the haciendas. . . . This fact came to radically change the life of the state. To augment their production of sugar, the hacienda owners naturally looked for an increase in the area of cultivation and this had to be, necessarily, at the cost of the free village lands. . . . In a word, one can say there was a complete revolution upon the definite establishment of the modern machinery. The land owners prospered, their cane gave them greater returns, the Government increased its income through taxes, only the (free) villages were obliged to cede their lands and waters. Little by little they were losing out. Some ended by disappearing, and the social disequilibrium intensified, breaking out in the Revolution of 1910.[2]

From 1870 to 1910, sugar production in the state increased steadily from 8,748,131 kilograms to 48,531,600 kilograms. During this period,

---

2 See Diez (1967), p. 130. Our translation.

the haciendas increasingly took over land from free peasants, aided by the government which abused the law concerning idle lands to justify the haciendas. The primary goal of the Zapatistas, stated in the *Plan de Ayala* of 1911, was return of land that had been usurped by the hacendados.

The dispossessed free villagers were the group that spearheaded the revolution in Morelos. In some cases, families which had held land for centuries were in danger of becoming landless peons. Rather than accept this, they were prepared to defend their property rights with their lives.

Zapata's goals were at first conservative, limited to defending the rights of small property holders. Those peasants whose families had been peons for generations were more likely to have been resigned and submissive, dependent on the hacienda, and unable to imagine another form of life. Only when the government of Victoriano Huerta radicalized the Morelos revolution by treating all peasants as Zapatistas and enemies of the state did Zapata open his army to *peones* (field laborers), and change his revolutionary goals to demand land for all and the abolition of the hacienda. Then, once the haciendas lay in ruins and the old life was gone, the peons' repressed hatred against their former masters added fuel to the explosion. However, there were free villages in which the Revolution was experienced as a threat to a peaceful existence, where no hacienda had encroached on land rights. A group of families within the village we have studied originates from one such village where the inhabitants fought against the Zapatistas.

THE HACIENDA

Before 1910 all the lands now belonging to the ejidatarios (holders of unalienable land) in the village we have studied were owned by the hacienda which employed them in the cultivation of sugarcane. A small community, no more than 40 to 50 families, lived in thatched huts (*jacales*) outside the hacienda walls. Some villagers were able to rent land from the hacienda, paying for it by sharecropping and labors (*faenas*) for the hacienda. A very few were small entrepreneurs, such as the muleteers (*arrieros*) who contracted to carry cargo from the village to the outside and back. The arrieros were particularly independent and brave individuals who constantly risked attack from bandits during their journeys. It is interesting to note that two of the five entrepreneurial villagers we encountered are sons of arrieros.[3]

Almost all of the villagers were dependent on the hacienda. While some of the employees worked as foremen (*mayordomos*) or supervisors

---

[3] It is also interesting that Emiliano Zapata was both a small landholder and had worked as an arriero. Known for his independence and incorruptibility, he was chosen by his village as a leader to defend small landholders from the haciendas. See Womack (1969).

(*capatazes*), the majority were field laborers (peones), who lived in total subjugation to the hacienda. Life for the peon was hardly distinguishable from slavery. Unlike the feudal manor, the hacienda offered no guarantees or legal protection to the peon. The hacienda made its own law. Those who were rebellious would be whipped and possibly expelled from the hacienda, from then on blacklisted in other haciendas. A peon who stole from the hacienda might have been executed.

The peon lived in perpetual fear of being beaten or of losing his source of livelihood. He learned to bow his head before his masters, to smile at small favors, to show abject submission. Even then, there was practically no hope for bettering oneself. Given the peon's poverty and perpetual indebtedness, there was no way of acquiring land, which in any case was scarce; and the hacienda owners or their managers (since some owners lived in Europe) had no interest in educating the peons who were for them most useful as submissive parts of an agricultural machine.

The peons were usually paid in kind, by land use or grazing privileges. The small sum of money due them seldom reached their hands, but went toward paying the account in the hacienda store (*tienda de raya*) where debts accumulated by fathers were inherited by their sons. Chained by these debts, most peons could not leave the hacienda even if they could imagine working on the outside, and, furthermore, they were fearful that life elsewhere might be worse. In return for total obedience and hard work, the hacienda saw to their subsistence and tranquilized them with cheap drink, occasional fiestas, and spectacles.

When the Revolution finally began to speak to the peons of independence and hope, the submissive, receptive attitudes moulded by centuries of hacienda life were not easy to erase. Once the peon became a landowner, he was not only psychologically handicapped for the post-revolutionary world, but he also lacked the training and experience to administer his land, to take account of costs and credit, and to consider problems of marketing. In adapting to the hacienda, the peons had become submissive and dependent and they did not have either the character or the knowledge essential to a free peasant. It will be seen that the peasants with character structure adapted to hacienda life have great difficulties adapting to the present-day circumstances.

Aside from these special historical influences, most villagers are subject to the present conditions of life which are similar to those of peasant societies throughout the world. For those who are fortunate enough to have land, cultivation is largely done by the same rudimentary methods which were in use centuries ago. The plots are too small to justify mechanized agriculture. The villager, like most peasants, is dependent on the city to buy his products and set the price, and he is powerless to influence the conditions that determine his profit and loss. Vulnerable to exploitation, the peasant distrusts, often with good reason, all those from the urban world. At the same time, he is dependent on the city, not only for markets, but also for the consumer goods he wants and the cultural stimulation he cannot create for himself.

THE INNER LIFE OF THE VILLAGERS

The villagers we have studied have many of the qualities described in accounts of peasants in other places and times. They are selfish, suspicious of each others' motives, pessimistic about the future, and fatalistic. Many appear submissive and self-deprecatory, although they have the potential for rebelliousness and revolution. They feel inferior to city people, more stupid, and less cultured. There is an overwhelming feeling of powerlessness to influence either nature or the industrial machine that bears down on them. Here are some dreams which are shared by many villagers and typical of their feelings.[4] One man's dream expresses this feeling: "I dreamt that I was in bed in my house with all my family, all in bed, when I saw a train, an engine that came over all of us. On seeing the engine, I jumped from the bed, yelling to the one driving that he stop his machine and not crush us all." Other dreams express helplessness against animals or the inability to defend oneself against attackers.

The peasant villager suffers from poverty and frustration. Many dream of riches, but are fearful that the dream itself will cause them bad luck. It is dangerous to hope. A woman of 32 years dreamed "that I found a little money. I asked myself what I'd do with it. Then I told my husband I'd found money and that I would give it to him so that he could work by himself without anyone ordering him around. I woke up happy, but at the same time I was disillusioned because it was not true. After this dream my husband failed in his harvests." A grown man remembers a dream provoked by hunger when he was a child. "I was five years old and asleep in my bed of straw when I began to dream I was eating a piece of bread. I took some delicious bites, because I felt the sensation of hunger. Suddenly I saw I was finishing and I gave a hard bite. I awoke and what I was biting wasn't bread but the fingers of my hand."

Dreams of women, especially, express the sense of being worn down by burdens, childbearing, and the heavy, constant work that prematurely ages the peasant woman. A woman of 30 said, "Sometimes when I am sleeping, I feel that I am carrying a heavy and cold burden, and that my feet are being pulled down. I want to cry out and I cannot. I am frightened. I think it must be ghosts or dead people that want to take me to the

---

[4] These dreams are taken from over 150 dreams we have collected from villagers.

cemetery." She feels that the burdens of the past and present are dragging her to an early grave.

The villager's world is hard and frightening. As many nightmares (*pesadillas*) show, there is a constant struggle against death. A man of 40 dreamt "that I was in bed and that death (*la muerte*) came. I felt I was seated in the bed, and it touched me and I cried out: 'Hija de la chingada! You are death.' And I gave it a blow in the head, knocked it over, and heard the bones hit the floor. I awoke frightened, looking for the bones, but I did not see anything." This dream symbolizes the reality of constantly fighting against hunger and disease. The villagers take pleasure in the conquest of death, even though they know that they will lose in the end.

The peasant's dreams express a sense of living in dirt, with the constant danger of infection from parasites and other diseases.[5] The dreams also reveal the wish to escape, to fly above the dirt and poverty, but the dreamer usually falls back into the mud. Even in dreams the peasant feels little hope.

Despite the shared misery of peasant life, deep friendships are rare, and the villagers spread gossip about each other which is often damaging and not always true.[6] An extreme distrust and fear of others, based in part on experience of being cheated or betrayed, limits the possibility that the peasant will open himself fully to others. Throughout life the closest emotional tie of the villager usually remains with his mother, a fact which will be discussed more fully in later chapters. The dream of an old man, age 80, expresses distrust which persists throughout a lifetime, even though in this case the distrust proved to be baseless. In fact, the dream itself was remembered by the dreamer as "evidence" against a potential friend. "A long time ago I had a dream that made me feel very bad. At that time I was 14 years old. I was still young. I dreamed that I was standing in the street, and an individual that was my friend came over. Then without any motive,

---

[5] Studies done in the village by Professor Francisco Biagi and his collaborators from the Medical School of the National University of Mexico discovered that over 90 percent of the villagers are infected with intestinal parasites. After the study, Dr. Biagi instituted a campaign for treatment and prevention of parasites. Dr. Adan Graetz had the idea for instituting the study and helped in setting it up.

[6] The use of gossip as a source of information is an ambiguous method. Certainly some gossip is true, but some other is not. To be able to know when one is dealing with either true or false gossip is exceedingly difficult. It would seem that a piece of gossip can be believed when all or the majority of the villagers believe it, but this assumption is by no means correct. It is notorious in small and large groups that a rumor will be believed by many, and yet the many, under the influence of suggestion and their sadistic pleasure, may be as wrong as only one individual may be. Not more trustworthy is the old maxim that "where there is smoke there must be fire"; or better, perhaps, if there is fire, it might be in the one who spreads the gossip rather than in his object. Considering the value of gossip one is reminded of Spinoza's saying: what Peter says about Paul tells us more about Peter than about Paul.

he stabbed me here in the breast where the heart is. Upon taking out the knife, I saw blood flowing out into a pool. I woke up frightened and nervous. I don't know why I dreamt that. He was a friend. Afterward he was even a *compadre* [a ritual co-parent based on being the godfather to a child or another important ritual role such as a godparent to a marriage]. There was never a single difficulty between us."

Mistrust, pessimism, and maliciousness are one side of peasant life. The villagers are also concerned about living a good life, about being good people. They are ashamed and unhappy about their egoism, the lack of trust and cooperation. Some of the villagers, those who are more active and productive, measure themselves in terms of Christian teachings. They would like to have faith in their fellow man, to love their neighbors, but their experiences and their own character make this difficult. To understand the inner life of the peasant, one must understand the constant conflict between cynicism and hopelessness on the one hand and faith, often a childlike faith, on the other. This is the same conflict that Huizinga (1950) describes as characteristic of peasants at the end of the middle ages in Europe, and it is sometimes expressed in the villagers' parables and sayings (*dichos*). Some of these sayings are almost identical to the ones Huizinga quotes. The medieval peasant said, "He who serves the common weal is paid by none for his trouble," and "No horse is so well shod it never slips." The Mexican villagers with good humor and resignation will say that "He who works in a soap factory should be prepared to slip," and "He who walks with the wolves will learn to howl." There are many stories and sayings to illustrate the dangers of trying to help the community.

Furthermore, despite the peasant's submissiveness, one is struck by his dignity and sense of self. The peasant knows who he is and has few illusions about himself. In his dealings with other peasants, he values both the forms and substance of respect. Villagers refer to a family head as *Don* José or to a married woman as *Doña* María, using the Spanish designations of nobility in their normal form of address. Although the peasant humbles himself before powerful individuals, it is often the case that a villager will leave job and risk starvation rather than accept a personal insult.

There are also unique satisfactions in being a peasant villager in Mexico. One of the most important is the sense of rootedness, of living in a small village where each person knows everyone else. While gossip is sometimes hostile, it is also a means of filling out one's knowledge of a common world. In our studies comparing the villagers' modes of thinking with those of urban Mexicans and Americans (Maccoby and Modiano, 1966, 1969), we found that the villager is more concrete, descriptive, specific, and less abstract or generalizing in his mode of ordering experience. The difference in modes of thought reflects differences in the demands of culture on cognition. In the industrial world, time is money and value is constantly converted into abstract terms. People must learn ways of approaching tasks rather than specific operations, so that as methods are continually modernized individuals will not have to learn them from scratch. The industrial world demands an approach to experience that is abstract, functional, and flexible. The peasant world does not make these demands. Methods of work have remained the same for centuries. Rather than seeking to understand abstract operations, the peasant is interested in the significance of concrete experience. He is concerned about the changes in the weather. He observes the state of a plant or an animal with a careful concern for its health and illness. He is extremely perceptive in observing the emotions of others and is often accurate in judging character, especially in those he has known for a long time. The villager spends his life learning to know a few things deeply. His knowledge is concrete and nontransferable, which is a reason that many peasants feel totally lost and helpless if they are uprooted. They have not learned the modes of thought and abstract principles which are useful in the industrial world, but what they have learned about their fellows and their physical world gives them a satisfaction of being related to their surroundings, of feeling at home. The peasant has a strong sense of the nontransferability of experience, even from one peasant village to another, and he will explain the lack of knowledge or strange conduct of someone who was not born in the village by saying "He is not from here" (*No es de aquí*) even if the person has spent his whole adult life in the village.

The Mexicans tell a story about a man from the city who arrives in a small peasant village, looking for a house on *Calle Revolución*. He asks a peasant standing by the road how to find the street, and the peasant answers that he does not know. "What?" says the city man, "You live in this tiny village and don't even know which street is *Calle Revolución?* You must be very stupid." "That may be," says the peasant, "but I'm not lost."

In terms of the comforts of modern society, and even in terms of the peasant's own aspirations, his life offers little pleasure in comparison with the hardship, scarcity, anxiety, and constant frustration. The Revolution gave the peons freedom and land, but today the growing population means that three-fourths of the men are again landless. Yet, one is struck by the villagers' good humor, their hospitality and tact, their realism and relatedness to life, and their ability to respond, despite suspiciousness and pessimism, to new opportunities.

As we shall see, one cannot easily generalize the villagers' attitudes and responses. While modes of thought and culture are held in common, significant variations in socioeconomic class and individual character influence important differences in behaving and experiencing life.

3

A Socioeconomic
and Cultural Picture
of the Village

In 1960, the study administered a census interview to each male villager over 16 and each female villager over 15 years of age. The socioeconomic and cultural picture of the village is based mainly on this census, combined with participant observation of village life.

AGE, PLACE OF BIRTH, AND FAMILY GROUPINGS

The census of 1960 lists 792 villagers, including 209 males over 16 and 208 females over 15 years of age who were interviewed. The remainder of the villagers, 375 children and younger adolescents, comprise 47 percent of the population. Although many young men of age 14 are full-fledged field workers and little girls do all the housework at an even earlier age, the cutoff point for age was decided mainly in terms of the ages when villagers begin to marry and form families. At age 16 boys are also legally eligible to receive land. The 417 individuals age 16 (15 in the case of women) or over, included in the census will be referred to as the adult villagers. As Table 3:1 indicates, a majority of them are less than 30 years of age and only 5 percent are aged 60 or over. As in other peasant societies, individuals grow up quickly, marry early, and die young.

Only 31 percent of the villagers were actually born in the village. As Table 3:2 reports, the largest percentage (36 percent) came from the neighboring state of Guerrero after the Revolution, particularly between 1927 and 1930 when land was partitioned. Other villagers migrated from other parts of Morelos and the State of Mexico. None of the villagers was born in Mexico City nor any other large urban center; all came from peasant backgrounds. The majority of immigrants were under the age of 25 when they arrived in the village (see Table 3:3). Some were brought by

TABLE 3:1   Age Composition of the Adult Villagers (in Percentages)

Age	Percent of Men (N=209)	Percent of Women (N=208)	Total Percent (N=417)
16-20 (women 15-20)	15	20	18
21-30	39	33	36
31-40	19	20	19
41-50	10	13	11
51-60	13	9	11
61-70	3	2	3
Over 70	1	3	2
	100	100	100

TABLE 3:2   Birthplace of Villagers (in Percentages)
(N=417)

Place	Percent Born There
The village	31
Other parts of Morelos	18
Guerrero	36
State of Mexico	10
Federal district	0
Michoacan	2
Other northern states	1
Other southern states	2
	100

TABLE 3:3   Age of Arrival in Village (in Percentages)
(N=417)

Age of Arrival	Percent
Born in village	31
Before age 6	9
Before age 15	13
Before age 25	22
After age 25	21
No data	4
	100

their parents. Others came in search of land or work, attracted by the climate and the abundant water that allow for year-round planting. Of the parents of the present villagers, even fewer were born there. As Table 3:4 shows, only 9 percent of the parents were born in the village, 46 percent in the state of Guerrero, and most of the rest either in other parts of Morelos or the nearby State of Mexico. This pattern is not uncommon for villages in this area of Morelos, which were depopulated by violence, famine, and disease during the revolutionary upheaval.

The majority of villagers come from large families where there is a

TABLE 3:4   Birthplace of Parents (in Percentages)
(N=417)

Place	Percent with Father Born There	Percent with Mother Born There
The village	9	9
Other parts of Morelos	19	21
Guerrero	46	46
State of Mexico	17	16
Federal district	0	0
Michoacan	2	2
Other northern states	1	1
Other southern states	3	2
No information	3	3
	100	100

median number of 5 children (see Table 3:5). Just 2 percent report they
had no brothers or sisters, while 14 percent are from families of 10 or
more children. Of the 133 families with children at the time of the census,
the median number of living children per family was 4 (Table 3:6), but
this does not include children who had died, and it includes many young
parents who had not yet completed forming their families. Of parents aged
30 or older, the median number of living children was 5, which would
indicate that the villagers do not differ from their parents in the size of
families they form.

Table 3:7 describes the civil status of the villagers. Twenty-four percent have never married or have not yet married. This percentage includes more men (61 individuals) than women (39 individuals) since
women marry at an earlier age. Of the unmarried men, 40 percent are
under age 20 and 90 percent under age 30. Of the unmarried women, 43
percent are under 20 and 80 percent under 30. Only 5 men and 8 women
over age 30 have never been married. Eight percent are single after having
been separated or divorced. Thirty-eight percent of the villagers have been
married officially in a civil ceremony, including 26 percent who have also
been married within the church and 12 percent married without a religious
ceremony. Another 9 percent were married in the church only, and have

TABLE 3:5   Number of Siblings (in Percentages)
(N=417)

Number of Siblings	Percent
No siblings	2
1-3	23
4-6	33
7-9	25
Over 9	14
No data	3
	100

TABLE 3:6   Number of Living Children of Families with Children

Number of Children	Number of Families	Percent of Families
1	26	20
2	17	13
3	19	14
4	23	17
5	20	15
6	13	10
7	8	6
8	2	1.5
10-12	2	1.5
N	130	98

Median = 4

TABLE 3:7   Civil Status (in Percentages)

	Percent of Women	Percent of Men	Total Percent
Single—never married	19	29	24
Single—separated	9	7	8
Married—civil and church	26	26	26
Married—civil only	12	12	12
Married—church only	9	9	9
Married—free union	13	15	14
Widowed	12	1	6
No information	0	1	1
	100	100	100

never signed civil documents. Fourteen percent of the villagers consider themselves married by free union. Generally, they are the poorest people, for whom the cost of either the civil papers or the more expensive church ceremony is prohibitive. Finally, 6 percent are widowed, including 25 women and only 3 men. This disproportion is in part due to a shorter male life span, for men can die as a result of violence, but the figures are also influenced by the tendency for some women who have been abandoned by their mates to then write them off as deceased and to call themselves widows.[1]

---

[1] From our observation, 8 of the 25 are real widows. Many of the others have been abandoned by a man who may or may not be alive. The tendency to consider the husband who has abandoned the family as dead is also reflected in the villagers' statements concerning whether or not their own parents are living. Thirty-three percent report both parents as living; 27 percent state that only the mother is living, as compared to 7 percent who state that only the father is living. In fact, there are a few cases in which we know the father deserted the family and has not been heard from since, but in most of these cases the children report the father as dead rather than missing.

Twenty percent of the villagers (60 percent women and 40 percent men) have been married more than once.

The 417 adult villagers can be grouped into 162 households or economic units, composed of the household head, spouse (if any), and dependents (if any). In some of these households, grown children also work or earn money, but they contribute to the household unit. In other cases, an individual, sometimes a relative but possibly a servant or a paying boarder, may live within the house or house site of a household unit without being considered part of their household. Such villagers (there are 11) are considered as separate household units. Of the total 162 household units, 127 (80 percent) are headed by men, and 33 (20 percent) are headed by women. The majority (70 percent) of female heads of household are "widows." The others are unmarried or abandoned mothers. As indicated, some of the widows were in fact also abandoned by one or more husbands. They are women who have a series of consorts who may leave them with children. Of the households nominally headed by a male, 6 are in fact dominated by a woman who has had a series of husbands in free union. The significance of the households headed by women will be considered in later chapters.

Of the 162 households, 79 (49 percent) own their house sites. Most of the others (42 percent) live on the house sites of parents, relatives, or friends. Only 14 households, or 9 percent, pay rent for their living accommodations. Due to a shortage of land in the village, it is not uncommon to find a house site with two houses, one belonging to parents and another belonging to a married son and his family.

LITERACY AND SCHOOLING

According to the census interview, 24 percent of the villagers read and write well, 44 percent can read simple notices and write their names and simple messages, while 32 percent are illiterate (see Table 3:8). Very few of the villagers read for enjoyment. No more than ten read newspapers, and fewer read books. Among the younger generation, comic books, in-

TABLE 3:8   Literacy by Sex

	Percent of Men (N=192)	Percent of Women (N=194)	Total Percent (N=386)*
Reads and writes well	29	19	24
Reads and writes a little	44	44	44
Illiterate	27	36	32
	100	99**	100

*No information on 17 men and 14 women.
**Since percentages were rounded off to nearest integer, some total 99 and others 101 percent.

cluding those that portray a soap-opera-type of love story with photographs and dialogue (such as *Doctora Corazón* and *Risas y Lágrimas*), have become popular in recent years. When the study opened a library in the village, these comic books along with illustrated magazines were the most eagerly sought by older as well as younger readers.

The level of literacy in the village corresponds to the demands of peasant life. The printed word has an economic function only for those who work in the nearby sugar refinery or the men who need a license to drive a truck or tractor. For the others, it may be useful to read notices or to do simple sums, but a high level of literacy would be a luxury. However, during the past decade an increase in school attendance is raising the level of literacy. Of villagers under 30, only 21 percent are illiterate compared to 43 percent of those over age 30. In observing Mexican peasants one is struck by their remarkably good memory. This suggests that perhaps when people do not write their memories are sharpened. If the memory is freed by the ability to write down what one wants to remember, one relies on the written word and the memory function is weakened. One might speculate that the art of writing and reading is not a one-sided blessing, especially when it does not serve to enhance the capacity to acquire valuable knowledge and to enjoy literature.

The men are slightly more literate than the women. Yet, as Table 3:9 demonstrates, there is no significant difference between the sexes in years of schooling. Rather, the men more than the women are likely to find literacy useful and practice it more, while women who have had one or two years of schooling may never again read or write.

Sixty-nine percent of the villagers have had some schooling, but only 16 percent finished primary school. Six percent, the sons and daughters of the richer peasants, have gone on to higher education, secondary school,

TABLE 3:9   Years of Schooling (in percentages)

Years of Schooling	Percent of Men (N=193)	Percent of Women (N=192)	Total Percent (N=385)*
No schooling	29	31	29
One year	11	7	9
Two years	8	12	10
Three years	13	12	13
Four years	16	15	15
Five years	7	7	7
Six years—finished primary school	9	10	10
Secondary school or beyond	7	6	7
	100	100	100

*No information on 16 men and 16 women.

technical training in a nearby town, or normal school to become village teachers. One villager was an agronomist, another was studying architecture, and a third started medical school shortly after the census was completed.

The tendency for more children to continue their schooling represents the determination of one group of villagers to give their sons and daughters the chance to achieve a better life in nonagricultural work. The shortage of land and the increasing population are factors which turn the villagers' attention to the city, to new industries nearby which demand a high level of literacy. The village first opened a primary school in the late 1930s after petitioning the government and contributing money that was saved by canceling some of the costly fiestas that had drained the village of its small surplus. Behind this campaign was a group of men, mainly immigrants of the late 1920s, who were particularly hard-working and "progressive." They have continued to support the school and encourage their children, especially the boys, to prepare for the future.

When age is correlated with years of schooling, we find that those in the age range of 16-30 have had significantly more schooling than any other age group ($r = .35$, $p < .01$), while the age range 41-50 ($r = -.30$, $p < .01$) and 51-60 ($r = -.30$, $p < .01$) are both negatively correlated with years of schooling.[2] The age range of 31-40 is in the middle, also

---

[2] All r correlations reported in this study are product-moment r's. A full understanding of the product-moment correlation can be found in any standard textbook on statistics such as McNemar (1955). However, since we shall have occasion to use the product-moment correlation often in reporting the results of the study, a general understanding of its meaning will be useful for the reader.

In the present example, the correlation between years of schooling and the age range 16-30 is .35. A possible numerical product-moment correlation can range from -1.0 to $+1.0$. If membership in this age range *always* implied a high level of schooling and not being in this age range implied a low level of schooling, the correlation between the two variables would approach $+1.0$. In contrast, if being in the age range 51-60 always implied a low level of schooling and not being in this age range implied a high level of schooling, the correlation between the two variables would move toward -1.0. If there were no systematic relationship between an age range and years of schooling, the correlation would be 0.0, meaning in effect that some people of this age had a high level of schooling, some had a low level, and that within this particular population there was no way of predicting whether a person of any particular age is likely to have had more or less schooling than the average adult.

In the following chapters, we shall also consider correlations between character traits and between character and socioeconomic variables.

In practice, correlations between character traits seldom approach the certainty of 1.0 or -1.0. Generally, the investigator looks for correlations large enough to be considered "significant," meaning that the value of the product-moment r cannot be attributed to a chance relationship. The significance level is found by a formula which takes into account the size of the correlation and the number of cases on which it is based to arrive at the probability that the correlation could be attributed to a chance relation, rather than a systematic relation between the variables, given the assumption

negatively correlated with years of schooling ($r = -.13$), but the correlation is not significant.

MEDICAL CARE

The census also determined the villagers' mode of treating illness, whether they turn to trained doctors or go to the traditional curandero or healer. This is not a question of poverty, since the healers and doctors generally charge similar fees. Furthermore, while some villagers who belong to the Sugar Cooperative are entitled to free medical care, they may still prefer a healer. As Table 3:10 reports, 52 percent of the villagers seek medical care exclusively from physicians. Thirty-six percent sometimes go to physicians, but also go to healers. These villagers may go to the healer first, and if he cannot cure them or the disease becomes very grave, they will look for a physician. In contrast, there are villagers who will seek help first from a physician, but if he fails to help them, which may be the case with psychosomatic ailments, they will then go to the healer, who often shows a better understanding of hysterical ailments and the use of suggestion or symbolic expiation as a way of alleviating symptoms. Twelve percent of the villagers go to healers only. These are generally the elder villagers who stick to traditional methods. The correlation between age and a scale ranging from 1 (indicating exclusive care by physicians) to 3 (indicating exclusive care by healers) is significant ($r = .39$, $p < .01$). Put

---

that there is only a chance relationship between the variables. This assumption is callled the Null Hypothesis, and traditionally in statistics it is rejected when the significance level is less than 5 chances in 100. Thus, a significant product-moment r (correlation) is large enough so that if there were really no systematic relationship between the variables, a correlation made from a random sampling from the same population with the same number of cases would produce an r that large or larger less than 5 percent of the time.

Besides looking at the significance of a correlation, we should also take account of the fact that it provides a way of determining the percentage of variance in one variable that can be accounted for by the other variable, or, in other words, the percentage of variability they hold in common. This percentage is found by squaring the correlation. For example, if the product-moment r between two character traits, masochism and submission, were .30, it could be stated that masochism accounts for 9 percent of the variance of submission or vice versa. It is important to keep in mind that a correlation may be significant but low. With 400 cases, a significant product-moment correlation can be as low as .12, meaning that, although only 1 percent of the variance between the variables has been taken into account, it is still true that a significant relationship exists between the variables. A significant but low correlation might indicate that the measures used to gather data were not fine enough to discover what is in reality a higher correlation. Or it might indicate that in reality the two variables account for a small but significant mutual variance that would remain the same no matter how fine the instruments used to measure the variables. It is important to stress the fact that even significant correlations must be understood in the light of both theory and the assessment of the instruments used.

TABLE 3:10   Mode of Medical Care (in Percentages)

Medical Care	Percent of Men (N=203)	Percent of Women (N=205)	Total Percent (N=408)*
Modern medicine – goes to physicians	54	50	52
Modern and traditional mixed–goes to physicians and curanderos	36	36	36
Traditional curing– goes to curanderos	10	14	12
	100	100	100

*No information on 6 men and 3 women.

another way, 61 percent of the villagers under age 40, compared to only 28 percent of the villagers over 40, rely on modern medical care only.

Reliance on modern medical care appears to be a result of schooling. Of those villagers with no schooling, 31 percent go to physicians and 25 percent to healers, with 44 percent mixing their mode of medical care between the two. Of those villagers who have finished primary school, 80 percent use physicians and none leave their medical care exclusively to curanderos. There is a similar relationship between literacy and the increased reliance on modern medical care. In other words, formal education and familiarity with the printed word turn the villagers away from traditional customs to the modern culture of the city.

OCCUPATION

The main work of the village is agricultural, and 85 percent of the men are engaged in farming as their main occupation (see Table 3:11). The rest of the men are scattered in a variety of occupations. Nine men are skilled workers, such as a carpenter, bricklayer, electrician, tailor, butcher (slaughtering animals), mechanic, or tractor driver. Sixteen men work as unskilled labor on nonagricultural projects, such as unskilled help in building, or caretaking the weekend houses owned by rich people from Mexico City.

A special category of agricultural workers are those men who frequently (three times or more) migrated to the United States as braceros or contract farm workers. This group includes 31 men (15 percent of the men). Working mainly in California or Arizona, these men used to do heavy farm labor at wages lower than American workers (70 cents to a dollar an hour), but fabulously high for the village, where at the time of the study a jornalero or day laborer seldom received more than a dollar

TABLE 3:11   Occupations

Occupation	Number of Men (N=209)	Number of Women (N=208)	Total Number (N=417)
Agriculture	172	17	189
Skilled labor	9	0	9
Unskilled, nonagriculture	16	0	16
Sugar refinery	8	2	10
Bracero (migrant labor)	31	0	31
Trade, selling, speculation	10	16	26
Stores or bars	10	11	21
Teachers	2	3	5
Students	9	8	17
Housework	3	159	162
Domestic servant	0	24	24
Seamstress	0	10	10
Nurse, midwife, injectionist	0	3	3
Does no work	3	8	11
	273*	261*	534*

*Individuals may be classified in more than one category

a day. Even a small land holder would make and save more money working for three months in the United States than farming his own land for a year. Shortage of land combined with the relatively high wages paid in the United States attracted 20 percent of the men at one time or another. Of these the 15 percent considered occupational braceros used to migrate on a regular basis. Another 17 percent of the men have left the village to find work in other parts of Mexico at one time or another, while 63 percent of the men have worked only in the village or nearby.

A few of the villagers work in the nearby sugar refinery. They include 8 men and 2 women. These jobs include caretaking, work in the stores run by the refinery, clerical work, and industrial work; one villager operates a mobile crane.

Villagers are occupied in three categories of nonmanual work: business, trade and speculation, and teaching. Twenty-one individuals, 10 men and 11 women, run seven small stores, six *cantinas* (bars), and the three *molinos de nixtamal* which grind corn into the *masa* used for making tortillas. The stores sell coffee, beans, sugar, eggs, canned food, soft drinks, beer, cigarettes, soap, and small hardware such as rope, nails, buckets, and electric light bulbs. Some also sell firecrackers and one specializes in cloth to make clothes. Most villagers shop for their essentials at these stores, usually making very small purchases and often on credit. Bills are normally settled weekly.

Another group of 26 individuals, including 10 men and 16 women, are occupied in trade and speculation. Some are very small business-women. Of this group, 2 women buy produce in the village to sell at a small profit in the markets of nearby towns and the state capital. Two women have small *puestos* or stands in the village zocalo where they sell candy, fruits, tacos, and tamales. On the weekends they are sometimes joined by 1 or 2 more women selling *carnitas* (cooked meats) and *pozole*. Two other women engage in selling milk and sometimes fruits from their orchards. Trade on a larger scale is practiced by 3 richer peasants with trucks who speculate by buying a complete harvest to sell in the large Mexico City markets. Others engage in such speculation on a smaller scale.

The teachers include 2 men and 3 women, 3 of them employed in the village school, the other 2 in nearby locations.

Another group of 17 younger adult villagers, 9 male and 8 female, were attending secondary school, training schools, or the university.

As the overwhelming majority of the men are engaged in agriculture, so the main occupation of most women (77 percent) is housekeeping. The other female occupations include working at the sugar refinery, in small businesses, in small trade, and in teaching. Besides these, another group of 24 women work as domestic servants, mainly in the weekend residences in the village, but some also in the houses of the richer peasants. Seventeen women work in the fields as agricultural workers, doing what is normally men's work. Ten women gain income as seamstresses, and 3 women are engaged in medical work: 1 injects medicines for a small fee, 1 is a midwife (*partera*), and the third is a nurse.

LAND TENURE

At the time of the census, 1936 *tareas* of land, both in the village and rented from nearby villages, were being cultivated by farmers who worked on plots ranging from 2 tareas to 180 tareas. The tarea is a common measure, meaning a task and perhaps referring to a good day's work. It measures 1,000 square meters or one-tenth of a hectare; a hectare is about two and one-half acres. The largest percentage of the land (54 percent) was planted with cane. Rice was the next most important crop, accounting for 23 percent of the land. The rest of the land was used for *maíz* (corn), *frijol* (beans), tomatoes, onions, melons, and other garden crops which are considered speculative since the market fluctuates so sharply. One hundred and seventeen tareas, belonging to villagers, lay fallow. It is notable that the villagers' crop preferences increasingly are determined by the market rather than by their own needs for consumption or the traditional and, in some indigenous villages, religious preference for corn. However, there are villagers who still feel a sentimental attachment to growing corn and plant some maiz on their house sites. The main reason more corn is not grown is that the yields have not been good in the area, and there are pressures from the sugar industry to plant cane, which is also easier and promises a guaranteed income (see Chapter 6).

Table 3:12 reports the distribution of cultivated land by households, and demonstrates that, although agriculture is the main village occupation and source of livelihood, the majority of households (53 percent) are landless. Some landless agricultural workers were braceros. The others either worked as peones for the richer entrepreneurs or sharecropped land for them. For those households with land in cultivation, the mean plot is between 11 and 19 tareas. The distribution of land by households forms a pyramidal structure, with a few villagers at the top controlling relatively large holdings (all of them are small in terms of the Midwest of the United States), a greater number with smaller plots, and the majority with nothing. To understand the inequality of land holdings, it is necessary to explain that some villagers were given land after the Revolution, while the others have had to be extremely fortunate and hardworking to accumulate the capital to buy or even rent land.

Those villagers who received land are called ejidatarios or members of the village ejido. The term ejido was used by free villages before the Revolution of 1910 to mean common grazing or farm land. It also referred to land given to floating Indian populations during the colonial period to induce them to settle down in villages. The term ejido now refers to a community which has received land to be used according to the rules of the Agrarian Code which has been developed during the past 50 years, based on Article 27 of the Constitution of 1917. As in the case of the village, the land may be given as an outright grant of land expropriated from the hacienda. In other cases, ejido land has been given back to a community which lost it through means which are judged to have been illegal (restitution). In still other cases, a community may receive confirmation of land that has been in its possession for generations. Ordinarily, the ejido con-

TABLE 3:12   Land in Cultivation in Tareas for Heads of Household

Tareas (= 1,000 sq. meters)	Number of Households (N=162)	Percent of Households
0	84	53
1-10	25	15
11-19	18	11
20-29	15	9
30-39	10	7
40-49	4	2
50-83	4	2
100-180	2	1

sists of at least 20 individuals who were eligible to receive land in accordance with the rules of the Agrarian Code.[3]

The two major economic classes in the village are the ejidatarios who control land given them after the Revolution in the partition of land previously held by the hacienda, and the nonejidatarios, most of whom are landless. There are 69 ejidatarios in the village, 54 men and 15 women. Thus, 26 percent of the adult men are ejidatarios and 74 percent are nonejidatarios. Of the 155 men who are not ejidatarios, 87 percent do not control any land. The other 13 percent have managed to accumulate capital to buy or rent farm land, but only 2 percent of the nonejidatarios work more than 2 hectares (about 5 acres), which is the average holding for the ejidatarios. The average land holding for the nonejidatarios with land is 1 hectare or 10 acres.

While the Revolution in Morelos began as a defense of land rights from the haciendas, during the fighting the Zapatistas turned toward a more radical goal, that each peasant should have his own *parcela* within the community ejido. The plot of land was meant to be large enough to provide a decent living for a family. It was to be unalienable, neither divisible nor subject to sale, and inherited intact by the ejidatario's chosen heir, either male or female. The peasant community would become an ejido, a society of free land holders, where decisions would be made democratically, each ejidatario with a single vote. Ideally, all the small farmers would be included within the ejido. The Zapatistas, themselves peasants, recognized that different villages had varying customs, and they left open the possibility that some villages might wish to have a communal ejido, while others would want to divide the land into small plots.[4] However, the national policy was at first based on Article 11 of the 1915 law which stressed the individual holdings of parcelas, although it recognized the villages' rights to hold communal land.[5] However, according to the Agrarian Code, a parcela given to an ejidatario can neither be sold nor rented and is to be kept by the ejidatario only so long as he farms it himself. The development of the Agrarian Code, especially in the 1930s under the presidency of Lázaro Cárdenas encouraged more cooperative structures. According to the Code, all pastureland, woodland, and other noncrop lands

[3] For a decripion of the organization of ejidos according to the Agrarian Code, see Whetten (1948), pp. 182 ff.

[4] In some villages even before the Spanish Conquest, the land system was similar to the ejido structure. Kinship groups (*calpulli*) administered communal land, and families had plots which were unalienable. See Tannenbaum (1929), p. 3.

[5] In 1929, Tannenbaum wrote of the agrarian laws, "It is important to see clearly that the legislation looks forward to individual use and enjoyment of the tillable soil and resorts temporarily to common possession and use for purposes of convenience and as a means of discipline and training for future individual ownership" p. 239.

are to be held and used in common. There is also the possibility that the ejido can take the structure of a collective farm, rather than a federation of small property holders. The new emphasis on cooperation had the purpose of trying to strengthen the economic power of the small farmer, and at the same time encouraging the production of extensively farmed cash crops, using modern methods. As we shall see, the peasant's character presents a stumbling block which must be taken into account in developing such cooperative structures. The overwhelming majority of Mexican ejidos are made up of small, individual land holders, with a community organization much like that of the village here described.[6]

In the village the partition of land began in 1924 and continued until 1935. The individual plots are of unequal size, ranging from 5 to 70 tareas. This is in part because some land was better irrigated and considered equivalent to a larger plot of nonirrigated land, and because some villagers accepted larger house sites rather than parcelas. Furthermore, at the time of partition, the peasant who claimed land had to have enough capital to work it and fence it, and some villagers lacked the capital or the ambition to claim a larger plot. Others, who had the capital, refused to take their share because they feared that the government or the former owners of the hacienda would someday return to take the land away from those who had worked it. Here, peasant suspiciousness and distrust put a brake on claiming land that was there for the asking. These fearful villagers did finally apply for land, but often had to settle for smaller parcelas. In the early 1930s when the population of the village was approximately 300 inhabitants there was land enough for everyone. Since then the village has more than doubled by birth and immigration. There is no longer enough land for the sons of the original villagers and the first immigrants. Of the 155 male nonejidatarios, 36 percent are the sons of ejidatarios and 64 percent include men and their sons who arrived in the village too late to receive land.

---

6 Whetten (1948) reports that 86.5 percent of the 5,650 ejidos in Mexico in 1944 were individually operated, while 12.3 percent were collectively operated, and 1.2 percent had a mixed organization. In 1960, the agricultural census reported that only 2 percent of 1.6 million ejido *members* were organized in collective ejidos. This percentage has not varied significantly since 1940. (See "Land Reform and Productivity: The Mexican Case: a Preliminary Analysis," Department of Agricultural Economics, Agricultural Experiment Station, University of Illinois, November 1966.) Article 200 of the Agrarian Code stipulates that the President of the Republic shall determine the type of farm organization. Lands which constitute economic units requiring the joint efforts of all ejidatarios for their cultivation, and ejidos in agricultural zones where products are homogeneous and intended for industrial purposes should be worked on a collective basis. Beyond this, collective organization may also be adopted in other ejidos whenever technical and economic studies show that such organization is feasible and that in this way better living conditions can be obtained for the villagers. See Whetten (1948), pp. 202-3.

To be an ejidatario in the village is to belong to a privileged social class. Most importantly, it means having the chance to work one's own land and rise above mere subsistence, not being dependent on others for work, not having to accept even the most menial tasks in order to stay alive. Beyond this, the ejidatarios are also eligible to become members of the sugar cooperative, which provides loans, medical services (under Mexico's Social Security program), life insurance (10,000 pesos), possibilities for scholarships for children of ejidatarios, and possibilities for work for landless family members within the refinery. All of this is denied the non-ejidatario. The ejidatarios dominate the village political structures, have more material wealth than the others, own most of the small businesses, and give their children more educational opportunities. Furthermore, most of the jornaleros are dependent on them for work. Thus, there are two basic socioeconomic classes within the village, despite the Revolution's breaking up of large land holdings and attempting to create a classless peasant society of free farmers.

There is no exact correlation between being an ejidatario and material wealth. The main reason for this is that some ejidatarios have been unsuccessful, either through bad luck or because of maladapted character structure. Ten percent of the ejidatarios regularly rent out all of their land, while another 20 percent rent or sharecrop a percentage of their land. The reasons for this will be considered in the chapters on Character and Socioeconomic Variables (Chapter 6) and Alcoholism (Chapter 8). Thus, it is more exact to state that the effective class of ejidatarios are those 70 percent who personally manage their own land.

HOUSING

Besides providing for the partitioning of farming land, the fruits of the Revolution included giving the peasants house sites in the village. The first ejidatarios could claim unoccupied land, but, unlike the unalienable ejidos, the house sites can be bought and sold. The census showed that 51 percent of the households have no house site. Fourteen percent own from 100 to 500 square meters; 11 percent from 600 to 1000 square meters; 9 percent from 1100 to 2000 square meters; 8 percent from 2100 to 3000 square meters; and 3 percent over 3000 square meters. The largest house site in the village is 7700 square meters. Almost all of those who have no farm land also lack property in the village; however, the correlation between the amount of ejido land and size of house site while significant ($r = .31$, $p < .01$) is low because some ejidatarios have small parcelas but larger house sites, which are sometimes used as orchards for fruit trees, especially avocados, or for raising animals, such as chickens or pigs. Also, since house sites, unlike ejido land, can be bought and sold, some of the villagers have sacrificed parts of their house sites while their parcelas have remained intact.

The census also rated different types of houses within the village. It was found that 24 percent of the households lived in minimal housing, jacales, huts made of sticks and mud with dirt floors and a straw-covered roof which gives little protection from the heavy summer rains. Another 29 percent of the households live in adobe houses, with dirt floors, and usually with a roof of straw or palm leaves, although in some cases the roof may be made of cardboard or asbestos strips. These adobe houses are nonpartitioned, so that as in the jacales, eating, sleeping, and cooking go on within the same room. Finally, 21 percent of the households live in houses made of concrete or adobe, with concrete floors, separate rooms for living, eating, and cooking, and roofs made of solid materials. Of this 21 percent, there are some houses (9 percent of the total households) which are not only solidly built, but are also really comfortable both in appearance and size.

OTHER CAPITAL POSSESSIONS

A few of the peasants have accumulated capital goods such as stores, livestock, machinery, or loan capital, which become a source of greater income. At the time of the study, even a television set was a capital investment, since the owner was able to charge a small admission price to the other villagers. Since then, there has been a significant increase in the number of television sets owned, and most villagers can now find a relative, *padrino,* or compadre who will invite them to watch television.

A scale of capital goods was constructed with each worth more than 10,000 pesos (or 800 dollars) considered as five points and each capital possession on the 2,000 to 5,000 level (160 to 400 dollars) considered as four points. Five points would be given for a truck, a tractor (which would be rented out with driver), a bar, a store, a billiard parlor, or loan capital worth 10,000 pesos or more. Four points would be given for possession of an old car (which might be used for a taxi service), a television set, a

TABLE 3:13 Possession of Capital Goods

Points	Households (N=162)	Percent of Households
0	142	88
4 (5,000 pesos or under)	7	4
5 (10,000 pesos)	7	4
9 (up to 15,000 pesos)	1	1
10-20	4	2
50	1	1
		100

corn grinder (*molina*), livestock, or loan capital worth from 2,000 to 5,000 pesos.

The scale (Table 3:13) showed that very few peasants were able to accumulate capital, either money or possessions. Eighty-eight percent (142 households) have none at all. The other 12 percent include seven households with one possession worth 5,000 pesos or less, seven with one possession worth 10,000 pesos or less, one household with two capital goods, and five households with three or four capital goods. One individual, who stands by himself at the top of the economic pyramid, has 50 points on the capital possessions scale.

All but two of the households with capital goods are headed by ejidatarios. The lack of capital among the majority, even the majority of those with land, illustrates the poverty of the villagers. Most live on the subsistence level, and those who produce a small surplus generally spend it first on improved housing, then on food, on costly fiestas for a saint's day, a graduation or a wedding, or on a few prestige items of consumption, rather than on capital investments.

CONSUMER GOODS

The consumer goods most valued by the villagers include a gas stove, a good bed with a mattress, or a sewing machine (which in some cases is a capital good). In the point scale constructed for prestige consumer possessions, each of these items was worth three points. Other valued consumer goods including electric lighting, a radio, kerosene stove, bicycle, and electric iron were scored as two-point items.

The scale of consumer goods (Table 3:14) shows 55 households (33 percent) with none of these valuable consumer goods. Another 16 families (10 percent) have one item such as a radio or a good bed. The scale reaches 26 points which are held by two families, one of which is also at the top of the capital goods scale.

TABLE 3:14   Possession of Consumer Goods

Points	Households (N=162)	Percent of Households
0	55	33
2	16	10
4	15	9
6	14	9
8	9	6
10	16	10
12	13	8
14-16	12	7
17-19	7	5
20-26	5	3
	162	100

Who are the owners of these consumer goods? Of the ejidatarios, 72 percent have consumer goods compared to 23 percent of the nonejidatarios. Of the 47 ejidatarios who work their own land, 43 percent have 10 points or more on the scale, while, of the ejidatarios who rent their land, 17 percent have 10 points or more. Fourteen percent of the nonejidatarios have 10 points or more on the scale, and 70 percent of these nonejidatarios worked as braceros in the United States, bringing either money or consumer goods home with them.

THE SOCIOECONOMIC SCALE

The distinction between ejidatario and nonejidatario is a good indicator of socioeconomic class in the village. On every economic measure, the ejidatarios have more than the nonejidatarios. However, we decided to construct a second measure of socioeconomic class, since there are a few nonejidatarios who have accumulated land or other capital, while among the ejidatarios some have dissipated their holdings and others have accumulated more land and possessions than the average. To take account of these differences in wealth, a measure of income might seem sufficient, but we did not attempt to measure income for three reasons. First of all, the peasant is reluctant to tell an outsider his income. After all, it might be used by the government as a basis of taxing him. But even if he trusted the interviewer, it would be difficult even for him to calculate his real income. Some of it includes what he consumes from his own planting and livestock. Other income may be made from occasional day labor, of which he keeps no record. Finally, the peasant's income varies considerably from season to season and from year to year. One year he may benefit from a shortage of the particular crop he plants. Another year he may plant the same crop and find the market glutted, the prices a fraction of what they were. The next year bad weather, crop disease, or insects may destroy most of his planting. For the day laborer also, income varies considerably with both the labor market, the season, and the type of crops being planted. An accurate measure of peasant income for any one period might be considerably misleading as to the average income, either overly high or too low.

We considered that a scale which took account of landownership, capital, and possessions would provide a more accurate measure of the peasant's real income than would any short-term estimate of earnings translated into money. In order to construct a more exact rating of socioeconomic class, for each unit head we combined scores for (1) capital goods owned, (2) consumer goods owned, (3) land under cultivation, (4) land owned in the village, and (5) type of house owned. These scores are weighted in such a way as to give each its relative economic value, as far as possible. Thus, we considered that 10 points of capital possessions would have similar earning power to 30 tareas of land; therefore capital goods points are multiplied by three, and land in use is scored by the number of tareas. For land owned in the village, one point is added for each 100 square meters, which apportions credit for the capital value of large house sites (planting orchards, garden plots). The type of house is scored by allotting 20 points for the best type of housing (brick or concrete, solid roofing, separate rooms, spaciousness, latrine); 12 points for the same type of house but on a smaller, less costly scale; five points for a one-room adobe house; and zero for jacales. Finally, the consumer goods points were added to the total scale.

The socioeconomic scale (SES) is an approximate measure of material wealth for village households. More weight is given to land and capital goods since they have earning power. Lesser weight is given to housing and possession of consumer goods which indicate past expenditures. The SES measures what each household has managed to accumulate, its current earning power, and its style of life as indicated by house type. The scale correlates with the subjective impressions of differential wealth by the participant observers who worked with the study. As we shall discover, the scale also proves to be a convincing measure in its significant correlations with other socioeconomic measures and with character.

Table 3:15 reports the distribution of the SES for unit heads. Forty-five units (28 percent) score zero, meaning that more than one-fourth of the households live in jacales, without electricity, sleeping on straw mats on the ground, landless, and with nothing to show for their labor. This is the population that lives on a bare subsistence level. This group also includes

TABLE 3:15 Distribution of Households on the Socioeconomic Scale

Points		Number of Households	Percentage of Households
0	1	45	28
1-3	} 2	11	7
4-5		9	6
6-10	3	12	7
11-18	4	12	7
20-25	} 5	12	7
27-35		17	11
36-39	} 6	10	6
40-45		9	6
50-70	7	8	5
70-90	8	8	5
90-100		3	2
133-150		2 }	3
160-163	} 9	2	
186		1 }	1
343		1	
		162	101

a few units which live with better-off families, including servants, boarders, and poor relatives who own no houses. Another 20 units (12 percent) score from 1 to 5 points. Households in this group may own a good bed with a mattress and a battery radio, but those who do not live with richer families have the same minimal housing, with much the same diet and mode of life that characterizes those with nothing.

The median of the scale falls at 12 points which would describe a family with an adobe house, a good bed, and a radio, possibly a sewing machine or gas stove, but unlikely to own land. On the upper part of the scale, there are 9 households (6 percent) with over 90 points. These are the individuals, most of them ejidatarios, who live in the best houses, control capital and land, and enjoy more consumer possessions than the others. Between this group and the median are degrees of relative prosperity which, it must be kept in mind, all represent poverty in comparison to a median American standard of living.

In order to use the SES for comparisons and correlations, it was coded in two different ways. One code makes the SES an ordinal scale with nine categories (see Table 3:15) ranging from one (zero points) to nine (90 points or more). All the product-moment correlations (r) between the SES and other variables are based on this coding.

Another way of summarizing the SES for purposes of comparison is to form three class groupings: a lowest class, a middle class, and a highest class. As far as possible, we attempted to make equal groupings, but the cuts were modified by taking into account natural groupings. Thus, the lowest class, including codes one and two, describes 41 percent of the households. The middle class, ranging from code three through code five, includes 32 percent, and the highest class, codes six through nine, includes 27 percent of the economic units. The lowest and the highest classes can be described most clearly. The lowest class is made up mostly of jornaleros or abandoned mothers who live in the most miserable circumstances. It also includes some servants, poor relatives, and a very few landowners who because of their alcoholism have sunk to the bottom of the social pyramid (see Chapter 8). The highest class includes families that live in brick or concrete houses, or in a few cases especially large adobe houses, and who have accumulated land and/or capital enough to raise themselves above the mere level of subsistence or dependence on others.

The middle class grouping is more difficult to describe, since it ranges from households with no more than a few consumer possessions (6 to 10 points) to households with some land, possessions, and perhaps a small amount of capital. This grouping should be considered as a middle ground, describing households which are neither prosperous (in relative terms) nor at the subsistence level, while the lowest and upper class groupings correspond more clearly to distinct socioeconomic classes, with different rela-

TABLE 3:16   Land Tenure and the Socioeconomic Scale for Households by Sex

	Ejidatarios who work their land		Ejidatarios who work part of land		Ejidatarios who do not work land		Nonejidatarios		
	Male	*Female*	*Male*	*Female*	*Male*	*Female*	*Male*	*Female*	*Total*
Lowest class (0-5 points)	2	0	0	0	2	0	47	14	65
Middle class (6-35 points)	11	1	8	3	2	1	24	3	53
Highest class (36-343 points)	26	7	2	1	3	0	2	3	44
N	39*	8	10	4	7	1	73	20	162

*Including two households headed by a man in which the wife is the ejidatario.

tions to property, different prestige in the village, different interests, and a different mode of life.

Ninety-four percent of the lowest class units, 50 percent of the middle, and 11 percent of the highest class are headed by nonejidatarios. In contrast, 89 percent of the highest class, 50 percent of the middle class, and only 6 percent of the lowest class are headed by ejidatarios.

Table 3:16 summarizes the distribution of households in the three classes in terms both of land tenure and the sex of the household heads. In Table 3:17, the percentages of households in the three classes according to land tenure is reported. We see that 70 percent of the ejidatarios who work their own land are in the highest class, 26 percent in the middle class, and only 4 percent in the lowest class. The ejidatarios who work only part of their land fall mainly (79 percent) in the middle class, with 21 percent in the highest class, and none in the lowest class. The ejidatarios who do not work their land fall almost evenly in the three classes, indicating that it is possible for an ejidatario to live on his rents without dropping to the bottom of society. Of the nonejidatarios, 66 percent are in the lowest class,

TABLE 3:17   Percentages of Households in Three Socioeconomic Classes According to Land Tenure

	Ejidatarios who work own land (N=47)	Ejidatarios who work part of land (N=14)	Ejidatarios who do not work land (N=8)	Nonejidatarios (N=93)
Lowest class (N=65)	4	0	25	66
Middle class (N=53)	26	79	37.5	29
Highest class (N=44)	70	21	37.5	5
	100	100	100	100

TABLE 3:18   Percentages of Households in the Three Socioeconomic Classes
According to Sex

	Male Heads of Household (N=129)	Female Heads of Household (N=33)
Lowest class (N=65)	40	42.3
Middle class (N=53)	35	24.3
Highest class (N=44)	25	33.3
	100	100

29 percent in the middle class, and only 5 percent in the highest class. All of the male nonejidatarios in the highest class are sons of ejidatarios who started out with backing and with possibilities for bettering their lot. One got his start from money made in the United States during World War II.

There is a significant correlation between the SES (1 to 9) and being an ejidatario ($r = .50$, $p < .01$). Indeed, the crucial element in socioeconomic class is being an ejidatario, and the ejidatario who works his own land, unless he is alcoholic, is practically certain to rise to the top of the village society (see Chapter 8).

Table 3:18 shows that the percentages of male and female heads of households in the three classes are similar. Of the 11 women heads of households in the highest class, 8 are ejidatarios and the others run stores. However, a greater percentage of households run by women have zero points (39 percent) than households run by men (25 percent). Some of the male households with zero points are older men who live with richer families or young men starting out with their families in the houses of their parents, while most of the female-headed households (10 of 13) represent unwed or abandoned mothers with little hope of changing their economic position by themselves.

Finally, both measures of social class (the SES and being an ejidatario) are significantly correlated with the age and civil status of male heads of households. The richest age group and the one with the highest percentage of ejidatarios is age 50 to 60 years. (The product-moment correlation between being 51 to 60 years of age and the SES is .29. The correlation between this age group and being an ejidatario is .41. Both correlations are significant at the 1 percent level.) On the other hand, the age groups 20 to 30 and 20 or under are both negatively correlated to the SES and to membership in the ejidatario class. Most richer female heads of households, generally ejidatarias, are also among the older villagers. Of the 11 women in the highest economic class, eight are age 50 or over, two are age 48, and one is age 34. Correlations are not reported, because there are too few cases for them to be meaningful statistically. In summary, however, the older villagers (with the exception of the very old) are more likely to be ejidatarios; 78 percent of the male ejidatarios and 80 percent of the female ejidatarias are age 40 or over.

For male heads of households there is also a significant correlation between the SES and being officially married, either in the church or by a civil judge ($r = .41$, $p < .01$). The poorer men are more likely to be single or to contract free unions, which do not demand either the large costs of a church wedding or the smaller costs of a civil marriage. (The product-moment correlation between the SES and free union is $-.23$, between the SES and being single is also $-.23$, both significant at the 1 percent level.)

We who live in the modern industrial society would expect to find a significant relationship between literacy and measures of social class. In fact, there is none. For a peasant, prosperity does not depend on being able to read and write; literacy is not saleable in a peasant economy. The rise of school attendance in recent years is a function of hopes for jobs outside the village, and it is notable that villagers with small aspirations for their children see no reason for them to continue their schooling. Neither schooling nor literacy increases the likelihood of becoming a prosperous peasant.

For both heads of households and their wives, schooling is unrelated to socioeconomic class. However, the sons and daughters of the richer families receive more schooling than the children of the poorer villagers. (The product-moment correlation between years of schooling for sons and the SES score of the family is .55; for daughters it is .34. Both correlations are significant at the 1 percent level. For heads of families and their wives, the correlations between schooling and social class are close to zero.)

CLASS AND PARTICIPATION IN VILLAGE AFFAIRS

On a number of occasions, the village must make decisions as a community. Meetings are held in the *ayudantía* (town hall) to decide whether the village will undertake a new project, which means cooperating with money and possibly work. It may be a new kindergarten, fixing the road into the village, beautifying the zocalo (town square) with cement so that it will look more "modern" and urban, petitioning the government to bring in piped drinking water, or electricity. These projects have been accomplished. In the future, the villagers may realize hopes for paved roads and a sewage system. All of the family heads, men and women, are invited to attend these meetings and each has a say, although formal votes are hardly ever taken. In practice, a few of the older and most respected villagers take a position and the rest of the villagers either accept it, if it is to their liking, or show their lack of enthusiasm, if they are opposed. Such a form of democracy can work only where the people know each other well and are keenly sensitive to their reactions. The Mexican peasant is very careful to avoid open conflict, if it is at all possible. He may agree to a proposal politely, but he expects others to understand whether or not his agreement is enthusiastic. If he disagrees strongly, it may be enough to voice a hesitant doubt. The few individuals who make it a practice to disagree vehemently embarrass the majority. In practice, the leaders are usually alert to the group feeling, and if they sense discontent, they will withdraw, holding back a proposal for another time, or abandoning it. The ideal is that the village unanimously support a project.

The ejidatarios and richer nonejidatarios are accepted as the leaders, the ones who propose. They initiate the projects, for they must be counted on for the largest contributions to any project that demands money from the village, and they are the ones who are more likely to donate their time and labor. (Both the piping for drinking water and the electrical equipment were paid for half by the village and half by the federal government.)

Very rarely are projects pushed through against significant opposition. The school was built by the enthusiasm of the "progressive" immigrants, oriented to the new opportunities of industrial society, who had to struggle against the traditional peasants' preference for fiestas. The streets of the town were broadened and straightened with the urging and direction of a schoolmaster in the late 1930s, following another schoolmaster who initiated a cooperative store and organized a basketball team and a youth club. With the support of most ejidatarios he was able to override strong opposition from those who lost parts of their house sites to the new streets. But such leaders are exceptional. More commonly, the leaders are careful to avoid dissension and count on a developing consensus to encourage the recalcitrant ones.

The villagers have succeeded in public works only when the ejidatarios have put their weight behind these projects, and when attempts at cooperative enterprises have failed (such as the store and a rice growers' cooperative), it has been due to dissension among the members of this same group. Progress on specific projects demands that one or two villagers take the main responsibility for leading the villagers and keeping the pressure of the consensus at an optimal level until the job is completed. Sometimes, the leaders may also be entrusted with the task of petitioning higher authorities for help. The villager most admired (and envied) is the one who speaks well, who has a talent for persuading his peers, and for making an effective impression on government officials or rich patrons who might help the village.

Through participant observation of village affairs, we rated 25 men (27 percent of the heads of families) as particularly active in village affairs, taking part in the meetings, offering their opinions, and following through in support of village projects. These men are generally ejidatarios, and older than the average (the highest percentage are in the age range of 40 to 60 years), and they are also among the richer peasants. Political activity is significantly correlated with both measures of social class; the correlation with the SES is $r = .42$, and the correlation between political activity and being an ejidatario is $r = .34$; both correlations are significant at the 1 percent level.

Another way of measuring political participation and leadership is to take account of the official offices held by villagers. Every three years an *ayudante municipal,* or mayor, is elected by all the villagers to preside over village meetings. Village committees for education (supervising the school plot of land and allocating funds to the school), *bienestar* (well-being), village betterment (beautifying the zocalo) are also chosen. The villagers also elect a *Juez de Paz* (Justice of the Peace) and *Comandante de vigilancia* (local police officer). Small disputes may either be settled by the judge or, as is often the case, carried to higher courts by the villagers. Most cases are settled at the level of the *municipio.*

Other important officers are elected by the Assembly of Ejidatarios, who comprise the elite community within the village. They elect principally the *Comisariado Ejidal,* the chief ejido officer in charge of overseeing and enforcing the agrarian law and, where necessary, referring disputes to higher authorities.

The political offices in the village were coded in terms of points to give an idea of the percentage of villagers who have occupied a few or many posts in the village government. The point scale was constructed as follows: four points were given if a villager had been ayudante municipal; three points were given if he had been Comisariado Ejidal; two points were given for the offices of Comandante de vigilancia and Justice of the Peace or for the presidency of a major village committee such as the committees on education or community betterment; two points were also given to the few villagers who had been *mayordomos* at major religious fiestas; and one point was given to villagers who had served on one of these major committees.

Most of the villagers, 74 percent of the men and 99 percent of the women, have held no offices. The formal political power of the village is controlled by the other 26 percent of the men, practically all of them older ejidatarios. Five percent (12 men) have over 20 points on the scale. Sixty-four percent of the men who have occupied offices are over age 40, and 70 percent are ejidatarios. The median number of points for the ejidatarios is seven; for the nonejidatarios, it is zero. Only 10 percent of the nonejidatarios have been given official positions in the village, and these are mostly sons of ejidatarios, the same men who have managed with capital gained as braceros and/or with backing from their fathers, to reach the highest socioeconomic class. For heads of family, there is a significant correlation between the scale of governmental posts and the SES ($r = .48$, $p < .01$).

As in peasant villages throughout the world, official power and wealth lies mainly in the hands of the older men. But there is by no means a one-to-one correlation between power and age for the men. To achieve material success and position in the village, a man must first of all have had the good fortune to have land. Furthermore, as we shall see in Chapter 6, he must have had the character structure oriented to material gain and profit.

PARTICIPATION IN RELIGIOUS AND CULTURAL ACTIVITIES

The peasant village offers few leisure activities, little cultural stimulation. We have seen that plays and regular band concerts of the past are no longer performed. The main fiestas are at Easter, the national holidays in September, and the Christmas *posadas*. Most of the time, there is radio and television, which some people keep on from the time they wake up until they go to bed. On Sundays a movie is shown in the rice warehouse for those who can pay two pesos. Some of the young men organized a basketball team 20 years ago and they take pride in their skill and in the trophies they have won in state competition. These players, 23 men, are an especially energetic group. Another 19 men are regular billiard players and often congregate in their free time at the village's one billiard parlor. Eleven men, most of them older men, still play in the village band at fiestas and sometimes practice in their spare time. The others may enjoy an occasional fiesta, either in the village or in nearby towns, but much of leisure time is spent in sitting around, the women and many men gossiping, some men drinking, others just "resting." The use of leisure time is in a great part a function of character, as will be discussed in later chapters. But it is important to emphasize that opportunities are limited, even for the most active and interested villagers.

A traditional source of stimulation is the Church and the religious ceremonies that center in it. Except for three Protestant Evangelists, all of the villagers considered themselves Catholics. Yet, it is notable that 34 percent of the villagers (40 percent of the men and 27 percent of the women) never attend Mass (see Table 3:19). Forty percent of the villagers attend Mass and other religious celebrations either frequently or most of the time. This included 34 percent of the men and 45 percent of the women.

While women are more frequent churchgoers than the men, there is no significant relationship between age and church attendance, except for a tendency on the part of the younger women to attend church more often during the years just after their first communion. For the older men, church attendance is related more to character than to any other variable.

**TABLE 3:19   Attendance at Mass and Other Religious Occasions
in Percentages**

Attendance	Percent of Men (N=204)	Percent of Women (N=200)	Total Percent (N=404)*
Regular attendance	20	27.5	24
Frequent attendance	14	18	15
Infrequent attendance	26	27	27
Never or hardly ever attends mass	40	27.5	34
	100	100	100

*No information on 5 men and 8 women.

For neither the heads of families nor their wives is church attendance correlated significantly for the SES. Nor is there a correlation between church attendance and the SES for daughters. However, the sons of the richer villagers are more likely to participate in religious celebrations ($r = .31$, $p < .01$ for frequency of church attendance and SES of the son's family). For these young men of the more prosperous families, church attendance may result from a somewhat higher cultural level, for in general there is no evidence that the church attracts the richer over the poorer villagers.

There is evidence, however, that the more literate villagers attend church more frequently. Of the villagers who read and write well, 57 percent attend church services regularly or frequently. Of those who are illiterate or read and write only a little, 35 percent attend church frequently or regularly. (The chi-square of this correlation is 9.9, significant at the 1 percent level.) In a society with so few cultural opportunities, it would appear that the church attracts those who are most interested in words, in ideas, and in moral precepts.

4

The Theory of
Character Orientations

Before we report the results of studying the character of the villagers, it will be necessary to outline the theory of dynamic character orientations which guided our investigation and led to the formulation of categories for scoring. The following discussion of modes of assimilation and productiveness is based largely on Fromm's (1947) formulation in *Man for Himself*.[1] For reasons of space we present in the following a short description of the various orientations. To the reader who is interested in a fuller exposition we must suggest reading *Man for Himself*.

As we have said in Chapter 1, the main difference in the theory of character proposed here from that of Freud is that the fundamental basis of character is not seen in various types of *libido* organization but in specific forms of a person's *relatedness* to the world. In the process of living, man relates himself to the world (1) by acquiring and assimilating things, and (2) by relating himself to people (and himself). The former is considered the process of assimilation; the latter, that of socialization. Both forms of relatedness are "open" and not instinctively determined. Man can acquire things by receiving or taking them from an outside source or by producing them through his own efforts. But he must acquire and assimilate them in some fashion in order to satisfy his needs. Also, man cannot live alone and unrelated to others. He has to associate with others for defense, for work, for sexual satisfaction, for play, for the upbringing of the young, for the transmission of knowledge, and for material possessions. But beyond that, it is necessary for him to be related to others. Complete isolation is unbearable and incompatible with sanity.

---

[1] Examples of responses to the interpretative questionnaire expressing these orientations will be found in Appendix A.

These orientations, by which the individual relates himself to the world, constitute the core of his character. Character can be defined as the (*relatively permanent*) *form in which human energy is structuralized in the process of assimilation and socialization.*

In the following analysis *nonproductive orientations* are differentiated from the *productive orientation*. It must be noted that these concepts are "ideal-types," not descriptions of the character of a given individual. Furthermore, while, for didactic purposes, they are treated here separately, the character of any given person is usually a blend of all or some of these orientations in which one, however, is dominant. Finally, in the description of the nonproductive orientations only their negative aspects are presented, while their positive aspects are discussed briefly in a later part of this chapter.

The following description of the nonproductive orientations follows the clinical picture of the pregenital character given by Freud and others. The nonproductive orientations correspond to Freud's pregenital stages of libido. Specifically, the receptive orientation corresponds to the oral-receptive; the exploitative to the oral-sadistic; the hoarding to the anal character; the productive orientation corresponds to Freud's "genital character" which he once defined as one endowing a person with the ability for love and work. No doubt Freud's description of the pregenital character types is much richer and more detailed than the description of the genital character. Our categories are based on Freud's, but systematically and genetically understood in a different way, which will become apparent in the following discussion.[2]

TYPES OF CHARACTER:
THE NONPRODUCTIVE ORIENTATIONS

THE RECEPTIVE ORIENTATION

In the receptive orientation a person feels "the source of all good" to be outside, and he believes that the only way to get what he wants—be it something material, be it affection, love, knowledge, pleasure—is to receive it from that outside source. As far as the acquisition of material things is concerned, the receptive character, in extreme cases, finds it difficult to work at all, and expects things to be given to him as rewards for his being so "good"—or perhaps because he is "ill" or "in need." In less extreme cases he prefers to work under or for somebody, and tends to feel that what he gets is given to him because of the boss's "goodness," rather than

---

[2] Another type of nonproductive orientation, that of the marketing, is described in Fromm (1947). However, we do not include it here because we do not find villagers who clearly have the marketing orientation.

as the result of his own work, and as something to which he has a right. In this orientation the problem of love is almost exclusively that of "being loved" and not that of loving. Such people tend to be indiscriminate in the choice of their love objects, because being loved by anybody is such an overwhelming experience for them that they "fall for" anybody who gives them love or what looks like love. They are exceedingly sensitive to any withdrawal or rebuff they experience on the part of the loved person. Their orientation is the same in the sphere of thinking: if intelligent, they make the best listeners, since their orientation is one of receiving, not of producing ideas; left to themselves, they feel paralyzed.

THE EXPLOITATIVE ORIENTATION

The exploitative orientation, like the receptive, has as its basic premise the feeling that the source of all good is outside, that whatever one wants to get must be sought there, and that one cannot produce anything oneself. The difference between the two, however, is that the exploitative type does not expect to receive things from others passively, but to take them away from others by force or cunning. This orientation extends to all spheres of activity.

In the realm of love and affection these people tend to grab and steal. They feel attracted only to people whom they can take away from somebody else. Attractiveness to them is conditioned by a person's attachment to somebody else; they tend not to fall in love with an unattached person.

We find the same attitude with regard to thinking and intellectual pursuits. Such people will tend not to produce ideas but to steal them.

The same statement holds true with regard to their orientation to material things. Things which they can take away from others always seem better to them than anything they can produce themselves. They use and exploit anybody and anything from whom or from which they can squeeze something. Their motto is: "Stolen fruits are sweetest." Because they want to use and exploit people, they "love" those who, explicitly or implicitly, are promising objects of exploitation, and get "fed up" with persons whom they have squeezed out. An extreme example is the kleptomaniac who enjoys things only if he can steal them, although he has the money to buy them.

THE HOARDING ORIENTATION

Since we have already dealt with the hoarding orientation in Chapter 1, we can be brief here.

While the receptive and exploitative types are similar inasmuch as both expect to get things from the outside world, the hoarding orientation is essentially different. This orientation makes people have little faith in anything new they might get from the outside world; their security is based upon hoarding and saving, while spending is felt to be a threat. They have surrounded themselves, as it were, by a protective wall, and their main aim is to bring as much as possible into this fortified position and to let as little as possible out of it. Their miserliness refers to money and material things as well as to feelings and thoughts. Love is essentially a possession; they do not give love but try to get it by possessing the "beloved." People with a hoarding orientation often show a particular kind of faithfulness toward people and even toward memories. It is a sentimentality which makes the past appear as more real than the present; they hold on to it and indulge in the memories of bygone feelings and experiences.

The character orientations which have been described so far are by no means as separate from each other as it may appear from this sketch. Each of them may be dominant in a person, yet blended with others. However, clinical data show that there are greater affinities between some orientations than among others. A great deal more research is necessary to arrive at reliable information about these affinities. The blending between the nonproductive orientations and the productive orientation will be discussed later on.

THE PRODUCTIVE ORIENTATION

Man is not only a rational and social animal; he can also be defined as a producing animal, capable of transforming the materials which he finds at hand, using his reason and imagination. Not only *can* he produce, he *must* produce in order to live. Material production, however, is but the most frequent expression of or symbol for productiveness as an aspect of character. The productive orientation of personality refers to a fundamental attitude, *a mode of relatedness* in all realms of human experience. It covers physical, mental, emotional, and sensory responses to others, to oneself, and to things. Productiveness is man's ability to use his powers and to realize the potentialities inherent in him. Saying *he* uses *his* powers implies that he must be free and not dependent on someone who controls his powers. It implies, furthermore, that he is guided by reason, since he can make use of his powers only if he knows what they are, how to use them, and what to use them for. Productiveness means that he experiences himself as the embodiment of his powers and as the "actor"; that he feels himself as the subject of his powers, that he is not alienated from his powers, i.e., that they are not masked from him and transferred to an idolized object, person, or institution.

Another way of describing productiveness (and like any other experience, it cannot be defined but rather it must be described in such a way that others who share the experience know what one is talking about [3]) is to say that the productive person animates that which he touches.[4] He gives soul to that which surrounds him.[5] The productive person gives birth to his own faculties and gives life to persons and to things.

By his own productive approach, he calls forth a productive response in others unless they are so unproductive that they cannot be touched. One might say that the productive person sensitizes both himself and others, and is sensitive to himself and to the world around him.

This sensitivity exists in the realms of thinking and feeling. What matters in the productive attitude is not its particular object, which may be people, nature, or things, but rather the whole approach. The productive orientation is rooted in the love of life (biophilia).[6] It is *being,* not *having.*

Generally the word "productiveness" is associated with creativeness, particularly artistic creativeness. The real artist, indeed, is the most convincing example of productiveness. But, on the other hand, not all artists are productive; a conventional painting, e.g., may exhibit nothing more than the technical skill to reproduce the likeness of a person (or fashionable images) in photographic fashion on a canvas, and a modern "expressionistic" painting may express regressive emotions with clever technical proficiency. On the other hand, a person can experience, see, feel, and think productively without having the gift to create something visible or communicable. *Productiveness is an attitude which every human being is capable of, unless he is mentally and emotionally crippled.*

Another approach to the nature of productiveness is to state that the productive orientation is characterized by *activity,* while all nonproductive orientations are characterized by "passivity." This statement is confusing for the modern mind because in our usage activity is usually defined as behavior which brings about a change in an existing situation by an expenditure of energy; it is synonymous with being "busy." In contrast, a person is described as passive if he is unable to change or overtly influence an existing situation by an expenditure of energy and is influenced or moved

---

[3] We found that it is easier to decide whether or not questionnaire responses express productiveness than to describe why this is so. It is similar to deciding whether an individual has a "mean" face. Two sensitive observers would be able to agree on the scoring, but it would be harder to define a "mean" face.

[4] This is in contrast to a character like King Midas who transformed everything he touched to gold, which is a symbol for death and, as Freud (1908) pointed out, for excrement.

[5] It is fortunate that the black radical movement has brought the concept of soul out of its disrepute by using it to mean a quality of animated activity rather than its traditional use as a metaphysical concept.

[6] See Fromm (1964).

by forces outside himself. This current concept of activity takes into account only the actual expenditure of energy and the change brought about by it. It does not distinguish between the underlying psychic conditions governing the activities.[7]

An example, though an extreme one, of nonproductive "activity" is the activity of a person under hypnosis. The person in a deep hypnotic trance may have his eyes open, may walk, talk, and do things; he "acts." The general definition of activity would apply to him, since energy is spent and some change brought about. But if we consider the particular character and quality of this activity, we find that it is not really the hypnotized person who is the actor, but the hypnotist, who, by means of his suggestions, acts through him. While the hypnotic trance is an artificial state, it is an extreme but characteristic example of a situation in which a person can be active and yet not be the true actor, his activity resulting from compelling forces over which he has no control.

The meaning of "activity" as characterizing the productive orientation is the same as that in which both Aristotle and Spinoza used "active" and "activity" vs. "passive" and "passivity." Thus for Aristotle contemplation was the highest state of activity and for Spinoza to be passive meant to be "driven" by irrational passions, while the degree of perfection in anything is commensurate with the degree of its "activity."

ORIENTATIONS IN THE PROCESS OF SOCIALIZATION

As pointed out in the beginning of this chapter, the process of living implies two kinds of relatedness to the outside world, that of assimilation and that of socialization. The former has been discussed in great detail in this chapter, because it proves of central importance in understanding the character of the villagers. The latter will be described still more briefly, and the reader who is interested in a more complete analysis is referred to *Escape from Freedom* and *The Heart of Man*.

We can differentiate between the following kinds of interpersonal relatedness: (1) *symbiotic relatedness,* (2) *withdrawal-destructiveness,* (3) *narcissism,* and (4) *love.*

In the symbiotic relatedness the person is related to others but loses or never attains his independence; he avoids the danger of aloneness by becoming part of another person, either by being "swallowed" by that person or by "swallowing" him. The former is the root of what is clinically described as *masochism.* Masochism is the attempt to get rid of one's indi-

---

[7] It might be better to speak of "activeness" rather than "activity" to describe the productive person.

vidual self, to escape from freedom, and to look for security by attaching oneself to another person. The forms which such dependency assume are manifold. It can be rationalized as sacrifice, duty, or love, especially when cultural patterns legitimatize this kind of rationalization. Sometimes masochistic strivings are blended with sexual impulses and are pleasureful (the masochistic perversion); often the masochistic strivings are so much in conflict with the parts of the personality striving for independence and freedom that they are experienced as painful and tormenting.

The impulse to swallow others, the *sadistic,* active form of symbiotic relatedness, appears in all kinds of rationalizations, as love, overprotectiveness, "justified" domination, "justified" vengeance, etc.; it also appears blended with sexual impulses as sexual sadism. All forms of the sadistic drive go back to the impulse for omnipotence, to have complete mastery over another person, and to make him a helpless object of one's will. Complete domination over a powerless person is the essence of symbiotic relatedness. It is rooted in and compensates for deep—and often unconscious—feelings of impotence and powerlessness.

While the symbiotic relationship is one of *closeness* to and intimacy with the object, although at the expense of freedom and integrity, the second kind of relatedness is one of the distance, of withdrawal, and destructiveness. The feeling of individual powerlessness can be overcome by withdrawal from others who are experienced as threats. In the phenomenon here described, withdrawal becomes the main form of relatedness to others, a negative relatedness, as it were. Its emotional equivalent is the feeling of indifference toward others, often accompanied by a compensatory feeling of self-inflation. Withdrawal and indifference can, but need not, be conscious; as a matter of fact, in our culture they are mostly covered up by a superficial kind of interest and sociability.

Destructiveness is an extreme form of withdrawal; the impulse to destroy others follows from the fear of being destroyed by them and from a hatred for life.[8, 9]

Destructiveness is the perversion of the drive to live; it is the energy of *unlived life* transformed into energy for the destruction of life.

Another form of withdrawal which varies considerably in degree of

---

[8] For a more detailed analysis of destructiveness see Fromm (1964) on the "love of death."

[9] It is important to note that the discussion of destructiveness has suffered greatly from the fact that theorists have hardly distinguished between destructiveness, sadism, and aggression in the defense of life and vital interests. They are all qualitatively different, and each has its own causes and conditions. Cf. E. Fromm, "On the Sources of Human Destructiveness," in *Alternatives to Violence,* Larry Ng, ed. (New York: Time-Life Book, 1968); a larger work under the same title is in preparation.

intensity is *narcissism.* The concept of narcissism is one of the most fruit-ful and far-reaching of Freud's discoveries. Because it is often misunder-stood, we shall describe narcissism in greater detail.

Freud sketched the main lines of the development of narcissism in the "normal" person, and the following paragraph is a short summary of his findings.

The fetus in the womb still lives in a state of absolute narcissism. "By being born," says Freud, "we have made the step from an absolutely self-sufficient narcissism to the perception of a changing external world and the beginning of the discovery of objects." [10] It takes months before the infant can even perceive objects outside as being part of the "not me." Individual narcissism is hammered into "object love" by the many blows to the child's narcissism caused by his ever-increasing acquaintance with the outside world and its laws, thus of "necessity." But, says Freud, "a human being remains to some extent narcissistic even after he has found external objects for his libido." [11] Indeed, the development of the individual can be defined in Freud's terms as the evolution from absolute narcissism to a capacity for objective reasoning and object love, a capacity, however, which does not transcend definite limitations. The "normal," "mature" person is one whose narcissism has been reduced to the socially accepted minimum without ever disappearing completely. Freud's observation is confirmed by everyday experience. It seems that in most people one can find a narcissistic core which is not accessible and which defies any attempt at complete dissolution.[12]

For those who are not familiar with the most drastic manifestation of narcissism in psychosis, it will be particularly helpful to give a picture of narcissism as it is found in neurotic persons. One of the most elementary examples of narcissism can be found in the person's attitude toward his or her body.

Let us look at two phenomena which are apparently extremely dif-ferent, and yet both of which are narcissistic. A woman spends many hours every day before the mirror to fix her hair and face. It is not simply that she is vain. She is obsessed with her body and her beauty, and her body is the only important reality she knows. She comes perhaps nearest to the Greek legend which speaks of Narcissus, a beautiful lad who rejected the love of the nymph Echo, who died of a broken heart. Nemesis punished him by making him fall in love with the reflection of his own image in the

---

[10] Freud, *Group Psychology* (Standard Edition), Vol. XVIII, p. 130.

[11] Freud, *Totem and Taboo* (Standard Edition), Vol. XIII, p. 89.

[12] For a full discussion of narcissism and of the difference between the libido concept and the energy concept used here, see Fromm (1964) on "Individual and Social Narcissism."

water of the lake; in self-admiration he fell into the lake and died. The Greek legend indicates clearly that this kind of "self-love" is a curse, and that in its extreme form it ends in self-destruction.[13] Another woman (and it could well be the same one some years later) suffers from hypochondriasis. She is also constantly preoccupied with her body although not in the sense of making it beautiful, but in fearing illness. Why the positive, or the negative, image is chosen has, of course, its reasons; however, we need not deal with these here. What matters is that behind both phenomena lies the same narcissistic preoccupation with oneself, with little interest left for the outside world.[14] While we chose here women as examples of narcissism, this self-absorption in one's body exists in the same way among men, only perhaps that under our social conditions male narcissism is more frequently centered around social position, prestige, or property.

What is common to all forms of narcissism is that only that which refers to one's own ego, i.e., body, sensations, feelings, thoughts, etc., is experienced as fully real, hence important. The reality outside, while perceived, has no weight, no importance, because one is not related to it. To the extent a person is narcissistic, the world outside is perceived without depth or intensity. In the psychotic person this often has reached such a degree that he cannot even perceive reality as it is, and the only reality is the subjective one; hallucinations and delusions are symptomatic expression of this fact.

In contrast to symbiotic relatedness, withdrawal, destructiveness, and narcissism, love is the productive form of relatedness to others and to oneself. It implies responsibility, care, respect, and knowledge, and the wish for the other person to grow and develop. It is the expression of intimacy between two human beings under the condition of the preservation of each other's integrity.

INCESTUOUS TIES

A further element that is essential to the understanding of character is the concept of incestuous ties, particularly the incestuous fixation to mother. Freud believed this concept to be one of the cornerstones of his scientific edifice and we believe that his discovery of the fixation to mother is, indeed, one of the most far-reaching discoveries in the science of man.

---

[13] Cf. the discussion of self-love in *Man for Himself,* which tries to show that true love for self is not different from love for others, that "self-love" in the sense of egoistic, narcissistic love is to be found in those who can love neither others nor themselves.

[14] Another form of narcissism is moral hypochondriasis, the constant concern with oneself in terms of having acted wrongly.

But in this area, as in those discussed before, Freud narrowed his discovery and its consequences by being compelled to couch it in terms of his libido theory, and thus to see as the core of incest the sexual strivings toward the parent of the opposite sex. Nevertheless, Freud saw the importance of the nonsexual tie to the mother in terms of the "pre-Oedipal" fixation, although the importance he gave it was small in comparison to the incestuous sexual tie which he dealt with in the bulk of his writings.

The tendency to remain bound to the mothering person and her equivalents—blood, family, tribe—is inherent in all men and women. It is constantly in conflict with the opposite tendency—to be born, to progress, to grow. In the case of normal development, the tendency for growth wins. In the case of pathology, the regressive tendency for symbiotic union wins, and it results in the person's more or less total incapacitation. In the majority of people in history so far, the incestuous fixation to family, tribe, nation, state, church, even when not extreme, has retained considerable force and is one of the most important factors working against human solidarity, and one of the deepest sources of hate, destructiveness, and irrationality. The patriarchal equivalent of fixation to mother, the obedient submission to father, has similar effects, although it seems that the depth and intensity of the fixation to or fear of the mother is greater. In fact, there are many clinical reasons for the assumption that submission to father is an attempt to escape the incestuous regression. Many rites of initiation seem to aim at cutting or reducing the ties to mother, although at the expense of forging new bonds to father and/or the male group.

Freud's concept of the incestuous strivings to be found in any child is perfectly correct. Yet the significance of this concept transcends Freud's own assumption. Incestuous wishes are not primarily a result of sexual desires, but constitute one of the most fundamental tendencies in man: the wish to remain tied to an all-protective figure, the fear of being free, and the fear of being destroyed by mother, the very figure with whom he has made himself helpless.

BLENDS OF VARIOUS ORIENTATIONS

In describing the different kinds of nonproductive orientations and the productive orientation, these orientations were considered as if they were separate entities, clearly differentiated from each other. For didactic purposes this kind of treatment seemed to be necessary because we have to understand the nature of each orientation before we can proceed to the understanding of their blending. Yet, in reality, we always deal with blends, for a character never represents just one of the nonproductive orientations or the productive orientation exclusively.

To understand the character system of any individual, it is necessary to take account of the interrelationship between modes of assimilation and relatedness, the quality of incestuous ties, and the degree of productiveness.

Among the combinations of the various orientations we must differentiate between the blend of the nonproductive orientations among themselves, and that of the nonproductive with the productive orientation. If one wants to characterize a person, one will usually have to do so in terms of which orientation is dominant and which are secondary.

The blending between the nonproductive and productive orientations needs a more thorough discussion. There is no person whose orientation is entirely productive, and no one who is completely lacking in productiveness. But the respective weight of the productive and the nonproductive orientations in each person's character structure varies and determines the *quality* of the nonproductive orientations. In the foregoing description of the nonproductive orientations it was assumed that they were *dominant* in a character structure. We must now supplement the earlier description by considering the qualities of the nonproductive orientations in a character structure in which the *productive* orientation is *dominant*. Here the nonproductive orientations do not have the negative meaning they have when they are dominant but have a different and constructive quality. In fact, the nonproductive orientations, as they have been described, may be considered as distortions of orientations which in themselves are a normal and necessary part of living. Every human being, in order to survive, must be able to *accept* things from others, to *take* things, *to save,* and to *exchange.* He must also be able to *accept authority,* to *guide others,* to be *alone,* and to *assert* himself. Only if his way of acquiring things and relating himself to others is essentially nonproductive does the ability to accept, to take, to save, or to exchange turn into the craving to receive, to exploit, to hoard, or to market as the dominant ways of acquisition. The nonproductive forms of social relatedness in a predominantly productive person—loyalty, authority, fairness, assertiveness—turn into submission, domination, withdrawal, destructiveness in a predominantly nonproductive person. Any of the nonproductive orientations has, therefore, a positive and a negative aspect, according to the degree of productiveness in the total character structure. The following list of the positive and negative aspects of various orientations may serve as an illustration for this principle.

The positive and negative aspects are not two separate classes of syndromes. Each of these traits can be described as a point in a continuum which is determined by *the degree of the productive orientation which prevails;* rational systematic orderliness, for instance, may be found when productiveness is high, while, with decreasing productiveness, it degenerates more and more into irrational, pedantic compulsive "orderliness" which actually defeats its own purpose. The same holds true of the change from

RECEPTIVE ORIENTATION (Accepting)

Positive Aspect	Negative Aspect
accepting	passive, without initiative
responsive	opinionless, characterless
devoted	submissive
modest	without pride
charming	parasitical
adaptable	unprincipled
socially adjusted	servile, without self-confidence
idealistic	unrealistic
sensitive	cowardly
polite	spineless
optimistic	wishful thinking
trusting	gullible
tender	sentimental

EXPLOITATIVE ORIENTATION (Taking)

Positive Aspect	Negative Aspect
active	exploitative
able to take initiative	aggressive
able to make claims	egocentric
proud	conceited
impulsive	rash
self-confident	arrogant
captivating	seducing

HOARDING ORIENTATION (Preserving)

Positive Aspect	Negative Aspect
practical	unimaginative
economical	stingy
careful	suspicious
reserved	cold
patient	lethargic
cautious	anxious
steadfast, tenacious	stubborn
imperturbable	indolent
composed under stress	inert
orderly	pedantic
methodical	obsessional
loyal	possessive

youthfulness to childishness, or of the change from being proud to being conceited. In considering only the basic orientations, we see the staggering amount of variability in each person brought about by the fact that

1. the nonproductive orientations are blended in different ways with regard to the respective weight of each of them;
2. each changes in quality according to the amount of productiveness present;

3. the different orientations may operate in different strength in the material, emotional, or intellectual spheres of activity, respectively.

If we add to the picture of personality the different temperaments and gifts, we can easily recognize that the configuration of these basic elements makes for an endless number of variations in personality.

SOCIOPOLITICAL ORIENTATIONS

To conclude this chapter, we would like to describe briefly the theoretical considerations underlying the concept of "sociopolitical character."

The first formulation of political-psychological character was the description of the authoritarian character, which was introduced into psychology about 40 years ago in the study of German political character described in Chapter 1. The concept combined a political category, that of the authoritarian structure in state and family, with a psychological category, the character structure, which forms the basis for such a political and social structure.

For our purposes now it may suffice to say that the authoritarian character structure is that of a person whose sense of strength and identity is based on a symbiotic subordination to authorities, and at the same time a symbiotic domination of those submitting to his authority. That is to say, the authoritarian character feels himself strong when he can submit and be part of an authority which (to some extent backed by reality) is inflated, is deified, and when at the same time he can inflate himself by incorporating those subject to his authority. This is a state of sado-masochistic symbiosis which gives him a sense of strength and a sense of identity. By being part of the "Big" (whatever it is), he becomes big; if he were alone, by himself, he would shrink to nothing. For this very reason a threat to authority and a threat to his authoritarian structure is for the authoritarian character a threat to himself—a threat to his sanity. Hence he is forced to fight against this threat to authoritarianism as he would fight against a threat to his life or his sanity. There are, however, significant differences within the range of the authoritarian character, depending on the degree of sadism (or masochism) which it contains. We find on the one end of a continuum the mild authoritarian character in which all the traits described are present, but with the absence, or with a low degree of sado-masochism. In this variant of the authoritarian character, the element of independence and productiveness is relatively high; while he will insist on his superiority, he will exercise it in a relatively benevolent way, and with a relatively low rage reaction when his authority is flaunted. On the other end of the continuum is the malignant authoritative character, with a low degree of independence and productiveness, whose predominant quality is sadistic control over those who are weaker and masochistic submission to those who are stronger. Between these two extremes we find all degrees of sadistic admixture. As far as social factors are concerned, there is good evidence for the hypothesis that the male authoritarian character's affective relatedness is primarily to other men, while his affective relationships to women are exclusively sexual; affectively, women are only either objects of domination, and/or submission (in the case of the type who is dependent on the mother). This, however, has nothing to do with homo*sexuality;* it may be called a *homoerotic* attitude, provided that we assume that eros and sexuality are not identical. (The confusion between the two, resulting from the libido theory, has done much damage to classic psychoanalytic thinking.)

On a social scale, the degree of the admixture of the sadistic and masochistic components to authoritarianism seems to be largely dependent on the socioeconomic function of a class or within a society. When a class has a productive function, like the lower middle class in the 19th century, or the Mexican peasant today, the sado-masochistic admixture seems to be relatively small; when, on the other hand, the class has lost its productive place in the economy and is slowly being destroyed economically and socially, the sado-masochistic admixture seems to be very high, as for instance among the German lower middle class after 1923 and the poor whites in the American south.

The authoritarian individual may sometimes appear to oppose authority and be a "rebel." But although he may look like a person who on the basis of inner strength and integrity fights the forces that block his freedom and independence, his fight against authority is essentially defiance. It is an attempt to assert himself and overcome his own feelings of powerlessness. However, the "rebel" usually attacks an authority whom he feels to be weak and, after the victory, submits to a new harsher and stronger authority. By identifying himself with this authority and playing the role of a harsh authority toward those who are weak, he can satisfy both the sadistic and the masochistic side of his authoritarian character.

The authoritarian orientation as described above needs to be distinguished from the attitude supporting traditional authority which is especially characteristic of peasant societies. The "traditional authoritarian" person is not sado-masochistic. He accepts a traditional authoritarian pattern. He does not challenge his fixed social structure, including the idea that those in power deserve respect, that children should subordinate their wills to the dictates of parents. Yet, the traditional peasant does not believe that force makes right, nor does his identity rest on identifying himself with power. The traditional pattern of relationships gives him a sense of continuity, security, and meaning, but he could probably accept a new social consensus without great difficulty as long as it did not threaten his life or livelihood. In Appendix A examples are given which illustrate the difference between authoritarianism and traditionalism.

In contrast to both the authoritarian and traditional orientations, we have defined the democratic individual as one who both affirms his rights and respects the rights and the humanity of others. He wishes to be free to pursue his own goals, and he expects others to want the same. He feels that decisions affecting the community should be made by all its members, taking account of each individual's feelings. The democratic individual does not necessarily believe the majority is right, since the majority decision might do violence to the rights of the minority. The democratic person does not separate humanity into unequal groupings of the powerful who are idealized and the weak who are seen as contemptible. The democratic individual feels that all people should have equal rights because they are equally human.[15]

---

[15] A final category, related to the democratic orientation is the most independent ("revolutionary") character, which is described in detail elsewhere (Fromm, 1963). We originally intended to include this category, but found only one villager who could be doubtfully scored as "revolutionary," and we concluded that the degree of productiveness required for the revolutionary character is absent in the village. Suffice it to say that in speaking of the "revolutionary" as a character type we do not refer to the purely political definition according to which anyone who aims at a social and political revolution would be called a revolutionary. The "revolutionary" in our characterological sense expresses a particular quality of independence and wish to liberate life from conditions that block its free growth. The revolutionary person does not oppose authority as a rebel. He is not motivated by resentment or hatred, but by the impulse to create a better social system, rather than avenging himself against the present one.

The revolutionary transcends the narrow limits of his own society and is able, because of this, to criticize his or any other society from the standpoint of reason and humanity.

The analysis of the specific blending between "revolutionaries" and "rebels" in any given revolutionary movement is an important key for the understanding of the dynamics of the movement as a whole.

5

The Character
of the Villagers

In this chapter we move from the theory of character to the results of our investigation into character. Just as we have reported the socioeconomic census in Chapter 3, we now can describe the distribution of character orientations in the village, the "census of character." What is the psychological makeup of the village? What is its social character?

We shall first outline the variables used in scoring the questionnaire. Next we shall report the two ways in which the data on character were analyzed: (1) in terms of the frequency with which the various traits are to be found in the population, and (2) in terms of a factor analysis. Finally, we shall summarize the social character of the village and consider its theoretical meaning.

VARIABLES OF SCORING CHARACTER

The interpretative questionnaire, which is reproduced in Appendix A, was scored for 406 adult villagers (200 men and 206 women), or 95 percent of the adult population. (Sample responses illustrating the dynamic orientations are given in Appendix A. In Appendix B, we report statistics on scoring agreement and comparisons between diagnosis of character traits based on responses to the questionnaire and two other projective tests —the Rorschach and the Thematic Apperception Test.)

In scoring the questionnaires, we distinguished between the dominant orientations and secondary tendencies, whenever this was possible. The following scales were constructed to score the variables of character that have been described in the previous chapter.

1. *THE MODE OF ASSIMILATION*

a. Receptive
b. Exploitative
c. Hoarding

Each questionnaire was scored according to which orientation, if any, was dominant. In cases where there was a secondary orientation, this was also scored as present but not dominant. The other orientations, the ones not expressed on the questionnaire, were scored zero.[1]

2. *PRODUCTIVENESS*

Productiveness was scored according to an ordinal scale ranging from six (high productiveness) to one (low productiveness) as follows:

(6) Active interest and involvement in one's work, family, and community, realistic and independent perceptiveness, maturity.
(5) Moderate interest, openness to new stimuli, but with other productive possibilities which have not been realized.
(4) Moderate interest but less active. These individuals can be stimulated, but they do not seek stimulation.
(3) Moderate interest, but unproductive traits are dominant.
(2) Passive and inactive.
(1) Rejecting and negative toward life.[2]

---

[1] For example, the scoring on the scale for a receptive exploitative individual on the data sheet would look as follows:

Dominant Receptive	0	①
Receptive	0	①
Dominant Exploitative	⓪	1
Exploitative	0	①
Dominant Hoarding	⓪	1
Hoarding	⓪	1

[2] Since maximal productiveness is rare in any society, or even a very high degree of productiveness most rare in an economically poor peasant society with almost no cultural stimulation (we found only one doubtful case of really high productiveness), we have adjusted our qualifications in terms of optimal productiveness within the limits of the village. This means that the score six in our scale would compare to a five or four in a much larger or less stagnant society, whereas the low degrees of productiveness would be the same as in any other society.

When the productiveness scores were tabulated we added additional scores for the presence or absence of both strong life-affirming tendencies or strong life-rejecting tendencies, since the overall productiveness score was sometimes a mixture of productive and unproductive tendencies. These additional scores were used in the factor analysis reported below.

3. *THE MODE OF RELATEDNESS*

a. Sadism

b. Masochism

c. Destructiveness

d. Narcissism I (indifference or low-grade narcissism)

e. Narcissism II (marked narcissism)

f. Love. From our observation of the villagers, we found it necessary to add two other categories which describe the way in which many relate to their children. These categories, which are more behavioral than dynamic, are the following:

g. Indulgence. Such individuals are basically dependent and passive, indulging children without setting limits for them and without reasoning whether or not such indulgence benefits the child. Indulgence implies a lack of firmness, moderate to low productiveness, and a strong wish to be loved.

h. Conditional love. This category implies a tending toward love, but the extent of paternal care given to the child depends on the child's obedience and respect for traditional authority.

Each questionnaire was scored according to which orientation or trait was dominant. In cases where there was a secondary or tertiary tendency, these were also scored. All other categories were scored zero.

4. *SOCIOPOLITICAL RELATEDNESS*

a. The Authoritarian Orientation.

b. The Orientation of Traditional Authority.

c. The Democratic Orientation.

d. The Revolutionary Orientation. This category was not found to be relevant for the village. There was only one villager with a revolutionary orientation.

e. Submissiveness.

f. Active rebelliousness.

g. Passive rebelliousness.

The scoring system for the scale of sociopolitical relatedness was identical to that of the Mode of Relatedness.

5. *PARENTAL FIXATIONS OR MOTHER VS. FATHER CENTEREDNESS*

a. Fixation to the mother was scored on a three point scale: zero (independence), one (moderate fixation), and two (intense fixation).

b. Fixation to the father was scored in the same way as mother fixation.

c. A third score was also calculated for mother centeredness by subtracting degree of father fixation from that of mother fixation. A score of two means extreme mother centeredness, a score of one means a tendency to mother centeredness, and a score of zero means the individual is not mother centered.

The questionnaire was also scored for the presence or absence of rebellious behavior against the mother and the father.

6. *OTHER BEHAVIORAL TRAITS*

Two other behavioral traits were also scored. Although these do not prove to be important to the study of social character, they are included in the factor analysis.

- a. Enterprise-energy. Individuals were scored in terms of how energetic they were in their work and leisure activities. A score of three indicated high energy; two, moderate energy; and one, low energy.
- b. Depression. The interviewer rated individuals for symptoms of clinical or subclinical depression, and these ratings were modified by the scorer in the light of the total responses. A score of two indicated extreme symptoms of depression; one, subclinical depression; zero, no symptoms of depression.

THE DISTRIBUTION OF CHARACTER TRAITS

1. *THE MODE OF ASSIMILATION*

Table 5:1 reports the distribution of the mode of assimilation in the village. Most of the villagers are either dominantly receptive (44 percent) or dominantly hoarding (31 percent). A smaller group is dominantly exploitative (11 percent). (We scored 14 percent as not having a clear-cut dominant mode of assimilation.)

When we consider the distribution of traits scored as either dominant or secondary, the relative distribution remains the same: 71 percent of the villagers have receptive tendencies, 55 percent hoarding tendencies, and 26 percent exploitative tendencies.

In terms of the mode of assimilation, the social character of the men is different from that of the women. While the women are somewhat more hoarding than receptive, the majority of the men are receptive. More women than men are hoarding and more men than women are receptive. This difference between the sexes will be analyzed in Chapter 7.

Given the distribution of the mode of assimilation, the next question is whether these modes are formed in their positive (productive) or negative (unproductive) aspects. The answer is different for men and women.

For the men, productiveness is significantly correlated positively with the dominant hoarding orientation ($r = .35$, $p < .01$) and negatively with the dominant receptive orientation ($r = -.33$, $p < .01$).

This means that the hoarding men tend to be productive, and the re-

TABLE 5:1   The Mode of Assimilation (N=406)
             (Percent scored)

Dominant Mode	Male	Female	Total
Dominant receptive	52	36	44
Dominant exploitative	13	9	11
Dominant hoarding	22	39	31
Dominant marketing	0	0	0
No mode dominant	13	16	14
	100	100	100

Dominant or Secondary			
Receptive	79	62	71
Exploitative	26	26	26
Hoarding	46	65	55
Marketing**	6	4	5
	157	157	157*

*Total greater than 100 percent because each individual may be scored as expressing either one or two modes of assimilation.
**Although we decided not to include the marketing orientation in the analysis of the results, the percentage scored for marketing is included in the tables in order to make them complete.

ceptive men tend to be unproductive. For women, on the other hand, there is no significant correlation between productiveness and either the dominant hoarding ($r = .06$) or the dominant receptive ($r = -.06$) orientations.

If we consider the villagers who are moderately or highly productive (with scores of 5 or 6), we find the following. Of the receptive men, only 9 percent are highly productive, while 48 percent of the hoarding men and 41 percent of the exploitative men are highly productive.

Of the receptive women, 17 percent are highly productive compared to 15 percent of the exploitative women and 21 percent of the hoarding women. In other words, highly productive village men are likely to be either hoarding or exploitative, while highly productive women are more evenly distributed in terms of the three modes of assimilation.

However, in terms of the overall scale of productiveness, there are no significant differences between men and women (see Table 5:3).

TABLE 5:2   Highly-Moderately Productive Percentage of Each Dominant Mode of Assimilation (Productiveness Score of 5 or 6)

	Men	Women
Receptive	9	17
Exploitative	41	15
Hoarding	48	21

TABLE 5:3 Productiveness (N=406)
(Percent Scored)

Level of Productiveness	Men	Women	Total
6. High to moderate (active interest)	10	10	10
5. Moderate (moderate interest)	14	10	12
4. Moderate (less active)	26	30	28
3. Moderate combined with unproductive traits	11	10	10
2. Low-passive (inactive)	32	26	29
1. Low life-rejecting	7	14	11
	100	100	100

Ten percent of the villagers were scored as highly to moderately productive; 12 percent as moderately productive; 28 percent as moderately productive but less active; 10 percent as moderately productive combined with unproductive traits; 29 percent as passive-inactive; and 10 percent as life rejecting.

We can conclude up to this point that there are two main types of male social character: the unproductive-receptive type which is the most frequent, and the (moderately) productive-hoarding type. There are also two smaller types: the productive-exploitative and the unproductive-exploitative.

For women, the distribution does not fall into this pattern. Most of the women are either hoarding or receptive, and more than is true for the men, hoarding tendencies are part of the female social character. These hoarding traits unlike those of the men are not correlated with productiveness.

2. *THE MODE OF RELATION*

Table 5:4 reports the distribution of the modes of relation in the village. The two most frequent of the dominant modes are narcissism I (33 percent) and conditional love (30 percent). Of the other dominant modes, only masochism (12 percent) is found in more than 10 percent of the population. Dominant sadism is found in 6 percent; dominant destructiveness in 5 percent; dominant narcissism II in 7 percent; dominant indulgence in 6 percent; and dominant love in one percent.

The relative distribution of modes of relation scored either dominant or as secondary tendencies are almost the same. The most frequent modes are conditional love (60 percent) and narcissism I (55 percent). The frequencies of the other modes are as follows: masochism (29 percent), sadism (26 percent), indulgence (25 percent), destructiveness (24 percent), narcissism II (13 percent), and love (13 percent).

TABLE 5:4   The Mode of Relation (N=406)
          (Percent Scored)

Dominant Mode	Male	Female	Total
Dominant sadism	7	5	6
Dominant masochism	4	20	12
Dominant destructiveness	2	8	5
Dominant narcissism I	40	26	33
Dominant narcissism II	9	5	7
Dominant indulgent love	7	4	6
Dominant conditional love	29	31	30
Dominant love	1	1	1
	99	100	100

Dominant or Secondary			
Sadism	30	23	26
Masochism	18	40	29
Destructiveness	21	27	24
Narcissism I	67	45	55
Narcissism II	15	12	13
Indulgent love	32	19	25
Conditional love	55	63	60
Love	13	13	13
	251	242	244*

*Total greater than 100 percent because each individual may be scored expressing one, two, or three modes of relation.

As we shall see in the discussion of the factor analysis, narcissism I and conditional love are related to different stages in life. Young unmarried villagers tend to have a narcissistic (I) mode of relatedness and those married, with children, are more likely to have a conditional loving mode of relatedness.

In terms of the mode of relation, there are also differences between the sexes. More men than women are narcissistic (I) and more women than men are masochistic. These statistically significant differences will be discussed in Chapter 7.

3. *THE MODE OF SOCIOPOLITICAL RELATIONS*

Table 5:5 reports the distribution of the modes of sociopolitical relations in the village.

The most frequent mode is submissiveness. Almost half (49 percent) of the villagers are dominantly submissive in their sociopolitical relations. The next largest categories are traditional authority (20 percent) and authoritarianism (16 percent). Seven percent are dominantly democratic, and 7 percent are dominantly rebellious.

TABLE 5:5   The Mode of Sociopolitical Relations (N=406)
(Percent Scored)

Dominant Mode	Male	Female	Total
Dominant authoritarian	17	15	16
Dominant traditional authority	24	16	20
Dominant submissive	45	55	49
Dominant rebellious (active)	3	8	6
Dominant rebellious (passive)	1	1	1
Dominant democratic	9	5	7
Dominant revolutionary	0	0	0
	99	100	99
Dominant or Secondary			
Authoritarian	29	28	28
Traditional authority	64	49	57
Submissive	77	81	79
Rebellious (active)	31	45	38
Rebellious (passive)	8	20	14
Democratic	46	30	38
Revolutionary	1	0	1
	256	253	255*

*Total greater than 100 percent because each individual may be scored as expressing one, two, or three modes of sociopolitical relations.

The relative distribution of modes scored as either dominant or as secondary tendencies is as follows: submissive, 79 percent; traditional authority, 57 percent; active rebellious, 38 percent; democratic, 38 percent; authoritarianism, 28 percent; passive rebellious, 14 percent; revolutionary tendencies, 1 percent.

There are also male-female differences in the frequency of sociopolitical modes. More men than women are traditional and democratic. More women more than men are dominantly submissive and have rebellious tendencies. These statistically significant differences will also be discussed in Chapter 7.

We can conclude that the sociopolitical character of the village is submissive, as combined with the attitudes of traditional authority. There is a minority of 16 percent who are authoritarian. However, there are underlying rebellious tendencies in about half of the villagers. Furthermore, a sizeable percentage of villagers, especially men, have democratic tendencies.

4. PARENTAL FIXATIONS

A key element in the character of the villagers is the fixation or dependence on the mother. As Table 5:6 reports, only 4 percent of the villagers are not mother fixated, and almost half (47 percent) were diagnosed as intensely fixated on the mother. The other 49 percent were scored

TABLE 5:6   Parental Fixations (N=406)
(Percent Scored)

Mother Fixation	Men	Women	Total
Little or none	3	5	4
Moderate	46	52	49
Intense	51	43	47
	100	100	100
Father Fixation			
Little or none	30	26	28
Moderate	53	58	56
Intense	17	16	16
	100	100	100
Rebelliousness to Parents			
Against the mother	1	9	5
Against the father	7	9	8

as moderately fixated to the mother. Fixation to the father is less common and less intense than fixation to the mother. Only 16 percent of the villagers are intensely fixated to the father, 56 percent moderately fixated, and 28 percent show no dependence on the father. Hardly any of these individuals who are not dependent on the father have become independent of the mother. Furthermore, very few of the villagers (7 percent) are more father fixated than mother fixated. Forty-one percent were considered as equally fixated on both parents, and 52 percent as more fixated on the mother.

The intense mother fixation is even more common among men than women (51 percent to 43 percent). However, practically as few women (5 percent) as men (3 percent) are not at all mother fixated.

The percentages of those who expressed rebelliousness to either parent were small. Five percent were rebellious to the mother and eight percent to the father. It should be kept in mind that from a dynamic standpoint, the emotional tie to a parent does not have to be a positive one. A person is as much bound to his father or mother if he is extremely attached to her as he is if his attitude to the parent is one of hate and rebellion.

Thus, virtually all of the villagers are mother bound to one degree or another. The question for each individual is whether or not there is a father influence also. We can distinguish two types of villagers: the mother fixated with or without the marked influence of the father.

5. OTHER BEHAVIORAL TRAITS

Table 5:7 reports the percentages of villagers scored according to the scale of enterprise energy and depression. In terms of enterprise energy we

TABLE 5:7   Behavioral Traits (N=406)
            (Percent Scored)

Enterprise-Energy	Men	Women	Total
High	11	6	8
Moderate	47	47	47
Low	42	47	45
	100	100	100

Depression			
Symptoms of clinical depression	3	4	3
Subclinical depression	35	45	40
No symptoms of depression	62	51	57
	100	100	100

find that 8 percent (11 percent of men and 6 percent of women) are highly energetic, 47 percent of both men and women are moderately energetic, and 45 percent (42 percent of men and 47 percent of women) manifest little energy. In terms of depression, 3 percent were diagnosed as being depressed. Forty percent (35 percent of men and 45 percent of women) had subclinical symptoms of depression, such as lacking interest in any activities. The majority of villagers (57 percent—62 percent of men and 51 percent of women) were not considered depressed. We shall see, in discussing Factor 2, that these traits are correlated with productiveness and unproductiveness.

THE FACTOR ANALYSIS

The second way of analyzing the data on character we used was a factor analysis (a Principal Components Factor Analysis with Varimax Rotation).

The inclusion of a factor analysis adds to the complexity of the study and the necessary information for understanding it will be reported in the following pages. However, a technical knowledge of factor analysis is not essential for understanding the results. Factor analysis is merely a labor-saving way of organizing the data and of clarifying relationships among variables. We found it useful for further understanding the data in the following ways.

First of all, it is a way of summarizing a large number of variables into a smaller set of variables called *factors*. If we did not use factor analysis, we could, of course, report all of the correlations of character variables with each other, but this would give us an overwhelming mass of information to digest. The factor analysis summarizes these correlations and makes it easier to see which variables go together. For example, Factor II (the productiveness factor discussed below) combines measures of productiveness, love, creativeness, and energy into one variable. The factor analysis and the intercorrelation of the traits allow us to consider all of these traits as related to a single underlying orientation, which we call productiveness. The decision of what to name the factor is not determined statistically, but theoretically.

Second, the factor analysis is useful in showing that certain character traits are rooted in different syndromes. A trait such as submissiveness may be related to different orientations. Submissiveness has one meaning when it is rooted in masochism. It has another meaning when it is rooted in passiveness and receptiveness. In the first instance, the individual has a passionate need to submit to powerful figures. In the second instance, he submits in order to be fed and cared for and because he lacks hope.

Third, there is the somewhat different case in which our scoring criteria failed to differentiate sufficiently between what are really two different traits. For example, the factor analysis shows that "love" is related on the one hand to a mothering syndrome (which also included masochism) and on the other hand to productiveness. In the first instance, it indicated the mother's unconditional love for her helpless, dependent children, a love which does not last when the children become independent and show minds of their own. In the second instance, it means respect, care, knowledge, and responsibility for an independent person. In both cases, the love is unconditional, but since we did not start out with scoring criteria for unconditional love limited to small children, the tendency was to score this trait as a tendency toward loving. The factor analysis calls attention to the different significance of love according to its rootedness in different syndromes of character.

It should be understood that the factor analysis does not automatically describe the most important syndromes of character found in the village. Rather, it summarizes relationships between the variables. In order to further delineate different types of individuals (beyond the frequencies of character orientations), we shall follow the practice of many factor analysts by interpreting combinations of the different factors.

THE MEANING OF FACTOR SCORES AND
FACTOR LOADINGS

Factors are fully described in mathematical terms. However, for our purposes it is sufficient to point out that factors are new variables that summarize the variables scored from the questionnaire; the factor analysis shows which ones are closely related to each other.[3] These relationships can be either positive or negative. For example, while productiveness is related positively with love, it is related negatively with destructiveness. The psychological meanings of these relationships are not automatically explained by the factor analysis, but must make sense in terms of theory; factors must be interpreted. The factor analysis we undertook resulted in six factors which can in fact be understood theoretically and which summarize the data in a meaningful way.[4] However, we feel we should emphasize the fact that the factor analysis does not prove that our scoring is correct. We do not want to give the impression that the factor analysis magically envelopes our subjective, diagnostic scoring (with its human fallibility) in a cloak of mathematical, computer-like precision.

We have stated that a factor summarizes variables. This is done in terms of the correlations between the original variables as we scored them and the new summary variable which is called factor. These correlations are called (factor) *loadings*. Each variable or trait that enters the analysis will have a positive loading, a negative loading, or a zero loading on each of the factors. A variable or trait with a high loading (about ±.30 in this

---

[3] For a technical exposition of factor analysis, see J. P. Guilford, *Psychometric Methods,* 2d ed. (New York: McGraw-Hill, 1954). The Varimax rotation is described in H. H. Harmon, *Modern Factor Analysis,* 2d ed. (Chicago: University of Chicago Press, 1967), pp. 294-300.

In semitechnical terms, we can report that a Principal Components factor analysis was performed on the domain of variables. This method first extracts a factor which according to mathematical criteria explains as much of the variance among the variables as is possible. The residual, the variance that remains unexplained by the first factor, is used to extract the second factor, and the process continues until there is so little variance left that it can no longer be meaningfully explained. In our case, the analysis stopped when the sum of the squares of the factor loadings would have been less than 1. These six factors were then rotated according to the Varimax criterion, a method aimed at encountering a maximum clarity of factors by means of purely formal criteria. There are a number of ways to rotate the principal component factors. One can decide to rotate so that a particular variable will have a high loading on a factor. Such a rotation naturally changes the loadings of all the other factors and produces a new factor. Rotations can be made according to theoretical requirements, or they can be made in order to examine the possibilities of dimensions slightly different from the principal components analysis. Such empirical rotations can produce syndromes centered around a particular variable that the investigator considers particularly significant, or they can be a means toward interpreting the "factor space" to explore possibilities of various syndromes or ideal types.

As it turned out, the Varimax method produced theoretically meaningful factors by mathematical criterion, so that it was unnecessary to resort to empirical rotation. The goal of the Varimax rotation is to clarify the factor structure by maximizing the variance in each factor, keeping the communality constant. What the Varimax rotation probably does is to emphasize ideal type syndromes in which particularly strong variables dominate the factor.

[4] Why were there just six factors, no more, no less? These six factors each explained more variance than any one of the original variables, and therefore met the criterion of scientific parsimony. Additional factors are possible, but they would individually explain less variance than any one of the *original* variables.

particular case) is considered as a main element in the factor. Variables with loadings of ±.20 to ±.30 are also considered as relating significantly but in a secondary way to the factor. When the loadings are on the order of ±.20 or even ±.15, they are, strictly speaking, statistically significant, but of less importance. The decision of whether or not to consider them as important depends in great part on their theoretical significance. A low-grade but still significant finding with a high-grade theoretical expectation is important and should be understood as fully as possible. This is different from a low-grade statistical finding combined with a low-grade theoretical expectation which we do not consider important. All of the factor loadings are presented in Table 5:8.

Just as each individual has a score in terms of each original variable, so too he has a (factor) *score* on each factor. These concepts can be illustrated in terms of Factor I. Factor I has positive loadings that include age over 20 years and character traits that describe adult adjustment to peasant culture. The variables that have high negative loadings on the factor, when taken together, describe the adolescent in terms of age and character. The factor, then, presents contrasting syndromes defined by its high positive and negative loadings: adulthood in one direction and adolescence in the other.[5]

Figure 5:1 illustrates the concept of factor loadings and factor scores. The factor loadings determine the contrasting syndromes of adolescence and adulthood. The individual's factor score indicates where he stands in terms of those dimensions. If individual A has a high score on Factor I, this means that he is considered to have the traits characterizing a mature peasant. On the other hand, if individual B shows a very low score on Factor I, we consider him to have the traits characteristic of the adolescent. A high score on the factor does not necessarily mean that the individual has all of the traits that are highly loaded on the factor. It means he has more of them than those with lower scores on the factor. For example, an individual might show some but not all of the traits associated with adulthood and still have a high score on the factor. The individual's factor score is a standard score, calculated by mathematical methods, which represents the degree to which the individual has the total pattern of traits represented by the factor.

THE SIX FACTORS

The result of the factor analysis performed on the 63 variables of character, behavioral traits, age, sex, and civil status for the entire group

---

[5] Mathematically, it would be just as logical to make either the adult or the adolescent pole the "positive" direction, but psychologically it is natural to think of the development from adolescence to adulthood.

TABLE 5:8 Rotated (Varimax) Loadings of Character Variables: Age, Sex, and Civil Status

Variable	I Adulthood vs. Adolescence	II Productiveness vs. Unproductiveness	III Exploitativeness vs. Nonexploitativeness	IV Hoarding vs. Receptive	V Masculinity vs. Feminity	VI Mother-Centered vs. Father-Centered
1. Sex: male = + Female = −	−.06	−.15	−.05	−.28	.38	−.02
2. Age: 13-16 years	−.42	−.04	−.05	−.01	.00	−.04
3. 17-20 years	−.38	.02	−.10	−.04	.12	.06
4. 21-30 years	.04	−.01	.03	−.14	.04	−.17
5. 31-40 years	.22	−.03	−.08	.16	−.06	.08
6. 41-50 years	.20	−.05	.10	.10	−.07	.14
7. 51-60 years	.22	.11	.09	.04	−.06	.02
8. 61-70 years	.17	−.01	.03	−.03	.01	−.03
9. Over 70	−.04	.04	.04	−.10	−.03	−.03
10. Unmarried	−.78	.07	−.00	−.07	.05	−.13
11. Married	.66	−.01	.01	.02	.12	.14
12. Widowed	.18	−.10	.08	.16	−.16	−.12
13. Separated	.00	−.00	.00	.00	.00	.00
14. Free union	−.00	−.01	−.06	.02	−.13	.09
15. Has children	.80	−.03	.04	.10	−.09	.10
16. Sadistic (dom.)	.11	−.08	.18	−.00	.04	.22
17. Sadistic	.19	−.15	.22	.01	.07	.08
18. Masochistic (dom.)	.04	−.05	−.07	.06	−.57	.03
19. Masochistic	.12	−.10	−.12	.03	−.54	−.06
20. Destructive (dom.)	−.03	−.21	.22	.24	−.11	.12
21. Destructive	−.09	−.27	.29	.24	−.05	.14
22. Narcissistic I (dom.)	−.47	−.11	−.12	−.11	.37	.05
23. Narcissistic I	−.34	−.13	−.26	−.13	.42	.06
24. Narcissistic II (dom.)	−.02	−.04	.55	−.08	−.01	−.11
25. Narcissistic II	−.02	.07	.57	−.04	−.07	−.11
26. Indulgent (dom.)	−.01	.03	.00	−.21	−.05	−.09
27. Indulgent	.13	.03	−.22	−.19	.07	−.23
28. Conditional loving (dom.)	.45	.24	−.24	.12	.09	−.16

96

29. Conditional loving	.46	.13	-.13	.12	.07	-.17
30. Loving (dom.)	.01	.79	.06	-.21	-.37	.19
31. Loving	.01	.79	.06	-.21	-.37	.19
32. Productiveness	.17	.64	.03	.10	.07	-.18
33. Creativeness	.07	.63	.14	.05	.05	-.02
34. No interest	.00	-.21	.15	.13	-.17	.07
35. Energy	.17	.47	.21	.25	.07	-.06
36. Receptive (dom.)	-.13	-.13	-.24	-.63	.05	.04
37. Receptive	-.12	-.15	-.30	-.58	.02	.02
38. Exploitative (dom.)	.00	-.04	.52	.02	.08	-.01
39. Exploitative	.01	.03	.54	.11	.07	.13
40. Hoarding (dom.)	.14	.12	-.12	.64	-.14	.01
41. Hoarding	.14	.04	-.15	.53	-.18	.01
42. Marketing (dom.)	-.04	.04	-.05	.07	.10	-.21
43. Marketing	-.16	.11	-.04	-.05	.04	-.28
44. Authoritarian (dom.)	.28	-.22	.60	-.06	.04	.05
45. Authoritarian	.34	-.27	.44	-.13	-.12	.04
46. Traditional (dom.)	.26	.38	-.01	.16	.29	.03
47. Traditional	.08	.38	-.25	.14	.30	.03
48. Democratic (dom.)	-.20	.35	.00	.09	.05	-.17
49. Democratic	-.00	.49	-.06	-.01	.20	-.26
50. Submissive (dom.)	-.22	-.24	-.45	-.27	-.29	.06
51. Submissive	-.13	-.18	-.39	-.21	-.24	.01
52. Rebel (dom.)	-.08	-.12	.10	.22	.00	-.12
53. Rebel	-.01	-.18	.16	.15	-.10	-.09
54. Passive rebel (dom.)	-.13	-.07	-.02	.09	-.02	.10
55. Passive rebel	-.23	-.24	.05	.12	-.21	.14
56. Revolutionary (dom.)	-.00	.00	-.00	-.00	.00	-.00
57. Revolutionary	.06	.16	.15	-.07	-.01	.04
58. Mother fixation	-.28	-.10	-.12	-.17	-.02	.42
59. Rebellion mother	.00	-.14	.03	.18	-.11	-.01
60. Father fixation	-.15	-.06	-.01	-.16	-.17	-.49
61. Rebellion father	-.08	-.11	.06	.02	-.11	.13
62. Mother vs. father fixation	.09	-.06	-.08	.02	.12	.71
63. Depression	.14	-.20	.17	.05	-.08	.12
Sums Squares	3.77	3.81	3.08	2.47	2.13	1.72

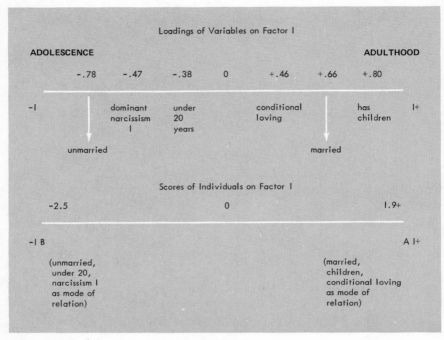

FIGURE 5:1

of 406 adult villagers was six factors. We gave these factors names in terms of the most important variables that are summarized by the factor, as follows:

Factor I—*Adulthood vs. Adolescence.* This factor summarizes traits that are related to the age of the villagers and suggests how character changes with development from youth to adulthood.

Factor II—*Productiveness vs. Unproductiveness.* This factor summarizes traits that are related to the productiveness variable.

Factor III—*Exploitativeness vs. Nonexploitativeness.* This factor summarizes the traits rooted in an exploitative orientation.

Factor IV—*Hoarding vs. Receptive Modes of Assimilation.* This factor indicates most of all that the villagers can be separated in terms of whether their character is basically receptive or hoarding.

Factor V—*Sex Role (Masculinity vs. Femininity).* This factor summarizes those variables that are significantly correlated with the sex of the villagers.

Factor VI—*Mother Centered vs. Father Centered.* We have seen that almost all of the villagers are at least moderately fixated on the mother. This factor contrasts exclusive fixation on the mother with the influence of the father.

FACTOR I—ADULTHOOD VS. ADOLESCENCE

On the side of adulthood, the main loadings include: being married, having children, conditional love, and a tendency toward authoritarianism. Traditionalism is a secondary loading.

On the side of adolescence, the main loadings include: being an adolescent (under age 20), being unmarried, and narcissism I. The secondary loadings include: fixation to the mother, submissiveness, and passive rebelliousness.

By summarizing and polarizing the traits associated with adolescence in contrast to traits associated with marrying and having a family, this factor presents a description of traits held in common by the average adult vs. traits held in common by the average adolescent. As it has been observed in general, in our material too, the narcissism of the adolescent gives way to a sense of greater relatedness and responsibility in the adult married person, and the new relationship between the spouses loosens the degree of the tie to mother. It is notable that this is the only factor of the six with high age loadings, suggesting that the other elements of character are more or less permanently structured by adolescence and do not change afterwards in the normal course of events. In this respect, it should be mentioned that Factor I includes narcissism I (rather than extreme narcissism) and hence can more easily dissolve with the assumption of family responsibilities.

Factor I does not imply that "normal" adults become more loving than adolescents. Conditional love, as we scored it, implies material care and affection, but conditional on obedience and respect for traditional authority. There are as few loving individuals among adolescents as among adults.

Adulthood in the village thus implies a more responsible relatedness and the adoption of traditional authoritarian attitudes in place of the submissiveness and rebelliousness of adolescence.

FACTOR II—PRODUCTIVENESS VS UNPRODUCTIVENESS

The high loadings related to productiveness are: love, creativeness, enterprise-energy, traditional authority and democratic modes of sociopolitical relatedness. The only secondary loading is conditional love.

On the other pole, related to unproductiveness, there are no loadings of more than −.30. But the secondary loadings of −.20 to −.30 show that unproductiveness is related to depression, no interest, destructiveness, authoritarianism, submissiveness, and passive rebelliousness.

Factor II presents no surprises. It reports that the productive villagers are the ones who tend to be either loving or conditional loving, creative and energetic, while the unproductive villagers are the most depressed and destructive, with no interest in village activities, in cultural events, or even in their own children. Beyond this, the factor shows that sociopolitical attitudes are rooted in productiveness. The productive villagers combine democratic and traditional attitudes. They are the ones who most respect the rights and wishes of others. In the context of a traditional society, they provide the emotional underpinning for the ideals of a community in which each of the village family heads shares in the process of making decisions. In contrast, unproductive villagers are authoritarian individuals who are contemptuous of the weak. These unproductive villagers are submissive to power, but they also tend to be passively rebellious.

The unproductive adults are authoritarian and depressed while the unproductive adolescents are mother fixated, narcissistic, and submissive-rebellious. In contrast, the most productive adolescents and adults are similar to each other in terms of character. However, the moderately productive adult has the traits that most represent the cultural norms of the village (see Figure 5:2).

The contrast between Factors I and II points to an essential difference between maturity defined by aging and adjusting to society vs. maturity defined by the development of the individual's unique human powers to produce and to love. We would expect to find these two different factors in other societies also, although it is likely that the specific variables that form the adult-adjustment syndrome differ according to varying cultural demands and social structures. In any culture, adjustment to the society's norms and to its characteristic mode of authority may be achieved only at the expense of optimal development of the individual's human powers. Adjustment to the society means compliance and acceptance of norms; the adjusted villager becomes what is expected of him. His uniqueness, his personal identity is submerged in the identity provided for him by his culture. The productive individual, on the other hand, becomes more and more individuated. His ideas, as we see in the examples of productive responses to the questionnaire in Appendix A, are not cultural clichés but are based on his own experience and powers of reasoning.

FACTOR III—EXPLOITATIVENESS VS. NONEXPLOITATIVENESS

This factor was one of the most difficult to name. The contrast between exploitativeness and nonexploitativeness seems the best overall description of the factor, although a careful analysis of the variables shows different kinds of exploitativeness and nonexploitativeness.

The main loadings related to the exploitative mode include authori-

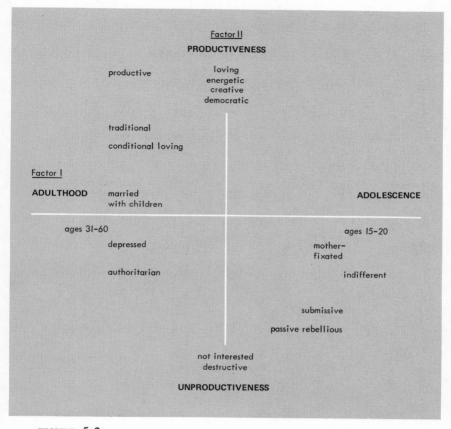

FIGURE 5:2

tarianism and extreme narcissism. The secondary loadings include sadism and destructiveness.

The main loadings on the side of nonexploitativeness include submissiveness and receptiveness. The secondary loadings include traditionalism, responsibility, indulgence, and narcissism I.

These loadings make sense only when they are considered in relationship to productiveness by combining Factors II and III as is shown graphically in Figure 5:3 which helps in differentiating the more positive and negative variations of exploitative and nonexploitative villagers.

The unproductive-exploitative villager is authoritarian and sadistic and/or destructive. Those with a clear-cut authoritarian-exploitative-sadistic or destructive orientation include approximately 10 to 15 percent of the population. We have seen that 6 percent of the villagers are dominantly

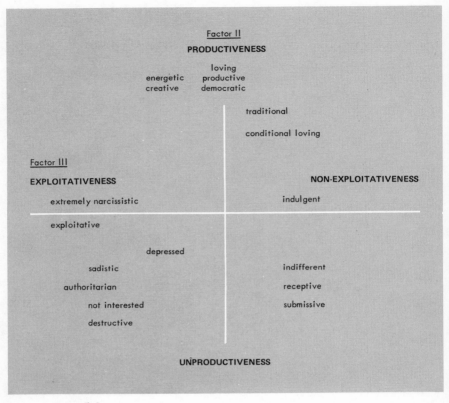

FIGURE 5:3

sadistic and 5 percent are dominantly destructive. Sixteen percent of the population is dominantly authoritarian.

The way in which the authoritarian-exploitative villager experiences life can be described as a feeling of living in a jungle where he must eat others in order to escape being eaten. This feeling is symbolically expressed in the responses of these individuals to the Rorschach test. They often see images of fierce carniverous animals combined with weak-destroyed figures (see Appendix B).

The authoritarian-exploitative's view of the world corresponds to his experience, and his perception of others' motives justifies for himself his own exploitativeness and destructiveness. At the same time, given his character, others fear him with good reason and thus confirm his beliefs. When intense narcissism is added to this syndrome, it describes an individual with an illusion of power and grandiosity, even though as a poor peasant he is rather powerless, subject to forces in nature and society over which he has no control. Furthermore, his narcissism may have the function of protecting him from facing his true motivations and allowing him to believe that his activities are motivated by more benign conscious values. However, we must keep in mind that in the peasant village, and indeed within most societies, even the most exploitative people wish to believe that their behavior is intended to benefit others or that at its most destructive, it is merely self-defense. The most authoritarian and sadistic parents in the village believe that their beatings are aimed at "getting rid of the child's badness," or at showing him the difference between right and wrong, and they would deny to themselves and others that they enjoyed the beatings, that punishing the child made *them* feel powerful, less depressed, more satisfied. What we find is that the most authoritarian and exploitative individuals are also the most narcissistic ones.

Being an authoritarian individual does not guarantee success in dominating others. Many with this character structure find themselves constantly frustrated in their authoritarian strivings. This leads often to violent behavior. Those men who were put on a list of violent individuals, known for getting into knife or pistol fights, are typical unproductive exploiters. The authoritarian-exploitative man lashes out if he feels threatened, if his narcissistic image of himself is challenged, and he must humble or destroy the other in order to maintain his self-respect.

Women, like men, have authoritarian-exploitative character traits. Such women unman their husbands, ridiculing them when they show weakness, and belittling them into despair and alcoholism (see Chapter 8). A high score for women of Factor III is correlated with the participant-observer ratings of women who fight each other on the streets of the village, either with fists, or with words, to see who can so insult the other that she is too shamed and speechless to continue. There are no limits to the ferocity of these word duels. The women save up all the malicious gossip they can find about the other women and their husbands and families to hurl at each other publicly.

In contrast to these unproductive sadists, the productive-exploitative orientation essentially describes a small group of about ten village men who are modern entrepreneurs. They are tough, energetic and innovative, the first to buy tractors which they rent out to others, the first to try out new methods of farming intensively, to rent new land to be farmed by persons under their direction, the most likely to become middlemen, thus taking over a role that used to belong largely to urban entrepreneurs.

The question arises whether this group of exploiters is really at all productive, or whether the group is merely more skilled, intelligent, and energetic than the other exploitative individuals. In fact, these individuals often exploit the weakness and desperate need of others. They sometimes sell labor-saving services that others do not need and cannot afford. They pay the lowest wages they can and often charge more for their services than is fair. They lend money at high interest rates. Unlike the traditional peasant, they are not *formal,* or respectful of others. Rather, others are used as objects for their personal gain.

In contrast to the unproductive exploiter, however, these entrepreneurs do not merely dominate by force and blackmail. The concept of the productive-exploitative individual implies someone who builds something that is an imaginative response to new opportunities which the majority do not use. This is particularly the case today, where there are opportunities to adopt new methods and use new agricultural technology. In the traditional village of the past, such entrepreneurs might have had less productive possibilities than exist today.

In the changing, developing society, the entrepreneur is the new man who can be considered the village "progressive." But he is this only in a certain historical perspective of intensifying the class difference in the village and destroying its traditional structure. The exploitative entrepreneurs are among the most alienated villagers. Despite their material success, our experience is that they seem to enjoy life less than anyone else. They do not like fiestas, they are not interested in others' welfare unless it helps them to profit. We found only one exploitative individual with a loving trait. Most of these men have destructive effects on their children, wives, and others in the village.

To summarize, the unproductive-exploitative syndrome characterizes the most violent and destructive men and women. The productive-exploitative syndrome characterizes the "new men" who are like small-scale robber barons in their character.

On the nonexploitative side of Factor III, two types can also be distinguished in terms of their productiveness: the more productive, traditional, responsible peasants, and the unproductive, passive, submissive, receptive peasants. The passive-receptive villagers submit to exploitation, not necessarily because they are masochistic, but because they feel powerless and have developed a protective indifference to life. The passive-submissive villager has given up hope, partly because he lacks the independence and energy to seek an alternative to his way of life, but also because such an alternative may be almost impossible for him to find.

The productive-nonexploitative peasant is traditional and responsible. Most of the more productive traditional-nonexploitative villagers are characterized by the hoarding orientation. For such individuals, traditional values now clash with those of the newer cash economy, and they are willing to go along with the new entrepreneurs in giving up many traditional forms such as costly fiestas for the sake of greater profit and modernization (see Chapter 6). (It must be noted that this attitude, while economically useful, contributes to the final destruction of what is left of traditional peasant values, which in this case is not too much!)

At this point, we see that the factor analysis suggests that some of the traits we scored must be interpreted differently in terms of the syndrome in which they are embedded. This can be concluded, for example, in the loadings on different factors of narcissism I, authoritarianism, and submissiveness.

The factor analysis indicates that our scoring of narcissism I as indifference did not distinguish between a "normal" adolescent narcissism and a deeper indifference which does not normally dissolve with marriage. There are two not mutually exclusive possibilities to consider. One is that we are justified in formulating narcissism in terms of degrees, and that what we call narcissism I includes a range of degrees. For example, if we conceive of a scale from zero (no narcissism) to 100 (psychotic narcissism), what we call narcissism I might include the range from, say, 20 to 60. Another possibility is that the narcissism associated with submissiveness and receptiveness (Factor III) is not in fact narcissistic indifference but the lack of interest based in the hopelessness of individuals who have been ground down and can expect nothing better from life in the future.

Authoritarianism has high loadings on Factors I, II, and III. On Factors II and III, authoritarianism is rooted in the sadistic character. This fits Fromm's (1941) theoretical formulation of the authoritarian as a sadistic, exploitative individual who expresses these character traits in the sociopolitical sphere as well as in his intimate family relationships. However, Factor I describes a responsible, well-adjusted, reasonably healthy adult villager who is generally not exploitative or sadistic. Here we are dealing with a different kind of authoritarianism which has to do with acceptance of a hierarchical social structure, conservatism, a strong reaction to deviation from the status quo. Even though we distinguished theoretically between sado-masochistic authoritarianism and "traditional" authoritarianism, the factor analysis shows that this theoretical difference was not made clearly enough. We find that one type of traditional attitude is authoritarian in the sense of supporting a hierarchical structure, while another type of traditionalism is combined with a democratic attitude. Both of these sociopolitical attitudes are different from exploitative, sadistic authoritarianism. The traditional democratic attitude approaches the concept of "rational authority," which Fromm (1947) has distinguished from the authoritarian-sadistic "irrational authority."

Submissiveness, also, has a different meaning in the context of adolescent dependence (Factor I), masochism (Factors II and V), and receptiveness (Factors III and IV). We have seen that 79 percent of the villagers were scored as submissive. Such a prevalent attitude can be considered as virtually a cultural pattern, but there appear to be different degrees of submissiveness according to the whole character system in which submissiveness is found. The most deeply ingrained submissiveness, and probably the most difficult to change, is that connected with masochism. In contrast, for the adolescents a certain submissiveness combined with rebelliousness is a part of dependence on the parents, and normally is weakened when the individual marries and has children.

In the third instance of the receptive character, the meaning of submissiveness is also somewhat different. It is the result both of the receptive orientation and also of the hopelessness of the receptive peasant due to his experience of being ground down by life. It is possible that this submissive attitude might change if the socioeconomic conditions of life provided for a better future and encouraged hope and initiative.

These three types of submissive character—rooted in masochism, adolescent dependence, and passive-receptiveness—are all different from the submissive behavior that even many of the more independent villagers exhibit in the face of powerful authorities. For these individuals, submissiveness is merely a *tactic* for getting along in the world, for pleasing powerful and dangerous people in order to avoid their wrath or secure their favor. (The different roots of submissiveness in the villagers are summarized in Figure 5:4.)

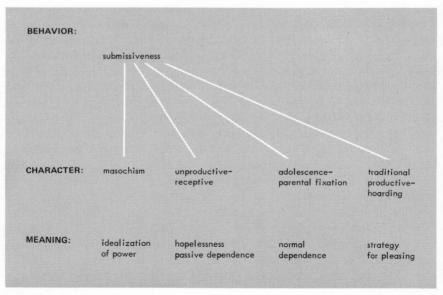

BEHAVIOR:

submissiveness

CHARACTER: masochism unproductive-receptive adolescence-parental fixation traditional productive-hoarding

MEANING: idealization of power | hopelessness passive dependence | normal dependence | strategy for pleasing

FIGURE 5:4

FACTOR IV—HOARDING VS. RECEPTIVE MODES OF ASSIMILATION

The contrast between the hoarding and receptive orientations which are the major loadings on this factor is a key element in understanding the character of this peasant population and perhaps of the peasant character in general. We have seen that 86 percent of the villagers are either hoarding or receptive in their dominant mode of assimilation (see Table 5:1). In contrast, only 10 percent of the villagers are dominantly exploitative.

The hoarding orientation is the single main loading on one side of the factor. The secondary loadings on this side include energy, active rebelliousness, destructiveness, and the female sex. The secondary loadings also indicate that the hoarding mode is related to independence from parents, rebelliousness to the mother, and the traditional orientation to authority.

The receptive orientation is the single main loading on the other side of the factor. The secondary loadings related to receptiveness include submissiveness, indulgence, and dependence on parents. A secondary loading also indicates that the positive receptive orientation tends to be more loving than the positive hoarding orientation.

Some reasons why women are more hoarding and men more receptive will be considered in Chapter 7. To understand the other loadings, Factor IV must be analyzed in relationship to Factor II. When this is done, as in Figure 5:5, we are able to differentiate the positive and negative aspects of the hoarding and receptive orientations.

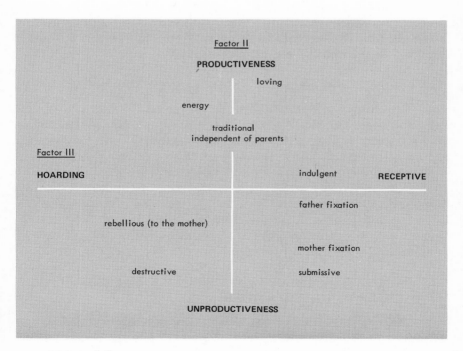

FIGURE 5:5

Those with the positive hoarding orientation tend to be the most independent, energetic, and traditional villagers. We shall consider why this is so at the conclusion of this chapter. Theoretically we would expect the hoarding character to be more independent and self-contained than the receptive character, for the reasons discussed in Chapter 4. Villagers with the negative hoarding character tend to fit Freud's concept of anal-sadism. Their rebelliousness describes the obstinacy that Freud (1908) associated with the anal character. Their tendency to destructiveness also is consistent with Fromm's (1964) theory of necrophilous destructiveness as rooted in an extremely regressive hoarding orientation.

According to the theory of character described in Chapter 4, individuals with a positive receptive orientation tend to be responsive, sensitive, and tender. It is consistent with this theory that the most productive-receptive villagers tend to have at least a secondary loving trait. The moderately productive-receptive villagers tend to be indulgent; they give in order to receive affection. Furthermore, they tend to be dependent on their fathers as well as on their mothers.

In contrast, the negative receptive character fits the "classic" psychoanalytic conception of the receptive, submissive, mother-fixated individual. We consider it theoretically significant that a receptive individual tends to be more productive if he is dependent on the father, while extreme dependence on the mother is likely to imply a more regressive and unproductive-receptive character. In the analysis of village social character and in the formation of character (Chapter 9) we shall see that the mother fixation is a key element in explaining unproductiveness.

FACTOR V—SEX ROLE (MASCULINITY VS. FEMININITY)

This factor summarizes traits that are correlated with sex. On the masculine side, the main loadings are narcissism I and traditionalism. The secondary loading is the democratic attitude. On the feminine side the main loadings include masochism, submissiveness, and love. The secondary loadings include passive rebelliousness and the hoarding mode.

Essentially, the loadings indicate that more men than women are indifferent, traditionalistic, and democratic, while more women than men are masochistic, hoarding, passively rebellious, and loving. These sex differences will be analyzed in relation to cultural and socioeconomic variables in Chapter 7.

FACTOR VI—MOTHER-CENTERED VS. FATHER-CENTERED ORIENTATIONS

This last factor can be considered a variable that describes at one extreme those individuals who are intensely fixated to the mother without any paternal influence. At the other extreme are those villagers who are fixated to the father as well as to the mother. Since virtually all of the villagers are mother-bound to one degree or another, the question for each individual is whether or not there is a father influence also. In the conclusion of this chapter we shall outline the theoretical significance of mother-centered vs. father-centered societies. Here, we shall consider only what the factor adds to the previous findings.

The main loading on the mother-centered side is the fixation to the mother. The secondary loadings are sadism and unproductiveness.

The main loading on the father-centered side is fixation to the father. The secondary loadings include the democratic orientation, conditional love, and productiveness.

In analyzing Factor VI we should keep in mind that extreme fixation to the mother has already been seen as related to the receptive unproductive orientation. On the side of mother fixation the factor adds the finding that sadism is frequently an element in the mother-centered personality. This finding is consistent with the theoretical formulation in Chapter 4. We stated that sadism is rooted in and compensates for deep—and often unconscious—feelings of impotence and powerlessness. The individual who remains fixated to the mother, without any paternal influence, would feel like a powerless infant if he did not compensate for these feelings in some way. One way that gives a sense of power is by means of a sadistic drive. This form of sadism, rooted in the mother-fixated and passive-receptive orientation, will be analyzed in relation to alcoholism in Chapter 8.

The secondary loadings connected with father influence indicate that, in the village society, it is associated with the positive character. Paternal influence is related to conditional love and to the democratic orientation. This finding is also consistent with our theoretical viewpoint as we shall outline it in the conclusion of this chapter.

CONCLUSION: SOCIAL CHARACTER

In the preceding parts of this chapter we have first reported the frequency of character traits and then described interrelationships among the traits as shown by factor analysis. This material provides the basis for formulating the social character of the village and for asking the question: What are the decisive influences that have formed these various character types?

We have distinguished three main types: first, the nonproductive-receptive character which is the most frequent one; second, the productive-hoarding character; and third, the exploitative character (which is composed of two numerically smaller types, productive-exploitative and un-productive-exploitative). In summarizing the major types, we put to one side some important male-female differences which will be analyzed in Chapter 7.

1. *THE NONPRODUCTIVE-RECEPTIVE CHARACTER*

The nonproductive-receptive orientation has its roots in the history of the feudal structure of the Mexican society as a whole. Even before the conquest, the Aztec society was organized in a feudal system. After the conquest, the hacienda system was organized according to what might be termed a modified feudal system, in which the peons were fixed in their positions for life, totally dependent on their masters, with no power to change, or any idea of changing their position. What makes the haciendas "semifeudal" was the fact that the peon lacked all the rights and that the hacienda owner, unlike the medieval lord, had no obligations.

However, there are key sociopsychological elements of the feudal system which characterize the sociopolitical structure of Mexico from the top down. The feudal structure implies that the individual of whatever social level is dependent on the superior, on the next level, and that there is a hierarchy of dependencies up to the top. Security and individual progress is not gained primarily on the basis of achievement and competence, as in modern society, but rather on the basis of total loyalty to the superior in return for the hope that the superior will do favors for and protect the inferior. Indeed, the inferior in Mexican society does not consider what he receives as something to which he is entitled but rather as favors or largesse on the part of the superior. We have observed in the village on paydays that receptive men who work as day laborers will come hat in hand to beg, as it were, the salary they have earned. In a feudal system, the inferior tends to look up to the superior patron as the one who can give or withhold, who feeds and nourishes him. One of the main efforts on the part of the inferior is to win the patron's favor by pleasing him. This reinforces the receptive orientation which we find not only among the villagers but throughout Mexico. The Mexican bourgeois has the same attitude toward a higher government official, up to the President. It is always the expectation that those above have favors to give, and one's energy is spent not so much in one's projects as in trying to manipulate the superior.

But it would be a mistake to think that this receptive attitude of the peasant or the bourgeois is nothing but a coldblooded, calculating attitude. It also has affective overtones, and often implies genuine warmth. It should be noted that the difference between the modern industrial society and the semifeudal society has important repercussions for the formation of personality traits. In an industrial society success depends primarily on achievement and competence, and being liked is only a secondary factor.

In the semifeudal society, being liked or pleasing the authority is a primary factor for success or even continuation of the same status, while achievement and competence are secondary. From this it follows that in modern industrial society a general friendliness is important but not always necessary to keep one's job and advance, provided one demonstrates competence; a certain amount of indifferent friendliness is usually enough to avoid antagonizing the boss. In semifeudal society, a great deal of knowledge of the other person is necessary to make him favorably disposed. This does not mean simply that one can flatter the patron, because he may dislike obvious flattery; rather one must be so aware of his subtle reactions and personality traits that one can say and do precisely what, considering his personality, creates a favorable impression. As a secondary consequence, one finds in the Mexican peasant as well as in the member of the middle class an extraordinary degree of tact and sensitivity to nonverbal communication which is rarely to be found in an industrial society.

Given the quasi-feudal structure, it is logical to expect that the peasants at the bottom of the hierarchy are receptive-submissive individuals.

The particular Mexican structure also has another key element which is decisive in the formation of the receptive character: the fixation to the mother. Mother fixation is part of the social character, so much so that we can consider the village (and the central plateau of Mexico) to be a society which in appearance is strictly father centered or patriarchal, but which in fact is emotionally centered in the mother. Some general theoretical statements are necessary in order to clarify this point. We start with the assumption that there are mother-centered and father-centered societies and individuals.

By mother and father centered is meant that the main emotional tie is to the mother or to the father. Within the father- or mother-centered personality there are significant differences of degree, ranging from an emotional tie to one parent with the exclusion of the other, to a tie to one parent accompanied by a tie to the other parent, although a weaker one. Seen from the dynamic standpoint, this tie does not have to be a positive one; a boy is as much bound to his mother if he is extremely attached to her, as he is if his attitude to her is one of hate and rebellion. The same, of course, holds true of the tie to the father. This distinction between father- and mother-centered individuals and cultures is gained from clinical material observed in psychoanalytic therapy, as well as from the study of cultures. We had been greatly impressed by Bachofen's work on matriarchal and patriarchal studies; while his hypotheses are hardly correct as far as the exact evolutionary scheme and its universality is concerned, there is no escaping the fact that not only anthropological data, but particularly the critical analysis of myth, demonstrate that Bachofen's and Morgan's basic idea of distinguishing between societies ruled by mothers and the motherly principle (matriarchal societies) and societies ruled by fathers and fatherly principles (patriarchal societies) is correct.[6] Even the full awareness of the fact that most anthropologists do not believe Bachofen's analysis, in fact hardly take it seriously, does not alter our conviction. Our concept of "mother-centered" and "father-centered" personalities and societies should make it somewhat easier to overcome the difficulties in accepting the main point.

If we speak of mother- and father-*centered* systems, we are able to leave out the arguable problem of social and political domination as it is presumed in the concept of matriarchy and patriarchy (mother and father *rule*). Furthermore the concept of father- and mother-centered systems has the advantage that it can be demonstrated in abundant clinical material, as we believe, also with regard to the social character.

What is meant by fatherly and motherly principles to which reference was just made must be explained. Basically these are the principles established by Bachofen, somewhat further developed by our clinical and social data. To put it briefly, the maternal principle is unconditional love, mercy, the natural equality of children, the prevalence of natural law over man-

---

[6] We would perhaps be more reluctant to hold such convictions in an anthropological question in which anthropologists are obviously more competent than we are, were it not for the fact that we are deeply impressed by the tremendous emotional bias which exists with regard to this point. It seems that even in a relatively mild form of patriarchate, as that of the United States, men and women find it extremely difficult to believe that the role of the sexes could be exactly the opposite of what the patriarchal society assumes to be natural. Consciously, of course, there is no prejudice, but like all prejudices, the unconscious reaction is quite different from the conscious one. One of the most drastic examples for the force of the bias is to be seen in Freud's theory about women. His whole idea that the libido is masculine and that half the human race is a crippled edition of the other half, is absurd, and this absurdity can only be understood if one takes into account the force of Freud's patriarchal bias (cf. discussion of this point in Fromm's *Sigmund Freud's Mission* [New York: Harper & Bros., 1959]). Freud's patriarchal prejudice appears also in another point. Because the devaluation of the woman's importance for the child had to be denied, Freud did not see the fact of a primary bond of the child (boy and girl) to the mother until ten years before his death. Although the evidence for a deep or intense non-genital tie (in Freudian language "pre-Oedipal") to the mother is overwhelming, practically all other analysts followed Freud in this error. (Cf. the excellent paper by John Bowlby, "The Nature of the Child's Tie to His Mother," *The International Journal of Psychoanalysis*, 34 [1958]: 350-73.) Because of this error in the evaluation of the mother's primary role, the important work by J. J. Bachofen was almost completely ignored by psychoanalysts. Fromm has since the early thirties pointed to Bachofen's work as contributing greatly to the understanding of the primary role of the child's tie to the mother.) Bachofen's work was for the first time (partly) translated into English in 1967 (*Myth, Religion and Mother Right*, Princeton University Press). Fromm's earlier papers on the social psychological significance of "Mother right" (1934) and on the Oedipus Complex and the Oedipus myth (1954) will be republished in *The Crisis of Psychoanalysis* (New York: Holt, Rinehart & Winston, 1970).

made law, and of natural groups like the family or the tribe over man-made groups like the state.

Mother's love is unconditional. This is a biological necessity, since her interest and love cannot depend on the infant's pleasing her. Because this love is unconditional, it also cannot be controlled or acquired; its absence produces a sense of lostness and utter despair since mother loves her children because they are her children, and not because they are good, obedient, or fulfill her wishes and commands; mother's love is based on equality.[7]

The fatherly principle is that of conditional love, depending on obedience and performance, abstract thought, hierarchical structure, justice, law, and order.

The nature of fatherly love is that he makes demands, establishes principles and laws, and that his love for the son depends on the obedience of the latter to these demands. He likes best the son who is most like him, who is most obedient and who is best fitted to become his successor, as the inheritor of his possessions: As a consequence, patriarchal society is hierarchical; the equality of the brothers gives way to competition and mutual strife.

As a result, fatherly love can be acquired by doing what father wants, in contrast to motherly love which is not acquired by anything, but which is there. The infant, indeed, is loved by his mother not because he pleases her, but because he is her child, and this experience of unconditional love has a euphoric character which remains as deep longing, almost ineradicable in the mind. If father's love is lost it is not so deep a tragedy, because it can be regained, but it also lacks the euphoric character of motherly love because it is always conditional and a reward, rather than an act of grace.[8]

The mother-centered and father-centered principles respectively mani-

---

[7] Cf. Fromm (1956).

[8] The Christian and Jewish religions were both essentially patriarchal religions, although in the Roman Catholic form of Christianity the matriarchal elements are much more manifestly expressed in the figure of the Virgin and of the mother Church. Luther's Protestantism, while it became the basis for the more patriarchal form of religion in Northern Europe, in its original form was a return to the desire for the unconditional love of mother, which cannot be gained and need not be gained by good works. Paradoxically, the Roman Catholic concept which Luther attacked was rooted in some extent more in the patriarchal concept of love, by its emphasis on good works as a factor contributing to God's grace. Luther, on the other hand, did not want to have anything to do with this "contributing factor." What mattered to him was the unconditional love without any contamination from man's need to deserve it or to prove anything. In the later development, however, Protestantism became more and more patriarchal and Roman Catholicism retained its blending between matriarchal and patriarchal principles. One may assume that it is precisely this blending to which Catholicism owes its deep appeal to people, because it synthesizes two principles and satisfies two basic desires in the hearts of men.

fest themselves in family life and in religious life. In a mother-centered family structure, the attachment is more or less exclusively to the mother. She is also one who dominates the family, even though the outward forms might be those of a father-centered façade. In religion, the role of the Virgin together with the Jesus Child is relatively emphasized against the relatively de-emphasized role of God the Father, and Christ the adult man. It has to be noted, however, that there are relatively unbroken father-centered cultures like those of Germany and southern Italy (although here with mother-emphasized traits blended with the patriarchal system), while there are other societies in which the father-centered system exists but *is undermined by rather than being blended with* strong mother-centered elements.

Blending of the two elements would imply stability. If the patriarchal and matriarchal principle were united, mercy and justice, order and equality, emotion and intellect, natural and man-made law, would cease to be mutually exclusive opposites. They would assume qualities which allow each pole to blend with its opposite. But if the two poles are torn apart, each side changes. Mercy becomes indulgence, justice hardness, order deadness, equality leveling, emotion unreason, intellect abstractification, natural law anarchy, and man-made law autocratic rule.

In Mexico we find that the father principle is undermined and at war with the mother principle. It is, in appearance, a strict father-centered society. In law and custom the man rules. Women are looked on as inferior and weaker. But it is also evident that interwoven with this patriarchal structure is a matriarchal system. It is manifested in a number of ways. First of all, in the family system the main figure of attachment, regardless of the individual's age, is his mother. As our data show, there are differences in degree of attachment but there are relatively few instances in which a son or daughter is more attached to father than to mother. The majority is more attached to mother. To hurt or offend the mother is perhaps the most real and severe crime, although not in legal terms nor even in terms of what villagers consciously think about crime.

The predominance of the motherly element can also be seen in the religious structure of Mexican Roman Catholicism. While its theology is, of course, not different from that of the Church in general, the emphasis and accent is heavily on the matriarchal side. The religious world is governed by the Virgin, the all-helping, all-forgiving merciful mother, while God and even the martyred Christ take a second place in the experience of the people. It is no exaggeration to say that for the Mexican peasant, the Virgin of Guadalupe (and many other Virgins of local significance) is at the center of religious belief.

So far, we have been describing a blend between father- and mother-centered elements in the Mexican structure, which appears similar in many ways to the religious structure of southern Italy; the Italian case reflects a constructive synthesis characteristic of the Roman Catholic religion.[9]

However, the patriarchal system in Mexico is not productively synthesized with matriarchal elements; it is in itself weak and shows symptoms of disintegration. Many Mexican men feel insecure, afraid of their wives, and instead of being in command they depend on their women. This was especially true for the receptive men, as we shall see in Chapters 7 and 8. Masculine inefficiency is also shown in the many instances of men abandoning their families, drifting and/or drinking. In contrast the Mexican mother takes care of her children with full responsibility and realism, hardly ever drinks or indulges in ways which could interfere with her responsibilities.

By and large it seems correct to state that the village represents a patriarchal façade, much of which, however, is undermined by matriarchal elements. Such a situation, as we shall see in further chapters, causes a great deal of antagonism between the sexes and has important social and economic consequences. When patriarchal and matriarchal principles clash instead of being blended, an intensified battle between the sexes is to be expected; our data show this to be true, which does not exclude the fact that there are also positive elements to be found which are the results of blending of both principles.

The interrelationship between the hacienda system, the matriarchal principle and the formation of the receptive character in the present can be traced historically in Mexico to the Spanish Conquest. The Spaniards destroyed the patriarchal Aztec society, and in doing so, left the Indian men, particularly in the haciendas, powerless to defend their women. The Spanish conquerors took Indian women as wives or concubines, and the offspring of this union were the mestizos. As a dependent peon in the hacienda, the mestizo lacked real patriarchal authority, and the hacienda masters were able at will to appropriate his women. We do not refer to the fact that the peon would not have succeeded if he had *tried* to defend his women, but rather that he was in a position of such powerlessness that he could not even dare to raise his hand against the Spanish masters and the hacienda owners. A man in this state of powerlessness is deeply affected. It gives him a sense of castration, of unmanliness, and deep shame. Clearly, a patriarchal system collapses if the men in it are totally or partly affected

---

[9] The Catholic religion, aside from its obvious patriarchal principle (hierarchy, male dominance, duty, etc.), has incorporated the matriarchal principle in the idea of the mother Church, in the role of the Virgin mother, and in the unmarried priest, who can function as both father and mother. (This holds true particularly for the image of the Pope as a just father and all-forgiving, loving mother.) In the Jewish religion the motherly element is less obvious but discernible. Protestantism seems to be the most patriarchal form of Christianity.

by this type of impotence, which is not the physiological one of not functioning sexually, but rather impotence in the larger sense of the traditional
male role, i.e., that the male is not capable of defending his women. Such
a conditioning makes the man feel humiliated and tends to make him
submissive before the women because he is afraid of their contempt. Sons
are unlikely to accept the patriarchal pretensions of their fathers. Rather,
they retain their primary attachment to the mother. In a situation where
men have felt impotent to fulfill the male role, the image of the mother is
strengthened as the one and only person who loves unconditionally, and who
will always give the feeling of being powerful, at least as long as the son
remains emotionally a child.

We would expect theoretically that the receptive-submissive orientation in the men would result in a strong although usually repressed sadistic
potential, that the men would feel the destroyed masculinity could be re-
solved only if they could show they could kill, that they could use weapons,
that they could destroy.[10] This might explain a reason for the extremely
violent blood-thirsty quality of Mexican civil wars. The revolution in
Morelos, led by Emiliano Zapata, was at first a limited struggle of free
land-holding peasants to retain their property against the developing haciendas. As Womack (1969) writes, in 1911 Zapata and his chiefs only
rarely recruited among the peons "who anyway preferred their bonded
security, and nowhere evidently did they excite these dependent peons
to rise up and seize the plantations they worked on" (p. 87). However,
once the haciendas were destroyed, the ex-peons entered the war literally
with a vengeance and blood lust. It would seem that since the receptive
peon's security lies in being fed, he would become depressed and/or furious
only when his source of supply was cut off. Then once he had lost his
security and fear of his masters, the potential for sadism was released and
he became violent and vengeful.

In the chapters that follow, we shall see that in the present the receptive village men are those who most lack the paternal principle. They
are the villagers most likely to fall into the feudal-type relationships of
dependency. And their repressed violence is likely to break out when they
drink.

2. *THE PRODUCTIVE-HOARDING TYPE*

From the consideration of the quasi-feudal nature of Mexican society
and the attachment to the mother one should expect that all peasants are
nonproductive-receptive. The fact, however, is that a sizeable minority

---

[10] Although the questionnaire scoring does not show this relationship between
receptiveness and sadistic tendencies, except in the case of the alcoholics (Chapter 8),
it is likely that the Rorschach responses provide a finer measure of repressed sadism.

of the village is productive-hoarding. Thirty percent of the villagers (22 percent of the men and 39 percent of the women) are dominantly hoarding. We have seen that in general the hoarding villagers, particularly the men, tend to be more productive and independent than the receptive villagers.

We can explain the presence of the productive-hoarding type by the specific influence of the peasant mode of production, which sometimes proves to be stronger than the general feudal influence, but *only* when the peasant possesses his own plot of land.

For the independent peasant with land, his mode of production favors a hoarding orientation, or to put it differently, the hoarding orientation is adaptive to his mode of production, and this for the following reasons:

1. The peasant can count on a small surplus at best, and the natural conditions essential to his production—good weather, lack of plant disease or insects—are uncertainties. His environment, unlike that of the tropics, provides few gifts of fruit or animals to be hunted. Saving part of one's crop for food and seed, hoarding rather than consuming, has been necessary since the beginning of farming. The peasant's stinginess is reasonable, since it is so hard to replenish a supply gained by slow hard work and good fortune.

2. The peasant generally works a small individual plot of land. Unlike many hunters and deep-sea fishermen, he works alone, planting, walking behind the plow, weeding, and harvesting. He must be independent and self-reliant.

3. The peasant's conservative attitude is based on his experience that time-saving new methods are usually no improvement over the old. With limited resources, the old methods work almost as well as new machinery, and why should he want to save time, the only commodity he has in abundance? Furthermore, for one living close to the level of subsistence, experimentation with crops is too risky. A society with limited resources that cannot be increased engenders the feeling that there is only so much to go around and all of it has been parcelled out and hence that one person's gain is likely to be another's loss. Thus, the cautious, conservative peasant has had little reason to question his distrust of change or economic development, and the values of peasant society reinforce his feelings.

4. Peasant work is repetitive. Row by row, the small farmer orders his land, and he must pay careful attention to each seed, each plant. He must be methodical and orderly.

5. The peasant cannot hurry the growth of his crops. He must wait for the natural process to develop. He must be patient.

6. When he sells his produce, the peasant is confronted by an uncertain market he cannot control and by middlemen who seek to maximize their gain at his expense. He must be suspicious.

Given these conditions, the hoarding peasant feels more secure, more prepared for the uncertainties of nature and the market, less likely to feel let down by others, less puzzled, frustrated, and stymied than the receptive peasant. His greater independence and mistrustfulness fit peasant reality more than the receptive individual's need for others and trusting openness, and he acts in ways that are more likely to be materially successful. These same conditions of work exist in peasant societies throughout the world (according to Foster [1967], with the exception of Southeast Asia), and they form the same peasant character in Southern Europe, India, the Near East, Latin America, and elsewhere.

Foster (1967) describes the free peasant as individualistic, suspicious, obstinate, stingy, hardworking—in short, with the traits rooted in the hoarding orientation. His conclusions are based on an examination of peasant ideas and world view. It is all the more striking then that we, applying very different methods based on psychoanalytic theory, arrive at the same conclusion. Our study goes even further to demonstrate empirically in Chapter 6 that the hoarding orientation, in contrast to the receptive orientation, equips the peasant with a better psychological basis for independent farming.

We should note, however, that this result, while it fits descriptions of peasants in other parts of the world, was a finding we did not expect when we began our study. We had accepted the stereotype that all Mexican peasants were passive and receptive, and we were at first surprised to discover that a sizeable minority of the villagers are characterologically like Greek, Italian, or Spanish peasants, and that the receptive peasant, which many people even in Mexico considered the only type, represents a less well-adapted alternative.

Furthermore, factors that undermined the patriarchal principle for the hacienda peon and led to the emotional dominance of the mother are less powerful or absent in the case of the free villagers. Where free villagers remained isolated from the domain of the hacienda, men were able to protect their women and they could present their sons a model of male effectiveness. In the village at the present time, the productive-hoarding peasants are less attached to their mothers than the receptive men and are better able to maintain the patriarchal role.

As we began to discover that a sizeable percent of the villagers were dominantly hoarding and to formulate the relationship between the productive-hoarding character and traditional peasant farming, we asked the question why most villagers came to be receptive and some hoarding. We reasoned that an important factor would be the different prerevolutionary backgrounds of the villagers. We arrived at the hypothesis that in general the receptive peasants came from the haciendas while the productive-hoarding peasants were from the free villages. This hypothesis was developed too late to include a question about prerevolutionary background in the questionnaire. But we were able to check on fifteen families (5 from free villages and 10 from the hacienda) and found that the hypothesis was in general supported. Indeed, those older men who had lived in the village when it was a hacienda are typically receptive. In contrast, there is a group of families that emigrated from a free village in a nearby state who are all headed by typical productive-hoarding men.

The question arises why we find in our material that the hoarding orientation is more frequently blended with productiveness and the receptive orientation with unproductiveness. This does not appear to be the case in the populations of all societies. Clinical data suggest that there are many productive-hoarding characters among shopkeepers, accountants, librarians, and engineers, and on the other hand, many productive-receptive characters among artists, artisans, physicians, employees, and intellectuals. We assume that if the hoarding or receptive orientations, respectively, are the best—or at least adequate—character bases for the exercise of a certain occupation or profession, they will have a greater affinity to productiveness than an orientation which is less apt to permit the successful exercise of the particular form of occupation. In relation to traditional independent agriculture, successful work demands attitudes which are based on a certain degree of productiveness, such as some initiative, interest, imagination, response to weather conditions and the market. Where a hoarding individual has land and the possibility of exercising his independent initiative, his productive qualities tend to be stimulated and reinforced by his mode of work.[11]

This is not the case for the receptive villager. Even when he has land, the receptive villager tends to fall into dependent relationships and lose control over his property. The requirements of peasant work do not engage his interest and do not mesh with his character. Hence his work does not stimulate him nor reinforce productive-receptive tendencies. Furthermore, the village culture has lost its cultural richness, and because of this, there is virtually no stimulation which would be conducive to the development of productive traits in the receptive peasant.

Productiveness in peasant society: We pause here, to consider the

---

[11] This is particularly true for men who are most involved in agricultural work. In the case of the women, where fewer hoarding individuals are productive, other factors having to do with the woman's work in the family and her differential upbringing enter the picture. These will be discussed in Chapter 7.

question: How productive are the productive-hoarding villagers we have studied? At the start of this chapter we stated that none of the villagers could be scored on the highest level of productiveness, and we noted that traditional authoritarianism, fear of individual expression, and lack of cultural stimulation were factors in limiting the level of productiveness in the village society.

The sociocultural factors stimulating productiveness appear to us weaker in the village than in some other peasant societies both in the present and past. If one compares the village culture—its lack of fiestas, dances, music, and handicraft work—with the culture of the Yugoslavian, Greek, or Russian peasant, then the village appears to be a very deteriorated peasant society, similar to Banfield's (1958) description of peasants in southern Italy. Even Tzintzuntzan, which Foster (1967) considers to be lacking in cultural stimuli, has a tradition of pottery-making and design. And the peasants of nearby Tepoztlán, as described by Redfield (1930) and Lewis (1951), still retain ancient dances and folk music.

If the village society is compared with that of the medieval peasant, the contrast is even more striking. According to the accounts of Sombart, Tawney, and M. Weber, the society of the medieval peasant was much more life centered than the material-centered village society, which is mainly oriented to monetary gain.

The ideal in the Catholic middle ages was, as Tawney (1926) stated it, *"that economic interests are subordinate to the real business of life, which is salvation,* and that economic conduct is one aspect of personal conduct, upon which as on other parts of it, the rules of morality are binding" (p. 31). In the medieval peasant society at its best, economic motives were suspect, unlike the village society, where these values determine the allocation of priorities and overshadow values of charity and personal salvation. Both in medieval society and among the Mayan peasants described by Redfield, work is meant to be spiritually satisfying. In the village, work is seen by all but the most productive individuals as a necessary evil and as a means for gain.

The art, folklore, and handicraft of both the Mayan and the medieval peasant suggest a higher level of productiveness and a greater enjoyment of life than in the village we have studied.

While our scoring of productiveness determines which villagers are more or less productive than the average villager, we do not have comparable data for individuals in other societies. In order to answer the question: how productive are the productive-hoarding villagers, we are limited to the impressionistic comparison of the villagers to descriptions of other peasants and the village culture to other peasant cultures.

Our theoretical viewpoint is that while the peasant mode of production favors and in large measure determines the hoarding character, the degree of productiveness varies according to the cultural stimulation in a peasant society. To the degree in which the culture is oriented to life, pleasure, humanistic values, art, play, and celebration, rather than to material gain and simple survival, there will be more productive individuals. In the village, the emphasis is on material gain and striving for a higher level of consumption, to feed appetites whetted by the lure of new products and the new style of life in the modern industrial society. Instead of celebrations and colorful fiestas, the pleasures of life in most villages now consist of drinking, watching television, and "hanging around" or doing nothing. Indeed, one may ask why the hoarding peasants are even moderately productive. The answer, as we indicated, is that agricultural work itself allows for a certain degree of activeness and creativeness, in contrast, for example, with the dead, mechanical repetition of assembly line work. The peasant is able to decide for himself which crops to plant, and in caring for his plants or animals he must respond to life and to nature. The most productive villagers recognize this and appreciate the opportunity their work gives them for active responsiveness. As one villager stated it, "Love is to respect all that is human. It is a sentiment one can have even toward a plant. I work my land with love because my children and I live from the plants." Or, as another villager said, "Even to raise an animal, one must love."

Given these characteristics of the village, in contrast to other peasant societies, we must also ask: How representative is it of other Mexican villages? First of all, it is not representative of those villages in the north of Mexico where farms are much larger and the mode of production is more characteristic of industrial agriculture. Nor is it representative of tribal villages, especially those to the south which are relatively independent of the urban society. As we interpret the evidence from reports of anthropologists, the village is in many ways representative of those in the central plateau of Mexico. However, in comparing the village to others, there are four variables that must be taken into consideration as probably making a difference in levels of productiveness and in the proportion of hoarding to receptive individuals.

1. The presence or absence of cultural traditions is a factor that may influence the level of productiveness in Mexican villages. We chose a village without a tradition. Like many villages in Morelos, this one was practically destroyed during the Revolution of 1910-1920, and afterwards was repopulated by many immigrants.

However, our evidence indicates that the most productive villagers are not notably different from the most productive inhabitants of another village in the central plateau which does have cultural traditions. Maccoby administered Rorschachs to thirty individuals selected by Foster in Tzintzuntzan. Some were the most creative potters in the village. His impression was that, while a higher percentage of Tzintzuntzeños may have productive-hoarding characters, these productive individuals are similar to the most productive villagers we studied.

2. The legacy of the hacienda, of semislavery, and of male impotence, was an important factor in the molding of the receptive character. We would expect, theoretically, that villages which have been free for centuries would have a smaller percentage of receptive individuals than those with a history of hacienda domination.

3. The percentage of landless peasants vs. the percentage of landholders is also a variable which may influence social character. Our evidence indicates that the village is not significantly different in this respect from other villages in the central plateau.

4. The extent of influence from the city is a factor that probably influences the rate of adoption of new values and the impact of new products. The village we studied is connected to nearby cities by fairly good roads and a regular bus service. It is close enough to have television. Furthermore, the accessibility, climate, and beauty of the village have attracted a few rich people from Mexico City who have built weekend residences. These influences from the city account for a strong pressure against traditional values and support for the materialistic values.

Thus, by its lack of traditions, its hacienda background, and its full exposure to urban influences, the "negative factors" found in many other Mexican villages may be intensified in the village we studied. However, the evidence indicates that the character types found in the village are characteristic of other peasant villages in the central plateau. As we shall examine in Chapter 8, the prevalence of alcoholism in the village does not differ significantly from general estimates for this region of Mexico. In order to determine the degree to which any of these variables makes an essential difference in the character of Mexican villagers, further study of different types of villagers would be necessary.

3. *THE EXPLOITATIVE CHARACTER TYPES*

Although only 10 percent of the population is dominantly exploitative, this percent grows to 25 percent of the population when we consider the total number of villagers with either dominant or secondary exploitative traits.

We have distinguished two types of exploitative villagers: the productive-exploitative entrepreneurs and the unproductive-exploitative individuals.

The unproductive-exploitative syndrome characterizes the small percentage of the villagers with a destructive character. The men are most likely to get into knife or pistol fights. The women are the most malicious gossip mongers. We would expect to find a small percentage of destructive people in any society, especially in one where the opportunity for individual development is so limited. Indeed, given the extreme poverty of the villagers one might expect many more villagers to be embittered, exploitative, and destructive. It is remarkable that the percentage of highly narcissistic, sadistic, and destructive individuals is as small as it is.

The productive-exploitative syndrome also characterizes a small percentage of villagers, no more than 15 individuals, but among them are the most powerful and richest men in the village. Despite the small number of individuals in this type, it is important socially.

The productive-exploitative villagers are the modern entrepreneurs who have been the first to exploit the new opportunities of capitalism. In the past, there were always a few entrepreneurial villagers, such as the mule drivers (arrieros) who carried goods between the village and the cities. In recent years, new factors favoring entrepreneurial activities have entered the village culture, including the following:

1. The values of capitalistic society—of material accumulation and fuller use of resources, of economic development by private enterprise— have been increasingly disseminated through the mass media and through the experience many have had of working in the United States as braceros. The entrepreneurs are the villagers who have most fervently adopted the "progressive" values for material development as opposed to spending money on fiestas. These values intensify the class differences in the village and work to destroy traditional structure, thus aiding the entrepreneur in dominating the village economically, politically, and ideologically.

2. The entrepreneur is aided by the new agricultural technology which allows the individual with some capital to accumulate more capital.

3. Some village entrepreneurs also have started to take advantage of the opportunities of tourism to set up small restaurants or to provide services for tourists from Mexico City. All this has begun to happen in the years since the study began.

We have stated that the effects of the new entrepreneurs on the village are in large measure destructive. They support the structures of domination that hold down other villagers. They take advantage of the unproductive-receptive villagers, most of whom become economically dependent on them. They have helped destroy the fiestas. In setting up large-scale farming, the entrepreneur breaks down the ejido system and justifies this in terms of greater efficiency and productivity. But he tends to re-create the values of the hacienda, to take over the role of a small-scale hacendado, even though he may increase the actual production of agricultural goods. One should ask, even in economic terms, whether he does not have a long-range negative effect, compared to other possible ways of building the economic system.

The productive-exploitative syndrome characterizes the "new man." In the medieval society, the humanistic values of the church tried to keep such men in check because they preferred material gain to religious values. In modern society people are more inclined to view such entrepreneurs from the viewpoint that they help the economy, that they are able to take advantage of the new opportunities.

In the chapters that follow, we shall explore the relationship of social character to the socioeconomic and cultural variables. At this point we can sum up our finding on social character in relation to theory in terms of Figure 5:6. Each main character type is molded by and adaptive to distinctive socioeconomic conditions. The receptive character was formed in the conditions of the hacienda. The productive-hoarding character is adapted to traditional small-scale agriculture. The productive-exploitative character is adapted to the new, industrializing society and to capitalism.

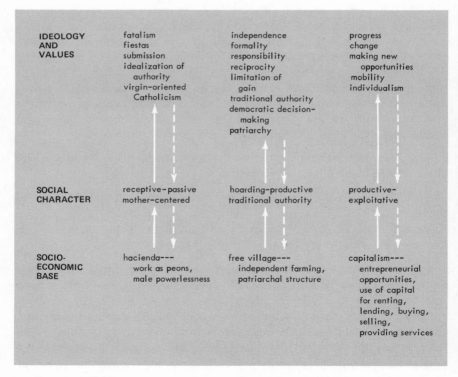

FIGURE 5:6

But secondarily, the values of each type both rationalize character and also support the economic system to which the character is adapted. (In Figure 5:6, we indicate this secondary tendency with dotted lines.) The values, the ideology of the receptive villager are fatalistic and submissive with the tendency to idealize both authority and the mother. These values supported the hacienda system. The productive-hoarding peasant values independence, responsibility, traditional relations of respect, and patriarchy, all of which support the social organization of the free village. The productive-exploitative villagers have the values of progress through schools and new technology and social mobility, which support the new industrial system.

6

Character, Socioeconomic, and Cultural Variables

In Chapter 1, we proposed that the social character is adaptive to the condition of life, and particularly to the mode of production, shared by a group, class, or nation. In terms of the theory, individuals develop the character structure that makes them want to do what is required by their mode of work. Now having established the data on the social character of the village population we can study its relationship to socioeconomic variables in order to see whether our data support this hypothesis.

Two main questions need to be explored. The first is whether there is evidence that a specific character is adaptive and that those villagers with the adaptive character are more successful and prosperous than those who lack it. The most crucial data bearing on this question show that ejidatarios with a productive-hoarding character are more successful as small independent landowners than are the unproductive-receptive ejidatarios.

A second question which arises from our theory is whether the mode of production is a decisive factor in forming the adaptive character. If those villagers who received ejido land after the Revolution included receptive ex-peons as well as typically hoarding free peasants, did the new requirements of free peasant work succeed in changing the character of receptive individuals who became ejidatarios?

Starting with the second question, one way of finding an answer is closed off to us, since it would require comparing the character of the peasants before they received land to their character after they spent years working the land as ejidatarios. However, we can attempt to answer the question by comparing the present-day character of villagers with land, the ejidatarios, to those who are landless. Does the fact of being an ejidatario have any significance in terms of character? The answer is no; our data show no significant correlations between character and membership in the ejidatario vs. nonejidatario classes. Some 50 percent of both the ejidatarios and nonejidatarios who head households are dominantly receptive and approximately 30 percent of both groups are dominantly hoarding. Furthermore, there are no significant differences in respect to any of the other character variables.

This finding calls for an explanation. Why did not all the receptive ejidatarios develop hoarding traits, if these are indeed the most adaptive to free peasant work? In terms of our theoretical viewpoint, one might expect that the radical change in the conditions of life after the Revolution, particularly the donation of ejido land to the villagers, would have influenced a change in character for at least a significant percentage of the new ejidatarios. Why does this not appear to be the case?

Of course, it is possible that the percentages of hoarding villagers, both ejidatarios and nonejidatarios, increased in the years following the Revolution, that is, that post-Revolutionary conditions increased hoarding tendencies throughout the population. However, even if this were so, one would still expect a differential effect, that a greater percentage of the ejidatarios would have become hoarding, most particularly those born after the Revolution.

That this was not the case results, we think, from the fact that after the Revolution the conditions of life did not change radically enough to result in character change for many peasants. This conclusion is based on considering the two main factors which influence the unproductive-receptive orientation, neither of which disappeared after the Revolution.

(1) Certain feudal structures continued to operate and offered the receptive ejidatario the possibility of choosing a mode of production providing greater security at the expense of both individual freedom and higher profit. The effect of this factor will be analyzed in the pages that follow. (2) The dependence of many men on the mother figure is intensified by the conflict between patriarchal and matriarchal tendencies in the society. The effects of this psychosocial factor will be explored in Chapters 7, 8, and 9. (3) Beyond these two considerations, another factor essential to the whole theory must be considered. Adaptation to the mode of production is not a matter of one or possibly even two generations. The old mode of production has led to forming the character of the parents, their value systems, ideology, and educational practices which continue to exist and exercise their influence while the new methods of production are already in operation. The past puts a stamp on the present by the fact that the character of the individual is formed through the established patterns; only through a much longer process do the new economic conditions weaken the old character structure and reduce the weight of the traditional value structure so that the new economic practice can exercise its full influence on the development of character in the new generation. We deal here with an important phenomenon: a lag between the socioeconomic change and the changes of the traditional character and its corresponding character. Marx-

ist theoreticians and modern economists have not taken account of the nature of this lag and hence often believed that economic changes would immediately result in personality changes. Only the study of the inter- mediary function of social character can show that while in the long run changing economic conditions bring about changes in personality, this process is slowed down by the still existing weight of the traditional char- acter structure. The extent to which this lag can be overcome by what might be called a cultural revolution, that is to say, the radical revolutionary change of all values and family traditions, and by the shock of confrontation be- tween the new values and the traditional character is a most important political psychological question which cannot be answered on the basis of our material.

CHARACTER AND THE MODE OF PRODUCTION

The correlation of character with the over-all measure of relative prosperity, the socioeconomic scale (SES), provides evidence that the productive-hoarding character is more adaptive than the receptive orienta- tion for free peasant farming. For ejidatarios (we shall discuss the non- ejidatarios later), the SES is positively correlated with productiveness ($r = .42$, $p < .01$) and the dominant hoarding orientation ($r = .31$, $p < .05$). In contrast, the SES is negatively correlated with the dominant re- ceptive orientation ($r = -.52$, $p < .01$) and with receptive tendencies ($r = -.43$, $p < .01$). In other words, productive-hoarding ejidatarios are significantly more prosperous than receptive ejidatarios. (See Table 6:1.)

It may not seem surprising that hoarding ejidatarios become richer than receptive ones, since they care about money more and are likely to hang on to what they have. But this is by no means as simple as it seems.

TABLE 6:1   Product-Moment Correlations of the Socioeconomic Scale with Character Traits For Ejidatarios and Nonejidatarios

Character Trait	Ejidatarios (N=48)	Nonejidatarios (N=73)
Productiveness	.42**	.46**
Dominant receptive	-.52**	-.39**
Receptive	-.43**	-.42**
Dominant exploitative	.07	-.08
Exploitative	.02	.14
Dominant hoarding	.31*	.48**
Hoarding	.21	.22*

*Significant at the 5 percent level
**Significant at the 1 percent level

The "miser" may save money or material goods, but in the pious legend, nobody becomes wealthy just by hoarding (we speak here, of course, of pure hoarding, and not of the investment of savings as capital). The miser may be somewhat ahead of one who spends whatever he gets, but he will not be a successful peasant or, for that matter, successful in any occupation. Success in traditional agriculture requires attitudes based in a degree of productiveness, such as, for instance, some initiative, interest, imagination, responsiveness to natural conditions and to the market. This blend between hoarding and productiveness is precisely what we find as a clear-cut trend in the character of those engaged in agricultural work. For male heads of household, there is a significant positive correlation between productiveness and the dominant hoarding orientation ($r = .35$, $p < .01$) and a significant negative correlation between productiveness and the dominant receptive orientation ($r = -.41$, $p < .01$).

In the previous chapter, we presented the reasons that the hoarding orientation facilitates the successful exercise of the traditional free peasant's work and why the hoarding peasant's character tends to be more productive in this particular society. We pointed out that where the hoarding orientation is the best, or at least an adequate character base for the exercise of a certain mode of production, it will have a greater affinity to productiveness than an orientation which is less apt to permit the successful exercise of the particular occupation.

Our observation of the villagers is consistent with these findings. The productive-hoarding ejidatarios are alert to ways of maximizing their material gains in their work. They keep track of the market prices and try to figure out which crops will be in scarce supply in the future and thus bring a higher profit. They are willing to work harder than the receptive ejidatarios.

The productive-hoarding peasant (or his wife) may also supplement income by opening a store when enough capital has been accumulated; in addition, there is satisfaction in having food and all kinds of goods close at hand, if they are needed. A few villagers store corn or other foodstuffs for their own consumption, but many sell their harvests and buy their basic needs from one of these small stores. (The storekeepers are very conservative in stocking their merchandise. It appears that they sell only what they themselves can use, and they have no interest in novelties that might or might not sell. If they stock two brands of cigarettes or canned goods, and one brand is sold out, most storekeepers do not order more of the brand that sold better. Rather, they wait until the less popular brand has been sold out.) Owning a store or bar, for men, is significantly correlated with the productive-hoarding orientation. The correlation with hoarding is $r = .36$ ($p < .01$); with productiveness, $r = .23$ ($p < .01$). However, the most decisive difference between the productive-hoarding and receptive ejidatario is in their modes of farming, the types of crops they grow, and the social relationships involved in the decisions they make about what to plant.

A key decision for the ejidatario involves the extent to which he will employ himself and his land in the production of sugar cane. Cane is much less profitable than other crops, especially rice. Cane takes 14 months to mature, while rice will yield a harvest in seven months of the rainy season, leaving the fields free to plant corn, tomatoes, or other garden crops in the dry season. Furthermore, after costs of planting, weeding, harvesting, and even insurance were paid, rice gave the ejidatario a profit of from 3,000 to 5,000 pesos a hectare in 1960 (or 240 to 400 dollars), while the average gain from cane, which occupied the land a longer time, was about 500 pesos (or 40 dollars) a hectare after the first year of planting. Other crops, such as corn and tomatoes, resulted in at least two or three times the profit of cane, even though the price of vegetables fluctuated much more than the price of cane or rice.

Why then would an ejidatario plant cane rather than more profitable crops? The village lies in land which is ideal for cane; before the Revolution the hacienda planted cane throughout the valley. Today, the refinery (*Ingenio*) has taken the hacienda's place, but in general it does not need to force the ejidatario to plant cane, although with regard to part of his land it can do so legally, since the government considers cane an important export crop. Rather than enforce cane production, the Ingenio tries to encourage it by offering special benefits. Those ejidatarios who plant a minimum of one-third (as long as it is one hectare or more) of their land in cane can become members of the sugar growers' cooperative. As members, they receive free medical care, life insurance, possibilities for scholarships to send their children to technical or professional schools, and jobs for their relatives. Furthermore, the refinery minimizes the amount of work for the farmer. The Ingenio sends tractors which plow the parcela. It plants the seeds, and 14 months later it sends migrant laborers to burn the leaves and cut the *zafra* (just as the haciendas employed migrant labor for the same purpose before the Revolution). All of these costs are deducted before the ejidatario receives his payment. Between plowing and harvesting, the cultivation of cane is much easier than working on other crops. The seed needs only a few fertilizations (*beneficios*), and it must be fertilized again only once when the plant rises. In the dry season, it is watered once a week, irrigated from the streams that course beneath and above the village land. The denseness of the plant drives out most weeds, and the toughness of the plant makes insecticides unnecessary. With fertilization, the cane will grow the next year from the same stalks, requiring even less work. (Cane can sometimes be cut for 10 years in a row.)

Rice, on the other hand, demands more and harder work. Shoots must be planted carefully, the farmer bending down in the cold water. Borders must be built around the field to keep the water in, and they must be watched continually for breaks and erosion. Even when the ejidatario hires jornaleros to help with the hardest work, he must supervise the water supply and borders. He must watch out for the birds and pests, and spray against the diseases that can destroy the delicate plants. Until recently, the ejidatario had to run a risk of losing his whole investment if a sudden hail storm, a very cold spell, or heavy rains ruined the crop. Only recently has the Ejido Bank instituted protection for the rice grower by insuring the crop by a payment of about 14 pesos ($1.10) a tarea. But the risks of partial loss from insects, birds, and disease remain. These same risks are even greater for other crops (such as tomatoes, onions, melons, etc.) which are also more profitable than cane and which also require more work, more care, and more protection from natural elements.

Considering the much higher profit from rice or garden crops, as contrasted to the profit from cane, the ejidatario may decide to plant a minimum of cane in order to secure the benefits of the Ingenio, while planting better paying crops on the rest of his land. Only in this way can he hope to increase his gains while also enjoying the services of the sugar cooperative. The ejidatario who plants cane exclusively receives the same services from the Ingenio and sacrifices his standard of living for a greater feeling of security and less need to work. Furthermore, the productive-hoarding ejidatario reports that he feels shame when he is not working, and he prefers work that demands more from him, especially if it is also profitable. He considers cane a lazy man's crop. In contrast, the receptive ejidatario is attracted to cane planting because he likes to have more time to lounge around the town plaza (*pasear*), to drink, gossip, and "rest," activities that the hoarding peasant would consider as "doing nothing."

The study was able to determine the exact percentage of land occupied by cane for 40 ejidatarios. Twenty-five percent had cane planted on from zero to 25 percent of their parcelas. Another 25 percent had cane on a quarter to one half of their land; 32 percent planted cane on 50 to 75 percent of their land; and 18 percent planted cane on 75 to 100 percent of their land. Based on the percentage of land occupied by cane, a scale from one to four was constructed. A score of one means that the ejidatario planted cane on one quarter or less of his land; a score of two signifies cane in 25 to 50 percent of the land; a score of three signifies cane in 50 to 75 percent of the land; and a score of four means that cane occupies 75 to 100 percent of his parcela. (See Table 6:2.) This scale was then correlated with socioeconomic variables and character factors.

Before discussing the relationships between cane growing and character, we might point out that the more land an ejidatario cultivates, the

TABLE 6:2 Sugar Cane Planting

Cane Scale Score	Percent of Land with Cane	Percent of Ejidatarios with Score (N=40)
1	0-25	25
2	26-50	25
3	51-75	32
4	76-100	18
		100

smaller will be the percentage of land devoted to cane ($r = -.39, p < .05$). This correlation can be explained in two ways. One, the ejidatario with a small parcela must employ a greater percentage in cane in order to meet the one hectare minimum and qualify for membership in the sugar growers' cooperative, while the ejidatario with more than three hectares can plant cane in a smaller percentage of his land, one-third, and still qualify for membership. Another explanation is that the ejidatario who plants a high percentage of his land in cane seldom gains enough profit to rent or buy more land; the more one plants cane, the less land he is likely to have.

These two explanations are not mutually exclusive. The question is whether the exclusive cane growers started out with smaller parcelas than the others. In fact, there is no correlation between the cane scale and the original sizes of the parcelas. The exclusive cane growers are people who have either lost part of their land or have not increased their holdings, while the villagers who plant more profitable crops have in general acquired more land over the years. As we shall discuss more fully in Chapter 8, those who plant cane exclusively are usually unproductive-receptive men who have become alcoholics and who have gradually lost possession of their land even though cane planting demands minimal work. On the other hand, those planting only a small percentage of land in cane are likely to be individuals who work the hardest and are most concerned with profit and accumulation. The cane scale is negatively correlated with the amount of land the peasant rents to increase his parcela ($r = -.42, p < .05$). As we would expect, the cane scale is also negatively correlated with the SES ($r = -.37, p < .05$) for the group of 40 peasants.

What is the relationship between cane planting and character? As we would expect from our findings about character and material accumulation, the productive-hoarding peasant works in a way that will maximize profit, while the passive-receptive peasant does not. The ejidatario who plants cane exclusively avoids hard work and risks, but does so at the expense of profit. His behavior implies a different attitude toward work and a different character structure from that of the ejidatario who plants a minimum of cane and uses the rest of his land for more profitable crops. The correlation between productiveness and the percentage of cane planted is $r = -.36$ ($p < .05$), and the correlation between the hoarding-receptive factor and the cane scale is $r = -.39$ ($p < .05$), which means that the productive-hoarding peasant tends to plant a minimum and the unproductive-receptive peasant a maximum of his land in sugar cane.

By understanding that character is a determining factor in the villagers' choice of crops, we have a clearer idea of how differences in the SES among landowners are influenced by character. Let us look more closely at the receptive-unproductive cane planters. It is notable that planting a greater percentage of cane is also significantly correlated with exclusive attachment to the mother (Factor VI: $r = .35$, $p < .05$). Furthermore, the cane planters tend to be more submissive ($r = .34$, $p < .05$). Cane planting indicates a receptive, unproductive, submissive, and mother-oriented peasant. This syndrome suggests to us that the decision to plant cane is not due merely to the wish to avoid tiresome work, but that those ejidatarios seeking maternal protection are attracted by the Ingenio's offer of security, even though they lose the opportunity for material gain and they give up their independence. They have the character structure that would have fitted the peon's mode of work in the hacienda, although in substituting the Ingenio for the mother, these peasants are not so different from individuals in modern industrial society who become dependent on government, large industries, or bureaucracies to provide them with a steady income, insurance, and retirement benefits in return for giving up their independence. The powerful organization has an irresistible attraction for those who remain emotionally like children in search of mothering.

The passive, receptive cane planters are oriented neither to independent farming nor to capitalistic production where the goal is to maximize profit and to work hard for material gain. The cane planter, like the traditional peon, is less concerned with profit than with minimizing strain. There is a story told in Mexico of the community development worker who finds a peasant resting by a lake. The community development worker, the representative of modern industrial society, is shocked by such unprofitable inactivity and asks the man why he does not at least tie a string to his big toe with a hook on the end and drop it in the lake. "Why?" asks the peasant. "Well, you can catch a fish and have something to eat." "I have enough to eat now," says the peasant. "Well then," says the modern man, "put strings and hooks on all your toes. Then you can catch enough fish to buy a boat. Then you can really go into business and perhaps catch enough fish to start a canning factory. Then you can become rich." "And what then?" asks the peasant. "Why, what then? Then, you can just relax, do nothing." "What do you think I am doing now?" answers the peasant.

This story touches upon a very important point which needs to be made explicit. The story tells us of a happy, satisfied peasant who is probably a receptive, rather than the hard-working and, as it would seem in our terms, productive-hoarding character. In our discussion thus far we have paid little attention to the problem of the happiness of the peasant. In fact, we have stressed the economic advantage of the productive orientation, but said little of the subjective factor of satisfaction and contentment. In order to understand this problem better, we must have in mind the important fact, mentioned in Chapter 5, that the village is a cultural and spiritual desert. The values which existed for the precapitalistic peasant, and which Tawney has described so succinctly, have virtually disappeared because they are in blatant contradiction to the spirit of a society in the process of industrialization. The friendly, purposeless conversation, the fiesta, the sitting around, and the sweetness of doing nothing, which in a society with precapitalist values and traditions were subjectively very satisfying, are rapidly losing their place within the Mexican village of the 20th century. This is so because such values and traditions cannot grow unless they are rooted in the spirit of the total culture; furthermore, the economically successful peasants, who are of the productive-hoarding type, and who dominate the village, have cut off the expenditures for fiestas and other forms of "uneconomical" recreations. Thus the receptive peasant is left with nothing except the cheap entertainment of radio, television, movies, and comic strips. The easy access to liquor (actively promoted by the industry producing alcoholic beverages) is all that is left to make use of his free time. The picture of the "good life" portrayed by television and radio increases even more the sense of worthlessness of the purposeless life, and increases the receptive peasant's sense of defeat and hopelessness. (It is interesting that the only productive form of recreation today is sports, which are not rooted in a receptive orientation.)

It is our experience that villages in which a richer cultural tradition is still alive (such as Tepoztlán or Tzintzuntzan) have probably a somewhat larger percentage of productive-receptive characters, and it is a legitimate speculation to assume that cultures like medieval society, in which man and living are the overriding goals, while not creating the characterological basis for hard and relentless effort, and not a great deal of individualism, offer the possibility for the development of the productive-receptive orientation. Both in the case of the village today, and in the case of a village in an unbroken, humanly rich culture, productiveness develops when the economic and the cultural reality permits and stimulates the kind of activity which is the essence of productiveness.

To return to the peasant of our village, while many are characterologically motivated for hard work, they have little enjoyment. Life is seen as a struggle to keep afloat. By orienting themselves more and more to the market, to profits and material gain, the productive-hoarding peasants are increasingly influenced by the new class of entrepreneurs to give up traditional fiestas as a waste of money, to work harder to buy more consumer goods, and to provide schooling for their children so that they can leave the village. While the cane growers cling to a way of life that leaves them increasingly vulnerable to exploitation, the productive-hoarding peasants do as much as possible to pull themselves into the modern society. A combination of factors including the values of the industrial society, pressures from the new entrepreneurs, rising prices, and new consumer demands all favor an orientation toward cash crops, capital investment, and status in terms of income. But the given limitations of their economic success are such that the vast majority of the productive-hoarding peasants can never earn enough to consider themselves successful in terms of the city economy, or even in terms of the new village entrepreneurs. All they have is hard work, little reward, and the constant risk of being run over by forces they can neither predict nor control. They must look at themselves in the eyes of the industrial world as underdeveloped.

THE NONEJIDATARIO

While the productive-hoarding orientation is the most adaptive for the ejidatario, which is shown in his greater material success, it is even more important for the nonejidatario to have if he is to escape the condition of virtual peonage. Since he starts without capital, he must accumulate a great deal to arrive at the level where most ejidatarios begin. And while a few receptive ejidatarios may become relatively prosperous by letting others —a shrewd wife, for example—manage their property, the receptive non-ejidatario is most likely either to become dependent on one of the richer landowners or on a woman who supports him (a wife or mother).

Although ejidatarios are on the whole much more prosperous than nonejidatarios (see Table 6:3), Table 6:1 shows the productive-hoarding orientation is significantly correlated with the SES for both ejidatarios and nonejidatarios. The hoarding orientation, however, is more crucial for the prosperity of nonejidatarios. A receptive jornalero lacks the traits that would make him try to accumulate capital or to buy or rent land. For the non-ejidatario, the correlation between the SES and the dominant hoarding orientation is $r = < .48$, significant at the 1 percent level.

We have already seen that for ejidatarios this correlation is also significant, but smaller ($r = .31$, $p < .05$). This is because the range of income distribution is narrower for the ejidatario who can be relatively prosperous even without the optimal character structure, because he has land. But it would be a mistake to assume that even with a productive-hoarding orientation the nonejidatario is guaranteed success. He may in fact find himself stymied by his poverty and inability to find capital. If, however, he has a prosperous father who gives him a start or he can accumulate some capital in the United States, he is likely to increase it. This holds true also for the small group of exploitative entrepreneurs who are more likely to get a start by taking over land from receptive and alcoholic ejidatarios and who then put their surplus capital into farm machinery which they lease out or into a truck which can put them into business as middlemen.

For both ejidatarios and nonejidatarios the passive-receptive character structure is maladaptive, and the negative correlations between receptiveness and the SES are highly significant. For the ejidatario the correlation between dominant receptiveness and the SES is $r = -.52$ ($p < .01$); for the nonejidatario $r = -.39$ ($p < .01$). The correlation between receptiveness as either dominant or secondary and the SES for ejidatarios is $r = -.43$ ($p < .01$); for nonejidatarios r is $-.42$ ($p < .01$).

One way a nonejidatario can accumulate capital is by seeking work as a migrant laborer in the United States. This was easier to do in the past, before the U.S. government passed laws against the importation of seasonal Mexican laborers. However, some of the villagers have been able to gain contracts as semiskilled workers in the United States. This route to gaining capital was taken by both productive-hoarding and productive-exploitative nonejidatarios. (The correlation between productiveness and working in the United States is $r = .35$, significant at the 1 percent level.)

The productive-hoarding peasant who gains some capital in the United States is then more likely to increase his land holdings and/or to open a small store. The productive-exploitative ejidatarios or nonejidatario entrepreneurs rent land, but they are also likely to offer new services to other farmers, such as trucking and tractor rental. Although there are not enough cases for a meaningful product-moment correlation, we can report that all of the men who provide these services have the productive-exploitative character. The difference between these men and those who emigrate to the city seems to confirm that going to the States as a bracero is, in psychological terms, the much bolder and more ambitious of the two decisions.[1]

_____

[1] During the five years 1960-1965, 21 younger villagers left to work in the city, because they had heard of opportunities. Some came back later, but the majority remain in the city, often visiting their families on weekends or holidays. In terms of our data, the young people, both men and women, who leave the village to work in the nearby cities show no significant characterological difference from the others. This is somewhat surprising, since one might have expected a significantly greater interest, adventurousness, etc., in this group. We are led to the conclusion that two factors may explain our data. (1) That going to the city is not so much determined by imagination and interest, as by opportunities (a friend, a relative, etc.). (2) That it is possible that a number of those who stay in the village are the more productive-hoarding ones who are interested in agricultural work and independence, while a number of nonproductive persons may go to the city because they expect, non-realistically, that the relative or friend on whom they rely will "take care of them." If both opposite tendencies were operative, the statistical evaluation of the sample—which is small anyway—would not show any clear-cut trend. In order to find out more about the motivation, one would have to evaluate the character orientation of each individual in this group.

CLASS AND CHARACTER

If class position were determined solely on the basis of the economic factor, we would expect that all of the ejidatarios would be richer than the nonejidatarios. The richer class would be composed of those who have land, and the poorer class would be composed of the landless. Clearly, the economic factor is the most important determinant of socioeconomic status, and membership in the ejidatario class generally determines relative wealth in the village. In Chapter 3, we reported that two-thirds of the nonejidatarios are in the lowest class, compared to only 6 percent of the ejidatarios. In terms of the highest class, the figures are practically reversed. Fifty-two percent of the ejidatarios compared to only 5 percent of the nonejidatarios are in the highest class. Furthermore, it was shown that an ejidatario who works his own land is practically assured of rising to the top of the economic pyramid. Putting it another way, 89 percent of the highest class is composed of ejidatarios and 11 percent of nonejidatarios. The middle class is evenly divided between ejidatarios and nonejidatarios. In contrast, 94 percent of the lowest class is composed of nonejidatarios and only 6 percent of ejidatarios. (See Table 6:3.)

TABLE 6:3   Composition of the Social Classes (in percentages)

	Lowest Class (N=65)	Middle Class (N=53)	Highest Class (N=44)
Percent of ejidatarios	6	50	89
Percent of nonejidatarios	94	50	11
	100	100	100

However, our data have shown that relative wealth within the ejidatario and nonejidatario classes depends on character and that character sometimes leads to a change in socioeconomic position. The few ejidatarios in the lowest class are unproductive-receptive men, and the nonejidatarios in the highest class are productive-hoarding or productive-exploitative men who have taken advantage of new opportunities to accumulate capital.

The relationship between the SES and character can also be presented in terms of percentages, as reported in Table 6:4. Of male unit heads in the lowest class, 54 percent are dominantly receptive and only 24 percent are dominantly hoarding. All of the receptive men in this class and all but two of the hoarding men in this class have nonproductive orientations; the only productive-hoarding members of the lowest class are jornaleros whose character has not overcome their lack of capital. The other 22 percent of the lowest class is composed of the nonproductive-exploitative men, all of them jornaleros.

TABLE 6:4 Character and Socioeconomic Class for Male Heads
of Household (N=122)

Dominant Mode of Assimilation	Socioeconomic Class		
	Low	Middle	High
Passive-receptive (N=55)	24	23	8
Nonproductive-exploitative (N=14)	9	3	2
Productive-exploitative (entrepreneur) (N=11)	1	3	7
Moderate to low productive-hoarding (N=25)	11	8	7
Productive-hoarding (N=16)	1	7	8
Total	46	44	32

In the middle class, 54 percent of the men are receptive, and almost all of these men are ejidatarios who plant cane. Thirty-four percent of the middle class is hoarding, the majority of this group made up of productive-hoarding nonejidatarios who have bettered their original class position. Fourteen percent of the middle class is composed of exploitative men (7 percent productive and 7 percent nonproductive). This group includes a few nonejidatarios who are entrepreneurs on their way up, and a few nonproductive-exploitative ejidatarios with receptive tendencies who are cane planters.

In the upper class only 25 percent of the men are receptive, and all of them are ejidatarios whose class position is maintained by wives who may run a store or help to manage their land. Forty-seven percent of the upper class is composed of hoarding men, almost all of them ejidatarios. Twenty-eight percent of the highest class is composed of exploitative men (7 of 9 are productive-exploitative). Of the 5 nonejidatarios in the highest class, 2 have a productive-hoarding character, and 3 have the entrepreneurial character.

THE CHARACTER OF WOMEN AND SOCIOECONOMIC VARIABLES

As in the case of the men, the character of the wives is also differentially related to socioeconomic class. Although a majority of wives are hoarding (for reasons which will be discussed more fully in Chapter 7), the percentage of hoarding wives in the upper two classes is greater than that of the lowest class (see Table 6:5). In contrast, most of the receptive wives are to be found in the lowest class.

The SES for wives is significanlty correlated with productiveness ($r = .30$, $p < .01$) and with the exploitativeness factor ($r = .27$, $p < .01$). The correlation with productiveness follows from the fact that husbands and

TABLE 6:5 Dominant Mode of Assimilation and Social Class
for Wives (N=102) (in percentages)

Mode of Assimilation	Social Class		
	Low	*Middle*	*High*
Receptive	40	22	8
Exploitative	13	13	28
Hoarding	47	65	64
	100	100	100

wives in general share the same level of productiveness.[2] The correlation with exploitativeness partly reflects the situation in which a receptive-unproductive ejidatario is dominated by an exploitative wife who is responsible for raising the family's economic level.

The receptive men in the upper class owe their economic position to wives who run stores or who lend out money for interest. (While such a partnership is beneficial economically, it often results in the man's becoming an alcoholic, as we shall discuss in Chapter 8.) There is a significant correlation between running a store or a bar and the exploitative orientation for women ($r = .26$, $p < .01$). (The men who engage in these activities are more likely to have a productive-hoarding orientation.)

In contrast, productive-hoarding wives tend to seek extra money by working at dressmaking, an activity which is more creative. The correlation between sewing for profit and productiveness is $r = .27$ ($p < .01$); between sewing for profit and the hoarding orientation, the correlation is $r = .21$ ($p < .05$).

Some of the women, married and unmarried, engage in other occupations to gain income, but these were not significantly correlated with character. A woman may work as a servant or even do a man's work in the fields (see Chapter 3), but these occupations are generally determined by economic necessity and/or opportunity. An ejidataria who is relatively well off may work in the fields, supervising her jornaleros. A poorer woman may work in the fields or take in laundry because she has no other way to earn money to feed her children.

CHARACTER AND EDUCATION

One of the startling, yet important, findings of our study was that neither education nor literacy was found to be correlated with material suc-

---

[2] Productive men and women are more likely to marry each other, while the unproductive also seek each other out. The product-moment correlation for productiveness of 102 husbands and wives is $r = .45$ ($p < .01$). A further discussion of relationships between the sexes is to be found in Chapters 7 and 8.

cess in the village. This actually should not be surprising, if one considers the fact that the peasant who reads and writes and who has had more years of schooling is no better fitted for small-scale agricultural work. Reading and writing have no importance for his work. It would be different if the mode of agricultural production changed. Learning new methods and communication with specialists might require that the peasant make active use of his ability to read and write. At the present time the school is favored mainly by richer peasants who see education as an avenue for their children to leave the village and qualify themselves for nonagricultural work. The children of the richer peasants have had significantly more schooling than the poorer children, and in some cases they have gone on to become school teachers and even professionals. It has been seen that those who support the school the most and lead the school committees are the new entrepreneurs (productive-exploitative) who want their children to prepare themselves for a well-paying job in the modern society.

Except by reinforcing patterns of authority (see Chapter 9), schooling makes little difference in the development of character. There is only one significant correlation between years of schooling and character. The women who have had more schooling are significantly more productive ($r = .21$, $p < .01$). This is probably not the *result* of schooling, but rather an indication that more productive girls stay in school. In general, the villagers, even the richer ones, prefer to educate boys and to keep the girls at home. The girls with a particularly strong interest in studying are more likely to prevail on the parents to allow them to continue attending school, and they are more likely to succeed if the parents have the money to pay for the books and school costs. For the girls, being allowed to study means a greater freedom from slavery within the home, and the more independent girls are the ones who seek an avenue out of traditional feminine servitude.

CHARACTER AND RELIGIOUS AND CULTURAL ACTIVITIES

The more productive villagers seek out the cultural stimulation that remains in the village. The evidence suggests that, among other things, productiveness measures the individual's responsiveness to such stimulation. For the productive men the church offers a source of cultural stimulation, of hope, and an affirmation of moral values that stresses responsibility. There is a significant correlation between attendance at Mass and productiveness ($r = .26$, $p < .01$). The productive men also tend to quote religious precepts.

For the women there are no significant correlations between productiveness, attendance at Mass, and the expression of religious ideology in the interview. This coincides with our observation that religion has a different function for women than for men. Church attendance is a more conventional female activity (especially for those women from the richer families) and does not seem determined significantly by character. This fits with the fact that, as we have observed in Chapter 3, a greater percentage of the women attend Mass than of the men.

At the start of the study we asked ourselves whether the villagers would respond to more cultural stimuli if they were offered to them. To answer the question, we brought experimental stimuli to the village; they included the choir of the National University of Mexico, folk dancers, and folk singers. A reading group was formed by Mrs. Marta Salinas, where each week those who were interested might come and listen to fairy tales, and to novels especially about Mexico and about peasants in other parts of the world. A group of 20 women and two men regularly attended the readings. They particularly enjoyed a novel about the peasants of the region during the Mexican Revolution of 1910 as well as Grimm's Fairy Tales and the stories by Tolstoy about Russian peasants. It was notable that they identified themselves with the attitudes, fears, and strivings of the European peasant. Furthermore, for the first three years of the study, motion pictures were also regularly shown by the study. At first the aim was to have comments and discussions about the films, some of which were feature films and others travelogues, films about farming, and instructional films about health and hygiene. Dr. Alfonso Millan, who selected and exhibited the films and who led these discussions, found that many villagers felt reluctant to attend a performance when they did not pay for it. However, when they were encouraged to comment on the films, their comments were sensitive and perceptive.

Each villager was rated in terms of his or her participation in the cultural activities introduced by the study. Thirty percent of the villagers participated at one time or another, while 70 percent never participated (64 percent of the men and 75 percent of the women [see Table 6:6]). A scale representing frequency of attendance, ranging from one to four (fre-

TABLE 6:6 Participation in Cultural Activities Brought to the Village by the Study (in percentages)

Participation	Percent of Men (N=196)	Percent of Women (N=200)	Total Percent (N=396*)
Frequent attendance	6	6	6
Occasional attendance	15	13	14
Infrequent attendance	14	5	10
Nonattendance	64	75	70
	99	99	100

*No information on 13 men and 8 women

quent, occasional, infrequent, and no attendance) was constructed for correlation with character variables.

For the men there was a significant correlation between productiveness and cultural participation ($r = .30$, $p < .01$). In fact, attendance at Mass and at the cultural events are significantly intercorrelated for the men ($r = .43$, $p < .01$). This finding adds support to the conclusion that productive men seek out cultural stimuli when they are offered and that the church service, with its music, color, sermons and parables satisfies the productive peasant in much the same way that a concert or a good movie pleases him. The more productive peasant also is more likely to seek meaning in life which he finds in the teachings of the church.

Why is it that the unproductive and receptive villagers do not respond to new cultural stimulation? First of all, the nature of the unproductive person is that he does not respond to stimuli, that he is passive. Furthermore, some of the particular stimuli might even have made him feel worse, in that they have reminded him of the values that represent the dominant ethic of material gain and progress and which would make him appear irresponsible and lazy. Even some of the folk stories tend to emphasize the values and moralizing of hoarding free peasants in Europe. In terms of these values the unproductive villagers would be seen as hopeless failures. If the passive-receptive villagers are to respond to cultural stimuli, it would seem that these would have to be of a different type, in the context of new economic conditions that promise a better future for these people. In Chapter 10, we shall consider such possibilities for change.

The figures on participation in cultural activities show that there is no difference in the percentage of men and women, respectively, responding to cultural stimuli. But in contrast to the finding that church attendance was not related to character in the case of the women, we found that the women who participated in the cultural experiments were significantly more productive than the others ($r = .29$, $p < .01$).

CONCLUSION

The correlations between character and socioeconomic variables are evidence that the hoarding orientation has been the one best adapted to the economic demands of peasant farming in the village. Furthermore, because his character and his work fit each other, the hoarding peasant is likely to be more productive and energetic, indeed more confident and hopeful, than the receptive peasant who finds himself increasingly out of tune with his world. There is little or no room for a productive-receptive individual in this culturally impoverished village, which has never had a professional storyteller, which has no tradition of dance or folk art, and which does not even support a professional band. The passive-receptive villagers can find work as peons, but they are likely to be exploited by the new entrepreneurs. Those receptive men fortunate enough to be ejidatarios may be able to survive with a certain degree of security by planting cane, but their position is precarious. As cultural traditions change, as status is determined by the values of the modern world, they are unable to defend themselves from the new entrepreneurs, and they are likely to feel inferior because they do not earn more money. Many such receptive individuals feel weak, overly dependent, and inferior. They may try to compensate for these feelings by acting tough, by trying to prove they are "men," but as we shall see in Chapter 8, this syndrome is likely to lead to alcoholism.

There is also evidence that the productive-hoarding peasant is being pulled away from traditional values toward those of the new industrial society. His position is still viable, as long as he is protected by the ejido system and by government policies which strengthen his bargaining position (see Chapter 10). However, he is threatened economically by the new entrepreneurs and psychologically by his appetite for new goods. As members of a dependent part of a larger society in the process of industrialization, the villages are beginning to experience new adaptive demands which will have an increasing effect on the new generation.

7

Sex and Character

In Chapter 5 we reported that one of the six factors (Factor V) summarized those traits which are correlated with sex. Tables 7:1 and 7:2 present the percentages of men and women who were scored as having those traits which are significantly correlated with the sex of the villagers.

TABLE 7:1   Character Traits that Distinguish Village Men
from Women

Traits	Percent of Men (N=200)	Percent of Women (N=206)	X^2
Sadistic tendencies	30	23	not significant
Dominant narcissism I	40	27	8.74**
Dominant receptiveness	51	36	8.72**
Receptiveness	79	62	14.08**
Traditional authority	64	49	9.21**
Democratic	45	30	10.80**
Indulgent tendencies	32	19	8.14**

**Significant at 1 percent level

The results show that, in general, men more than women (Table 7:1) are dominantly receptive (51 percent to 36 percent); with receptive tendencies (79 percent to 62 percent); narcissistic-type I (40 percent to 27 percent); traditional (64 percent to 49 percent); and democratic (45 percent to 30 percent). They also tend to be more indulgent (32 percent to 19 percent) and to express sadistic tendencies somewhat more than the women (30 percent to 23 percent), although the difference is not statistically significant.

More women, on the other hand (Table 7:2), have a dominant

TABLE 7:2   Character Traits that Distinguish Village Women
from Men

Trait	Percent of Men (N=200)	Percent of Women (N=206)	X^2
Masochistic tendencies	18	40	22.44**
Conditional loving (material care)	55	63	not significant
Dominant hoarding	22	39	13.81**
Hoarding	46	65	14.49**
Rebellious tendencies	32	45	8.37**
Passive rebellious tendencies	8	20	12.21**

**Significant at 1 percent level

hoarding character (39 percent to 22 percent); hoarding tendencies (65 percent to 46 percent); masochistic tendencies (40 percent to 18 percent); active rebellious tendencies (45 percent to 32 percent); and passive rebellious tendencies (20 percent to 8 percent). More women are also conditionally loving (63 percent to 55 percent), but not statistically significantly so. We might note here that, while there is no difference in the percentage of men and women who are loving or submissive, in the factor analysis love and submissiveness are part of a female syndrome when combined with masochism and rebelliousness.

The conditions that influence the character formation of men and women will be discussed more fully in Chapter 9. Suffice it to say here that the villagers are likely to express the traditional attitudes of patriarchy which allots to men the right to govern the women, responsibly but firmly. Women should not have the same rights as men, most villagers state, because the husband should be like a new father who protects his wife. In support of traditional values, they cite the patriarchal viewpoint of the Bible, which states that God gave men the right to command women when he told Eve that Adam would rule over her.

The narcissism characteristic of the village male (which seems related to this attitude of superiority to women) implies a certain isolation and self-protectiveness. Our results tend to confirm the picture, which has been described so eloquently by Octavio Paz (1959), of the Mexican male's resistance to being touched, to being made open and vulnerable. He suggests further that the "hermetic" quality of the male Mexican has resulted as a defense against the humiliation of the Spanish Conquest and more particularly from the undermining of the patriarchy, a point which will be discussed in more detail below.

For the Mexican male, according to Octavio Paz, to be open is to be opened by force and made defenseless, like the "inferior" woman. Closed off by his defenses, the Mexican male, he writes, "does not transcend his solitude. To the contrary, he buries himself in it. . . . We oscillate between intimacy and reserve, between shouts and silence, between the fiesta and the funeral vigil, without every fully committing ourselves." [1]

In understanding why more women than men are hoarding, this trait must be seen as a part of different syndromes, responsive to distinct social conditions. As we have shown in Chapter 5, the hoarding men tend to be more productive than the hoarding women; 48 percent of the dominantly hoarding men compared to 21 percent of dominantly hoarding women are highly productive. For the men, given their mode of production, the hoarding orientation has an affinity to productiveness. This is not clearly the case for the women.

The fact that in women unproductive-hoarding tendencies, combined with submissiveness, masochism and/or rebelliousness, are more frequent than in men can be understood in terms of the role the culture offers women, which is in many ways different from that of the man in terms both of work and social relationships. Women are expected to treat themselves as property that belongs to men. They are supposed to hoard, as it were, both their virginity and their love, saving the first for a husband and the second for their children. The female traits most admired are those of abnegation, suffering without complaint, fierce mother love, modesty, and submissiveness. This type of hoarding syndrome is reinforced not only by attitudes toward sexuality and love, but also by the work a woman is trained to do. Essentially, she is confined to the home, which she is expected to keep clean and ordered. Washing and sweeping take more of her time than cooking. Most wives are limited to a small budget, normally provided by the male, which the woman cannot increase by her own work (unless she is employed outside the home). Often she must submissively beg her husband for money. The cultural traditions also stress female submissiveness, dependence, and inferiority. Even at birth, girls are less valued. (The partera, or midwife, charges up to twice the price for delivering a boy). As the children grow up, the boys are favored, indulged more, and allowed more freedom to roam the streets of the village and to play, while at age six or earlier their sisters are cleaning the house and caring for their younger siblings. Even though both boys and girls must obey their parents without question, the girls are expected to be more modest, self-sacrificing, and more concerned with cleanliness and order.

Furthermore, folklore expresses the theme of male strength and female weakness, the need for the woman to protect herself, to wall herself in. We have observed that in the games of the girls from the age of 8 to 12, the dominant theme is defense against attack from sexually destructive male figures who try to penetrate the ring of female solidarity to take possession of the pure and defenseless maiden, such as *María Blanca* or *La Monjita*

---

[1] Paz (1959), p. 58 (our translation).

(the little nun). Many of these games may be descendents of European roundelays which ritualized the theme of marriage by capture. In some, such as *Naranja Dulce* (sweet orange), the meaning expresses the idea that a girl who opens up and gives in to the men will be abandoned and left to die. The song is as follows:

> Sweet orange, parted lemon
> Give me the embrace I beg
> If my promise were in vain
> Quickly would I forget
> Play the march, my heart cries out,
> Good-bye my lady, now I leave.
>
> Sweet orange, celestial lemon
> Tell Maria not to lie down.
> But Maria has already given in
> And death has come to take her away.

As is to be expected, theoretically, the women also have rebellious tendencies which can be understood both as obstinacy rooted in the hoarding orientation and as reactive resentment against the demands made on them.

PRODUCTIVE AND UNPRODUCTIVE MEN AND WOMEN

In Chapter 6 we discussed the fact that the more productive men tend to be hoarding while the unproductive men tend to be receptive. While the productive men are responsible and traditional as well as independent, unproductive men are submissive-dependent (receptive and mother-fixated) and have sado-masochistic tendencies.

There are also differences between the more productive vs. unproductive women (see Table 7:3).

Productive women are likely to be significantly more affectionate and giving (conditional love) and traditional-democratic than unproductive women, who tend to be more rebellious and mother-fixated. However, while the men are polarized into two different types of social character—the productive-hoarding (independent and responsible) vs. the unproductive-receptive (dependent and irresponsible) types—the social character of the women is not polarized. Rather, there is one dominant type of female character which is a syndrome of submissive hoarding, and responsible traits. Its positive (productive) aspect has the quality of maternal love and traditionalism as well as greater independence. Its negative (unproductive) aspect has the quality of passiveness, obstinacy, and a type of mother centeredness which, as we shall see, although it does not imply irresponsibility toward children, implies rejection of men. Hence while the unproductive men tend to be receptive, basically "soft," and only superficially

TABLE 7:3 **Productiveness Correlated with Those Character Traits that Differentiate the Sexes**

Trait	Men (N=200)	Women (N=206)
Sadistic tendencies	-.25**	.00
Masochistic tendencies	-.17*	.04
Dominant narcissism I	-.12	-.15
Dominant conditional loving (material care)	.40**	.18**
Indulgent tendencies	-.02	.02
Dominant receptive	-.33**	-.06
Receptive	-.30**	-.17*
Dominant hoarding	.35**	.06
Hoarding***	.32**	-.01
Traditional authority	.29**	.24**
Democratic	.31**	.31**
Submissive	-.31**	-.11
Rebellious tendencies	-.12	-.18**
Passive rebellious tendencies	-.21**	-.27**
Mother fixation	-.24**	-.19**

*Significant at 5 percent level
**Significant at 1 percent level
***For heads of family only, these correlations are slightly different as reported in Chapter 6.

manly, unproductive women tend to be hard and unyielding and fiercely protective of what they consider part of themselves, which includes their children. While the productive woman tends to build an inviting house, the unproductive woman constructs a psychological fortress which excludes anyone who is not a part of her.

THE RELATIONSHIP BETWEEN MEN AND WOMEN

In considering relationships between the sexes, it is important to take account of the different ways in which the two types of men—hoarding and receptive—relate to women.

We noted in Chapter 6 that husbands and wives are likely to have the same level of productiveness. This is true equally for younger and older couples, suggesting that level of productiveness is a factor in choosing a marriage partner, rather than a result of two people living together. It is not surprising that this should be the case. The more productive individuals share a responsible, more independent attitude, while the unproductive individuals are more likely to "fall in love" on the basis of symbiotic, sado-masochistic attachment.

In families headed by productive men, there is dignity and concern for fulfilling one's obligations, for being *formal y cumplido*. The wives are modest and submissive, but protective and loving, especially to small children. One is struck by the rather cool formality that is maintained between the members of the family, even between husband and wife. The village patriarch is suspicious, guarded, possessive of what he owns, which includes his wife and family. He may be unfaithful to his wife, but he does not feel he has betrayed her, as long as he supports his family. In some cases, the richer men may even set up a second household (*casa chica*) with a common-law wife. The double standard prevails. He considers his obligation to his wife is responsible material care and protection, but not deep love. In fact, there are very few families in the village where husbands and wives are loving partners. The other villagers observe these loving families and consider them remarkable, admirable, but exceptional. This situation is by no means limited to Mexican peasants. Thomas and Znaniecki (1958), for instance, report that Polish peasants feel that the ideal relationship between the sexes is that of traditional dominance by a responsible and firm man and that marriage has the function of forming a viable economic unit.

What is the relationship between unproductive husbands and wives

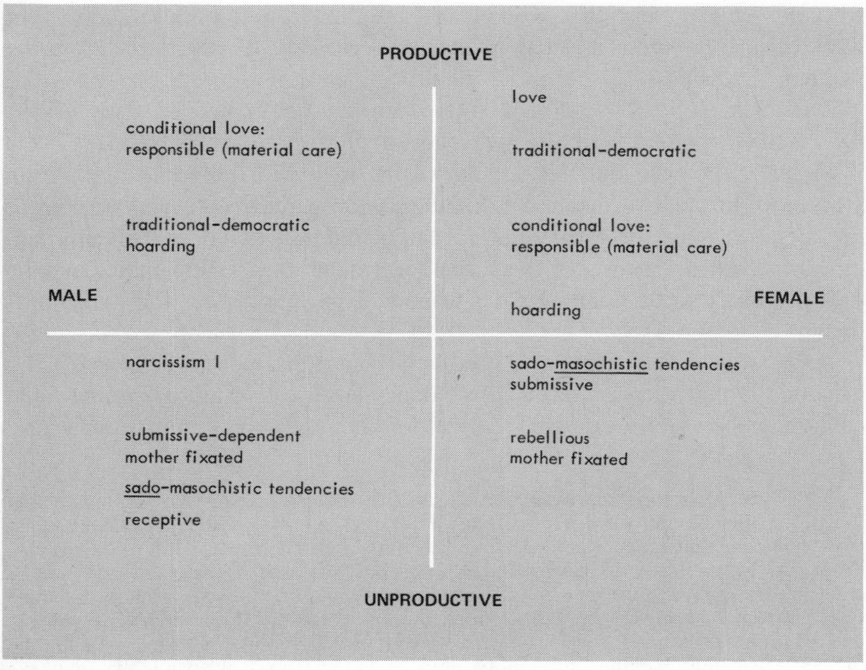

FIGURE 7:1
(BASED ON TABLE 7:3)

in contrast to that between productive couples? One measure bearing on this relationship is that of dominance in the family. Independent of the projective questionnaire a behavioral rating was made by Drs. Theodore Schwartz and Lola Romanucci Schwartz of 68 percent of the families composed of husband and wife (86 of the 127 families) in terms of who was the dominant individual and who was more submissive, i.e., who made the decisions about spending money, child rearing, taking sides in village conflicts, participation in village projects, etc. This sample was representative of the full population in terms of both social class and character.

The results show that approximately two-thirds of the husbands (66 percent) are dominant. But this figure has to be taken with a good deal of skepticism. In some instances it includes men whose wives allow them to appear dominant, but who privately dominate or even sabotage their husbands.[2]

These results show that, while the majority of husbands appear to fit the patriarchal model, a sizeable minority of families contradict the official values of the culture. If we consider further that some 20 percent of all families are headed by women without husbands we can calculate that at least about 48 percent of the families are dominated by women rather than men. This contrasts strikingly with the ideal of patriarchy. It contrasts also with the official view that women are inferior by nature and should not have the same rights as men, which was asserted by 80 percent of the women in response to the questionnaire.

Which men are dominant and which are dominated by their wives? By correlating dominance to measures of character and behavior (Table 7:4) it can be seen that 88 percent of the men with hoarding orientation (the more productive men) are dominant, compared to only 54 percent of the men with receptive orientation. These differences are statistically significant. They are consistent with the theoretical expectation that receptive men are likely to be dominated by women, especially those who are hoarding.

What is it that allows the productive-hoarding men to dominate? The evidence is that they are firmer, less dependent, less afraid of women, and economically more successful. An important factor in domination is also

---

[2] This fact is referred to in the joke of the village *cacique* who wanted to find out if the men or the women ran things in his village. He asked an assistant to go from house to house and where he found a man in charge present him with a horse as a gift, but if his wife governed the household he was to be presented with a chicken. The poor man found himself giving away chickens only, but finally he came to a house presided over by a big, tough man. He asked, "Who runs things here?" and the man responded, "I do." A small woman came out and meekly confirmed this. The assistant happily left a horse, but as he was walking away, the man ran after him and called, "You gave me a brown horse, but my wife wants a white horse." "All right," said the assistant sadly, "here is your chicken."

TABLE 7:4   Male Dominance Related to Psychological
and Economic Variables

Traits	No. of Husbands with Trait	Percent Who Dominate Wives	Product-Moment Correlation Between Dominance and:	
Moderate to high productiveness	44	75	Productiveness =	.28**
Low productiveness	42	57		
Dominant receptive	50	54	Receptive character =	-.35**
Dominant hoarding	17	88	Hoarding character =	.27*
Intense mother fixation	47	55	Mother fixation =	-.23*
Moderate or no mother fixation	40	80		
High machismo	41	59	Machismo =	-.12
Low machismo	43	77		
Violent (behavioral rating)	25	56	Violence =	-.12
Not violent	62	71		
Alcoholic	26	25	Alcoholism scale =	-.41**
Heavy drinker	16	69		
Moderate drinker	32	72		
Abstainer	32	94		
Lower Economic Class	26	58	Socioeconomic scale =	.28*
Middle Economic Class	33	67		
Higher Economic Class	22	77		

*Significant at 5 percent level
**Significant at 1 percent level

the degree to which men are fixated on their mothers. Of those men who remain intensely fixated on their mothers, 55 percent are dominant, while 80 percent who do not show extreme mother fixation are dominant.

Men who are productive and hoarding, with less dependence and less fear of women, are thus able to conform to the patriarchal role. Such men do not fit the pattern of *machismo*. They drink less than the average (see Chapter 8) and they are less likely to be aggressive.

These data also support the finding that the patriarchal role is different from sadistic machismo, which is usually a compulsive compensation for feelings of weakness and dependence on women. This is confirmed by the striking fact that only 59 percent of the husbands who scored high on machismo dominate their wives compared to 77 percent who scored low on machismo. Aside from this, we assume that a large percentage of wives of the macho-type man pretend that he dominates the family, because they know that he needs this conviction in order to function well, or at least without too much violence. Many of the women interviewed stated that in their opinion machismo is an expression of weakness and immaturity. There are good reasons for the assumption that these women would never reveal this "secret" knowledge to their husbands. We have also observed in the village that such men dominate their wives by force while young and strong, but as they age, the woman gradually takes command of the family. This same process has been observed by Lewis (1951) in Tepoztlán.

Octavio Paz has suggested a different root of sadism in the Mexican male. He writes that this sadism "begins as vengeance for the feminine frigidity or as a despairing attempt to obtain a response from a body we fear is totally insensitive."[3]

How do our data bear on this hypothesis? It seems, from reports by Dr. Lola Romanucci Schwartz of her conversations with village women, that their attitude is not too different from that of Victorian women. Sexual enjoyment by women is regarded as unnatural or indecent. The village women consider the sexual act as one in which they are "used" by the man. While this does not necessarily prove that women with this opinion do not have sexual enjoyment (although they may hide it or feel ashamed about enjoying sexual relations), nevertheless it tends to confirm Paz's statement.

As far as male sadism is concerned, our data do not seem to support Paz's general statement which seems to indicate that all Mexican men are sadistic. According to our data, only 30 percent of the men have sadistic tendencies. However, there may not be as much difference as it seems. For one reason, our scoring may have underestimated the prevalence of sadism in men (see Appendix B); for another, Octavio Paz's statement is not a statistical one that claims to fit all of the men. As to the reasons for the widespread feminine frigidity, not having any detailed data on sexual behavior, we can only speculate. One reason is undoubtedly the repressive cultural pattern; another may have to do with the prevalence of the hoarding character orientation in women. The most important psychological condition for the female orgasm is that the woman let go and open herself. This is difficult for the hoarding character whose security is built on being closed up, in a self-sufficient fortress-like position.[4, 5]

---

[3] Paz (1959), p. 60 (our translation).

[4] These considerations further develop a trend of thought expressed by Fromm (1963) in "Sex and Character."

[5] One might ask why the hoarding men are not impotent, if hoarding women tend to be frigid. Aside from the fact that the male physiological functioning seems better secured against failure by powerful physiological mechanisms, it should be emphasized that the act of penetration is not one of opening oneself. Therefore only the extreme hoarding male who does not want to give up his semen is likely to become impotent.

THE CHALLENGE TO PATRIARCHY

The crucial question arises why are so many men dominated by women in a society with patriarchal values, where women are brought up to consider themselves inferior?

In Chapter 8 we shall describe in detail how many of the men with a receptive character are crushed by their poverty and their weakness vis-à-vis the women and become alcoholics. However, this process cannot be fully understood without taking into account the contrast between the cultural values of patriarchy and the reality of a powerful matriarchal tendency. We have stated in Chapter 5 that we consider the village culture as a broken patriarchal system, in contrast to that of the Spanish or Southern Italian peasant societies or that of the pre-Conquest Aztecs characterized by unchallenged male rule.

The Southern Italians, like the Aztecs before the Conquest (Soustelle, 1964), dealt harshly with an unfaithful woman. In the village, while more wives are still faithful to their husbands than vice versa, there are a few cases where women openly make fools of their husbands, who in turn seldom become indignant, either because they are afraid of their wives or because they can expect no support from the society.

While in other societies, for instance in Japan, the patriarchal values have such force that a wife will go to great lengths to make others believe that a weak husband is strong, because her prestige depends on others' believing that her husband dominates the family, in the village this is by no means the case, generally. If a woman does pretend to defer to a weak man and to accept the patriarchal values, it is because she understands that he is like a child who can be managed better by feeding his narcissism or by protecting his sensitivity.[6] Nevertheless a number of women do not disguise their contempt of receptive, dependent men, especially when the man is an economic failure.

In considering the factors which determine whether the village male will rule his family, it is difficult to separate character from economic position. Both factors are important and, as we have observed (Chapter 6), they are intercorrelated. The higher the man is in terms of economic position the more likely he is to maintain the traditional authority of the male (Table 7:4). Of the men in the upper class, 77 percent rule their households, compared to 67 percent in the middle class and 58 percent in the lowest class. In each class the men with receptive characters, the de-

---

[6] For example, a man responded to question 42 that a woman "should be very good with her husband, care for his honor, his work but especially his honor. If the woman does not guard the man's honor, then he is nothing."

pendent and mother-fixated men, are more likely to be dominated by their wives. But the outcome of male weakness is more often total defeat in the lowest classes, where the man has no weapon other than brute force against a contemptuous wife. The more prosperous men, even when they are dominated by their wives, still have an important function as wage earners in the household. But in the poorest families the wife may work, and a defeated man may also feel economically useless and may end up deserting the home. In the hacienda the peon felt impotent in terms of the male role because he could not defend his woman from the master. In the lowest classes, the village men feel a similar impotence because they cannot provide for their families. Sometimes a wife may leave such a man and she will return to her mother's house. In other instances the woman will simply tell the man to leave, giving as a reason that he demands too much without giving anything in return or that he is a bad example to her children (some of whom may be offspring of earlier free unions).[7]

One village woman of the lowest class who lives without a husband asked, "Why should I have a husband? He would be no more than another child to take care of, and I have enough to do supporting my family." Another, who has had a series of consorts, in responding to a question of the father's role in her family, said, "Look, I am everything, father and mother, because the father is a drunk. He never occupies himself with them. In everything I am father and mother because the father is a drinker." Later she admitted that the children do not obey her husband, and he in turn hits them. "I don't like the way he educates them," she said. "He only knows how to hit them, and because of that they don't obey him or love him." Her solution was to drive the husband away. "We have now spoken together," she said, "and I told him he should leave us. We have arrived at a decision. I have decided that he leave us." This woman, like many others who live without men, supports herself by washing clothes, sometimes by selling, and at times by doing a man's work in the fields.

A number of Mexican authors, some of them psychoanalysts, have written about the intense conflict between the sexes in Mexico and its pathogenic effect on character. These authors, including Aniceto Aramoni (1961), Francisco Gonzáles Pineda (1961), and Santiago Ramirez (1959), point out that many families in Mexico lack fathers, and children are raised by women alone. These women have either been abandoned by their husbands or have thrown out men not able to support the family. The men, in turn, try to assert their masculinity by brute force against wives

---

[7] This pattern is not limited to the Mexican village. It is found among the poorest families in the United States, especially among Negroes but also among the white rural migrants to urban areas, where "matriarchal" households are formed by the desertion of men whose self-esteem has been crushed by economic failure.

who are outwardly submissive but in fact closed up, reserving their love for their mothers and children, and passively rebellious against male domination and indifference.

One important factor in this picture may be that in many instances men are less submissive and weak when they marry, but are made more so by their wives. The masochistic women might, as Aramoni notes, want to submit to tough, authoritarian men. When instead of finding strength they encounter receptiveness and submissiveness behind the image they formed in childhood of the powerful, predatory male, they are often defiant and contemptuous, and they may ridicule the male, making him furious and impotent.[8]

---

[8] In his article, "Sex and Character," Fromm (1963) suggests that the weapons men and women use against each other are determined in part by their biological vulnerabilities. "The man's position is vulnerable insofar as he has to prove something, that is, insofar as he can potentially fail. To him, intercourse has always the coloring of a test, an examination." "The woman's vulnerability, on the other hand, lies in her dependency on the man; the element of insecurity connected with her sexual function lies not in failing but in being 'left alone,' in being frustrated, in not having complete control over the process which leads to sexual satisfaction." The man's first defense against his vulnerability is power, either physical force or prestige. But his craving for invulnerability makes him sensitive to ridicule from the woman, and "the man's fear of losing his life may be less great than his fear of ridicule." To protect himself from ridicule, from being deflated and symbolically castrated, the man may try to dominate the woman, for "If she is afraid of him—afraid of being killed, beaten, or starved—she cannot ridicule him." In the village the clash between the sexes brings out these weapons. The men, when humiliated, resort to force and then abandonment, while women are highly skilled in the destructive art of ridicule which they may turn against each other as well as against the men. It is interesting that in a game played by girls, *Matarili,* the object is to ridicule and shame a person so that she can no longer stand it and must join the leader. The game continues until all the girls have joined the leader, the aggressor.

There are cases in which dreams reflect violent conflicts between men and women, in which each is afraid of the other. A woman who has been at war with her husband for years told the interviewer: "A month ago I dreamed that he arrived drunk, that he took out a pistol and shot me and that instead of going to my father's house, to complain to him, I went to the *ayudantía.* I arrived bathed in blood. Then I told the judge: 'Look what he did to me. I come to give you evidence so that you know what it is like. Now you are advised that if something happens to him or I do something to him some day, you know why.' He shot me in the breast. I awoke full of fear and began to think. I believe I dreamed that because he has threatened me and any day he might do something. Twenty days ago when he was drunk, he told me that for three nights he had dreamed that I strangled him with my hands."

8

Alcoholism

Alcoholism is a critical problem for the village. Drinking plays a part in most fights and murders.[1] Those who drink neglect families and work. The alcoholics, including 18 percent of the male population over 20, abandon responsibility as farmers, husbands, fathers, and members of the community. By abandoning his land, renting it or selling it, and drinking up the proceeds, the alcoholic damages the ejidal system which was meant to free him from exploitation. In other words, alcoholism results not only in violence and broken families, but also in the undermining of those institutions that might improve the villager's life.

Before probing into the causes of alcoholism in the village, we shall consider the alcoholism in the village in comparison with that of the country as a whole.

In terms of alcoholism and violence, the village is known through the court records of the area (*municipio*) as somewhat less troublesome and less alcoholic than its neighbors. It is difficult to estimate alcoholism precisely. However, the available estimates indicate that the State of Morelos in which the village is situated is considered among the most alcoholic states in Mexico.

How is the prevalence of alcoholism estimated? Three different methods are commonly used by investigators: per capita expenditure for alcohol, the Jellinek formula based on the number of deaths due to cirrhosis of the

---

[1] According to a report by Dr. Miguel Silva Martinez, the sale of alcoholic drinks and the crime rate are highly correlated throughout Mexico. In the City of Mexico, 66 percent of the acts of violence, including fights and accidents, involve people who have been drinking. See "El Alcohol en la Salud Individual y Colectiva," *Higiene,* 2:70–85, 1963.

liver,[2] and field studies using interviews. In the village, we used a field study method only, because we considered it the most reliable one. This viewpoint was also taken by the Latin American Seminar on Alcoholism sponsored by the Pan American Sanitary Office of the World Health Organization at Viña del Mar, Chile in 1960.[3] The seminar concluded that estimates of alcoholism based on per capita expenditures for alcohol provide only a crude comparison. First of all, they lump together unequivalent types of drinks, when in fact hard liquor produces stronger alcoholic effects than beer and wine. Second, they do not include unregistered alcohol, such as homemade distilled cane (*aguardiente*) or pulque, which makes up a high percentage of what is drunk by alcoholics in peasant and Indian villages. Indeed, while most village men begin as beer drinkers, the alcoholics end up drinking pure cane alcohol which is stronger and cheaper (about 50 centavos or 4 U.S. cents for 2 ounces) and which is unregistered. Sometimes the alcohol is mixed with Coca Cola and called *teporocha*. With this problem of accuracy in mind, it can be noted that the State of Morelos has the third highest per capita expenditure for alcohol in Mexico, exceeded only by that of the bordering States of Mexico and Puebla.[4] We do not have figures on per capita expenditure for the village.

The seminar on alcoholism also concluded that while the Jellinek formula was the best indirect estimate of prevalence of alcoholism, it tended to underestimate the number of alcoholics. This is because it assumes that reliable data can be gathered from autopsies, a factor which cannot be counted on in peasant societies. Indeed, they report that in Chile prevalence estimates based on the Jellinek formula were consistently smaller than those based on field studies.[5] Beyond this, the formula itself has a weakness; it assumes that the percentage of cirrhosis cases that are fatal does not vary from one culture to another, an assumption which the seminar on alcoholism did not accept. The report points out that "the malnutrition in the Latin American countries can be responsible in producing variations in the factors that make up the Jellinek equation, that deaths from cirrhosis may be due to an etiology of malnutrition rather than extreme alcoholism."

According to the report of the Pan American Sanitary Organization in 1960, the prevalence of alcoholism among adults age 20 or over in Mexico, based on the Jellinek formula, is about 3.5 percent, which is

---

[2] For a description of the Jellinek formula and its use, see Jellinek (1960).

[3] *Seminario Latinoamericano Sobre Alcoholismo,* Informe Final, Oficina Sanitaria Panamericana, Oficina Regional de la Organizacion Mundial de la Salud, con la colaboracion del Servicio Nacional de Salud y el auspicio de la Universidad de Chile y el Colegio Medico de Chile, Santiago, Chile, 1961.

[4] See Miguel Silva Martinez, "El Alcohol en la Salud Individual y Colectiva," p. 73.

[5] *Seminario,* p. 68. In a 1958 study in Chile, the Jellinek formula gave an estimate of 3.4 percent while the interview study indicated a percentage of 5.1.

almost the same as that of Chile but lower than that of the United States (4.5 percent) or France (5.2 percent). Although we do not have estimates based on the formula for the different regions of Mexico, both the figures on per capita expenditure for alcohol and our own observation indicate that alcoholism is more prevalent in the area in the central plateau near Mexico City than in most other parts of the country.

Again, keeping in mind the problems of accuracy, it is still interesting to report that the Jellinek formula resulted in an estimate for male alcoholism in the City of Mexico which was greater than the national average and also similar to that found in the village by the method of field observation. Using the Jellinek equation, Silva Martinez (1963) estimated that 8.7 percent of the Mexico City population over age 20 are alcoholic. Since the Pan American Sanitary Organization calculates the ratio of male to female alcoholics in Mexico as 5.3 to 1,[6] the estimate based on the Jellinek formula would be that about 15 percent of adult men in Mexico City are alcoholic. While the Jellinek formula was never employed in the village, we found by observation that 18 percent of the men age 20 or over are alcoholics.

Our data are based on participant observation, not interviews. We considered that even most field studies run the risk of underestimating the problem, since they are based on interviews only. Although the villagers, in answering interview questions, were frank about many intimate details of their lives, the alcoholics tended to underestimate or misrepresent their drinking habits. Clinical experience confirms the impression that alcoholics either consciously or unconsciously distort the extent of their drinking. Our ratings of alcoholism in terms of drinking habits were more exhaustive than studies based on estimates, and a valid comparison of prevalence in other areas would demand equivalent methods and controls.

In defining degree of alcoholism, either the physiological aspects of the disease or its social results can be emphasized. Since this study focuses on social pathology, the social effects of drinking are primary. Degree of alcoholism was determined by the extent of failure, due to repeated drinking, to meet social obligations. This definition does not take into account the amount of alcohol consumed nor the injury to the drinker's health. Yet, it is consistent with Keller's (1962) carefully analyzed definition of alcoholism as "a chronic disease manifested by repeated implicative drinking so as to cause injury to the drinker's health or to his social and economic functioning." [7] Although the operational definition used in this study is

---

[6] *Ibid.,* p. 67. However, the report notes that the field studies in Chile show a much higher proportion of male to female alcoholics than is indicated by studying deaths by cirrhosis. The same may be true for Mexico.

[7] Mark Keller, "The Definition of Alcoholism and the Estimation of Its Prevalence," in David Pittman and Charles R. Snyder (1962).

based on social and economic functioning, all of the villagers whose health has suffered due to drinking are included in the classification of alcoholism.

The men of the village were divided into five categories: alcoholics, excessive drinkers, moderate drinkers, abstainers, and ex-drinkers.[8] The "alcoholics" are defined by the fact that they lose several working days each week because of drinking. (It also happens to be the case that these men drink whenever they have the chance.) On the basis of our observations confirmed by interviews with older villagers including the owner of a cantina, 30 men or 14.4 percent of the male villagers age 16 or older were judged to be alcoholic.

The "excessive drinkers" differ from the alcoholics only in degree. Excessive drinking during the weekend is not considered abnormal in the village, but the excessive drinker exceeds the cultural norm by losing Mondays and sometimes other workdays because of his drinking. Twenty-seven men, 13 percent of the males over 16, were judged to be excessive drinkers.

The "moderate drinkers," including 109 (47 percent) men, are villagers whose drinking does not conflict with their responsibilities. They are likely to drink beer or brandy (few villagers drink *tequila*), and never touch pure cane alcohol. The moderate drinker may occasionally get drunk during the weekend or at a family reunion or fiesta, but he generally stops after one or two drinks. The "abstainers," including 34 (16 percent) men, do not touch liquor at all. The final category of "ex-drinkers," including 8 persons or 4 percent of the adult men, includes men who were either alcoholics or excessive drinkers but then stopped drinking. This category is too small for statistically meaningful comparisons, but it will be useful for illustrating the importance of psychological factors.

On the average the alcoholics and excessive drinkers are older than the moderate drinkers and abstainers (Table 8:1). Of the alcoholics, 60 percent are over 40, compared to 34 percent of the excessive drinkers, 24 percent of the abstainers, and only 16 percent of the moderate drinkers. Indeed, of the male population over 40, 32 percent are alcoholics and 16 percent heavy drinkers, so that almost one-half of the older men suffer problems of alcoholism. These data reflect the observation that many villagers become alcoholics or excessive drinkers later in life and that the majority of young men start out as moderate drinkers.

There is no significant difference in the civil status of alcoholics, excessive drinkers, and abstainers, with married men predominating in all three groups. A higher percentage of moderate drinkers are unmarried, reflecting the predominance of young men in this group (Table 8:2).

What causes alcoholism in the village? As many studies have shown,

---

[8] No female alcoholics were discovered in the village. The first four categories correspond to those suggested by the *Seminario Latinoamericano Sobre Alcoholismo*.

TABLE 8:1   Age of Alcoholics as Compared to other Groups (in percentages)

Age	Alcoholics (N=30)	Excessive Drinkers (N=27)	Moderate Drinkers (N=109)	Abstainers (N=34)	Total Male Population (N=209)
16-30	27	33	70	53	54
30-40	13	33	14	23	19
40-50	33	8	2	12	10
50-60	20	22	11	6	12
60-70+	7	4	3	6	5
	100	100	100	100	100

	r	probability
Correlation: Alcoholism vs. age	.29	.01

it is not possible to pick out a single trait which invariably causes alcoholism. Rather, as Jellinek (1960) suggested, there are "vulnerabilities," social and psychological, that increase the likelihood of excessive drinking. These factors have, however, different weight within different cultures. In extreme cases one factor may be so weighty that even a very small vulnerability in another factor will tend to produce alcoholism. Vulnerability in the village, as in other societies, is a combination of cultural, psychological, and socioeconomic factors.

We have distinguished four types of vulnerability: (1) Cultural vulnerability, this includes institutions that encourage drinking and cultural activities which involve drinking. It also includes the degree of cultural stimulation, since where there is little, drinking becomes more attractive as a leisure activity. (2) Psychological vulnerability, the psychological, and mostly unconscious, motivation that characterizes the alcoholic. (3) Psychosocial vulnerability, the interpersonal patterns and conflicts, particularly between the sexes, which reinforce or trigger the impulse to drink. (4)

TABLE 8:2   Civil Status (in percentages)

Civil Status	Alcoholics (N=30)	Excessive Drinkers (N=27)	Moderate Drinkers (N=107)	Abstainers (N=34)	Total Male Population (N=209)
Unmarried	27	18	37	23	29
Free union	6	4	23	12	15
Married (by church or civil law)	60	78	27	62	48
Widowed or divorced	7	0	13	3	8
	100	100	100	100	100

Economic vulnerability, the economic pressures which interact with character structure and increase the likelihood of alcoholism.

CULTURAL VULNERABILITY

Although there is a cultural pattern for drinking associated with special events such as fiestas, *jaripeos* (local rodeos), dances, and weddings, there is no accepted pattern for drunkenness. Almost without exception, the villagers consider drinking a harmful vice. Even the alcoholics state that alcohol is a great danger to health and it is liable to lead to violence and enmity between friends. One villager who drinks rarely sums up the feeling of the majority: "The vice of drinking makes a man lose his chance to gain money for his family. If he is a worker, he does not earn money. He harms his body and his family. If he is a peasant, it is the same, and he also neglects his crops." Yet, this man adds that drink makes him feel happiness, great pleasure, and the desire to communicate with others. Some of the alcoholics say that drinking is the only thing that gives them the joy of being alive, the desire to sing and shout.

The attractions of drinking increase through the boredom of village life and the almost complete lack of cultural activities, other than passively listening to the radio or watching television. There are six cantinas in the village, and when men congregate in the plaza in the afternoon, they often find themselves drawn to a cantina for want of anything else to do. For many villagers, drinking is the most attractive activity the village has to offer.

Those who do not drink, the abstainers, are among the peasants who have rejected traditional cultural patterns. They support new recreational activities imported from the city. Many of them either play on the town basketball team or did so when younger; the team was formed 25 years ago by the progressive schoolmaster who with a group of the villagers campaigned against the jaripeos and fiestas that they felt encouraged drinking and wasted money. The abstainers are the villagers who prefer modern sports such as basketball and soccer football to bullfights. Their concept of manliness is not the hard drinking, touchy, and violent "macho" figure, but the well-trained, disciplined athlete or the successful businessman. Thus, they not only reject traditional forms of recreation, but they also seek new forms of cultural stimulation both to make their lives more interesting and less monotonous and also to put themselves more in contact with the city world. When our project brought movies, musical performances, and readings to the village, 60 percent of the abstainers, 36 percent of the moderate drinkers, 27 percent of the excessive drinkers, and only 7 percent of the alcoholics attended at least one of these events. (See Table 8:3.) The chi square of alcoholics vs. abstainers is 20.1, significant at the 1 percent level.

There is no significant correlation between age and attendance $(r = -.06)$, showing that the difference is not due to the younger age of the abstainers. Neither is the difference due to educational level, since approximately half of both alcoholics and abstainers have had no schooling (Table 8:3).

TABLE 8:3 Level of Education (in percentages)

Level	Alcoholics (N=28)	Excessive Drinkers (N=26)	Moderate Drinkers (N=97)	Abstainers (N=34)	Total Male Population (N=193)
No schooling	50	35	15	44	29
1-6 years of primary	43	61	64	35	55
Graduated primary	7	4	21	21	16
	100	100	100	100	100

	r	probability
Correlation: Alcoholism and education	-.15	insignificant
Age and education	-.18	.05

There is also a clear-cut relationship between church attendance and sobriety; 67 percent of the alcoholics compared to only 18 percent of the abstainers never attend Mass (chi square $= 15.2$, $p < .01$). (See Table 8:4.) It is not that the alcoholics do not consider themselves good Catholics. Possibly, many of them seek to avoid the moralizing of the priest. But in general they take no part in activities that do not involve drinking. They have become dependent on drinking as their sole diversion.[9] The only alcoholics who have any interest outside of the cantinas are members of the village band where the traditional reward for their services is drinks. And, as we have noted, interest in the band has been diminishing in the village.

PSYCHOLOGICAL VULNERABILITY

Clinical studies of alcoholics in the United States have produced an essential agreement as to the psychological traits that characterize the alcoholic. As summarized by Zwerling and Rosenbaum, these include oral-receptive dependency, deep mother fixation, narcissism, extremely aggressive

---

[9] Lack of interest in cultural stimuli also characterizes alcoholics in other parts of the world. Jellinek (1960) writes of the Swiss alcoholic that he is a "primitive hedonist," a person "with an extremely narrow field of interests and a veritable inability to take interest in anything else but himself and a narrow circle around him. There is also, generally, an inability to respond adequately to the finer stimuli of life. The narrowness of interests constitutes a psychological vulnerability which is the source of the 'mere habit' of heavy drinking" p. 387.

TABLE 8:4   Attendance at Mass and at Cultural Events (in percentages)

CHURCH ATTENDANCE

Attendance	Alcoholics (N=30)	Excessive Drinkers (N=26)	Moderate Drinkers (N=107)	Abstainers (N=33)	Total Male Population (N=204)
Regular or frequent	6	27	37	49	34
Infrequent	27	19	27	33	26
Never	67	54	36	18	40
	100	100	100	100	100

		r	probability
Correlation:	Alcoholism and church attendance	-.32	.01
	Church attendance and age	-.04	insignificant

ATTENDANCE AT MOVIES, CONCERTS, READINGS

Attendance	Alcoholics	Excessive Drinkers	Moderate Drinkers	Abstainers	Total Male Population (N=196)
Frequent or occasional	7	23	19	36	21
Infrequent	0	4	17	24	14
Never	93	73	64	40	64
	100	100	100	100	100

		r	probability
Correlation:	Alcoholism and attendance	-.32	.01
	Attendance and age	-.06	insignificant

impulses, and the wish to escape the anxiety of aloneness.[10] Yet, it cannot be said that these traits constitute an "alcoholic character," since they also characterize people who do not become alcoholics but develop other serious personality disorders. What these character traits appear to represent is a syndrome of psychological vulnerability which fits the majority but not all of the village alcoholics.

Knight's (1937) description of this character syndrome in Freudian terms is generally cited as the psychoanalytic interpretation of alcoholism. According to Knight, the alcoholic's childhood experiences with a characteristically overprotective mother have produced excessive demands for indulgence. Disappointment and frustration of these oral needs trigger rage, but the individual feels guilty about his hostile impulses and punishes himself masochistically. He needs excessive indulgence to pacify his guilt, thus

[10] For a review of clinical studies of alcoholism see Israel Zwerling and Milton Rosenbaum, "Alcoholic Addiction and Personality" in *American Handbook of Psychiatry,* Silvano Arieti, ed. (New York: Basic Books, 1959).

stimulating a vicious cycle. Alcohol smothers the rage and disappointment, and it is a symbolic substitute for affection. But it serves also to spite those who withhold affection and results in masochistic debasement.

Our findings suggest that the indulgent attitude of mothers to boys (see Chapter 7) may help to explain why male vulnerability to alcoholism is greater than female vulnerability. However, our dynamic interpretation of alcoholism is different from that of Knight. Furthermore, our data point to the importance of psychosocial factors other than the frustration of receptive needs.

The alcoholics in the village do not report feeling guilty about their aggressive-hostile impulses, although as we shall see, these are generally strong. Rather, they express fear that their rage will make other people abandon them and refuse to satisfy their receptive needs. Some of the alcoholics frankly admit that drinking leads them into arguments or fights with their wives which is dangerous because the wife then refuses to feed the alcoholic. Others say they fear drinking because their friends avoid them when they become hostile. In the light of our material, we interpret the renewed need to drink not as a means to pacify guilt, but to produce a symbolic satisfaction of the alcoholic's needs for total well-being and a sense of potency. The alcoholic wants to feel that he is independent of others, especially women.

The second point is that although some of the alcoholics drink when they are frustrated in their receptive needs, this interpretation is over-generalized. The impulse to drink for many village alcoholics is determined mainly by frustration of their sense of manliness. These alcoholics are the men who only start to drink later in life, after marriage. Although they share the receptive-passive traits of the more mother-fixated alcoholic, their needs for indulgence in themselves are not great enough to cause alcoholism.

RECEPTIVE CHARACTER

Our study demonstrates the connection between a receptive character orientation and vulnerability to alcoholism. Although 79 percent of the men have receptive tendencies and 57 percent are dominantly receptive (see Table 8:5), this orientation is most characteristic of alcoholics and heavy drinkers. Over 80 percent of the alcoholics, 60 percent of the heavy drinkers, 47 percent of the moderate drinkers, and only 37 percent of the abstainers were scored as dominantly receptive in their mode of assimilation.[11] The comparison between alcoholics and abstainers produces a chi square of 12.3 significant at the 1 percent level.

---

[11] Of those 208 men scored for alcoholism, 199 or 96 percent had been administered the interpretative questionnaire at the time the analysis was carried out. This included 28 of the 30 alcoholics, 26 of the 27 heavy drinkers, 107 of 109 moderate drinkers, 30 of the 34 abstainers, and the 8 ex-drinkers.

TABLE 8:5 Alcoholism and Character (percent scored as having trait)

Trait	Alcoholics (N=28)	Excessive Drinkers (N=25)	Moderate Drinkers (N=107)	Abstainers (N=30)	Total Male Population (N=208)	r
Sadistic	43	36	17	27	30	.17*
Dominant receptive	82	60	47	37	51	.19**
Receptive	93	84	78	70	79	.08
Dominant hoarding	11	16	22	37	22	-.19**
Hoarding	18	48	46	60	45	-.26**
Aggressive	67	68	36	27	43	.28**
Strong machismo	63	60	31	35	39	.25**

*Significant at 5 percent level
**Significant at 1 percent level

The receptive-passive orientation of the alcoholics can also be inferred from their answers to the interview question: "What are the forces that determine the destiny of man?" Of the alcoholics, 68 percent saw man as passive, dependent on God's will or on accidents of birth. Of the abstainers, 45 percent took this view, while more than half felt that man's decision and energy are factors in determining his destiny. The difference between alcoholics and abstainers results in a chi square of 4.6, significant at the 5 percent level.

The receptive person also seeks "magic helpers." If this is so, it might be expected that the alcoholic would turn to curanderos rather than medical doctors when he is sick. The curandero, more than the doctor, is likely to take seriously the peasant's fears and depressions, and not tell him that there is "nothing wrong with him." He presents an image of magic authority and concern for even those ailments which appear to have no physical basis. On the basis of the villagers' statements, 74 percent of the alcoholics as compared to 39 percent of the abstainers seek help from curanderos. (See Table 8:6.) The chi square of this difference is 8.4, significant at the 1 percent level. Although using curanderos is also correlated with age, 60 percent of the alcoholics under 40 compared to only 28 percent of the younger abstainers employ curanderos.

MACHISMO, NARCISSISM, AND SADISM

The village alcoholic's narcissism is expressed not only in his lack of interest and activity, but also in his need to present himself as invulnerable, irresistible to women, without sentiment, yet always capable of defending his honor by force if necessary. These traits as they show up on the responses to the interview are the basis of scoring a four-point scale of "machismo," including extreme machismo, marked machismo, and few or no indications of machismo. Machismo is inversely correlated to ratings of responsibility, cooperation, satisfaction in work, and productiveness. It

TABLE 8:6 Use of Curanderos and Modern Medicine (in percentages)

	Alcoholics (N=29)	Excessive Drinkers (N=26)	Moderate Drinkers (N=107)	Abstainers (N=33)	Total (N=203)
Modern medicine only	24	39	66	61	54
Use both curanderos and medicos	59	46	28	27	36
Curanderos only	17	15	6	12	10
	100	100	100	100	100

		r	probability
Correlation:	Alcoholism and use of curanderos	.22	.01
	Age and use of curanderos	.39	.01

is significantly correlated with aggressiveness and belligerency. The correlation with age is not significant ($r = .08$). Of the alcoholics, 63 percent were scored as extremely or markedly machistic, compared to 60 percent of the excessive drinkers, 31 percent of the moderate drinkers, and 35 percent of the abstainers. (See Table 8:5.) The correlation of alcoholism and machismo is $r = .25$, significant at the 1 percent level.

Machismo indicates an attitude of male superiority, a wish to control women and keep them in an inferior position. One of the interview questions asked whether women should have the same rights as men. Of the alcoholics, 79 percent say *no* compared to 45 percent of the abstainers. The chi square of the difference is 6.8, significant at the 1 percent level. In their explanations of why women should not have the same rights as men, the alcoholics express more a fear of women than a conviction of superiority. They imply that unless men receive an advantage, the women are liable to control them. In other words, the alcoholic's machismo is a reaction to his fear of women, a compensation for his feeling of weakness, dependence, and passiveness.

If the alcoholic's machismo is contrasted to the reality of his relations with women, it becomes perfectly clear that his attitude of toughness is a façade. As we saw in Chapter 7, of the alcoholics, 15 of the 20 married men (75 percent) were judged as dominated by their wives, while only one of 17 abstainers (6 percent) was dominated by his wife. The unmarried alcoholic men are also submissive to women. Just as the married alcoholics are dominated by their wives, those who are unmarried are dependent on their mothers.

Of the alcoholics, 43 percent were scored as having sadistic tendencies, as compared to 36 percent of the excessive drinkers, 17 percent of the moderate drinkers, and 27 percent of the abstainers. The correlation of alcoholism and sadism is $r = .17$ ($p < .01$). Like all sadistic impulses, those of the alcoholics are rooted in the sense of powerlessness which in them are engendered by the passive-receptive orientation. This type of sadism is likely to be rather weak because it conflicts with dependent strivings.

In addition to the specific sadistic satisfaction, the state of being drunk gives a sense of strength and narcissistic satisfaction, which is in drastic contrast to the bored and low-key feeling of the nonproductive receptive person. Passive, bored, and empty, the alcoholic tries to overcome feelings of impotence by dominating others, especially the women he depends on. Outside of his fantasies, he is seldom successful. However, he may be made to feel his impotence and frustration by a well-aimed insult, and the alcoholic will then explode, lashing out against someone he feels has challenged the reality of the macho image. Most of the village violence, including murder, has resulted from sudden flare-ups in a cantina, sometimes caused by an imagined insult but often by an intentional one which is magnified by self doubts and by the fear of backing down and being shown up as a fraud, a "nobody."

THE MOTHER FIXATION

Dependence or fixation on the mother is consistent with the character syndrome of the passive-receptive individual who never grows up. As long as the individual seeks mother's unconditional love, he does not become a man who produces actively, and continued fixation on the mother weakens him so that the task of developing his own powers becomes more difficult.

Very few of the village men were neither intensely nor moderately fixated to their mothers. (See Table 8:7.) This reflects the central position occupied by the mother in Mexican peasant society which we have described above.

Of the alcoholics, 57 percent were scored as intensely fixated, compared to 44 percent of the excessive drinkers, 56 percent of the moderate

TABLE 8:7   Fixation to the Mother (in percentages)

	Alcoholics (N=28)	Excessive Drinkers (N=25)	Moderate Drinkers (N=107)	Abstainers (N=30)	Total Male Population (N=208)
Intense fixation	57	44	56	33	51
Moderate fixation	39	48	42	60	46
Independent	4	8	2	7	4
	100	100	100	100	101

drinkers, and 33 percent of the abstainers. Although the abstainers differ markedly from the other groups in the low percentage of intense mother fixation, the association between alcoholism and mother fixation is not as great as clinical evidence would lead one to expect. Furthermore, moderate drinkers are just as intensely mother fixated as the alcoholics. To explain this discrepancy between theory and data it is necessary to refer to the two different types of alcoholics and excessive drinkers.

The villagers most psychologically vulnerable to alcoholism are those with passive-receptive character traits, compensated by narcissism and machismo, and who are intensely fixated on their mothers. These villagers usually do not marry, but remain with their mothers, sometimes entering into unstable and brief liaisons with other women. There is another type of alcoholic, however, who begins to drink heavily later in life, after he has married. These are men whose psychological vulnerability as far as mother fixation is concerned, is less great, but when other factors intrude, especially conflict with their wives, they are driven to alcoholism. An indication of the greater dependence of the unmarried alcoholics is revealed by comparing the mother fixation of married vs. unmarried drinkers. Of the 10 unmarried alcoholics 8 are intensely mother fixated, while of the 16 married alcoholics only 7 were scored intensely mother fixated. Similarly, of the unmarried excessive drinkers 5 of 6 are intensely mother fixated while of the married group, the proportion is only 6 of 19. Combining the alcoholics and excessive drinkers, 81 percent of the bachelors are intensely mother fixated, as compared to 37 percent of those married, producing a chi square of 8.6, significant at the 1 percent level.[12]

THE ABSTAINERS

The abstainers' resistance to alcoholism calls for explanation. The abstainer is as much a deviant from the village norm as is the alcoholic. Up to this point, the abstainer has been described mostly in contrast to the alcoholic. The abstainer is more responsive to cultural stimulation, and he rejects those activities which reinforce patterns of drinking. Psychologically, he is less receptive, less macho, less sadistic, and less mother fixated. Describing the abstainer more positively, his underlying character structure is the productive-hoarding mode.

The median score for the abstainers on the scale of productiveness is 4 indicating moderate interest and activeness; for the moderate drinkers,

---

[12] Of the abstainers the proportions of bachelors and married men intensely mother fixated are the same, approximately one-third, which serves as a control to indicate that the lesser fixation of the married drinkers is not a result of marriage, per se.

the median is also 4; for the excessive drinkers the median is 3 indicating moderate interest with nonproductive traits predominating; and for the alcoholics the median is 2 indicating the inactive, nonproductive individual. The correlation between alcoholism and productiveness is $r = -.30$, significant at the 1 percent level.

The abstainers are also characterized by traits of orderliness, conservatism, saving, and concern for cleanliness that are lacking in the alcoholic. While the alcoholic seeks security by having others feed him, the abstainer seeks to build a protective wall around himself and his possessions. The abstainer's hoarding mode of assimilation makes him feel less dependent on others, since he guards against anxiety by accumulating supplies as well as people.

Thirty-seven percent of the abstainers are dominantly hoarding, compared to 22 percent of moderate drinkers, 16 percent of excessive drinkers, and 11 percent of the alcoholics. The correlation between alcoholism and the dominant hoarding orientation is $-.20$, significant at the 1 percent level.

Of the abstainers, 60 percent have hoarding tendencies, compared to 46 percent of the moderate drinkers, 48 percent of the excessive drinkers, and only 18 percent of the alcoholics. The difference between alcoholics and abstainers can be expressed in a chi square of 10.7, significant at the 1 percent level. The correlation between alcoholism and the hoarding trait is $r = -.26$, significant at the 1 percent level.

PSYCHOSOCIAL VULNERABILITY:
THE UNDERMINED PATRIARCHY

What is it that makes the men in this society so vulnerable to alcoholism? The conditions of life in the village, the boredom of work, and cultural barrenness are not different from those peasant societies where alcoholism is not a serious problem, for instance Southern Italy.[13] Although drinking is a traditional part of fiestas, in other societies there is also festive drinking but without alcoholism. Furthermore, the villagers disapprove of excessive drinking and consider it a disease. Neither is alcoholism explained by the propaganda of the alcohol industry, since it is not so intense as to make people drink if they were not impelled to do so.

In two distinct types of primitive societies male alcoholism is absent, because it is either psychologically unnecessary or forceably suppressed. These, according to evidence reported by Field, are societies characterized by either a strong "matriarchal" or "patriarchal" social structure, as de-

---

[13] For a description of a village in Southern Italy see Edward C. Banfield (1958). He notes there are few cases of family heads who are "wine-bibbers (p. 57). Danilo Dolci has commented that the rare alcoholic in Sicily is usually a man dominated by his wife, but that this is exceptional (personal communication).

fined by residence (patrilocal or matrilocal) and economic and political power.[14] Why should alcoholism be absent in both types of clear-cut and unmixed societies? The general answer to this question may be that in cases of either clear matriarchy or patriarchy, respectively, there is no manifest war between the sexes, so that there is no reason for either sex to undermine the other; on the contrary both sexes feel relatively secure and hence there is no need for escape into alcoholism.

Furthermore, in a matriarchal society where there is no ideal of male dominance, men would not feel the need to dominate women and show the traits of machismo, while in a patriarchal society there seems to be good reasons also for the absence of alcoholism.[15] First, drinking undermines discipline, respect, and order which are characteristic of traditional patriarchal societies, such as the peasant societies of the Mediterranean area, and are indeed the stated ideals of Mexican peasant society. Second, on a deeper psychological level, the impulse to drink and alcoholic euphoria express a yearning for the mother which must be stamped out in patriarchal society.

The following are examples of patriarchal societies which insist on the elimination of alcoholism. The elders of the Bantu Tiriki, a patriarchal society, only allow initiated men to drink within male meetings, and there are severe penalties for drunkenness and disruptive behavior.[16] In the strongly patriarchal Aztec society, only old people or captured warriors about to be sacrificed could get drunk. Otherwise, repeated drunkenness was punishable by death.[17] One can interpret the Aztec symbolism as seeing alcoholism as fixation to the mother. In the Fejérvary-Mayer Codex, Mayahuel, the goddess of pulque, is represented as a woman within a maguey plant, suckling a male child.[18]

It is our hypothesis that the breakdown of the patriarchal structure makes the male vulnerable to alcoholism. In Mexico, the Spanish Conquest weakened the patriarchal structure. Although he held onto the *ideal* of male dominance, in reality the Indian male and later the mestizo lost their dominant role, politically, economically, and psychosexually. The Conquest also wiped out the Aztec religious and legal system which held alcoholism in check. Concluding his study of the Conquest, Charles Gibson (1965) writes, "what we have studied is the deterioration of a native em-

---

[14] See Peter B. Field, "A New Cross-Cultural Study of Drunkenness," in Pittman and Snyder, eds. (1962), pp. 6-22.

[15] Bachofen has pointed out that the mature matriarchal society is monogomous and well stabilized. While permeated with the matriarchal principles, it is not one in which men are dominated by women.

[16] Walter H. Sangree, "The Social Functions of Drinking in Bantu Tiriki," in Pittman and Snyder, eds. (1962), pp. 48-75.

[17] See Jacques Soustelle (1964), p. 164. Soustelle quotes Sahagún.

[18] Oswaldo Gonçalves de Lima (1956), p. 130.

pire and civilization. The empire collapsed first, and the civilization was fragmented into individual communities. . . . One of the earliest and most persistent individual responses was drink. If our sources may be believed, few peoples in the whole of history were more prone to drunkenness than the Indians of the Spanish colony." [19]

We found an important confirmation of our theory in the cross-cultural study of drunkenness in primitive societies by Field (1962) who demonstrates the relationship between sobriety and social structure. Field shows that there is no consistent relationship between drunkenness and measures of anxiety, aggression, sexual problems, orality, or any of the other traits that make up psychological vulnerability. He concludes that "drunkenness increases markedly if the authority of the man in the household is lessened or diffused, and if the nuclear family is less integrated into larger kin structures through bilocal or neolocal residence." [20]

The hypothesis about the role of the undermined patriarchal structure helps to explain both differences between societies and increased individual vulnerability within the village. The economy of the Mexican peasant village is similar to that of villages in Southern Italy. The two societies share many psychological characteristics. The main difference lies in the fact of the minor role of alcoholism in Southern Italy and in the fact that men rarely leave their families. It is our hypothesis that the reason for this difference is that Italy has had centuries of unbroken patriarchal dominance, while the Mexican patriarchy has been undermined.

In this context, we may distinguish between two types of alcoholics. One attempts to live according to the patriarchal ideal, but he is defeated by a wife, in part because he is receptive and dependent. The other belongs essentially to the "matriarchal" subculture; he is centered in the world run by the women, and he is more dependent than the other men. Both types have in common their weakness in relation to women. Both substitute sadistic aggressiveness for independence and manliness.[21]

---

[19] See Charles Gibson, *The Aztecs Under Spanish Rule* (Stanford: Stanford University Press, 1964), p. 409. For further discussion on the undermining of the Mexican patriarchy due to the Conquest and the problems of *mestizaje,* see Aniceto Aramoni (1961), Octavio Paz (1959), and Santiago Ramirez (1960).

[20] Field, "A New Cross-Cultural Study of Drunkenness," p. 60.

[21] Indirect evidence for the alcoholic's lack of manliness or "paternal" strength can be observed in the responses of alcoholics and abstainers to Card IV of the Rorschach, which has been described by various investigators as the "father image," the symbol of paternal power and authority. Of the abstainers, 74 percent see integral images of force and firmness (monkeys, men, elephants, bears, etc.) compared to 29 percent of the alcoholics. The alcoholic images are skeletons, lungs, a dead chicken, a spine, and symbols of decay and defeat. The chi square of the difference is 4.29, significant at the 5 percent level. This difference is not due to a general tendency of alcoholics to perceive destroyed figures, since there is no difference between the two groups on other cards.

The first type of alcoholic attempts to carry on the patriarchal ideal, but he is ill-equipped for the battle between the sexes. He acts tough and aggressive, but inside he lacks authority. If he is unfortunate enough to marry a sadistic or destructive woman, he is easily dominated and made to feel impotent and defeated. His impulse to drink gains strength from his wish to get out of the house, to drink artificial courage, and to regain a joy in living. Sometimes an alcoholic will only have the courage to beat his wife when he is drunk, as appears the case in Bunzel's (1940) description of drinking in Chichicastenango and Chomula.

The comparison of the character traits of the wives of alcoholics and those of the wives of abstainers supports this interpretation. The dominant mode of relation of two-thirds of the alcoholics' wives and 60 percent of the heavy drinkers' wives is either sado-masochistic or destructive as compared to only 30 percent of the abstainers' wives. The chi square comparing alcoholics and abstainers is 4.45, significant at the 5 percent level.

Another way of expressing the character traits of the wives is in terms of the proportion of wives whose dominant mode of relation with their husband and children is giving material care and affection (conditional love). Of the alcoholics' wives, 27 percent were scored as relating dominantly in this way, compared to 36 percent of the excessive drinkers' wives, and 60 percent of the abstainers' wives. The percentage whose dominant mode of relation is conditional love (material care) is even greater among the wives of those village men who are ex-alcoholics. Of the six ex-drinkers who are married, none has a wife who is dominantly sado-masochistic or destructive. One of these men stopped drinking after marrying a motherly and gentle woman 10 years older than he. In another case, an alcoholic divorced his wife who was generally considered a sadistic and malicious woman and remarried, also to an older woman. Although the number of cases is small, it appears that despite psychological vulnerability, if a man has a mothering wife who does not attack his sense of manliness, he is not likely to become an alcoholic.

The second type, the "matriarchal" alcoholic, is characterized by the most intense mother fixation. He remains unmarried and dependent on a mother who hates strong men and treats him emotionally as a child. These mothers have raised their children by themselves. They too may have been brought up in fatherless families. With their sons, they are both indulgent and sadistic, overprotective and intolerant of independence or disobedience. Fiercely they defend their sons from the outside world, but they crush initiative and self-confidence. They demand unconditional loyalty, forbidding their sons to have anything to do with other women, and destroying any relationship that might develop. They complain constantly about having to feed and care for grown sons, but they are only satisfied when these men remain at home with them. Thus, they smother the manliness of their sons, yet constantly frustrate the receptive yearnings they have encouraged.

These men drink in order to have the illusion of power and in order to feel they can independently satisfy their receptive yearnings.

ECONOMIC VULNERABILITY

Historically, drinking served the interests of the hacienda which encouraged alcoholism by making liquor cheap for the peon and letting it flow liberally at fiestas. This was another way of keeping the peon passive and docile. The spectrum of economic variables relating to alcoholism in the village today ranges from pressures of the alcohol industry to the influence of social class and forms of work on the individual's readiness to drink.

The major effect of the alcohol industry is to reinforce those cultural patterns which are traditionally associated with drinking. In their publicity the breweries in particular identify themselves with bull fights and fiestas, by sponsoring broadcasts of the *corridas,* and by sometimes donating musicians (*mariachis*) to enliven the fiestas. The breweries also loan money to set up cantinas and may help to make them more attractive by also lending money for buying jukeboxes (*sinfonolas*). Thus the efforts of the breweries and bar owners succeed in coloring the atmosphere of drinking with an illusion of excitement and gaiety missing in other village activities.

What is the effect of the villager's own economic situation on his drinking habits?

Socioeconomic class and alcoholism are not related in a simple way. The aim of the following discussion will be to present possible relationships in the light of the evidence, rather than to attempt to arrive at final conclusions.

We shall start out by considering the relation of alcoholism to material wealth (SES) separately for ejidatarios and nonejidatarios, since they are subject to different pressures and have different opportunities for earning income. For the jornaleros, the nonejidatarios, alcoholism is directly related to poverty; among them 85 percent of the alcoholics fall into the lowest class, compared to 47 percent of the heavy drinkers, 30 percent of the moderate drinkers, and 32 percent of the abstainers. None of the alcoholics and only one heavy drinker, compared to 27 percent of the moderate drinkers and 20 percent of the abstainers are in the highest class. Furthermore a smaller percentage of alcoholics (14 percent) are in the middle class than the percent of excessive drinkers (47 percent), moderate drinkers (43 percent), and abstainers (48 percent). These statistics are reported in Table 8:8. These figures show that practically all of the alcoholic nonejidatarios live on a bare subsistence level. The excessive drinkers are somewhat better off, but poorer than the moderate drinkers and abstainers who are similar to each other in terms of wealth.

These statistics raise important questions. Does extreme poverty lead

TABLE 8:8 Socioeconomic Class and Alcoholism–Comparison of Ejidatarios and Nonejidatarios (in percent)

Socioeconomic Class	Alcoholics		Excessive Drinkers		Moderate Drinkers		Abstainers		Total Men	
	Ejid. (N=16)	Nonejid. (N=14)	Ejid. (N=10)	Nonejid. (N=17)	Ejid. (N=21)	Nonejid. (N=89)	Ejid. (N=7)	Nonejid. (N=25)	Ejid. (N=54)	Nonejid. (N=149)
Lowest	25	86	0	47	0	30	0	32	7	37
Middle	56	14	30	47	43	43	0	48	41	41
Highest	19	0	70	6	57	27	100	20	52	22
	100	100	100	100	100	100	100	100	100	100

to increased drinking? Does drinking impoverish the nonejidatario, or does the same passive receptiveness that leads to drinking also lead to poverty?

The attractiveness of drunkenness is increased by the boredom of peasant life and, more so, by the hopelessness of individuals who have no way to better their lives. But within the context of generalized poverty, some individuals are more attracted to alcohol than others. The fact that they are slightly poorer is not a convincing explanation of their drinking habits. All but the richest third of the population live on a level close to subsistence, and the less poor might prefer the comparative gaiety of the cantina as much as the poorest. We have already seen that most of the jornaleros are in the lowest class. Indeed, even the most sober nonejidatario is likely to be in the lowest class unless he is both lucky and oriented to hard work and accumulation (productive hoarding character). Among the nonejidatarios poverty would seem to incline against alcoholism, since the jornalero must work to survive. It is more likely that the excessive poverty of the alcoholic jornalero reflects the fact that his character and hopelessness override the economic factor. This conclusion is supported by the contrast with the ejidatario whose economic situation is the opposite.

At first it seems surprising to discover that there is a higher percentage of alcoholics among the ejidatarios than among the nonejidatarios. As Table 8:9 reports, there are three times as many alcoholics among ejidatarios as among the nonejidatarios. Furthermore, over half the alcoholics (53 percent) are ejidatarios, compared to 37 percent of the excessive drinkers, 20 percent of the moderate drinkers, and 20 percent of the abstainers. Considering the greater economic security of the ejidatario, it seems puzzling that he should be more vulnerable to alcoholism. However, this surprising picture changes somewhat if we examine the relation between alcoholism and economic position within the ejidatario class which turns out to be the same as observed for the nonejidatario, even though the ejidatario on the average maintains a higher socioeconomic level. As Table 8:8 reports, the only ejidatarios who fall into the lowest class are alcoholics, and even among the alcoholic ejidatarios only 25 percent (compared to 85 percent of the alcoholic nonejidatarios) are to be found in this category. On the other hand, the excessive drinkers who are ejidatarios do not appear to suffer at all economically, since 70 percent score in the highest class and none in the lowest class. Indeed, except for the alcoholic ejidatarios, none of the other ejidatarios fall into the lowest class.

Two questions confront us here: (1) Why is the socioeconomic factor of being an ejidatario positively correlated with higher alcoholism, when we should rather expect the opposite, considering the general affinity between poverty and alcoholism? (2) Why is the socioeconomic difference between alcoholics and excessive drinkers so sharp for ejidatarios, when it was not so sharp among jornaleros?

TABLE 8:9 Percent of Alcoholics Among Ejidatarios
and Nonejidatarios

	Ejidatarios *(N=54)*	*Nonejidatarios* *(N=149)*
Alcoholics	28	9
Excessive drinkers	17	12
Moderate drinkers	36	58
Abstainers and ex-drinkers	19	21
	100	100

The answer to both questions suggests the great importance of the difference between the category of wealth-poverty in distinction to that of the mode of production.

The most important distinction is that the jornalero has to work in order not to starve, while the ejidatario will, in general, not starve even if he works little, since in this case the Ingenio will have the work of cane planting and harvesting done for him (see p. 130). This means that the economic penalty for alcoholism and especially for excessive drinking, is considerably greater for the jornalero than it is for the ejidatario. Hence the economic vulnerability of the ejidatario is greater than that of the jornalero.[22] The particular mode of production explains also the sharp economic difference between ejidatarios who are alcoholics and those who are excessive drinkers.

Once the ejidatario becomes an alcoholic, he may be so disorganized that he may not be capable of working even half the year. He may fall into debt and be forced to rent or sell his land, even though this is against the law. In fact, of the 16 alcoholics who are ejidatarios, 8 rent out some or all of their land to others and the other 8 plant cane exclusively. The excessive drinkers, on the other hand, who usually do not work on weekends and Mondays, are in no way similarly handicapped. They can still take care of their plot without any difficulty.

There is another factor which makes the ejidatario vulnerable: he has more free time on his hands than the jornalero. This free time increases the temptation to drink, unless the ejidatario is sufficiently strongly motivated to spend his time in an economically more productive way. (The possibility that he would spend his free time in a humanly more productive way is pretty much excluded by the cultural poverty of the village, as we have indicated before.)

---

[22] An interesting analogy is the clinical observation that among American alcoholics from the middle and upper class, there seems to be a relatively higher percentage of those who have mothers with enough income and willingness to support their sons when they are incapacitated and unable to work, often for the rest of their lives. It seems that the mothers' capability and willingness for material support constitutes not only a psychological factor, but also an increasing economic vulnerability.

This leads to another factor which is related to drinking-character, namely the kind of crop which the ejidatario cultivates. Recalling the discussion of Chapter 6, we found that the extent of the ejidatario's free time varies with the type of crop he plants and with the way he employs time not spent on his ejido. Some crops such as rice and garden vegetables demand a great deal of time and care. In contrast sugar cane calls for much less work, but the profits are only a tenth as great as those from an equivalent rice harvest. However, the crop alone does not determine the amount of free time. An ejidatario may plant cane because he wants the time to raise animals or to work at jobs that interest him more than farming.

We found that the decisions about what to plant and how to employ free time are essentially functions of character. The passive-receptive and mother-fixated ejidatarios are satisfied to plant cane only, while the productive-hoarding peasant plants only the minimum needed to be a member of the cooperative.

Thus, it turns out that the ejidatario with the most free time is likely to be just the type of person who has the least use for his time and who is most likely to loiter around the plaza and be drawn into a cantina. By planting only cane, he has to work less than half the year. If he lacks other occupations or economic interests, which is likely the case for one who limits his planting to cane, he will be idle most of the time. Since the same character traits that make him idle also make him vulnerable to alcoholism, it is logical to suppose that the prevalence of alcoholism would be greater among these ejidatarios who plant cane only and who have no interest other than drinking.

What is the difference in crop cultivation among the various types of drinkers? The pattern of work of the excessive drinkers differs from that of the alcoholics. Of the 10 ejidatarios who are excessive drinkers, only 1 rents land to others and only 1 plants cane exclusively. The other excessive drinkers work at their ejidos when they are not drinking, which explains their prosperity. Thus, from the economic point of view, excessive drinking, unlike alcoholism, does not imply a significant deviation from the cultural norm for the ejidatario.

Of the 21 ejidatarios who are moderate drinkers, only 1 plants cane exclusively. Of the 7 abstainers who are ejidatarios, 2 plant only cane, but both of these men employ the time they gain in other economic activities.

It now becomes clearer why the ejidatario is more vulnerable to alcoholism. It is not because his character structure is different from that of the nonejidatario, but because the economic system offers a bait which appeals especially to those ejidatarios who are psychologically more vulnerable to alcoholism. This is the bait of limiting planting to cane, and the trap for men who have no interests other than drinking is idleness. Once they do not have to work, these men are lost, since they are not driven to accumulate and do not have the capacity or the cultural stimulus to develop productive activities. The nonejidatario with the same psychological vulnerability lacks this temptation. His psychological vulnerability must be stronger, if he is to become an alcoholic, since he ordinarily does not have so much idle time, and perhaps because the economic risks he faces are greater if he does not seek work every day.

In summary, alcoholism in the village is a widespread disease which both reflects the social pathology of the society and is, in itself, a cause of violence, abandonment of families, economic stagnation, and the undermining of the ejidal system. Of the men over 16, over one-quarter are alcoholics or excessive drinkers. Of those age 40 and over, almost one-half suffer from drinking. The roots of alcoholism are to be found in character structure, in cultural patterns, and in the psychosocial vulnerability of the whole society. The character traits which make a man most vulnerable to alcoholism are receptiveness, fixation to the mother, and narcissism, combined with aggressiveness and sadism. Depending on the strength of the mother fixation, there are two types of alcoholic, one who drinks in order to maintain symbolically and independently the "symbiotic" ties with the mother and another who drinks to repair the damaged image of male force and patriarchal power. What both types share is: (1) an inability to carry on the patriarchal tradition, due to their receptiveness and passiveness, their fear of women blended with their resignation to the hopelessness of peasant life, and (2) the fact that they are not characterologically oriented to the ethic of material accumulation. In a society where others are becoming increasingly oriented to profit and opposed to "useless" pleasure, it is likely that the alcoholic individual feels even more hopeless and more a failure in the eyes of his world. Significantly, the villagers who do not drink have rejected traditional cultural patterns for the new ethic of material progress and have fought boredom through basketball and soccer, in cultural activities that draw them to the modern society, and in their work. These men have also rejected the machismo pattern, with its implications of drinking and violence, for an image of manliness based on skill and profit rather than aggression.

9

The Formation of
Character in Childhood

How does the villager's character develop from birth to adulthood? When do fundamental changes take place, and what are the factors that influence the formation of character? Our evidence so far shows that a change takes place after the age of 15 or 16, between the end of adolescence and the beginning of young adulthood, when in the normal course of events the villager's bond to mother becomes weaker and he or she becomes less narcissistic and more responsible. However, the mode of assimilation, the degree of productiveness, and the deeper modes of relatedness have already been formed by adolescence.

In the village, the conditions of life and the demands on the child to adapt vary at different ages. This is due to the combination of the child's own development, his changing consciousness and capability, and the cultural expectations of how a child should behave. Adaptational demands are modified by both the character structure of the parents and by their socioeconomic class. Most villagers state that they are bringing up their children in the same way that they were brought up themselves, but they interpret cultural patterns in terms of their own character orientations. Furthermore, the social class of the family is also an important factor. As we shall see, the psychological climate in the poorer families is different from that in the richer families.

We have distinguished three distinct periods in which the growing villager feels different pressures for adaptation. The villagers themselves recognize these different stages and explain them in terms of the child's natural development. The first period is infancy when the newly born is referred to as a *nene* or baby. During the second period, roughly from two to six years, the child is a *niño* or *niña,* a young child. The third period lasts from age six or seven, when the boy or girl is called *muchacho* or *muchacha* until some time after puberty when the young man (*joven*) or young lady (*señorita*) begins to prepare for marriage and new responsibilities. (Adolescence is not a separate stage, except for some richer villagers who can afford to go to schools in a nearby city.) In describing these three periods, we shall indicate how both the character of the parents and their social class modify the conditions of life for the village child.

INFANCY

Infancy is the only time the child's wants are met quickly, with warmth and indulgence, when the individual is the focus of affectionate attention by all members of the family. It is the period when a strong bond is forged between mother and child in all families. Village mothers state that they love their children best at the age of six months to a year because they are so "pretty" and "funny." Some admit to a reason that seems to us more relevant, that during the first two years the child is totally dependent and docile. Mothers begin to feel ambivalence when their children begin to act independently. The character of the mother is a crucial factor in development during this period. Some mothers pressure their children to maintain a symbiotic attachment beyond the period when symbiosis is biologically necessary.

Almost all women nurse their babies from the third day of life; until the milk comes in strongly, babies are fed sweetened teas. Nursing is done upon demand; the first response to almost all crying is to offer the breast, either for nourishment or as a pacifier. Women cradle their nursing children, sometimes in their arms, often in a *rebozo*. The rebozo is an essential part of a woman's dress (only some of the richest women now go out on the street without one); it is a specially woven shawl, about two by six feet, with long, delicately tied fringes at both ends, and it is used as a head covering, for warmth, as an adornment, for hiding and carrying possessions, but most importantly, for transporting infants. Babies are carried in it; put to sleep in it when away from home, cradle, or hammock; and nursed in it (at which time both the baby's head and the mother's breast are covered). With the rebozo babies can be tied on a mother's back, but more often they are held in front, in a somewhat upright position, close to the heart. A nursing mother must be more careful about her diet and activities than when she was pregnant. She should avoid sour fruits and nuts and should not go out in strong sunlight for fear of heating and drying her milk.

At about the age of six months the infant's diet is supplemented with corn gruel (*atole*) and soda, then broths, and later semi-solid foods such as softened tortillas, noodles, or rice. When they are able to grasp well and have enough teeth for chewing, they are given tortillas and other soft solids such as beans, which form a regular part of the adult diet. Feeding is always upon demand; there is little attempt to accustom children to adult meal schedules during early infancy.

Most babies are nursed for about a year or a year and a half; others have been known to continue for as long as three years although this is not an approved custom. By the end of the first year it is expected that the mother will have become pregnant again and will stop nursing in order to protect the new baby's milk. Often the mother weans the infant by withdrawing the breast, letting the baby cry for two or three nights. Another common form of weaning is to send the baby to his grandmother's home for a few days. He is already accustomed to her home for he has visited there often; only the absence of his mother and accustomed milk is new. He is treated very gently, indulged, handled a great deal, and warmly soothed, until he apparently forgets his need for the breast. After a few days he returns to his mother, who also soothes and indulges her by now *chipil* (jealous) child. Another, and older, form of weaning is to smear some unpleasant tasting substance or chile on the breast and then let the baby nurse in order to show him that he no longer likes it. This is a practice followed by many Mesoamerican groups but not preferred by more productive mothers.

In the poorest families, mothers try to breastfeed as long as they can because they cannot afford to buy milk. In better-off families, mothers are more likely to decide earlier that it is time for weaning.

Some people interpret the baby's first cry as the first true sign of life, others consider that it begins with the first movement in the womb, and a few, following conventional Catholic dogma, consider the moment of conception as the beginning of life. One older woman, a descendent of the hacienda peons, said, "A baby's first cry shows all the suffering in the world; he is alive from the time he is born and has awareness (*conocimiento*) after a year."

Beyond this first wail, all crying is discouraged. As soon as a baby cries the breast is offered; for children who have been weaned, a commercial nipple-shaped pacifier is substituted. Crying infants are also fondled, rocked in the cradle or hammock, bounced in the rebozo, or distracted, and the cause of their complaints is attended to as soon as possible.

Most babies appear to be silent and serious most of their waking time. Whether in a rebozo, hammock, or in a small packing crate on the floor near their mothers, they appear to be relatively immobile but busily watching all that is going on about them. Apparently passive, their motor development is in fact encouraged and they begin to walk at the age of about one year, stimulated by the approval of the family.

At the end of this first period of childhood, almost all children appear happy, active, and alert. We found on developmental tests that they scored as high or higher than U.S. norms.[1]

EARLY CHILDHOOD

From age 2 to age 6, the young child is expected to become more independent, to do things for himself that were done before by the mother. Children learn mainly by imitation and prodding by mothers (who will say, for example, "Now you are big enough to use a spoon"). Children also learn to urinate and defecate in appropriate places, often, by observing older siblings. The child is expected to learn gradually how to clean himself and play by himself. He is also expected to learn to follow simple orders and to differentiate between what is his and what is not his, although he is usually allowed to play with his siblings' things, and although within the family, individuals freely share their property.

Village families are not preoccupied with the child's sexual behavior. Children may walk around without clothes and no one takes notice. Toilet training is not rigidly enforced nor charged with emotion. Masturbation is generally ignored, except by extremely destructive mothers who sometimes threaten a little boy with castration. The child's body is his own, and most villagers do not deny children what pleasure they can find as long as it is not at another's expense. Furthermore, since in most families everyone sleeps in the same room, children learn to take sexuality for granted. Although the parents are not openly demonstrative of affection with each other, they still hug and kiss the child and caress him to sleep.

Although the two-year old's care is left more in the hands of older siblings and young aunts, the mother still keeps a close watch. At age 4 or 5, children may be sent on errands to the store or to the grandparent's house, but they are not allowed to wander off to play. The cultural pattern stresses staying close to mother. However, the quality of the relationship between mother and child depends most of all on the mother's character. Productive mothers are more likely to stimulate the child's sense of autonomy, by teaching him to take care of himself and by sending him on errands. (There is little difference in treatment of boys and girls at this age, except that many mothers are more indulgent with boys, stricter with girls.) Unproductive, symbiotic mothers become anxious if the child strays from her or appears too independent.

---

[1] The results of the developmental tests, together with an earlier version of the findings on the children, is reported in N. Modiano and M. Maccoby, "Cultural and Sociological Factors Relating to Learning Development," final report, Project No. 6-8636, Grant No. OEG-1-7-068636-0191, U.S. Department of Health, Education and Welfare, Office of Education, Bureau of Research, 1967.

Some mothers insure that children will stay nearby by scaring them with visions of strangers, ghosts, or devils who will kidnap them if they stray from the home, or of wild animals such as the *gato* (the cat), the coyote, or the *cocodrilo* (crocodile) who will eat them up. This may explain why responses of some children aged 6 to 8 to the CAT (Childrens Apperception Test) express fear of being eaten.

But more important probably is that in many children there is a deep-seated fear of mother in her role as destroyer—not as life giver—fears which often find expression also in dreams of adults in which the destructive mother is symbolized as crocodile, lion, tiger, and serpent, animals which strike swiftly and are deadly and toward whom the individual feels totally helpless.

The cultural emphasis on obedience begins to be felt by children increasingly from the age of 2 on. The two-year old finds that people now express mild annoyance if he is stubborn or gets under foot. Although little children are free to express their anger in temper tantrums (*berrinches*), or their sorrow by crying, they find that the adults are increasingly unmoved by such displays. Parents are deft at distracting the child when he is angry or crying. If this doesn't work, the child may be left alone. Anger directed against the parents themselves is not allowed. Even the more productive parents are likely to respond with a threat to spank the child which usually is enough. If this fails, the child may be slapped sharply.

Productive parents, however, are more likely to concentrate on understanding what is troubling a child and to do whatever they can to help him. They distinguish between real hurts that need tending and temper tantrums or plays for attention. Unproductive parents are more likely to punish any disobedience.

At this age (from 2 to 6) children begin to learn strategies for pleasing authorities. Tattling is frequent, as is whining, and children learn to protect themselves from older siblings by threatening to complain to the parents. Children use the same technique later with their school teachers. Quarrels with siblings tend to be short-lived because of the threat that parents will punish the older child. By encouraging tattling, parents break up the possibility that children will band together against authority, and they try to make sure that vertical relationships to authority remain more important than horizontal bonds among equals. The result is to strengthen traditional authoritarian attitudes.

From the ages of 2 to 6, parents feel that obedience is not in fact difficult to secure. While children may be stubborn, they never question the fundamental rightness of adult authority. But the parents are careful nonetheless to do nothing that would encourage disrespect. Less than 4 percent of the parents who were interviewed believe that a parent should be indulgent (*consentidor*) with their children, while 70 percent felt that the ideal way to be is strict (*seco,* which literally means "dry"). The rest, including the most productive parents (26 percent), thought that one should be neither too strict nor too lenient. When we asked parents how they actually behaved with their children, only 54 percent considered themselves in fact strict, while 10 percent called themselves lenient, and 35 percent as neither one nor the other. Despite the ideal of strictness, it is our observation that the true percentage of indulgent parents is probably closer to the 25 percent who were scored on the interview as having indulgent tendencies. Why is there a discrepancy between ideal and actual conduct? The answer is that most parents try to follow the ideal of strong traditional authority handed down by their parents and generally accepted by the culture, and that indulgent parents often feel they are failing to live up to proper standards and may even deny their behavior. Thus, some parents with indulgent tendencies do not allow themselves to express these tendencies in their behavior. Impulses to play with the children are controlled by most parents, because they feel the child will not respect a parent who shows such levity. Only 35 percent, the most productive parents, play with their children under the age of 6, although most enjoy playing with infants.

By the age of 6, the average village child has learned that he will be left alone in his play and that he will be protected by his family, provided he stays close to home and does not get in the way of parents. His adaptation has been in large measure that of acquiring social skills and control of his own body. By age 2 or 3 he is toilet trained. By age 4, he dresses himself and by age 6 bathes himself. The average village child of 5 or 6 expresses a rather independent self-affirmative attitude with other children. Only where the mother is extremely unproductive and symbiotic does the child feel deep fears about leaving her side, fears which she has communicated to him. On the other hand, children with productive parents are more active and self-confident than the others at this age.

Despite demands for obedience (which are still relatively mild at this age), and despite widespread malnutrition in poorer families and intestinal parasites, most little villagers of 5 or 6 appear remarkably contented, although reserved. When spoken to by a stranger within their own houses, they are likely to answer confidently. They spend most of their time playing by themselves, or in the company of a sibling close to them in age. All but the poorest families provide one or two toys, commercially manufactured, and usually of cheap plastic: little cars, dolls, or trains, which they use over and over again. These they supplement with tin cans, old spoons, sticks, stones and other scrap objects they find lying about their yards. Their play is rarely imaginative but is a combination of imitating adult activities and seeing what can be done with their playthings. Unlike American children, they do not create imaginary worlds of castles, battles, or monsters. Rather, they stay close to concrete reality, as though examining their own world in the most minute detail. (We find that they are likely to describe the CAT cards in concrete detail, rather than making up imaginative stories.) When not playing they seem to watch what is going on about them with considerable interest and attention.

For those children we observed up to age 6 or 7, the dominant orientations were not yet fixed. The children still had a great deal of flexibility and practiced different modes. This is borne out in the responses of six boys and eight girls of this age who were administered CAT's and Rorschach tests. There were no clear patterns in the responses to indicate a crystallized character structure.

However, some of the children at this age have strong symbiotic tendencies which will resist the adaptational demands that are made on the child at the next stage. (In Freudian terms, one would say that for some children libido has been fixated in such a way that they are likely to regress as pressures for adaptation become stronger at age six or seven.)

MIDDLE CHILDHOOD TO ADOLESCENCE

At about the age of 6 or 7 the child begins to develop a sense of self. In meeting the requirements of the culture, he is also concerned with his growing needs for potency and self-determination. Erik Erikson has observed that during this period the child tries to develop a new sense of initiative.[2] Jean Piaget has shown that children at this age begin to think for themselves and to question the authority of adults.[3]

At about age 6 for girls and 7 for boys a combination of both external and internal demands mark a new stage in development. The relatively healthy child is flexible enough to adapt without losing his freedom for further change and development. However, children who have been made frightened and overly dependent by sadistic or symbiotic mothers are more likely to respond to these new pressures in a rigid, pathological, and regressive way.

Village mothers have commented to us that at this age the child changed from being relatively docile and obedient to being a person with a mind of his own. Before the age of 6, children might be stubborn, but now they become critical of the parents, and disobedience takes on a new meaning. While before this age the child's responses to the parents are essentially limited to yes or no, now there is a new sense of self and of alternatives. The 6- or 7-year old may suggest doing things differently. He is capable of pointing out that parents do not live up to their threats or follow their own rules. He asks questions and wants to know why things

---

[2] See Erikson (1963), p. 255.
[3] See Piaget (1955, 1967).

are done. Some parents feel the child of this age has suddenly become bad, obstinate (*terco*), and disobedient. The comments of more productive parents show deeper understanding. Speaking of her son, one mother told us that "he changed at seven years because he began to think for himself." Another said her daughter "began to think" at that age.[4]

For the villagers, this new development is threatening. While wilfulness in the small child may often be considered laughable, at this new stage it is taken more seriously. The general cultural response to the questioning child is twofold. Disobedience is punished more severely, and the child is put to work (so that his new initiative can be molded into adaptive pathways). School also begins at this time, but it does not have the importance as a socializing agency that it has in the United States. Except in the richer families, parents do not consider it important how well a child does at school, nor are the children vitally concerned with grades or progress. Although they are proud when children do well, it is common to repeat years; and little shame is attached to such failure, although the parents will most likely express disapproval or anger and blame the child for laziness. Inasmuch as school does serve a socializing function, it reinforces the cultural concern with strict obedience. Children are not expected to be original, imaginative, or to reason for themselves, but rather to repeat exactly what they are told by the teacher, and to memorize lessons. In the schoolroom, the child who does not obey is ridiculed or made to stay in during recess. When the teacher is away, children become more active and playful. At home, the enforcement of obedience depends in great measure on the character of the parents. A sizeable minority (40 percent) of parents are explicitly authoritarian in their treatment of children at this age. They believe that the disobedient child should be beaten and made to fear them. The majority of villagers prefer to give *consejos,* to use reason, but most will spank the child if these fail. Only 27 percent of the most productive villagers stated that it was bad to beat children. In fact, productive parents can usually command respect and obedience without the use of force.[5]

---

[4] Piaget's investigations show that the child at this age does begin to think for himself. He writes (1967) that "At about the age of seven the child becomes capable of cooperation because he no longer confuses his own point of view with that of others," p. 39. Also see Sheldon H. White, "Evidence for a Hierarchial Arrangement of Learning Process," in *Advances in Child Development and Behavior,* Lewis P. Upsitt and Charles C. Spiker, eds. (New York: Academic Press, 1955). White summarizes evidence that shows that children at the age of 5 to 6 begin to learn in new ways, employing abstract thought and logic in contrast to the associational learning of younger children.

[5] One might note here that the extreme concern about whether or not one should spank a child is symptomatic of the behavioristic orientation in the United States. In fact, some of the cruelist and most sadistic parents do not spank their children, but threaten to abandon them if they do not obey. On the other hand, a productive parent may occasionally spank a child without causing hate or resentment on the part of the child.

At this age, from 6 or 7 on, most parents make it a policy not only to punish disobedience (which is the only behavior that is always punished) but also not to show any pleasure when the child does something well. (They may speak well about the child in another's presence, but they do not praise the child directly.) The cultural pattern is to punish often but to reward only minimally. A mother describes her attitude toward an 8-year-old son. "I say that it is important that they obey immediately. If he does things immediately, I *think* to myself that he is a very intelligent child, but I *don't say* anything. If he doesn't obey me, then I have to get angry, because he will only obey if he sees me angry. I don't spank him much. . . . Sometimes later I feel sorry. I feel it, but I don't tell him, because he would only say to himself: 'it isn't serious if she spanks me and then repents.'"

Village parents are serious about obedience, and they feel that to be playful or to show enthusiasm about the child at this age would undermine respect. We asked the parents how they react when the child brings home good grades and bad grades from the school. In response to good grades, 80 percent of the parents would feel pleased but say nothing at all to the child. Fifteen percent, the most productive and loving parents, say they would show their pleasure. Five percent say they wouldn't care one way or the other. In response to bad grades, only 15 percent—again the most productive—say they would try to find out from the teacher what was wrong or help the child to do better. The rest would feel angry or disillusioned with the child. Thirty percent say they would punish the child either by spanking or withholding privileges.

At the same time that children are being made to obey forcibly, they are also being put to work, not only at school but as helpers to their parents. Girls must learn to cook, care for babies, clean house, wash and iron, sew, mend and embroider, and care for houseplants, kitchen, garden, and small domesticated animals. Boys get up at 6 a.m. in the morning to go to the fields with their fathers before school starts. They begin to learn the skills involved in the cultivation of sugar cane, rice, corn, and other vegetables; the care and use of farm tools such as machetes and sickles; the care of farm animals; fruit culture; and the application of fertilizers and insecticides. They also learn something about house building and maintenance.

The child is expected to learn, with a minimum of questioning, by careful observation and imitation of the parent. Although, as we have noted, parents do not reward the child for mastering a new skill, they are generally quite patient in allowing the child his own time to learn it. Once the child knows how to do something, parents may then punish if the child fails to do it.

During this period of childhood, differences in sex roles are stressed not only in work but in play and leisure as well. We have noted in Chapters 7 and 8 that boys are often allowed more freedom to roam away from the house and to play, while parents are stricter and more protective in relation to their daughters. At this age, boys and girls begin to play in separate groups. In the girls' play, especially from age 8 to puberty, the emphasis is on games which symbolically represent the threat of the predatory male to the pure and defenseless female (see Chapter 7). During this same period boys play games of skill and central-person games that are of two symbolic types. In these games—tag, hide-and-seek, and "burnt leather" (*cuero quemado*)—either the central person (the *"it"*) has no authority at all and is chased by the group, or he has full permission to punish the others, who must try to escape.

If we contrast the structure of village central-person games with those played by children in Western industrialized societies, we find that in the United States, England, or Australia, the symbolic content of central-person games teaches the child that the central person, the authority, can be vanquished if the children are able to cooperate with each other. For the child in these societies, central-person games have the function of dissolving the infantile submission to adult authority and reinforcing the ethic of fairness and reciprocity. (In later childhood and adolescence, many games, such as football, have the function of fitting children into their social role and of developing an attitude of competitive teamwork and efficiency.) [6]

In village games, the child does not learn this attitude. Rather, the traditional authority of parents and the group is impressed upon him. The individual is shown to be weak when he stands alone, strong when he can use force or is part of the group. In the game of burnt leather, a belt is hidden and the one who finds it chases after the others, who flee to the base line. The one with the belt may whip all those who have not reached safety. The moral is that authority is irrational and punishing; one can neither reason with it nor overcome it. The best strategy is to get as far away from it as you can, unless you can join it. In a village version of hide-and-seek, the central person is chased and hunted down by the others. The moral is that the deviant is not tolerated; one must join the consensus.

In many games, the boys express ambivalence toward authority that later can be seen in their political attitudes. In these games all authority is considered irrational and exploitative. As grown-ups, some men refuse positions of leadership because they do not wish to be disliked and distrusted. Although the authority of parents is considered necessary in order to get rid of the child's "badness" it is not considered proper to enjoy exercising power over others. We found that the most capable older boys would refuse to be captain of the soccer team or president of the boys' club that was started by the study (see Chapter 10), even though they would do

---

[6] For a more detailed analysis of the role of games in the formation of social character, see M. Maccoby, N. Modiano, and P. Lander (1964).

more than their share at play and work. (In contrast, a few of the girls are eager to accept positions of authority and even fight over who will be captain of the girls' volleyball team.)

THE VILLAGER AT THE END OF CHILDHOOD

In evaluating the outcome of childhood in the village, we should bear in mind that despite the negative aspects of village child-rearing, there are also positive elements which can be contrasted to practices in the United States. The village culture does not pressure children to achieve beyond their ability, even though on the other hand there are few stimuli to develop intellectual or creative abilities. Although no attempt is made to develop cooperation, no emphasis is placed on competition with others. Children do not find it necessary to repress sexual feelings, to feel shame about bodily functions, although the culture does not value sensuality and, as we have seen, relations between the sexes are characterized by a good deal of hostility. Furthermore, although the child is forced to be obedient and submissive to parents, no effort is made to manipulate his feelings. Village parents do not tell their children that feeling angry at having to obey is bad, nor do they demand that the child express love when he does not feel it. A clear distinction is often implied between proper social behavior and the child's feelings and impulses which are his own.

While the village culture is impoverished in the sense that it does not stimulate and develop the child's creative powers, traditional authoritarian attitudes do not always result in crushing the child's sense of self. The degree to which the village child can maintain his sense of self depends on: (1) the degree of sadism and intimidation brought to bear on him; (2) his inner strength and ability to resist authoritarian demands; and (3) whether or not the child feels loved by his parents and senses that while they demand formal obedience, they do not cease to love him when he is independent. In fact, where the child feels that his parents love him, he may submit to traditional authority and still maintain a strong sense of self.

By the age of 13 or 14, the process of adaptation—to the parents and the requirements of work—has resulted in the formation of the child's mode of assimilation, in the degree of productiveness, and in the quality of submissiveness.

Some character tendencies which we considered had the same significance for adults and children and could be scored with confidence from the projective responses. On the other hand, there were character tendencies which we did not consider comparable for children and adults respectively. The children seemed still to be experimenting with different modes of relatedness, and in the test responses these did not seem sufficiently fixed to score them with confidence. Hence, we decided not to score these dynamic tendencies in the children.

How does the character of children compare to that of adults? To answer this question, we administered projective tests, including the CAT, cards from the TAT, the Rorschach, as well as interview questions.[7]

A basic sample of 50 children—5 boys and 5 girls each at ages 6 to 7, 8, 9, 10 and 11—was randomly selected. Some children were added to the sample later. The difficulties of finding children and limitations of time led us to decide to increase the sample at the cost of randomness. The final sample included 16 children (6 boys and 10 girls) ages 6 to 7; 14 children (6 boys and 8 girls) ages 8 to 10; 28 children (12 boys and 16 girls) ages 10 to 12; and 52 adolescents (22 boys and 30 girls) ages 13 to 17. Thus, there were 110 children (46 boys and 64 girls), half the population of children in these age groups, included in the sample. Of these, we found we could score 92 cases with confidence.

The interpretative test responses were scored in terms of mode of assimilation, a scale of productiveness, attachment to mother and father, the quality of aggressiveness, and for self-affirmative vs. passive-submissive attitudes. Again all the scoring was done by one of us (Maccoby). The tests were scored "blindly" in the sense that the names of the children were hidden. Furthermore, the scorer did not administer any of the tests. We also scored the following themes as expressed in stories given by the children: the expression of hostility and against whom (father, mother, siblings, self, men, women, others in general) it was directed; the child's fears (physical harm, hunger, abandonment, being eaten, ridiculed, loss of possessions, loss of integrity, sexual fears, fears of the father or mother); and the child's view of the mother (as loving, responsible only, or rejecting).

In comparing younger with older children, and children with adults, the ideal method would be a longitudinal developmental study. Such a study would indicate when in the normal course of development dynamic tendencies become firmly rooted and whether or not they remain so. Lacking longitudinal data, our alternative was to compare the distributions of orientations at different ages and to consider significant changes in these distributions as indications of either normal development, or possibly as changes in social character due to specific changes in the society. We have already shown that from adolescence to adulthood and old age, the distribution of the modes of assimilation, degrees of productiveness and modes of relatedness (other than narcissism) remain invariant. Thus, if we are able to find the same distributions in childhood, particularly of the mode of assimila-

---

[7] Tests were also administered for cognitive development, including the development of concepts of moral judgment. These results are reported in Maccoby and Modiano (1966, 1969).

tion, further evidence is added to support our theoretical viewpoint that once the nucleus of character has been formed in childhood it remains more or less fixed for life unless new circumstances arise which mobilize what were formerly only potential orientations.

The data in Table 9:1 present a startling picture. In contrast to what one might expect, the process of education in both home and school tends to weaken rather than strengthen the child's character. From age 6 to 16 there is an increasing prevalence of submissiveness, receptiveness, and exploitativeness.

Although the percentage of highly productive children does not change after age 6 (possibly because they are protected by a favorable constitution), significantly more of the older children are characterized by unproductive traits (Table 9:2). If we consider productiveness as a measure of

TABLE 9:1   Age Trends in Personality and Character Traits
Between Ages 6 and 16 (Significant Correlations)
N=96

Trait	r (age)
Receptiveness	.18*
Exploitativeness	.18*
Hoarding orientation	-.15
Productiveness	-.20*
Submissiveness	.23*
Self-affirmation	-.23*
Generalized hostility	.41**
Fears	
Abandonment	.36**
Being eaten	-.30**
Being ridiculed	.49**
Loss of integrity	.24**
Sexual fears	.38**
Fear of the father	.15
Fear of the mother	.25**
General intensity of fear	.20*

$*p = <.05$
$**p = <.01$

the child's ability to relate himself actively to new situations, this means that younger children are more *themselves* and that they could respond more readily to new favorable conditions. Later the stimuli will have to be stronger. At age 6 the village children are more active and self-affirmative than at age 13 or 14. From age 7 to age 13, the process of dynamic adaptation and submission causes increased hostility which, while often

TABLE 9:2 Comparison of Character at Three Ages
(Percent with Trait)

	Age Range		
Character Trait	6-12 (N=44)	13-16 (N=52)	Over 16 (N=415)
Highly productive	27	26	26
Low productive	27	32	40
Receptive	55	73	71
Exploitative	64	69	26
Hoarding	61	54	55
Destructive	23	23	24
Submissive	71	89	79

suppressed behaviorally, is increasingly expressed in projective stories and Rorschach images of older children. The children have also become more fearful during this period. While there seems to be a decrease in fears of being eaten, the fear of the mother may be transformed in later years to fears of being abandoned and being ridiculed if one does not conform. These new fears reflect the methods parents have used on older children to enforce obedience. Older boys and girls also begin to fear sex and intimacy. Furthermore, we observe an increasing direct fear of the parents, especially the mother who is seen as more dangerous and potentially destructive than the father by the majority of the children.

Our findings are consistent with the Freudian viewpoint that healthy development requires independence from the mother and, in the case of boys, an acceptance of the father as a positive model for identification. As we shall see, those boys who maintain a deep emotional symbiosis with the mother are the ones who develop pathological and maladaptive character structures.

COMPARISON OF CHARACTER OF CHILDREN AND ADULTS

Table 9:2 compares the percentages of individuals with the various modes of assimilation, and with destructive and submissive traits at three different age ranges: 6 to 12, 13 to 16, and over 16. These comparisons show the following:

1. The percentage of highly productive individuals remains constant from age 6 through adulthood, at a little over 25 percent of the population. The percentage of unproductive individuals increases from 27 percent at ages 6 to 12 to 32 percent at adolescence and 40 percent in adulthood. The percentage of individuals with destructive traits remains constant from ages 6 to 12 through adulthood, at about 23 percent.

2. The percentage of individuals with receptive traits increases from age 6 to 12 (55 percent) to age 16 (73 percent), but then remains constant through adulthood (71 percent).

3. The percentage of hoarding individuals decreases somewhat but not significantly from ages 6 to 12 (61 percent) to ages 13 to 16 (54 percent), but then remains constant through adulthood (55 percent).

4. The most striking difference between adult and child character is to be found in the percentage with exploitative tendencies. While 64 percent of those from ages 6 to 12 and 69 percent from ages 13 to 16 have exploitative traits, only 26 percent of the adults were scored as having exploitative tendencies. Why are the children more exploitative? There are two possible explanations.

The first explanation is that the greater powerlessness and frustration of the child is likely to engender exploitative tendencies in him. According to this explanation, as children grow up and become less powerless when they leave their families, their exploitative tendencies would tend to be replaced or dry up, as it were.

A second possible explanation is that the society is changing as the new exploitative entrepreneurs are rising to positions of power, by accumulating capital, and by taking advantage of new technological opportunities. As the entrepreneur rises to the top of the society, he increasingly becomes a model for the young people,[8] and his values, those of progress and utilization of resources, increasingly are accepted. And young people, witnessing the success of the entrepreneur and impressed by his prestige and power, may even reject the example of their parents in favor of this new model. This modeling process does not change character but rather behavior. However, since children have a good deal of exploitativeness as part of their character, the model might serve the function of keeping this tendency alive, as opposed to the past, when the model villagers were nonexploitative.

CHARACTER FACTORS IN CHILDHOOD

As with adult character scoring, we were interested in discovering the syndromes of personality variables for the children. In this case, factors were derived using McQuitty's method of analysis.[9] For the purposes of

---

[8] For the evidence concerning variables including success that determine who the child takes as a model, see Albert Bandura, "Social-Learning Theory of Identificatory Processes," in D. A. Goslin, Ed. *Handbook of Socialization Theory and Research* (Chicago: Rand McNally, 1968).

[9] See McQuitty (1961). In analyzing character variables, we experimented with different types of factor analysis. McQuitty's method is simpler to employ than the Varimax method reported in Chapter 5, and the results are similar. On theoretical

this factor analysis, we also added personality measures of 24 adolescents (9 boys and 15 girls) between the ages of 14 to 17 to our sample of 86 children aged 6 through 13. Eight syndromes emerged from this analysis.[10] One was characteristic of the 6-year-old children only. It included fear of being eaten, extreme hostility to sibling rivals, and unquestioning acceptance of adult authority. This syndrome characterized the child who has not yet begun to think for himself, who is still in what Piaget (1951) calls the "egocentric stage" of development. The other factors represent dynamic outcomes of the demands made on the child after the age of 6.

Of these other seven factors, four represent unproductive orientations, all of them significantly intercorrelated. One represents a syndrome of traits that was common to all of the unproductive orientations. Two represent productive orientations which were also significantly correlated with each other.

The unproductive orientations include:

The receptive syndrome. These children are receptive, dependent, and unaggressive. Their adaptation is submissiveness at the cost of initiative and independence. It corresponds to the unproductive-receptive type of adult.

The authoritarian-destructive syndrome. This syndrome represents the most extreme psychopathology found in the village. Authoritarian attitudes are combined with extreme hostility and malignant destructiveness (*necrophilia*). Many Rorschach responses of these children were images of decay and death. The projective responses also indicated grandiose ambitions for prestige, money, and power, characterizing extreme narcissism. At the same time, the children expressed acute fears of starvation and abandonment, combined with a regressive fixation to the mother, who was seen as more powerful and destructive than the father. This syndrome represents a pathological and nonadaptive character, caused by intense fixation to a destructive mother. It corresponds to the unproductive-narcissistic-destructive adult.

---

grounds, we would have preferred to employ his more advanced methods of typal analysis (e.g. McQuitty, 1968), but at the time we were analyzing the data, these methods had not yet been fully worked out. The advantage of these newer methods is that they isolate *types of individuals* rather than summarizing variables into factors. Thus, one may determine the percentages of individuals that are similar to each other in terms of a syndrome of traits. Furthermore, the method allows one to distinguish which traits are important to a syndrome both in terms of presence and absence. We feel that McQuitty's methods contribute significantly to the possibilities of employing quantitative statistical techniques to the study of social character, because they are designed for the better understanding of types of individuals rather than types of traits.

[10] These syndromes in some ways seem richer in content than the adult factors reported in Chapter 5. This is because they include more variables (e.g. types of fears, objects of hostility). In the earlier scoring of adult character, we limited the variables to the modes comprising the nuclear character.

The exploitative-rebellious syndrome. While this syndrome has common elements with that of the destructive orientation, it is less pathological. It characterizes the "lone wolf," who is exploitative, predatory, and rebellious. The lone wolf's adaptive solution is to steal what he can, to try and incorporate and use other people. Underlying his character traits is intense fearfulness, especially to the mother, who is seen as destructive and castrating. But rather than submit to her, the lone wolf rebels and attempts to fend for himself. If this syndrome is combined with more productive traits, it becomes that of the independent entrepreneur.

The submissive-ingratiating syndrome. This syndrome describes children who adapt by a particular type of ingratiating submissiveness. About 10 percent of the children have this attitude, which appears to be a new development in the village since its prevalence is negligible in the adult population. It is similar to Fromm's description of the marketing orientation and is characteristic of children who are oriented to the modern world and who find models on TV and in the movies. In trying so hard to please others, these children are also fearful of feeling their own impulses for self-expression and are resentful of those they try to please. In their Rorschach responses they express anxiety concerning wholeness (integrity). It appears that they sense they are sacrificing integrity by making themselves into attractive packages.

It is noteworthy that the four unproductive orientations are all significantly correlated with a syndrome of traits indicating rejection of the father. This syndrome includes fear of the father, rejection of the father's influence, rebellion against the father, hostility to the father, and identification with the mother. For boys, this syndrome also implies intense feelings of self-contempt and fear of being ridiculed. In rejecting the father and identifying with the mother, boys betray their own sex. Their fear of ridicule reflects their underlying feelings of shame, and the fear that others will see them as feminine.

In contrast to the unproductive outcomes of childhood adaptation, there are two productive orientations. One is the *democratic self-affirmative syndrome,* which implies strong self-affirmation. The other is the *productive-hoarding orientation,* which includes a strong tie to the father and the child's perception of the mother as loving. Children characterized by this syndrome express the productive-hoarding mode that is most adaptive to the peasant situation yet most open to new stimulation.[11]

---

[11] Productiveness is also significantly correlated with I.Q. as measured by Ravens Progressive Matrices ($r = .36$, $p < .01$). The Ravens Progressive Matrices tests the child's powers of concentration and reasoning ability, which are aspects of productive peasant intelligence. Productiveness is not significantly correlated with scores on the Stanford-Binet I.Q. test, which measures the verbal-abstract type of intelligence not generally developed in the villager (see Maccoby and Modiano, 1969).

CORRELATIONS OF PARENTAL AND CHILD CHARACTERS

The factor scores of the children were correlated with their parents' scores on the adult factors. We found that all of the unproductive orientations were significantly correlated with the mother's character, while only exceptionally with the father's. The key character trait was the mother's own mother centeredness. Those mothers who remain intensely fixated on their own mothers tend to keep their children weak and dependent on them, discouraging independence and growth. Whether these *symbiotic mothers* undermine their children by pampering or frighten them into submission, the result is to cripple the child's ability to adapt actively to the world outside the mother. We were able to discover certain relationships between the character of the parents and the specific type of unproductive traits that develop. In the case of the receptive children, a particular family constellation is often encountered. While the mother is symbiotic, she also tends to be loving to very small children. Furthermore, our data show that the receptive child's father is also likely to be passive and receptive with the conditional loving orientation, indicating a certain amount of material responsibility and affection. In contrast, significant positive correlations indicate that when the father is extremely unproductive and lacking responsibility and the mother is symbiotic, the child's character is more likely to be either authoritarian or exploitative.

In contrast to unproductive parents, productive parents influence the development of productive traits in children. The democratic self-affirmative syndrome is significantly correlated with having a productive father (Factor II) and a responsible mother (Factor I). The productive-hoarding factor is significantly correlated with having a mother who is loving and productive (Factor II) and a productive-hoarding father who is also economically successful. These correlations are higher for boys than for girls (see Table 9:3). (It is noteworthy that the child's perception of the mother as loving in his projective stories given to the TAT is significantly correlated with our scoring of the mother as loving from the projective interview.)

CORRELATIONS OF PARENTAL AND ADULT OFFSPRING CHARACTERS

Of the adult population scored for character, 146 individuals (76 male and 70 female) had living parents, so that in these cases it was possible to intercorrelate the character factors of parents and grown children. In making these correlations, we have separated males and females and have made separate correlations for 53 individuals (32 sons and 21 daughters) from fatherless homes.

TABLE 9:3   Child Character Factors (Ages 6-16) Correlated
with Parents' Character Factors (N=92)

Parental Factors Mothers (N=10)	Receptive	Authoritarian-Destructive	Child Factors Exploit-ative	Ingrati-ating	Self-Affirmative	Productive-Hoarding
Mother's responsibility (Factor I)	-.15	-.05	-.01	.05	.24*	.11
Mother's productiveness (Factor II)	.10	-.03	-.05	-.07	.07	.19
Mother's mother fixation (Factor VI)	.26**	.20*	.20*	.30**	.05	-.04
Fathers (N=83)						
Father's responsibility (Factor I)	.26**	.08	-.09	.08	-.09	-.02
Father's productiveness (Factor II)	-.02	-.14	-.19	-.11	.23*	.12
Father's hoarding mode (Factor IV)	.00	-.04	-.06	.05	.15	.21*

*Significant at 5 percent level
**Significant at 1 percent level

The results essentially confirm the pattern shown for the younger children and adolescents. Productive individuals are more likely to have parents who are loving, productive, and economically successful. Unproductive children are more likely to have unproductive parents.

We shall consider separately the correlations for sons and daughters.

PARENTS AND GROWN SONS

There are positive correlations between the character factors of young men and the same traits in their fathers (Table 9:4). The highest correlation shows that fathers and sons are alike in terms of the hoarding-receptive factor. The correlation of sex role is also significantly high. With the exception of Factor I (the adolescent vs. adulthood factor) the other correlations, while not significant, still indicate a consistent positive pattern. The correlations of parent character factors with those of adult sons support the finding that the productive-hoarding young man is likely to have a productive-hoarding father and a productive-loving mother. Furthermore, this father is likely to be among the richer peasants. The correlation between the productiveness of sons and the high socioeconomic status of their fathers is $r = .41$, which is significant at the 1 percent level.

TABLE 9:4   Positive Correlations Between Character
of Grown-Up Sons and Parents

Factor	Father-Son r (N=45)	Mother-Son r (N=45)	Mother-Son, Fatherless Families r (N=32)
Adulthood	—	—	—
Productiveness	.23	.18	.55**
Exploitativeness	.26	.21	—
Hoarding-receptive	.41**	—	.23
Sex role	.31*	—	.31*
Mother fixation	.26	.34*	.36*

*Significant at 5 percent level
**Significant at 1 percent level

In contrast, the unproductive son is more likely to grow up in a family suffering extreme poverty, with a receptive-unproductive father and a mother who is likely to keep him dependent on her.

These results permit various theoretical explanations:

1. That boys inherit the productive qualities of their parents.[12]
2. That boys take productive and successful fathers as models.
3. That boys are stimulated by and respond to the productive atmosphere in their families, and become more productive themselves.

While our data do not allow us to decide on the relative importance of the three explanations, one further element must be kept in mind: in addition to these three possibilities, another one—the economic factor—is also of considerable importance. We have learned that a crucial question for character development in the village is whether a boy is mother centered or father centered. While father centeredness is significantly correlated with the degree of the parents' productiveness, *the father's economic status is of equal weight* (for girls as well as boys) (see Table 9:5).

A very important question arises. How much is the father's influence due to his economic status and how much is it due to his character? We know that richer men are usually more productive men in this population. An important clue to answering this question is that when the father's productiveness is partialed out of the correlation between mother centeredness and economic status, class is still significantly correlated with father vs. mother centeredness. This means that even among sons of less productive men, the father's high socioeconomic status is a factor in attracting the son

[12] As shown in Chapters 6 and 7, productive men are usually married to productive women.

TABLE 9:5   Grown Sons' Productiveness and Mother-Father Orientation
Correlated With Parents' Character and Social Class
(N=45)

Parents	Sons	
	Productiveness (Factor II)	Mother Fixation (Factor VI)
Father's productiveness	.23	-.36*
Father's mother fixation	—	.26
Father's socioeconomic status	.41**	-.49**
Mother's productiveness	.18	-.17
Mother's mother fixation	-.18	.34*

*Significant at 5 perecnt level
**Significant at 1 percent level

away from the mother (while in poorer families even a productive father often fails to attract the son away from the mother).[13]

This would not be the case if the strength of the mother attachment were determined primarily by psychosexual factors, if the outcome of the Oedipus Complex depended mainly on the intensity of a libidinal cathexis. Our findings are not consistent with Freud's main position, which emphasizes the fear of castration as the decisive factor in the boy's renouncing his primary attachment to the mother. It is our view that the breaking of the primary tie with the mother, which is necessary if a boy is to become a man, depends more on socioeconomic than on psychosexual factors. Where the father is unsuccessful in his adaptation to society, he presents a model of failure. He has failed to provide for the family, and he fails to live up to the patriarchal role. In this case, the mother becomes the dominant one in the family, while the father is demoralized and humiliated. In these conditions, it would be almost impossible for a boy to become free of a mother who did not wish to relinquish her hold on him. Why should he leave the safety of a mother's protection to become like a father who has been crushed by failure?

Furthermore, one must be careful not to put too much emphasis on the explanation of character formation as being based exclusively on identification or modeling. When a boy's character development is explained solely in terms of identification with the father, the part played by the child's own active adaptation to his environment is ignored. Also, it implies that a boy without a father would be unable to develop productive mascu-

---

[13] The correlation between mother fixation for sons and the father's socioeconomic status is $r = -.33$ ($p < .01$). If the father's productiveness is partialed out, the correlation is $r = -.22$ ($p < .05$).

The correlation between mother fixation for sons and the father's productiveness is $r = -.36$ ($p < .01$). If the father's socioeconomic status is partialed out, the correlation is $r = -.26$ ($p < .05$).

line traits unless he found a father substitute as a model. This is not the case. We find (Table 9:4) that in fatherless households, the mother's productiveness and her lack of symbiosis vis-à-vis the child are the key factors in the development of productive character traits in boys. In this case, the mother's socioeconomic status plays no part in the equation. The results indicate that even where there is no father, if the mother is productive, a son is more likely to develop a productive character structure than if he had an unproductive father. On the other hand, if his mother is symbiotic and unproductive, a productive-successful father (even a nonproductive but successful father) can often help him to achieve independence from her.

Let us summarize in the light of our findings the reasons why some boys become productive-hoarding and others passive-receptive. The productive boy is more likely to have been stimulated by supportive parents. He has a successful productive-hoarding father and a productive mother. He has been neither crushed and frightened nor babied into submission. Thus, he can respond actively to the real world. In doing so, he is likely to develop the productive-hoarding orientation which best fits the socioeconomic conditions of his society.

In contrast, the receptive boy with an unproductive-receptive and unsuccessful father is unable to break the bonds of dependence on a symbiotic mother. Although emotionally he rejects his receptive father as a model, he becomes just like him, because he is unable to become independent from his mother. This outcome may be even more regressive and pathological in the case of intense fixation to a destructive mother.

Although boys are normally tied to their mothers until the age of 5 or 6 (and in the village, until marriage), in the normal development in most cultures it is the function of the father to help the boy to cut this tie. The father helps by offering himself as a guide and helper, bringing the boy into the life of the larger society. He does so partly by being a model, but also by offering his son the possibility of an affectionate tie with him that dilutes or replaces the earlier affectionate tie with the mother. [14] Social class may be a crucial factor in determining this outcome. The poorest children have no hope of ever becoming more than peons. They feel looked down upon, inferior to the richer children. Storekeepers refuse to give them credit when their mothers send them on errands. Their world, even more than is true of other villagers, is one of suspiciousness and hostility. Only inside the family and close to the mother do they feel "at home."

---

[14] This hypothesis differs essentially from Freud's hypothesis that the boy gives up his incestuous love of the mother because he fears the father and then becomes like the father by internalizing him in the form of the superego.

In fact, and according to our observations, more frequently the unconscious guilt feelings are often produced by the mother's threats and not by the father's.

PARENTS AND GROWN DAUGHTERS

The relationship between the character of grown daughters and that of their parents has not yet been fully discussed. In fact, it follows a similar pattern to that of the boys, although there are some important differences. As with sons, the productiveness of grown daughters is significantly correlated with having productive-loving parents (Table 9:6), although the

TABLE 9:6   Positive Correlations Between Character of Grown Daughters and Parents

Factor	Father-Daughter (N=55)	Mother-Daughter (N=55)	Mother-Daughter (Fatherless Families) (N=22)
Adulthood	—	—	—
Productiveness	.28*	.49**	.30
Exploitativeness	—	—	—
Hoarding-receptive	—	.32*	—
Sex role	-.34**	—	—
Mother fixation	—	.32*	.54**

*Significant at 5 percent level
**Significant at 1 percent level

productiveness of the mother seems even more important for the daughter than for the son. Just as the son tends to develop the hoarding or receptive mode of his father, the daughter's mode of assimilation is likely to be that of her mother.

Both the father's character and his socioeconomic status influence the development of one factor in his daughter's character. When fathers have hoarding traits (Factor IV), masculine traits (Factor V), and are economically successful, the daughters become less mother fixated. On the other hand, when fathers are receptive-submissive, "feminine," and economic failures, the daughters' mother fixation is strengthened (see Table 9:7). This leads to a vicious circle in which these girls will grow up to be unproductive-possessive mothers who hate men.

We should also note that, at the other extreme, girls find it difficult to break away from a possessive father, especially when he is relatively rich. Some girls in this situation never marry, while others find it necessary to elope. In such cases, the possessive father, often furious, refuses ever again to speak to his daughter.

In fatherless families, the strength of the daughter's mother fixation depends most of all on the mother's own mother fixation (or symbiotic tendencies). However, socioeconomic factors also play a crucial role in the development of productive traits in girls. The correlation between the

TABLE 9:7   Daughters' Productiveness and Mother-Father Orientation
Correlated With Parents' Character and Social Class
(N=55)

Parents	Daughters	
	Productiveness (Factor II)	Mother Fixation (Factor VI)
Father's productiveness	.28*	—
Father's mother fixation	—	—
Father's socioeconomic status	.22	-.27*
Father's hoarding-receptive	—	-.46**
Father's sex role	—	-.34**
Mother's productiveness	.49**	—
Mother's mother fixation	—	.32*

*Significant at 5 percent level
**Significant at 1 percent level

mother's socioeconomic status and her daughter's productiveness is $r = .73$, significant at the 1 percent level. The reason for this is not hard to see in the village. In the few families headed by women where there is sufficient income, daughters are encouraged by productive mothers to develop themselves, to go as far as they can in school. They are not forced to work at the age of six or seven, nor to look forward to a life of servitude.

The findings reported in this chapter point to an important element in the process of widening the class differentiations in the village. While we have seen (in Chapter 6) that for economic reasons the gap between the poorer and richer villagers is increasing, the data presented in this chapter show that this process is further intensified by the psychological factor. We see that the productive parents (and that means to a large extent the richer parents) have more productive children, while the unproductive parents (and that means mostly the poorer parents) have unproductive children. Since these children, according to the same process, will in turn again have more productive and unproductive children, respectively, the social cleavage will increase for psychological as well as for economic reasons.

10

Possibilities for Change:
Character and Cooperation

What are the possibilities for the future of the village? The most likely possibility, if the social and economic conditions remain the same, is that the current trend will continue. The new entrepreneurs will further consolidate their control over the village. The ejidatarios will increasingly become dependent on them as middlemen and as political leaders. The landless either will leave for the cities or, since good jobs are scarce and they are not qualified for them, many will continue to work as day laborers.

If conditions remain the same, this will mean that most villagers will live their lives in poverty and that there will be no alleviation of their hopelessness and alcoholism. Various suggestions have been made by experts concerning how to better the situation of villagers in Latin America and throughout the world. In the light of our findings, we shall consider three such proposals.

1. It has often been proposed that the peasant be given technical training to use more modern agricultural methods and to learn new skills (e.g. handicraft, poultry-raising) that will increase his income. Such training is often of value, especially to those peasants with larger land holdings and some capital. However, it is only a limited solution.

New technology requires different attitudes on the part of the peasant, as we have noted in Chapter 1. To be more than minimally effective, technical training must be combined with change in the character structure of the peasant.

Such a change could be accomplished to some extent through entirely different methods in schooling. (A most impressive and ingenious program for peasant education which not only conveys knowledge, but affects the whole personality is that of Freire,[1] who experimented with his program of alphabetization of adults with peasants and urban workers first in Brazil, and then in Chile. Freire's method can be applied to the education of children as well as adults. But so far there are only a few groups experimenting with it in this way.) As far as the rural school system in Mexico is concerned, it is saddled with very traditionally oriented teachers, and unless one could bring in a sufficient number of teachers who know how to stimulate interest and activity, nothing much can happen.[2] Another way of influencing character would be to change the traditional socioeconomic system of the village in the direction of a greater amount of cooperation and initiative, but this too is a remote goal under the given circumstances.

Furthermore, one could think of an integrated program of cultural stimulation. Attempts in this direction were made under President Lazaro Cardenas, but later petered out. Nevertheless, as we shall indicate later in this chapter, we think that while the difficulties are great, serious efforts in the field of education, cultural stimulation, and cooperative methods—if they went to the roots and were integrated in a new system of life—would have a significant effect.

Another way of changing the peasant's deep-rooted emotional attitudes has been suggested by David McClelland (1961) who proposes a method of training villagers to have a higher "need for achievement." He suggests that individuals with this need are more likely to become entrepreneurs who will adopt and develop new methods and create new industries.

But the facts indicate that entrepreneurs do not solve the village's economic problem. A few entrepreneurs have prospered, but they do not raise the general economic level. In fact, their prosperity is gained at the cost of others. Lacking resources for large-scale economic activity, they become middlemen, money lenders, and storekeepers. While they may employ others as day laborers, the result is to increase the dependency and powerlessness of the landless.

Thus, it seems to us that changes in peasant attitudes in the direction of making more of them small-scale entrepreneurs rigidifies a new class structure and increases misery for the majority. The question which will be considered further in this chapter is whether peasant attitudes can be changed in a way that favors both economic development and life-centered values.

---

[1] Paulo Freire, *Educação e Conscientização* (Cuernavaca: CIDOC, Cuaderno No. 25, 1968).

[2] We want to refer the reader to the writings of Ivan Illich on the problem of compulsory schooling in Latin America. He questions the validity of the modern trend for more extended schooling as being conducive to a more alienated and automatized character structure. See Everett Reimer and Ivan Illich, "Alternatives in Education, 1968-69," *CIDOC, Cuaderno No. 1001,* Cuernavaca, Mexico, 1970.

2. Albert O. Hirschman (1967), an economist specializing in problems of development, cautions that new programs must take account of the peasant's cognitive attitudes which often block economic development. He suggests that development projects be of two types: those that are "trait taking" and those that are "trait making."

A "trait taking" project is built by taking into account the existing traits and does not demand that the peasant change in any way, while a "trait making" project is one which demands that the peasant develop new traits. It requires more from him than does his normal work. In responding to the demands of an exacting job, an individual must develop new traits in order to maintain the project.

We agree with Hirschman that trait making projects are desirable. We want to stress, however, that it is important to be aware of which traits one wants to make, those of the entrepreneur type of modern farmer or those of the productive-cooperative type. As is clear from our overall discussion, we do not think that all psychological traits which serve to speed the process of economic development are desirable from a human standpoint.

3. Programs of education, trait taking, and trait making alone leave certain problems unsolved. Even if the peasant were to increase his earning power somewhat, he would still remain economically powerless in relation to the city, unless he were able to cooperate with other peasants in buying and selling. A cooperative movement which fits this requirement has begun in Mexico under the direction of CONASUPO and has been achieved in other countries such as Sweden in a more extensive and systematic form.[3]

However, an even stronger cooperative movement would be necessary to prevent the trend in this village and others toward a new class stratification, to protect the small independent peasant from the entrepreneur. A cooperative organization, such as the Israeli kibbutz, or some of the cooperative ejidos developed in the Lagunilla area, allows for greater differentiation of work, a higher level of technology, and more rewarding work for the landless peasants. To organize this type of cooperative ejido on a large scale requires changes in the system as well as the support of the government which would have to buy or expropriate the land for these projects and provide the technical leadership.

In considering this third alternative, of a strong cooperative movement, we must keep in mind the fact that peasants throughout the world are extremely individualistic and suspicious of others. When cooperatives

---

[3] An example of a trait-making project which also has increased peasant cooperativeness and his economic and political power is Danilo Dolci's project in Sicily. One aspect of the program is the construction of a dam which requires new skills and traits on the part of the peasants. Dolci has found that he needs not only to train villagers technically, but also to make them aware of their passiveness, fatalism, and submissiveness before their attitudes and work habits change.

are introduced by outside agencies, they almost always fail, even when they promise the peasant greater profit, more power in the market, and new technical training. The kitbbutzes comprise a special case, since they were founded not by peasants, but by urban intellectuals, motivated by the ideals of socialism, who set out to create an agricultural community which would maximize not income but the quality of life for its members. In contrast, failures have been reported in cooperative peasant projects in Latin America, Italy, and India, as well as in many communist countries.[4] The question remains, however, whether the peasant will inevitably reject cooperative projects or whether their success depends on more adequate methods of introduction and structure.

In this chapter we shall consider the villagers' attitude toward cooperative activities as it relates to character. Then we shall report experiments which demonstrate ways of developing cooperative projects and cooperative attitudes.

COOPERATION IN THE VILLAGE

In the recent past the village has sporadically organized cooperative enterprises which have lasted only for brief periods. A cooperative store prospered only so long as it was supported by strong-minded and respected rural schoolmasters. A rice growers' cooperative which promised the ejidatarios higher profits as well as protection against loss collapsed as individual members became suspicious that they would be cheated by the others and fail to receive their proper share. In both cases these cooperatives benefitted a large group of villagers at the expense of the entrepreneurs whose gains were threatened by the projects. Those who stand to lose from the cooperative have the natural tendency to play on the suspicions and fears of the villagers that the cooperatives will cheat them, that the ideals of cooperatives hide new forms of domination from the outsiders.

Public works projects rather than cooperative enterprises are the kind of activity in which the villagers do work together successfully. The leaders of the village, all of them richer peasants, have organized movements to bring electricity and piped drinking water to the village. As we have already described, these "modern" entrepreneurs, oriented to the market economy and away from traditional practices, succeeded in doing away with the most costly fiestas and collected money to build a school. For most villagers the concept of "cooperating" (*cooperar*) means contributing money for such public works, or if they are not rich enough, donating their labor to clean the ditches or fix the roads (*faenas*), always with the hope that the au-

---

[4] Yugoslavia is a notable exception (see below).

thorities or some rich patron who wants to be governor will also "co-operate" in return for the village's gratitude and political support.

Foster (1967) suggests that, traditionally, the richer peasant spends part of his wealth on fiestas, musical bands, masses in the church, and food for the others who in turn are expected to give him the respect due such a generous individual. In this way, the rich also try to avoid the envy of the poor. In the village we have studied these traditional practices are being replaced by more modern practices, but the goals of gaining respect and avoiding envy remain the same. Since the richer villagers consider money spent on fiestas and fireworks as wasted, they prefer to put money into building a new road that will bring more tourists and weekend residents to spend money in the village or a new school that will give their children a chance to better themselves. In supporting these public works projects, they emphasize their own public-spirited, "cooperative" attitude in order to make the case that they are using their wealth for the community benefit. To visitors they express the wish that the village were more truly cooperative instead of being so egoistic and divided. In fact, they justify their leadership by organizing the others only for projects which promise profit for themselves, and they are the first to withdraw from the institutionalized cooperatives.

By making a show of "cooperating" more than others, they also try to soften the envy of the poor. Here is another example of how misleading it would be to judge character on the basis of stated ideals. Most villagers will state that they favor cooperation, and they may even cite the cooperative ideology of the Mexican Revolution, but their character and their actions contrast sharply with this ideology.

One notable exception to lack of cooperative activity is that villagers will join together to oppose a common enemy. They have worked together against a neighboring village in a struggle over water rights. And a number of villagers banded together to oppose an ejidatario who tried to use for himself what they considered to be communal land. But these cooperative groups dissolved as soon as the struggle had ended.

ANTICOOPERATIVE ATTITUDES

While the few entrepreneurs are likely to oppose any cooperative effort which might limit their own opportunity to make money (a credit union would compete with their money lending, a buying or selling cooperative would limit their activities as middlemen), this does not explain why many of the nonexploitative, traditional peasants are opponents of cooperatives.

It is our conclusion that the reluctance of these villagers to put effort into maintaining cooperative ventures, even when they promise them material gain, is influenced in large part by attitudes rooted in the hoarding character and in the traditional sociopolitical orientation. These attitudes must be taken into account in any form of cooperative planning.

First, the peasants distrust each other and are afraid that both fellow villagers and outsiders will steal from them if they have the opportunity. Sometimes these suspicions have been justified, but even when they are not this intense distrust and fear of being robbed are understandable in terms of the hoarding character syndrome. The hoarding individual's security system is based on protecting himself and his possessions. His fear is that others will take what he has, and he is constantly on the lookout for thieves. A small incident or evidence of dishonesty which might seem unimportant to another type of person is enough to convince him that his fears are justified.

The peasant's willingness to work jointly for public works projects contradicts the above only apparently. The hoarding individual can contribute small sums for public works despite the risk that they will be stolen, because it is a small sum, and it is only a one-shot affair. Furthermore, to exclude himself from public works would mark the villager as an egotistical person and do harm to his standing with others.

In contrast to the productive-hoarding peasant, the passive-receptive villager might remain in a cooperative with the hope that others will give him something, but he is too irresponsible and inactive to contribute to the venture. It is a telling fact that, comparing the 14 men who first opposed the rice cooperative with those who remained in it, the ones who left first were those with productive-hoarding characters, while those who stayed were passive-receptive ejidatarios.

Second, the hoarding peasant has a strong sense of private property, and feels happier and more secure when he has his own piece of land and feels that he depends on himself alone for his livelihood. It is difficult for him to take part in a cooperative which appears to threaten his security in controlling private property. The original followers of Zapata were willing to die rather than lose their land. For the hoarding individual, his property is part of himself. The more property he has, the more of a man he feels that he is. This does not mean, however, that it is not possible to organize cooperatives which respect the peasant's wish for private property, from which he can withdraw if it is not to his advantage to remain.[5]

_____

[5] One of us (Maccoby) visited such a peasant cooperative in Yugoslavia where individuals maintained legal possession of their plots but worked together in a cooperative in which they bought seed and sold their produce as a unit, divided labor according to different skills (e.g., tractor driver, bricklayer, expert on poultry, etc.), and received profits in terms of differential work and the amount of land contributed to the cooperative. Although decisions were made by a board of managers according to requirements of scientific agriculture, the members of the cooperative could replace

Third, we have observed that the productive-hoarding peasant does not like to take orders and is at the same time unhappy about telling others what to do. The first trait is related to the compulsive need for independence and the obstinacy that is part of the hoarding character. The second trait is related to the productive-hoarding person's fear of having to reciprocate. He feels that if he asks something of another person then he owes that person something in return. In a complex cooperative project, tasks must be allocated and someone must be responsible for their completion. Many peasants who have the capacity for leadership and are themselves responsible are unwilling to demand such discipline from others, because they do not want to feel under obligation, and also because they are sensitive to the dislike others feel in taking orders. As they see it, why should someone risk the enmity of others for a project which is, in any case, unlikely to succeed?

In the village the more productive peasants sometimes accept positions of responsibility but most do not want to be considered as leaders (*lideres*), a word which has a strong negative connotation throughout Mexico suggesting exploitative bosses. They are aware that the villagers distrust all leaders and suspect them of using their positions to get what they can from others. In fact, those who have accepted leadership roles complain that they always end up making enemies. Some villagers refuse to accept posts in the village government, and there was even a case of a villager who became sick with a psychosomatic back ailment on being chosen comisariado ejidal. Consciously, he considered that he could not refuse the responsibility. The ailment, which allowed him to avoid taking office, resisted both medicines and curings until another man was chosen in his place. The reluctant villager, no longer faced with a conflict between duty and desire to avoid trouble, got better shortly afterward.[6]

When a villager does accept a position of leadership, he hardly ever tries to force others to comply with their legal obligations. Although by law all heads of families must attend the assemblies called by the ayudante or pay a fine for absence, the authorities never attempt to collect the fines. If a villager refuses to "cooperate" on a project, he may be asked to contribute once or twice, but if he expresses strong opposition, his refusal to cooperate will be respected. The loose political structure of the village allows an individual to refuse to go along with the majority as long as his

---

the managers by vote at any time. It was proven to the peasants that they profited more by belonging to the cooperative than by remaining independent. However, some peasants were allowed to apply for limited membership in the cooperative for the purpose of buying seeds and selling produce only, while farming their land by themselves. In this way, the Yugoslavians made it clear that the peasant was not forced to join the cooperative, and he could wait until he was convinced that full membership would be beneficial to him.

[6] Foster (1967) reports a similar case in Tzintzuntzan.

behavior does not imply an attack against the majority (see Chapter 3). While this type of political structure avoids conflict, it minimizes the possibilities of organizing the villagers for many kinds of cooperative activities.

Once in a while a charismatic individual, like the two schoolmasters in the late 1930s who organized the cooperative store and other cooperative activities, will animate and stimulate the villagers to forget their fears and work together, but the cooperative spirit lasted only so long as the teachers remained. It was not possible to institutionalize their charisma.

There is always the danger that a cooperative project introduced by outside authorities who provide leadership may be treated as a semi-feudal setup, requiring submission to new patrons in return for favors. Anyone who tries, as we did, to create cooperative projects runs up against the peasant's attempt to place him in the category of hypocritical do-gooders seeking admiration or political support. And if the outsider does not want this, the villagers think he must be seeking to exploit them in some other way. It is deceptively easy to fall into the role of patron, cushioned by the flattery of the village and by the feeling that only in this way can anything get done.

Often outside authorities are convinced that their projects will benefit the peasant and they are taken in by the seeming submissive acceptance of the new plan. But this "submissiveness" is generally a way of avoiding conflict, and the peasants have no intention of following through. By not taking account in their plans of peasant suspiciousness, the authorities ignore the need to construct conditions which reassure the hoarding individuals. Such conditions would demand knowledge of the peasants' attitudes, as well as patience and ingenuity to change them. Many well-intentioned projects are constructed on shaky foundations. They may last as long as the outside authorities remain and the peasant feels it is worth his while to please them in return for benefits, but as soon as the authorities leave, many peasants automatically withdraw behind their walls.[7]

POSSIBILITIES FOR COOPERATION

Yet, well-structured cooperative projects could be profitable for the majority and benefit the village as a whole. Cooperatives for buying and selling would give peasants more power against the markets and the middlemen. Cooperatives based on the division of labor would allow individuals with talents outside of agriculture, masons, mechanics, and artisans, to

---

[7] Foster (1967), in commenting on the failure of community development projects in Tzintzuntzan, describes such a project and blames bureaucratic structures of community development agencies for demanding a level of cooperation that clashes with the peasant personality.

specialize and develop their abilities and would be an alternative to developing large farms under the control of entrepreneurs. The question remains whether the peasants' attitudes and character structure are insurmountable obstacles to the construction of institutionalized cooperative projects. Our study cannot provide a definitive answer to this question, but before citing our own experimental evidence, we want to give two examples which demonstrate that peasant individualism and suspiciousness can be overcome to a great degree, if a project is well organized. The Mexican government's CONASUPO program is an example of a project that has been successful, because it has built-in safeguards that take account of the peasant's suspiciousness. Beyond these experiments, the orphanage *Nuestros Pequeños Hermanos* (Our Little Brothers) is an example of another possibility of changing the peasant character by organizing a community on the basis of cooperative, life-oriented principles. Our own experience with a boys' club suggests the possibility of achieving higher levels of cooperation in villages such as this one by educating the peasant to become aware of irrational attitudes in himself, especially those having to do with traditional authority.

The CONASUPO program (*Compañía Nacional de Subsidios Populares*), until recently directed by Professor Carlos Hank Gonzáles, has two major goals. The first is to guarantee a fair price to the peasant for his harvest, and the second is to make available consumer goods to the peasants and the city workers at the lowest price possible, which is done through a network of CONASUPO stores which undersell private retailers while still making a small profit.

CONASUPO and the agencies that preceded it began by offering to buy the peasant's harvest (corn, grain, rice, beans, etc.) at a guaranteed price, paid in cash, and avoiding all bureaucratic procedures. The price was usually above the one private buyers would pay. The price was set both to protect the peasant from speculators and exploiters and to encourage the planting of crops which were either needed for national consumption or which could be exported by the government. It was expected that CONASUPO would provide a minimum price which would protect the peasant but not affect the possibility of a higher price being offered by private buyers. If there was an overproduction of certain crops, the government would store or export the surplus.

It was soon discovered, however, that many peasants were unable to transport their produce to CONASUPO centers. Speculators who owned trucks were still able to take advantage of the small farmer, buying his harvest at low prices and then transporting it to CONASUPO centers. The speculator benefitted, but the average peasant did not. CONASUPO was willing to send trucks to the villages, but it ran up against the problem that most villages lack storage facilities, and that peasants did not want to store their grain in a common warehouse for fear that they would be cheated out of their proper share.

The response of CONASUPO was imaginative and ingenious. A cone-shaped silo, based on a colonial model, was designed. It was cheap to make from local stones or brick, simple and beautiful, and extremely practical for protecting grain from animals and dampness. (The cone shape solved the problem of roofing materials which are often not durable and disintegrate during the rainy season.) Together with the offer of a loan for building a cooperative silo, CONASUPO proposed a system that protected individual property rights, demonstrated a way of making a greater profit, and offered safeguards against stealing.

A peasant who would act as a CONASUPO representative would be chosen by the village to be in charge of weighing the corn, grain, or whatever the village harvested. He would be sent first to a CONASUPO school to be trained in methods of judging the quality of the produce. Weight and quality would be recorded, with a copy remaining in the peasant's possession. This employee (and CONASUPO offered to train any peasant interested in learning) would be subject to discharge by the village assembly at any time. Furthermore, CONASUPO representatives would periodically visit the village to check on the operation.

As a way of guaranteeing to the peasant that he would profit by selling to CONASUPO, the village was told that they could keep the money loaned to build the silo, if they did not in fact benefit from the system after the first harvest.

Finally, as a dramatic safeguard against theft, the silos were sealed with three different locks, and the village was told to choose three men to hold the separate keys. Hence the silos could be opened only in the presence of all three. Most villagers were convinced that, while one man would probably be dishonest, and two might join forces, it would be unlikely that three men would conspire to rob the rest of the village, since that would demand too much cooperation. This was an ingenious way of trait taking, using the villagers' suspiciousness to reassure them.

The first step in instituting the CONASUPO system in a village is for the representative to speak to any assembly and explain the program. If possible the peasants are invited to visit other villages where the system has been established. The CONASUPO representative then rates the village's reaction, whether it is "very interested," "moderately interested," or "uninterested." There is a follow-up only when the village is very interested, but increasingly villages, which on their own have observed the success of the system and the profits to the participants, have petitioned for help in building a silo and instituting the CONASUPO system.

By instituting conditions that overcome peasant suspiciousness, CONASUPO has succeeded in creating a minimal system of cooperation with clearly demonstrable benefits for the peasants and safeguards against their fear of being cheated. Rather than attacking the hoarding character or traditional authority, it gives those with this character the chance for more effective organization; in other words, it does not change character but rather behavior. That the negative traits of the peasant character, such as extreme distrust and egoism, can be changed by a radical reorganization of social and cultural conditions is demonstrated by an orphan community under the direction of Father William Wasson in Cuernavaca, Morelos, called "Our Little Brothers and Sisters."

Around 1954, Father Wasson started a home for orphans, some of them young adolescents already with prison records. This home developed into an institution, or rather a community, that now comprises about 1000 boys and girls from the ages of 3 to about 20, living in Cuernavaca or in a branch of the institution in Mexico City. The boys and girls come from the poorest classes, from families in which the mother has died, and, in about 80 percent of the cases, in which the father has abandoned his children. Considering these conditions, one would expect a great many behavioral difficulties—either destructiveness or sexual problems—since they are prevalent among children and adolescents of the poor in Mexico as in many other countries. But contrary to such expectations, no major behavior problems exist among these children. There are practically no cases of violence in the sense of serious physical assault against either another member of the community, teachers, or outsiders, nor are there any serious sexual problems, in spite of the fact that the boys' dormitories are not far from those of the girls, and the kind of supervision is such that secret meeting would not be impossible. What is remarkable, however, is not only the absence of major behavioral problems but the presence of a spirit of cooperation and mutual responsibility. The boys and girls feel themselves to be members of the "family" and are proud of this membership, although this family is not based on the common tie of blood and is so large that it exceeds the limits of what could even be called an extended family. It is actually a community with life-centered values, characterized by a spirit of cooperation and responsibility.

The following is but one example of this spirit. "From time to time benefactors write and ask the boys to pray for them or some other person in trouble or seriously ill. For the boys the praying takes a special form: instead of kneeling to pray, they do a special act of kindness. Sometimes this takes the form of helping a friend or a stranger, volunteering to clean some place, or any little thing that takes a bit of extra time and consideration." [8] In fact, even aside from the Catholic character of the institution

---

[8] This, like the next quotation, is from a personal communication from Mrs. Robert Conti, wife of the Director of the adolescent group.

(although no boy's religious activities are controlled and no pressure is exerted to make him go to Mass or confession), the personality of the director expresses his sincere love for the children and his fellowman, and makes his teachings credible—teachings centered around the command to love one's neighbor, and the evil of selfishness and egotism.

It is interesting to study the conditions under which boys and girls coming from peasant stock not different from the people we studied in the village could change their attitudes in essential areas, especially those of cooperation versus selfishness and suspiciousness. Following are the most important principles which seem to us to be responsible for making this change possible.

1. *The principle of unconditional acceptance.* No child once accepted in the community is ever expelled, for whatever reason. There is nothing the child or adolescent can do which could lead to expulsion. This principle is carried so far that even when they are through with high school (the institution has a high school of its own, which is actually one of the best in the region) they are not forced to leave the community, but can go on to study at the university provided they devote as much time as their studies permit to working in the community. Even if they do not study, there is no fixed time limit by which they are forced to leave. This situation expresses the principle of motherly love which is unconditional, and which never excludes a child, regardless of what he may have done. Children are also not given away for adoption, in spite of many pressures in this direction.

2. This motherly principle of unconditional acceptance is balanced by the paternal principle of demanding from the child *respect for the rights of others and fulfillment of his obligations to the community in accordance with his age.* And what is done to enforce obedience to this demand in cases where the children violate or flout it? It is true that mild forms of punishment, mainly the withdrawal of certain privileges or spankings, are used. But these disciplinary measures are so mild that they would certainly not deter strong destructive or asocial impulses. The fact is that such impulses hardly ever manifest themselves, and hence there is no need for stricter disciplinary measures. In fact, the disciplinary measures are of relatively small importance for the control of behavior in comparison with what the institution produces, an atmosphere of solidarity and realism, with an absence of threat or any kind of brutality. It should be added that if any behavior problems arise they are "talked over" in a realistic, friendly, yet unsentimental manner.

3. Another principle which seems to us of great importance is that of the extensive participation of the children, especially the adolescents, in the

management of their own affairs. Every two weeks a "house director" is appointed in the unit of boys who attend secondary school. "This boy assumes complete charge. He assigns boys to their various chores: sweeping, cleaning classrooms, mopping halls, dorms, and windows. He also makes out the work staff for the kitchen, and *he* appoints any overseers. The boy in charge sees that bells are rung for Mass and breakfast, that study hall is on time and everyone present. He is the 'acting director'; if he sees that someone is not doing his job, he finds out why. The boys he appoints for kitchen duty plan the meals and cook them. They also make out the shopping lists and give them to the boy in charge of buying. Washing of clothes, ironing, and mending are done by each individual boy in his own spare time. Also, making his bed and keeping his locker clean. The boy in charge will see that the dorms are clean and neat. Very few need to be reminded of this duty."

The children cultivate their own vegetable garden and take care of the animals (chickens, cows, ducks, pigs). Aside from cooking, they also bake their own bread. While the system of participation, formally speaking, goes on under the general supervision of the director of the adolescent group, and does not constitute a co-participation in which formally the children have equal voice with the administrative staff, practically speaking they are independent and take responsibility for the management of the affairs with which they have been entrusted. It must be added that this system functions very well, and that there are no difficulties, for instance, arising in the self-management of the kitchen and other departments. We believe that this degree of responsibility and self-management is very important for the understanding of the low degree of aggressiveness and the spirit of cooperation which exists.

4. In relation to this, another factor must be mentioned which is crucially important. In spite of the fact that this is a rather large institution, it is conducted in a *nonbureaucratic spirit*. The children are not treated as "objects" to be managed by a bureaucracy, but are loved and cared for as individuals by Father Wasson and his assistants, in spite of the fact that by now they number 1000. This tends to show that where a loving attitude is genuine, it becomes credible and that what matters is not the amount of time that is spent with children, but the atmosphere which is created. Characteristic of this nonbureaucratic spirit is, for instance, the fact that in contrast to most Mexican school children, these children do not wear uniforms, and also the fact that the rooms are not numbered but instead are given names.

5. Another factor of considerable importance is the *degree of stimulation* which the children receive. There is a folkloric dance group, a mariachi band (string instruments and trumpets), and children play individual in-

struments too. All this was first taught by a music teacher who came from Mexico City, but now the older children teach the younger. The children also learned to make their own costumes, and the boys as well as the girls enjoy sewing. There is a carpentry shop, and there are classes in painting, sculpture, and ceramics. There are good soccer and baseball teams; a library of books and records is being developed, again under the supervision of older boys. The richness of stimulation compares well with that of a good high school or junior college attended by children from the middle and upper classes. In an institution attended by the poorest children in Mexico it is unique.

We have mentioned the five principles which in our opinion make it possible to have the remarkable results in behavior and attitude and to some extent in character which this institution shows. It is important to stress that these various principles form a unity or, as we might say more technically, a system. Many attempts for change are made on the erroneous belief that a certain symptom has a certain cause, and that if one changes *the* cause, one cures the symptom. This kind of thinking is based on a linear model of cause and effect. Stimulated by the progress in the natural sciences, and to some extent in the social sciences, it has become ever more clear that one cannot change a symptom by changing *the* cause which produces it. This is precisely so because every symptom is part of a system in which every factor is related to every other factor in such a way that if you change one factor you have to change all, or at least many others. Any system shows such a tremendous inertia and resistance against change precisely because it is so completely integrated that it has the tendency to continue in its particular structure. However, while on the whole one cannot cure one defect by changing its "cause," it is possible to change the system if one creates another set of conditions which in themselves have a systemic character and can produce a change in the system as a whole. To give an example, if one would apply the principle of unconditional motherly love and acceptance only, children would probably react in such a way that would make it impossible to conduct a large-scale institution. The situation would be different in a relatively small group, but even then we believe the motherly principle has to be complemented by the fatherly principle of realism and responsibility. On the other hand, if one employs only the principles of realism and responsibility without the motherly principle of unconditional acceptance, one creates a hard, bureaucratic structure which may force children to behave dutifully, but which at the same time will create a great deal of antagonism which, while repressed at the moment, will cause havoc in the child and, on the whole, lower the level of his energy and inner freedom. If the two principles, however, are fused, something new emerges which results in changes that each of the two principles by themselves could not achieve.

The two other features characteristic of the conduct of this institution are also important as part of the new system. The principle of self-management and the nonbureaucratic spirit stimulate a sense of responsibility, rather than enforcing a sense of duty by the use of threats and rewards. Eventually, the active intellectual and artistic stimulation intensifies the productive elements in the character of the members of the community; hence the hoarding and receptive tendencies are changed from their more negative to their more positive qualities. Or, to put it another way, the atmosphere of the community tends to dry up the destructive and suspicious elements in the personality and to feed the loving and cooperative elements. As a result those who have more negative traits than the average do not express them, because they would lose the respect and affection of their peers.

Needless to say that the success of the community would have been impossible without the authenticity and strength of Father Wasson's personality but this probably makes the difference between success and failure in many intentional and other communities, especially those in which most of the members have not developed a critical and independent attitude. As is to be expected in a traditional Catholic institution, the element of stimulating critical attitudes toward authority seems to be absent in this community, except in an indirect way in that the children can compare the reality of Father Wasson's attitude with both sadistic-authoritarian conditions and the ideological unreality to which they have been exposed all their lives.

THE VILLAGE BOYS' CLUB

Can individuals living within a village such as the one we studied develop more cooperative behavior? With the aim of seeking the answer to this question experimentally, the study introduced cooperative projects to observe the reactions to them, and to discover whether and which new methods of achieving cooperation could be instituted. The first attempt was a cooperative chicken-raising venture which ended with some of the richer villagers selling the community chickens. They claimed the money was needed to pay for school expenses, but most of the villagers had their doubts that the profits were used for this purpose. The second experiment was organized more carefully. The study formed a Boys' Club with the help of volunteers from the American Friends' Service Committee. The club, including about 20 boys ages 12 to 16, started by planting hybrid seed corn on land belonging to the school which was loaned by the village school committee, based on the agreement that the boys would get half of the profits with half going to the school. Later the club started raising chickens for egg production; milk-producing goats, Jersey Duroc pigs, and a cow were given by an American organization, the Heifer Project, to the club which paid only the transportation of the animals from the United States.[9] The aim of the club was to teach the boys new methods of farming and animal raising, to give them the opportunity of earning some money by their work, and to stimulate a sense of responsibility and an experience of cooperation.

At first the club suffered from the lack of cooperation characteristic of community development projects. The boys treated the study as a new patron which could bring unheard-of riches to them. They took no initiative in feeding the animals or in caring for the crops, but waited for orders from the bosses. The village boys did not believe they would ever receive the profits, and some took eggs, milk, or tools to compensate themselves for their work. When they became convinced that they would receive the income from the sales of produce, each began to accuse the others of laziness or irresponsibility, of trying to get more than his work deserved. In response to the discontent of those productive-hoarding boys who did more work than the others, we introduced a system of *bonos* or credits for the number of hours worked. At the end of the month half of the profits were reinvested, and the rest were distributed to the boys in proportion to their work. This resulted in greater satisfaction and harder work from the more productive members, but the boys still depended on the orders of the "authorities" and they would not take personal responsibility.[10] A schedule had been made indicating the days each boy would feed the animals, collect the eggs, milk the cow and goats, clean the pens and the chicken coop. But if one boy forgot his chores or did not feel like doing them, the others would neither pressure him nor do the chores themselves, even though they knew this negligence endangered the animals and the whole project. The more responsible boys did their work, but they were increasingly discouraged by setbacks due to others' irresponsibility. At this time, they felt unable to do anything about the situation. They were reluctant to pressure anyone else to comply with community obligations. Furthermore, they considered our study as the owners of the animals, and when their companions neglected tasks, their reaction was a passive discouragement with the expectation that the "patrons" would eventually assert authority and save the project.

The club had begun on the wrong basis for a cooperative venture, because the boys had received too much as gifts, and they did not feel they had earned anything by their own work. We first had to overcome the

---

[9] Our total contribution for materials to build a chicken coop and buy feed and tools was about $400, which was supplemented by other donations from Mr. Dewey Lackey (chickens), the Heifer Project directed by Mr. Paul Stone, and CARE directed by Mrs. John Elmendorf.

[10] The Boys' Club was organized and supervised at first by Dr. T. Schwartz. After he left the village this work was taken over by Maccoby, who was in constant contact with the boys, while the daily work was supervised by AFSC volunteers who moved to the village.

idea that we were rich patrons who would continue to feed the project. After some of the boys had begun to work and to feel a sense of ownership and after the system of bonos had been introduced to divide profits according to the amount of work done, the projects still remained in danger, because many of the boys did not work if the supervisors of the study left the village for a day or two.

At this point we instituted a weekly discussion of two hours with the aim of making the boys more conscious of these anticooperative attitudes so that they could see for themselves how they sabotaged their own possibilities for greater profit.

At first the boys blamed their neglect of the animals on lack of time and lack of knowledge, but they soon recognized this as a rationalization, since they had plenty of time to play or to sit around the plaza, and they avoided learning what we were eager to teach them.

What blocked their energy and self-development were the submissive-authoritarian attitudes which marked the peasants' relation both to government authorities and potential patrons. Each boy felt his only bond within the club was his tie with us, the patrons. Despite the new system of profits based on individual work, the boys still saw their fellows as rivals who were trying to get as much as they could from the club with as little work as possible. Even in our meetings, when one boy spoke to another, it was to accuse him, never to support him. When the boys spoke to us, they always sounded guilty, as though they feared that whatever they did we would be dissatisfied.

During the first meetings most of the time passed in painful silence. We asked them to say what was on their minds but we refused to follow the pattern they expected, to lecture them and give new orders. At one meeting no one spoke for an hour until finally one boy, the bravest and most responsible of the group, admitted that he had been thinking of going to a dance that had just begun. But he was afraid to say it, sure that the "patron" would be angry. The boys were told that we did not want to schedule meetings conflicting with dances and that they were free to go, but it was suggested that they talk some more at the next meeting about the fear of saying what was on their minds.

Discussions at the next meetings centered on the ever-present guilt that each boy felt before his parents and any other authority. The boys had been taught that to anger the authority for whatever reason meant punishment. Therefore, with parents, with employers, or with us, it was better to remain silent, to do what one was told to do, and hence to avoid any initiative. It was suggested to them that this attitude was the way a peon felt in the hacienda, but that it no longer was necessary for them to be this way. Indeed, with such a fearful and submissive attitude, they would be peons in their souls and never feel like free men; by accepting the idea that the right thing to do depends on another's judgment, they could never develop their own sense of right, they could never be the masters of their own activity, and they would always be more interested in escaping punishment than in the work they were doing.

After this meeting there was a surge of initiative and responsibility. We suggested that the Friends' Service Committee volunteer, who was living in the village supervising the work, leave for a few days to give the boys a chance to work on their own and then to examine the results. At the next meeting the boys were asked how they had managed by themselves, and they all turned their eyes sheepishly to the floor. This reaction was quite surprising to us since in fact they had done a good job by themselves, but they were unsure the authorities would be satisfied. They were unable to decide for themselves whether their actions were good or bad. Traditionally, authorities in their village show their approval by not scolding or punishing. Seldom do they stimulate children to feel satisfaction in a job well done. This attitude of always expecting failure is common to peasants in Latin America; Hirschman makes the significant suggestion that for many Latin Americans success is disconcerting because it demands a radical change in one's view of the world.

At this point, we tried to interest the fathers of the boys in the club so that when we left they would support the project. The club had now become a small business with valuable animals and some 350 chickens which produced 220 eggs a day. But we had failed to reckon that the parents were likely to feel, fatalistically, that like every other cooperative enterprise begun in the village this one would fail. Naturally the parents' point of view, well known by the boys, weakened their confidence.

In a last attempt to enlist the support of the parents we asked the ayudante municipal to call a meeting. When the parents heard about the difficulties the boys had in cooperating, and the losses due to negligence, they were all for giving up the club. Their immediate response was to express the characteristic self-deprecation of the peasant. "These boys are just egoistic," one father said. "You should move the club to a village that will appreciate it." "Why do you waste your time?" another asked. "These boys are not worth it." We assured the fathers that the boys had done a great deal, and that we would not leave until the club was financially solid, but privately we wondered how the club would carry on without help from the older generation and how the boys who were present at the meeting would react to their fathers' fatalism and lack of hope.

At the next reunion the boys were asked what they had thought of the meeting. By this time the group of boys who came to these discussions had shrunk from twenty to a hard core of six of the older boys who always came and one or two others who came from time to time. One boy said the meeting seemed fine. He was immediately challenged by the others. "What do you mean, fine?" one said. "They have no interest in helping us, they think we are no good, and they want the club to end." This boy and the others realized they could expect no support from their parents, and they decided they could do without it. "Already we know more about chickens than they do," said one boy, "and we have learned how to market the eggs. Even if they were to help, they would only order us around and take the profits."

This discussion marked the turning point in the boys' attitude. After this discussion the boys began for the first time to cooperate in setting a day in which each one took the others' animals to pasture. Before this, they had refused even to keep their goats in the same pen, even though this was necessary for breeding purposes. Each one carefully kept his own goat at home. Now they decided to build a roof for the goat corral. They demanded that others cooperate or leave the club. Those older boys who had before shunned leadership in order not to seem to put themselves ahead of the others accepted the fact that if they did not lead, nothing would be done. They organized a dance to raise money; and, taking advantage of the Mexican love of lotteries, they sold chances on a pig, realizing a greater profit from the lottery than they would have made in the market. They began to think of new projects, such as fixing up a village bath house, long run down by disuse, and charging a few cents for soap and a shower. They petitioned and received village approval for the project.

Shortly afterwards, three years after it began and after a year and a half of the discussion meetings, the study withdrew from the village and the boys' club continued to prosper under its own steam for over a year, which in itself is remarkable for such a project. However, the boys had grown older and were no longer able to spend time at the club. By this time one productive-hoarding boy had gone away from the village after passing examinations to enter officers' training school. Another of the same character type was attending medical school. A third was playing football professionally. Another of the boys who had at the start been typically receptive and passive was now taking a technical training course at a high school in a nearby city. Another boy from a fatherless family whose receptive traits had become more positive was taking a course in horticulture and was organizing a rock band in his spare time. Another boy with an entrepreneurial character had gotten papers to work in the United States. Only one of the original group, a very intelligent but, at the start, extremely rebellious and mother-fixated boy, was working as a day laborer, and he was trying to find a job in a newly-opened factory. Thus, one result of the club was to stimulate the development of more productive traits and a new sense of possibility in the boys, rare among peasants, to train themselves for more demanding and rewarding work.

The boys then decided that it was necessary for them to prepare a new generation to take over the club, but they found themselves stymied by the same lack of cooperation that had characterized the beginnings of the project. Finally a group came to discuss these difficulties with us. One of the boys remarked that he now understood what we must have felt with them, their irresponsibility, egoism, and rebelliousness. But he did not know how to change this behavior in the new members and asked that we hold meetings for the younger boys just as we had done for them. This was not possible, and it became evident that the club could not continue. With regret the boys sold the communal animals and the club was closed, some of the boys keeping the animals they had earned, to raise at home.

The aim of the project was experimental, to see first of all whether the young people could respond to a new opportunity and, second, to help the boys become conscious of deeply-rooted attitudes that made responsible cooperation impossible.

The first barrier to cooperative work was the feeling on the part of the more productive boys that the others would take advantage of them. This was solved by the trait taking bono system which gave greater profits to those who worked more. The second barrier was the attitude of defeatism and fatalism which was shaken by the experience of managing the club successfully during our planned absence and then analyzing the inability to feel satisfied and hopeful about it. The third obstacle was the authoritarian mode of relation which made the boys submissive to the new patrons and at the same time rebellious when they were away. The authoritarian mode of relation implied an egoistic, suspicious, and hostile attitude toward each other and a lack of responsibility for the communal enterprise.

The decisive and most important point in breaking through the authoritarian-submissive attitude was the meeting in which the boys criticized their fathers; this was not an emotional, "rebellious" criticism. It was a criticism in which they saw the fathers realistically, as they were; and they saw, furthermore, that the authorities were stifling their chances to grow. This intellectual and affective insight was the crucial point in changing their attitude. Although we did not plan this confrontation, we had prepared the boys for their new awareness that their submissiveness and fear of punishment made them passive and unable to judge for themselves, that they had been irresponsible because they were unable to respond to life. While before they could react only to commands, their new awareness produced a new kind of responsiveness. After the confrontation with the fathers, one of the boys opened the next meeting by saying: "Now I know what you mean about the difference between fear and the ability to respond. Before I always fed our cow because I was afraid that my mother would beat me if I didn't. But last week I looked into the cow's eyes and for the first time I realized she was alive and that if I did not feed her she would die, and I knew that I would never again forget to feed her."

How shall we describe the weekly discussions which were an integral part in the process of dissolving authoritarian attitudes? Were they psychoanalysis? Or group therapy? Not in the usual sense. The boys were not encouraged to talk about their personal problems or private hangups; no one complained about not receiving enough love from his mother; neither was there a discussion about individual goals in life, although some of the boys came to talk about these privately. There were three essential factors in the effectiveness of the discussion group:

1. The boys were trying to respond to a new possibility (reality) which would allow them to do interesting work with animals and gain material profit. They could see that their attitudes limited their efficiency, and they wanted to change them.

2. The discussion group offered the boys a way of critically analyzing both their work and the psychology of the villagers. In part the discussion group was a type of educational seminar very different from traditional village schooling, or, for that matter, conventional education throughout the world.

3. The whole study, including the village doctor and the supervisors of the club, had created an atmosphere of trust and confidence that contrasted sharply both with the authoritarian and fatalistic atmosphere of the home and the expectations concerning outside authorities. The boys had the emotional support first from us and later from each other, to confront authority. But we also made it clear that we respected their right to remain as they were. We did not push them to confront authority. Unlike group therapy, they did not have to work through a "transference" of their fear of authority with the group "leader," because they "worked through" the real thing with their parents.[11] Nevertheless there was an element of psychoanalysis in this session: but not in the conventional way. Here the analysis was restricted to one problem, the attitude toward au-

---

[11] Such a confrontation rarely happens without outside support. We know of an isolated village, Cuauhtenco, in the State of Tlaxcala, in which a strong spirit of cooperativeness prevails. One of us (Maccoby) who visited the village (with Ed Duckles of the AFSC) was struck by the uncharacteristic peasant cooperativeness and asked whether the village had always been this way. The village leaders, all of them young men in their late twenties, replied that up to five years ago the village had been run for centuries by the old men, and that in those days there was little or no cooperation. Then a rural school teacher had encouraged a group of young men, the present leaders, to dig a well, since the village had no supply of water, except what was collected during rains or imported. Using the crudest methods, they began to dig with shovels, scraping the earth out and, as the well became deeper, raising the earth in baskets mounted on handmade wooden pulleys. The elders ridiculed them, saying they were fools and that if water were under the ground it would have been found centuries before. But they persisted and found water at about 300 feet. Their achievement exploded the traditional authoritarianism, overturned the authority structure, and made them the leaders. They then demanded cooperation from other villagers in digging more wells, building a road to the village, and instituting a cooperative weaving project. The result has been to increase both hope and prosperity in the village.

thority, and not carried out with conventional methods but by explaining a good deal about the problem of authority. Even so, the decisive break-through might not have happened had it not been for the fact that in the meeting with the fathers they saw the clear proof of what had been told to them before. This session had a cathartic quality; the various pieces of their own experience and our explanation "gelled," as it were, and a real, though limited change occurred in their character structure.

The result was increased productiveness and cooperativeness and in-creased independence as shown by the subsequent careers followed by most of the boys. It is also notable that the boys did not become resent-ful and vengeful toward their parents. They did not blame them for their troubles, but rather took the realistic attitude that they had to become independent. They saw their parents more clearly and decided, *"así son"* (that's the way they are), and "we must be different."

Similar methods of opening the peasant's mind, of broadening his consciousness, have been described by Danilo Dolci in his work with the Sicilian peasant and by Paolo Freire with the Brazilian peasants and urban slum dwellers. Both men have described how the passivity, submissiveness, and egoism of the peasant can be overcome when he becomes aware of these attitudes and when he begins to think creatively about his culture and himself.

The experiment demonstrated that the development of critical aware-ness about reality, in this case especially about traditional authority, leads to a transformation of character, to greater activeness and responsiveness, which also resulted in greater cooperativeness among the boys. How such critical awareness can be furthered on a large social scale is a political and cultural problem of such dimensions that it transcends the scope of this study. Our experiment tends to confirm the thesis that not hate nor accusations, but radical critical thought which dissolves paralyzing illu-sions, is the way to change the peasant's traditional submissiveness and passivity.

Does the experience of the orphanage contradict our findings about the crucial importance of critical thinking? We do not think so, mainly because the case of the orphanage consists only of young, hence more malleable people. It is guided by an extraordinary personality in whom love for children is completely real. Such personalities are exceedingly rare, and all the more so since it is necessary that they also have great practical and organizational talent. In a sense, the orphanage is a life-oriented traditional community, more like the ideal medieval village than the modern world.[12] Eventually, the village is led by authoritarian men

---

[12] To what extent the adolescents who graduate from the orphanage will sus-tain the cooperative spirit they show as adolescents remains to be seen; one might suspect that they may adapt too well to a competitive, alienated society, precisely because their critical attitude has not been sufficiently awakened.

oriented to material gain who dominate a majority of submissive, passive people, and use this domination to continue the existing village system. Without the awakening of the capacity for critical thinking, the social structure will hardly change. On the other hand, in the orphanage there are no obstacles of an economic or social nature to be overcome. There are no problems of law, scarcity, modes of production, or exploitation by one class of another.

However this may be, we have given the example of the Pequeños Hermanos not because we want to recommend it as a solution of the peasant problem, but because we believe it is relevant for two reasons: first, because it shows to what extent children and adolescents are capable of undergoing important changes when adequate methods are employed; second, because the methods employed—even without their particular religious frame of reference—show that changes must be brought about by introducing a number of new conditions which are interrelated, these being a spirit of unquestioned human acceptance, unsentimental realism, stimulation, and active responsible participation. By comparing the principles employed in the boys' club and those in the orphanage, it can be easily recognized that they are very similar, except in the point of assisting critical thinking.

As far as the special problem of adolescents is concerned, Father Wasson's methods show that neither the principle of letting adolescents act out and thus "get rid" of their aggressiveness, nor that of threats of punishment is adequate to cope with actual or potential aggressiveness: making life interesting, stimulating activity, and a group spirit which does not admire violence or force all have an effect that neither indulgence nor threats can produce.

In short, what this experiment shows is that, given a new set of conditions, the traditional peasant character can to a considerable extent undergo changes, and traditional peasant behavior can change from antagonism and selfishness to cooperation. The main problem is to find those new conditions which in a systemic way are able to bring about these changes. And this is only achieved by an organization of social life that is conducive to an increase in the productive elements of the character structure.

11

Conclusions

This study was undertaken with three purposes. The first was to test a new method which permits the application of psychoanalytic theory to the study of social groups without psychoanalyzing the individual members of the group. The second was to test the theory of social character. The third was to discover data which might be useful for prediction and planning of social change in peasant society.[1]

THE METHOD

We started out with the premise that statements made by individuals when taken at their face value show us only what people think and feel consciously at the moment, that is to say, what *opinions* they have. Unless these statements are *interpreted,* they tell us little about the underlying psychic and usually unconscious forces that determine feelings, thoughts, and actions. Hence the results of polls and social psychological inquiries that deal only with *conscious* data tell us at best what people think and feel under the given circumstances and what they might think and feel if the circumstances remained unchanged. They do not throw light on what people might feel if circumstances were to change drastically. In contrast, if we understand the unconscious elements of the character structure, we are able to recognize which character tendencies can emerge under the influence of new circumstances, and even make predictions about such changes.[2]

---

[1] This problem has been considered in Chapter 10 and hence will not be further discussed here.

[2] The emergence of Nazism in Germany would have surprised anyone who had taken an opinion poll among Germans two years before Hitler came to power.

Our main tool for the study of the social character was the interpretative questionnaire as it had been first developed in the Frankfurt Study in 1932. But during our work on the present study we learned more about methodology. In the process of interpreting the questionnaire we had to struggle with the difficulty of distinguishing between ideology and conventional opinions on the one hand, and emotionally rooted attitudes or character traits on the other. Despite our theoretical sensitivity to the difference, we found that it was not always possible to distinguish between the two with confidence. The tests for agreement, the results of the factor analysis, and the significant correlations between character and socioeconomic variables provide convincing evidence that the method of the interpretative questionnaire is generally valid for scoring character. Even so, the data suggest that the Rorschach test appears to be a more sensitive method for scoring the dynamic tendencies that are most deeply repressed (such as sadism).

Ideally, we conclude it would be better to base a diagnosis of character on both the interpretative questionnaire and the Rorschach test.[3] However, one must keep in mind that while the interpretation of the questionnaire requires a good deal of psychoanalytic training, the Rorschach requires additional training and experience. Those investigators who have been able to analyze character from Rorschach responses—E. Schactel and R. Schafer are the most notable—were trained as psychoanalysts as well as in the use of the Rorschach test. Clearly, for the study of large social groups, the application of both questionnaires and Rorschach would require much more personnel and indirectly greater expense than would the use of the interpretative questionnaire alone. But even aside from this practical consideration it seems to us that if one had to choose between the interpretative questionnaire and the Rorschach, the questionnaire is preferable, since it allows one to observe the discrepancy between conscious and unconscious attitudes, between ideology and character, which is much less possible from the Rorschach.

Another approach which in some ways may facilitate the study of social character is the use of a projective questionnaire with precoded answers. Such a questionnaire would be based on the same theoretical considerations underlying the interpretation of answers to the questionnaire we used. Obviously such a method would be much easier to administer to large populations, and much less costly.

A projective questionnaire might include a number of items, such as the following:

---

[3] The TAT would be of further value. However, in choosing between the Rorschach and TAT, we found the former a better method for interpreting the most deeply repressed dynamic tendencies.

"Which is a better quality for a wife to have, to cook well or to keep a house neat?"

"What annoys you most, a person who is too messy or one who is too neat?"

The individual who prefers good cooking to neatness and who is bothered by extreme order is likely to be more receptive, while one who prefers order to good food and who is bothered by messiness is likely to be hoarding.

However, this method presents certain difficulties:

1. The projective questions must in fact touch deep-rooted emotional attitudes, rather than merely describing the ideology of a particular group. (The precoded answers used in *The Authoritarian Personality*, for instance, have been justly criticized because they do not sufficiently distinguish between ideology and character.) One should not underestimate the patience and ingenuity as well as theoretical understanding required to formulate good projective questions and a choice of answers which poll emotional attitudes, rather than conventional opinions or ideology.

2. It may be necessary to change precoded questions as the consensual attitudes within a group or society change. A question that elicits an emotional attitude at one period may not do so a few years later. For example, we developed a set of projective questions to study biophilia and necrophilia in large populations (Maccoby, 1969). The precoding of the answers was based on the theory of biophilia and necrophilia (Fromm, 1964), and the hypothesis that the set of questions were all related to the same variable (biophilia-necrophilia) was supported by the results of a factor analysis. In our early testing, in 1966, we found that the following question and alternative answers served to distinguish between people with biophilic and necrophilic orientations:

"Suppose a man whose family was starving was caught stealing food. What do you think the judge should do?"

1. Give him a heavy sentence.
2. Give him a light sentence.
3. Reprimand him.
4. Let him go.
5. Help him to get food and a job.

While in 1966 necrophilics indicated that the man should be punished, by 1968 almost all Americans said that the poor man should be helped to find a job. This change seems to imply a new national consensus in relation to poor people.

3. Any particular question (like any particular behavior) may mean something different for an individual (or social group). For example, we

found that among white Americans an indication of necrophilia was the greater number of times a year they felt one should visit the cemetery where loved ones are buried. However, in Harlem, New York, some biophilic individuals liked to visit the cemetery often, not because they were attracted to death, but because in the cemetery, in contrast to the slums, one could see trees, grass, and flowers.

To study any character orientation with precoded questions it is necessary to have enough items to get a clear-cut trend, so that one or two items which may have an idiosyncratic meaning for an individual do not make any great difference in the overall measure. Furthermore, one must show by intercorrelations and/or factor analysis that the various questions do in fact measure the same underlying character tendency.

Clearly, precoded questions lack the advantage of both the interpretative questionnaire and the Rorschach, in that one cannot discover new character tendencies because one ends up with responses relevant only to the tendencies into which one is probing with the questions. There is also a further danger in the use of precoded questions, in that it may be easier for the intelligent respondent to sense what a "good" answer would be and hence to be influenced by his wish to show his best side. While this is also a danger in the interpretative questionnaire (and less so in the Rorschach), the requirement of spontaneous, unstructured answers makes it harder for the respondent to control his answers. In responding to the interpretative questionnaire, unlike one with precoded answers, the individual does not have a range of possibilities before him, but must formulate his full answer by himself.

In spite of all these considerations we believe that precoded questions are useful for many types of sociopsychological investigation. The essential requirement is that, like the interpretative questionnaire, the formulation of precoded questions must be based on theoretical expectations, rather than expecting a theory to emerge from the responses.

In the formulation of precoded questions, a promising *strategy* for investigating social character would be to study a few key individuals intensively and, on the basis of this, to formulate projective questions to use with a large population. The precoded questions would be constructed to probe for the tendencies which had been found to be of importance in determining the attitudes and behavior of the key individuals who were previously studied in depth. For example, in the present study, we might have chosen a small group of both highly successful and extremely unsuccessful ejidatarios and on the basis of studying them intensively, devised precoded questions to probe specifically for the hoarding and receptive orientations.

The method of precoded questions would facilitate the study of dynamic tendencies in large populations. However, it would require the same theoretical knowledge, clinical sensitivity, and understanding of socio-economic factors as the two other methods. But only those who formulate the precoded questions and answers need to have this knowledge, not the people who do the scoring; this would not be the case with the interpretative questionnaire and the Rorschach.

The conclusion at which we arrive is that the ideal method is a combination of the interpretative questionnaire and the Rorschach; the second choice is the application of the interpretative questionnaire alone; and the third choice is the method of the precoded questionnaire.

THE THEORY OF SOCIAL CHARACTER

The study was an attempt to test the theory of social character. This theory postulates that in the social process human energy is structuralized into character traits common to most members of a class and/or of the whole society; the social character motivates them to behave in such a way that they fulfill their social-economic functions with an optimum of energy and a minimum of friction. The social character is the result of the adaptation of human nature to the given socioeconomic conditions, and secondarily tends to stabilize and maintain these conditions.

In the case of the village we found this theory confirmed. Our data show three main types of social character—the productive-hoarding, the unproductive-receptive, and the productive-exploitative—which are adaptations to distinct socioeconomic conditions: that of the free landowner, the landless day laborer, and the new type of entrepreneur. We also found that the individual's character in turn affects his behavior and its outcome within the framework of his socioeconomic situation. Those individuals whose character coincides with their class role tend to be more successful, provided that their class role objectively allows the possibility of economic success. Examples for this are the productive-hoarding and the productive-exploitative types. On the other hand, when the economic situation of a class does not provide the basis for economic success, as in the case of the landless day laborer, only exceptional individuals whose character differs from the social character of their class can escape from a level of extreme poverty and dependence into the land- or capital-holding class. The influence of character on economic activity was shown clearly in the fact that among the land holders the choice of crops planted is a function of character: furthermore, that alcoholism is largely dependent on individual character. Both factors, the choice of crop and alcoholism, in turn largely contribute to increasing the class division in the village.

The three main character types mentioned above are to be understood only in terms of syndromes in which other elements play an important part, particularly the mode of relatedness to others (love, sado-masochism, destructiveness, narcissism) and the relationship to father and mother respectively (mother and father centeredness). Only in terms of whole syndromes can one appreciate the full interaction of character, socio-economic conditions and cultural traditions.

While these findings have in general confirmed the theory of social character, our study has led to new insights into the dynamics of social change. First of all it shows that character is one of the elements which contribute to increasing the gap between poorer and richer villagers: this occurs in two ways.

1. The landholder with a productive-hoarding character becomes richer, while the alcoholic landless peasant—and even some alcoholic landholders—with an unproductive-receptive character, fall to the bottom of the economic pyramid.

2. Usually people marry a partner with a similar character struc-ture: as a result, children of productive, and in general richer, couples in turn tend to be productive, while the opposite holds true for the children of unproductive, and in general poorer, couples. Thus both the elite and the poorest classes perpetuate themselves and move further apart in terms of both character and material resources.

Second, our study shows that the new economic opportunities tend to attract individuals with a character structure which in the past was a deviant type with a limited social function. These are the villagers with a productive-exploitative character. To be sure, in the past there were also villagers who made use of others or tried to introduce new services. But they were looked upon with suspicion, or were disliked, and further-more their social role and their economic activities were strictly limited within the precapitalistic agrarian society. Today the capitalistic economy opens up much greater possibilities for such men by allowing them to own capital goods and to use the facilities of the modern economy. More important than this is the fact of their growing prestige. Instead of being suspected or disliked, they become the models, not primarily so because of what they do for the village, but because the movies, television, radio, and other forms of mass communication make them so. The adventurous, individualistic entrepreneur has become a symbol of progress, of the better and glamorous life which the villager sees only on the screen. But the entrepreneurs are by no means only symbols. They take the lead in pro-moting those changes in village life and its institutions which destroy traditional culture and replace it by the modern principle of rational purposefulness.

What we have just described leads to an hypothesis about the role of character in the process of social change. This hypothesis is an answer to the question of *how* social change is possible if we do not think only in terms of machines, techniques of production, political institutions, and scientific discoveries, but also in terms of human beings who have to function under these conditions.

We believe that a central principle in the process of social change is what might be called "social selection."

What is the nature of social selection? In a relatively stable society (or class) with its typical social character, there will always be deviant characters who are unsuccessful or even misfits under the traditional conditions. However, in the process of socioeconomic change, new economic trends develop for which the traditional character is not well adapted, while a certain heretofore deviant character type can make optimal use of the new conditions. As a result, the "ex-deviants" become the most successful individuals and the leaders of their society or class. They acquire the power to change laws, educational systems, and institutions in a way that facilitates the development of the new trends and influences the character formation of succeeding generations. Thus the character structure is the selective factor which leads to the successful adaptation of one part of the population and the social failure and weakening of another. The "superior" sector will have the advantage of greater wealth, better health, and better education, while for the "defeated" sector the opposite will be true. The stability of such characterological classes will, of course, be all the greater the longer the period of social stability. But however long it is, historical evidence shows that deviant and secondary trait personalities never fully disappear and hence that social changes always find the individuals and groups which can serve as the core for a new social character.

Our description so far does not do full justice to the complexity of the process of social selection. It would seem to be sufficient in the case where a small group becomes dictator over the whole population, imposing new laws and institutions: after one or two generations, new men whose characters have been molded by these new arrangements would have emerged. However, this case is purely hypothetical. In reality, even a gifted dictatorial elite could not remain in power for any length of time without a social and psychological basis in a considerable part of the population. What happens in fact is that the ex-deviants succeed in polarizing the whole society and attracting within a short time, if not the majority, at least a critical mass of the population; in this way their dominant position becomes increasingly a popular one.

In order to understand this process fully one must consider the fact that aside from the extreme deviants who form a small minority, there are much larger minorities whose social character is different from that of the majority, but not enough so to make them unable to function in their society. They may be said to have "secondary character traits" which are latent as long as the social structure remains unchanged, but which become activated when new socioeconomic conditions attract and mobilize them. A simple example of this difference is a primitive agricultural society dedicated to a peaceful and cooperative mode of life. The few individuals whose character is dominantly destructive and suspicious are likely to be failures in this society, because they are totally unable to function under the given conditions. Many others with secondary destructive tendencies, that is to say, with a greater admixture of hostile traits than the majority—but not intense enough to prevent them from functioning—will tend to encounter more difficulties in adaptation to socioeconomic conditions and be less successful than the majority.[4] Let us assume, however, that through changes in the external conditions the peaceful cooperative system was no longer able to function. The tribe might be then forced to organize itself for warfare against other invading tribes, or the scarcity of land may have led to competition and hostility among the members of the society. In such a case the former deviants might become the new leaders, the minority with the secondary traits might become their most successful followers, while those whose character was most like the former social character might eventually play the role of the former deviants and become a minority representing a secondary trait.

While this example was constructed in order to illustrate the process of social selection in its simplest form, there are plenty of specific empirical examples which, although more complex, show the same process. An example is the new merchant class that developed in Europe and North America from the 17th and 18th century onward. This class was characterized by the hoarding-productive attitude. It was adapted to the need for capital accumulation (rather than consumption), personal industriousness, sobriety, the obsessional drive for work, and the absence of compassion.[5] Only those who shared all, or at least some elements of this

---

[4] The reason for the assumption that the majority shares the typical social character, that only a small minority has a totally different character structure (the deviants) and that a larger majority has different secondary character traits, lies in the very concept of "social character." Over generations the majority's character becomes adapted to its social function, but because of constitution and individual factors, a small minority is not molded by the social needs at all. In the case of many others, although still a minority, character adaptation has not been fully established only because of these idiosyncratic factors of constitution and individual experience.

[5] Cf. Benjamin Franklin's list of virtues: moderation, silence, orderliness, decisiveness, parsimony, activity, sincerity, justice, cleanliness, quickness, chastity (later he added humility); but characteristically charity, love, or kindness are not even mentioned. Cf. Fromm, "Psychoanalytic Characterology and its Significance for Social Psychology" (1932), English translation in *The Crisis of Psychoanalysis* (New York: Holt, Rinehart & Winston, 1970).

"obsessional-hoarding-productive" character syndrome could become successful under the new conditions of developing capitalism. The same social character would not have been adaptive for the medieval artisan whose character grew out of the precapitalistic mode of production in which not saving and obsessional work, but a tendency to enjoy life, including work, was outstanding. With the new economic opportunities, the many whose character had a more or less strong admixture of obsessional hoarding traits became the successful group, because their character fit the new circumstances. That this process of adaptation was mediated by Protestant ideology is by now widely recognized.[6] Luther, the key figure in effecting the transition from Catholic to Protestant ideology, can be characterized as representing the radically deviant character: obsessional, hoarding (anal), father centered, unloving, and isolated.[7] While medieval in his views he stamped Protestant thought with his personality, and thus indirectly became a pioneer for the emergence of the new hoarding character.

In the same way that the deviant character and the "secondary character trait minority" rose to the dominant position, those who most fully represented the traditional social character became less successful under the new social conditions, and the purest types of the old dominant character became the new deviants. The same process of social selection can be found in the change that occurred from the 19th-century, independent small-businessman to the managerial entrepreneur in today's large advanced technological organization. The successful new managerial type is not hoarding and authoritarian, rather he tends to be flexible, team oriented, detached, treating life in the spirit of a highly competitive game, and ready to switch his full loyalty to any organization (team) he works for. Those men who were most successful in business a hundred years ago would probably not be successful today, and vice versa.

The process of social selection can occur in evolutionary forms or be mediated by political revolutions. Revolutions might accelerate the process of social selection, but they will not lead to lasting changes unless new socioeconomic conditions have developed sufficiently to attract the latent "characterological minorities." A similar process can be found in the quasi-revolutionary Nazi regime that polarized the population and attracted the character types which had already been socially discarded. A small core of intensely sadistic, destructive people attracted a larger group whose destructive traits were secondary tendencies. Once Hitler was close to seizing power (a fact made possible by a number of industrialists who

---

[6] Cf. the work of Max Weber on Protestantism and the Spirit of Capitalism, and Fromm's *Escape from Freedom* (1941).

[7] Cf. the brief analysis of Luther's character in Fromm (1941) and the fuller and more detailed analysis in Erikson's *Young Man Luther* (New York: W. W. Norton, 1958).

thought of him as a useful tool to combat communism and to enhance profits by large-scale rearmament, although they did not like his vulgar personality and ideology), this minority (essentially recruited from the lower middle classes) was enlarged by a still larger sector who had enough of the Nazi admixture in their character so that opportunities and fear could make them lukewarm adherents. The cut-off point was where the destructive admixture was so absent that not even opportunism and fear could motivate people to join the Nazis. Those with strong democratic-revolutionary characters opposed the regime and even became active fighters against it.[8]

While we have seen that in the process of social selection the social character is a dynamic element facilitating social change, it must also be stated that social character may be a delaying factor for social change since it is responsible for the "lag" between economic change and human adaptation to it.

The social character is formed by socioeconomic conditions which have existed over centuries and have resulted in the formation of ideologies, customs, and methods of child-rearing. This cultural tradition determines the character of parents, so that even though traditional culture no longer fits changed economic conditions, the children—through the mediation of the traditional social character of their parents and the old educational methods, ideologies, and values—are still determined by the past. Even if they acquire the *knowledge* necessary to be effective in a changed economy through a school system, their traditional character stands in their way. In the case of peasant society, punctuality, discipline, rationality, risk taking, satisfaction gained from work, and income as aims in themselves, cannot be learned: they are elements of a new social character which it took Europe approximately 300 years to develop. We do not mean to say that such changes necessarily take such a long time if instead of being left to the blind process of historical change they are planned intelligently. But we do mean to stress that the failure to understand this characterologically conditioned lag is one of the factors which Marxist theory overlooked, and that this led to the overoptimistic view that changed conditions would *immediately* produce a changed man.

---

[8] There are, of course, many individual cases which do not fit this general scheme. A good example is Albert Speer, Hitler's minister for armament production who, though a character without a destructive admixture, became a leading Nazi partly through the temptation of extraordinary success and partly because of his emotional ties to Hitler, whose relationship to Speer was perhaps the only relatively human one he had with any man. Cf. Speer's autobiography, *Erinnerungen* (Propylaen Verlag, 1969). These memoirs give many examples that reveal Hitler's necrophilous character. The basic character difference can be seen when Speer, risking his life, sabotaged Hitler's orders for a scorched earth policy at the time the Allied troops invaded Germany.

This general principle of the "lag" needs, however, an important qualification. It seems to be contradicted by the fact that the hoarding character of the European and American middle class which was prevalent until about the 1930s has changed drastically into a consumer character within one generation. In this case, the influence of economic conditions on character was practically instantaneous. Why did this happen?

The most important element to make this rapid change possible seems to be the unprecedented possibility of influencing man's character through the new communications media. These media do not appeal to the intellect, but have a suggestive power through their ability to put audiences into a passive mood by endlessly repeating the same theme and thus creating a situation which in many ways resembles that of hypnotic procedure. Never before had it been possible to reach and penetrate people of all ages so effectively as by the electronic media, which required no active effort on the part of the individual and satisfied his desire for effortless diversion. Other elements furthering the rapid change in character were the new abundance of consumer goods, advertising, and buying on the installment plan, that is to say, a system of constant and insistent temptation and seduction.

Does this not lead us to hope that through the use of these new methods of mass communication, characterological progress could be achieved as easily as regression? It is impossible to answer this question with any degree of certainty, but some considerations are conducive to skepticism. First of all, the mass media are in the hands of private enterprises, which themselves represent the prevailing spirit of an alienated society, and which, for reasons of maximizing profit, appeal to the characterological *status quo*. Of no less importance is the fact that it seems to be much easier to effect character changes for the worse than for the better. It is much more difficult to stimulate the development of a productive, humanly mature character, to find methods which appeal to the aliveness, reason, and independence of individuals, and which help to overcome inertia and emotional laziness. Such methods can be devised and applied only in societies whose aim is the full development of man, and not where man has become an instrument for achieving the maximum development of the Gross National Product.

Once such an aim is present and effective, the new means of communication may accelerate the process of character change, provided the methods are so radically transformed that they motivate and stimulate, rather than alienate their audiences from their deepest sources of productiveness, thus making them passive. But this medium is a dangerous one because by its very nature it appeals more to receptive than to productive attitudes.

OUTLOOK

The process of industrialization, increasing alienation and hunger for commodities, and the new values of industrial society, profoundly influence the mentality of the peasant in spite of the fact that economically he hardly participates in the new structure. What we find in the village, as in many peasant societies all over the world, is the victorious march of the spirit of technological industrialism destroying the traditional values and replacing them with nothing except a vague longing for the good life represented by the city. Cheap movies replace joyous fiestas, television replaces amateur theater, radio replaces the local band, and the cement plaza replaces one of grass, trees, and flowers. The peasant is at a double disadvantage: he has lost his own culture and does not gain the material advantages of the more affluent city population.[9] He not only is materially poor, but is made to feel humanly backward, "under-developed." He

---

[9] Our conclusions are in essential agreement with Rodolfo Stavenhagen's analysis of "Seven Erroneous Theses About Latin America" (*New University Thought*, Vol. 4, Number 4, Winter 1966/67). Stavenhagen in refuting the thesis that "Progress in Latin America will come about by the spread of industrial products into the backward, archaic, and traditional areas," writes the following:

A. While it is certain that a large number of consumer goods have been distributed to the underdeveloped areas in recent years, this does not automatically imply the development of these areas, if by development we mean an increase in per capita output of goods and services, and in the general social welfare. Often this diffusion of products is nothing but the diffusion of the culture of poverty into the backward, rural areas, for it involves no basic institutional changes.

B. The spread of manufactured industrial goods into the backward zones often displaces flourishing local industries or manufacturers, and therefore destroys the productive base for a significant part of the population, provoking what is known as rural proletarianization, rural exodus, and economic stagnation in these areas.

C. The same process of diffusion has contributed to the development of a class of merchants, usurers, middlemen, monopolists, and moneylenders in the backward rural areas, in whose hands is concentrated a growing part of the regional income; and who, far from constituting an element of progress, represent an obstacle to the productive use of capital and to development in general.

D. The "diffusion" is often nothing more than the extension into rural areas of monopolies and monopsonies, with negative consequences for a balanced and a harmonious development.

E. The process of diffusion of capital has taken place from the backward to the modern areas. Constant decapitalization of the underdeveloped areas in Latin America accompanies the migration of the best trained part of the population out of the backward zones: young people with a bit of education who are looking for better opportunities in other areas. It is not the presence or absence of factory-made goods, but this unfavorable outward flow from the backward zones which determines the level of development or underdevelopment of these areas.

F. This process of "diffusion" to which are attributed so many beneficial results, has been going on in Latin America for more than 400 years—and aside from certain dynamic focal points of growth, the continent is still as underdeveloped as ever (pp. 29-30).

dreams of the good life for his children, yet only very few of them can ever attain it. And if they attain it, is it the good life? All attempts to "improve" the peasant by making him better adapted to city life only reinforce the process of human deprivation, without giving him more than, at best, the belief in the paradise of consumption that his grandchildren might enter some day.

Is there a way out of this dilemma? Any attempt to answer this question would far transcend the scope of this study. However, we do believe that the future of the peasant depends, among other factors, on a better understanding of his character, and on a greater awareness of his needs and anxieties as they interact with his economic situation. We hope that this study will stimulate others to continue the research into character and socioeconomic conditions.

Appendix A:

The Interpretative Questionnaire and Examples of Scoring

In this appendix we reproduce the interpretative questionnaire used in the study.[1] We then cite examples of responses that are expressive of the various orientations. We found this no simple task. In many cases, it is difficult to find any single answer which expresses a particular orientation or trait convincingly. The reader will recall that our method was to score each trait after having read the whole questionnaire. Hence, the interpretation of each answer is influenced by all other answers. In practice, the scorer often finds that any particular answer may reflect more than one orientation, or it may be an ideological response. The final scoring decision depends on the evaluation of the overall evidence.

INTERPRETATIVE QUESTIONNAIRE

GENERAL DATA

1. Name.
2. Age.
3. Place of birth. (Where were you born?)
   Where were your parents born?
   In what year and at what age did you arrive at the village?
4. Civil Status.
5. Can you read and write?
   What schooling did you have?
6. Who are the members of your family?
   (The group that lives together now.)

THE INTERPRETATIVE QUESTIONNAIRE

7. a) Is your mother still alive?   a) Is your father still alive?
   b) How old is she?   b) How old is he?
   c) Where does she live?   c) Where does he live?

---

[1] The numbering of questions is not consecutive, since some original questions were withdrawn during the study.

8. a) How frequently do you see your mother now? (Or the person who takes the place of your mother.)
   b) For what reasons, if any, have you consulted her during the last year?
   c) Would you act against her wishes?
   d) On what occasions have you done so?

Question 8 is then asked in terms of the father.

9. a) How many brothers (or half-brothers, etc.) and sisters (or half-sisters, etc.) have you?
10. When you are in trouble or have problems, whom do you ask for help? Why?
12. a) Give a brief description of your mother (or mother figure) as you see her.
    b) Give a brief description of your father (or father figure) as you see him.
13. a) How did your mother treat you when you were a child? (Did she ever punish you when you did something bad? Did she ever console you or comfort you?)
    b) And your father? How did he act?
14. Describe your idea of a good mother.
15. a) Do you believe that your wife (or husband) is a good mother (or a good father)? Why?
    b) Do you believe yourself to be a good father (or a good mother)? Why?
16. a) When you were a child, did you fear the anger of your father more, or that of your mother?
    b) Do you think that children should fear their parents?
18. a) What do you think of corporal punishment as a means of educating children?
    b) Do you ever beat your children?
    c) Do they ever bleed when you hit them?
    d) Who is stricter in punishing them, you or your wife?
19. a) If you could choose, what job or profession would you like for yourself? Why?
    b) For your children? Why?
    c) Who do you think should decide which job or profession the children will choose? Why?
20. What is your work and what does it consist of?
21. a) What do you like most about it?
    b) What do you like least about it?
22. a) Besides your main occupation, what other work do you do?
    b) What do you do with your free time?
23. If you had the time, what would you like to do the most, and why?
24. If you had the opportunity, what would you like to know, or study?
25. What diversion or amusement do you like best? Why?
26. What film have you liked the best? Why?
27. What stories or novels have you liked best? Why?

28. a) What work in common have you done with others of the village?
    b) What would you like to achieve or do in terms of community work?

29. What other opportunities, besides the present ones, should the village offer to its inhabitants?

38. If it were necessary to create a new industry, for example, a big fish tank, or a chicken farm, how would you like to do it? Individually, or in co-operation with others?

30. In what do you find the greatest satisfaction? (In work, family life, leisure, amusements?)

31. a) How often do you drink (alcoholic drinks), and when you do, how often do you get drunk?
    b) And your husband?

33. What effect does the drink have on you? (Become aggressive, become very sad, mental blackouts, do absurd things, feel incapacitated, fearful.)

36. What is your concept of the worst results of drinking?

39. a) What was the saddest situation you have experienced?
    b) What was the most embarrassing?

40. What experience in your life has been the happiest?

41. What should a man defend as his honor?

42. a) What are the qualities or virtues a man should have?
    b) And what are the qualities or virtues a woman should have?

43. What do you think of "machismo"?

44. Which individual or individuals, present or past, do you most admire? Why?

45. a) What is your opinion of Pancho Villa?
    b) of Cuauhtémoc?
    c) of Jorge Negrete?
    d) of Emiliano Zapata?

46. a) What should a man do when his wife is unfaithful (betrays him)?
    b) What should a woman do when her husband is unfaithful?

47. Should women have the same rights as men? Why?

48. What do you consider the worst crime a person can commit? Why?

49. What are the forces that determine the destiny of man? (Birth, circumstances, etc.)

50. a) Do you think the day will come when humanity has abolished war? Why?
    b) Poverty? Why?
    c) Corruption? Why?

51. What do you believe love is? (What is your concept of love? Give your opinion in your own words and without limitations.)

52. a) In what manner does a father express his love? (In respect to his children.)
    b) A mother?

55. How do you interpret the commandment: "Love your neighbor as you love yourself"?

56. a) Are you a jealous person?
    b) Under what conditions are you jealous? Give examples.
57. a) Do you think there are remedies or good luck charms or anything else that make someone more loved or loving? (What are they?)
    b) Have you used them?

QUESTIONS FOR PARENTS ONLY

58. What things do you have to sacrifice because of your children?
    b) What would you do if you didn't have children?
59. a) When was the last time that your children made you lose your patience (temper)?
    b) Do your children make you suffer much? If so, how?
60. On what occasions do you feel happiest with your children? (Amplify the answer to describe the pleasure you have with your children.)
61. What do you do when your children cry because other children hit them?
62. When your child cries because you have beaten him or scolded him, what do you do?
64. a) What is best to educate children: to be strict or to be lenient?
    b) Which are you?
67. a) What games do you play with your children?
    b) What stories do you tell them?
    c) Do you make their clothes?
68. a) Do your children progress in school?
    b) Do you help them with their homework?
    c) What do the teachers say about your children?
69. a) What is your reaction when you see good marks on their school reports?
    b) When you see bad marks?
70. Describe each of your children.
71. a) Which child do you prefer? Why?
    b) Which one needs your help the most? Why?
73. a) What bad habits do your children have? (Help the person interviewed to understand the question, specifying factors such as lying, robbing, destructive behavior, bad sexual habits.)
    b) How do you explain these defects?
    c) How do you correct them?
79. With what do you generally threaten or frighten your children? (The police, the bogeyman, God, and devil, etc.)
80. What would you do if your daughter married against your wishes?

FINAL QUESTIONS FOR ALL RESPONDENTS

81. For what purpose do you believe we were born into this world?
82. In your opinion what is the worst vice?
83. Do you feel superior or inferior to others? In what ways?

STORY QUESTIONS

1. A mother is ill and sends her son out to buy the food for the whole family. Because he stops to play, the boy loses the money and cannot buy the food. What do you think the mother did?
2. A boy liked very much to paint but his father would not buy him the paints. One day he was given money to buy a schoolbook that he needed and bought paints instead of buying his schoolbook. What do you think the father did?
3. Various soldiers, armed and drunk, grab or caress the wife of a farmer who walks with her on his arm in front of a canteen (bar). What do you think about that? How do you feel about it? What do you think the husband did? What did the woman feel?
4. A young man marries a woman of whom his mother disapproves, and he must go to live far away from the village where his mother lives. His mother becomes sick because of the separation and finally dies. What do you think of the young man? What did he feel? And the wife?
5. A church in the village is robbed. The jewels of the Virgin are taken. How did the mother and father feel when they discovered that their son was the person who stole them and that they are the only ones who know of the robbery?
6. A farmer goes to the city to buy an expensive medicine, one hard to obtain and desperately needed for his sick son. He finds a friend and gets drunk with him, carouses and spends all his money. When he returns home 24 hours later, his son is dead. What do you think of this? How did the father feel? How did the mother of the dead boy feel? How did the friend who accompanied him and got drunk with him feel?

At the end of the interview, the duration was noted, and the interviewer wrote down his impressions of the subject's attitude and conduct. He also made observations on physical or mental conditions that might have affected the responses given.

EXAMPLES OF SCORING

A. THE MODE OF ASSIMILATION

1. The Productive Orientation. The responses that best typify the most productive villagers are their views on love (Question 51). The following are examples:

"There are many kinds of love, for a plant, for the land. First, there is love of God. Second, for a father or mother. Love is to love a woman, the love that one's sons grow and develop. One has many loves."

"Love is to respect all that is human. It is a sentiment one can have even toward a plant. I work my land with love because my children and I live from the plants."

"It is the nature that is one's self, that lets us live in the world."

"It is necessary, because to live without loving anybody is like not living."

"One can interpret love in different ways. A person can love a piece of land in which he has put the work of almost his whole life. Also it can be the love of one's family, of work, of all the things one does with sacrifice and feels true love. I believe then that love is all that I achieve with sacrifice and that it is a sentiment that is born in the most profound part of the soul."

"Love is very sacred because without love there would not be the world we would have if we loved each other, because even though there is friendship, it is not enough. One must love. Beginning with love of parents, of sweethearts, love of a husband, love of children, love of a good friendship; even to raise an animal one must love. It is incomparable, because people even commit suicide if they do not know love. The love of a father is eternal. One retains the love of friends even when they are away. Love of God, one must have also, for God sends us love in the form of understanding."

A loving man said that if the wife betrays the husband, "he should learn why this happened and try to change her way of seeing things, if he loves her." Loving men also have a more democratic attitude toward women. One man said, "Women should have the same rights, because they feel the same as one does. Besides that they are our companions in life." Another said, "They are also human beings. They have the same feelings as the men. When one marries, the priest says, 'I give you a woman, not a slave.' "

In these responses the villagers also expressed greater openness, interest, and activeness than the majority gave in their other responses. We should note here that in general the villagers' concepts of love strike us as particularly genuine and deeply felt. Unlike answers we have received from individuals in Mexico City or from urban Americans, the responses of the villagers are not repetitions of what they have heard or read. They are not attempts to give the "right answer," but in practically every case they express the individual's *experience*.

Many villagers, unable to read or write, have an "emotional literacy" which gives a poetic quality to their words and makes the city man's phrases sound empty and conventional by contrast. Even unproductive individuals often express a profound understanding of themselves and others when they speak of love, such as the young man who said, "Although you feel that you love a girl, you can never be sure that they pay sufficient heed to you. Love does many things to you. You even rob to please the girl who has captured you. You commit many barbarisms for love, and the illusion never ends. All your life in this world, you see some good things, but mostly you make illusions for yourself and you get no further than that."

It may be surprising to find so many productive answers to the question of what love is when in fact there are so few loving individuals in this population. But one must consider that it is one thing for a person to feel and express love in his real relationships and another thing to sense or "know" what love is; beyond that, he wishes strongly to be loved and to love. Even though these people do not love actively, love has not yet been completely alienated as is the case with the more "developed" populations of the city. Even in their fantasies about love, villagers express what they really feel it is, or could be.

2. The Receptive Orientation. A concept of love often stated by unproductive-receptive villagers reflects the feeling that all good things of life lie outside oneself, beyond reach; that one must await passively the experience of happiness or love, being grateful if it arrives but without power to keep it. For these receptive people, joy exists only momentarily, if at all. It may remain no more than a dream, a promise that never materializes, but which soon sours into disillusion. For one abandoned woman, love has become "violence, no more than that. It fills you for a moment and then you have nothing. Since it has never made me feel happy for long, I believe it does not exist, that thing love. Since the father of my children left me, I don't believe there is love."

In one young, receptive girl, the concept of love reflects oral imagery. "Love is a pretty thing. Drinking it in one feels fine. Not having it, there is no faith; one can do nothing."

Love for another moderately productive young man essentially is being loved by women: "Love is love of women, you can't have anything better. Tell me what other thing you can have that is better than the love of women. What else can one love? Only children, also. The woman that loves you, of course you have affection for her, you love her." (The "of course" is the key phrase in this sentence, since it trivializes what follows.)

Receptive individuals show this quality not only in regard to love, but they often refer to their satisfactions in getting food and to their frustrations in terms of inner emptiness.

One moderately unproductive-receptive man described a job he had at age 13. His response expresses gratitude at being loved and fed, and pleasure in not having to work.

"He [the employer] loved me like a son, not a servant, and he trusted me. He bought me fruit. I ate what I wanted. He brought me my shoes, my little clothes, my hat. I ate my fill. And I only had to stay in the house and care for the animals. I didn't have to worry about anything."

Now, as an adult age 37, this man still works for others, but longs to own his own property, "because even though the farmer doesn't see the results of his work right away, afterwards when there is fruit, one can go freely to pick oneself an ear of corn or squash to eat."

For him, as for many unproductive-receptive villagers, free time is "to rest in the house a while and then to go out in the street to walk around awhile (*pasearse*) and chat with friends." A common activity is drinking: "When I drink in a gathering of friends, I feel full of pleasure; I feel the impulse to continue drinking and to buy them another beer."

It is notable that the receptive villager may express values that are in contrast to his own character. The man who drinks a great deal, who gets into fights, and who loves to talk, admires those men "who never get drunk, never cause scandals and don't talk too much."

A rare example in the village of a productive-receptive person is a young married woman whose responses express generosity and loyalty, but a concern for maintaining her dignity.

The kind of work she would most like is "to be a cook in a restaurant." She likes to cook at home and to prepare the dishes that her husband likes. Furthermore, she volunteered to work in the breakfast program sponsored by the Rural Welfare agency, where she enjoyed "preparing and serving breakfasts to the little children." She adds, "if I were trained, I would be happy to work as a nurse."

This young woman left her first husband because he was too possessive. She stated "that she felt as though she were in a prison, and although the cage may be of gold, it is still a prison." The happiest experience of her life (Question 40) has been her second marriage, her feeling that it has not failed, that her husband does not fight with her, that there is harmony, and that he provides for her. She believes that "love is the care and the faith that one puts in a plant or in a creature."

It is notable that she expresses many of the values of the patriarchy, of submission and obedience to man. She says (Question 47), "The woman should not have the same rights as the man, because the man is to give orders and the woman is to obey them." Yet, both her character and her conduct indicate that in reality she is more independent than one would infer from judging her on the basis of conscious values alone.

3. The Hoarding Orientation. Hoarding individuals tend to "store" love as if it were a valuable and limited quantity which should be given only to those who merit it or have a special right to it. Furthermore, the hoarding individual generally tries to possess the beloved. The following are concepts of love expressed by hoarding villagers:

"I believe it [love] is composed of different forms, for work, a woman, for money—more exactly it is affection. I don't understand more than that and all that is good for one is love: a friend, a *compadre.*" This productive-hoarding man is reserved and formal. Like many hoarding individuals, he turns love into a more diluted and measurable affection, and he puts love for money in the same category as love for people.

"Love is what one feels for all the things one loves and belongs to one, like the land that gives us food and other things like that."

Here again, love is equated with possessiveness, as in the following example:

"Love is when one has one's children with one, in the home, and they do not go away." For this mother, love is possessing her children.

"I have only so much affection to give, and I give it to those children who are good to me." Here love is apportioned by an unproductive-hoarding mother like a limited supply of money to those who have earned it.

"A woman should respect herself in order not to be like the flowers. . . . The young men are like butterflies that seek flowers with honey. When honey is sucked, they go, and it should not happen to a woman that she lose her honey. Then the men will seek another. In any event, the men love the land more than they love their women. Women love their parents more, because they remain with them while the men leave." This woman remains unmarried and is becoming an old maid, guarding her love as if it were honey. She sees all men as exploitative, which further justifies (rationalizes) her own hoarding attitude to herself.

The positive values of the hoarding individual are the ones most characteristic of peasant societies in Latin America and Europe.

Men and women with the hoarding orientation state in the interview that they admire qualities such as formality (lack of intimacy), hard work, saving, cleanliness, efficiency, respect for law, traditions, and obligations. A virtuous man or woman is one who owes nothing to anyone, who is self-sufficient and independent, and who does not indulge himself or fall victim to vices such as drinking. (It is characteristic of the hoarding mode that ideals are so often expressed in negatives rather than in positives.)

In order to distinguish between individuals who merely repeat conventional peasant hoarding values and those whose values are rooted in their character, the scorer must always consider the total context of questionnaire responses. A receptive person may repeat hoarding ideals, but he may do so without conviction, and there may be contradictions between his conscious values, e.g., "independence," and his dynamic needs, e.g., for magic helpers or "good patrons." Furthermore, hoarding individuals express their orientation in statements about what most satisfies them, what shames them, and what makes them sad. Unproductive-hoarding individuals often express their greatest satisfaction not in any concrete activity, but in the state of having possessions and/or family safe and secure, as if they were planted behind walls. Their most intense experiences of shame or sadness involve losing their goods, being left empty-handed. Satisfaction for productive-hoarding peasants is in active work. They are ashamed when they feel they have lost their values or failed to comply with their obligations.

The positive qualities of the hoarding individual are expressed in responses that affirm independence, patience, dedication, and interest in preserving and building. A productive-hoarding farmer stated that what he most likes in his work is "that which needs care, which is pretty and happy, to raise a plant, to see that one produces something." Another productive-hoarding man spends his leisure in sports, "because in sports there are no vices or betting, where you can lose money." Productive-hoarding women often sew to earn extra money, but at the same time they enjoy doing the fine needle work.

In contrast, the negative hoarding traits are expressed by individuals who work just to make money ("what I most enjoy is harvesting, especially when I am going to make a good profit") or those even more unproductive villagers whose ideal is owning a store and making money without much work, spending leisure time resting so as not to "use up" limited energy. Unproductive-hoarding women prefer cleaning and ironing (cleanliness and order) to cooking. In contrast to productive-receptive women who enjoy cooking, a hoarding wife states (Question 21), "What I dislike most is the kitchen, being always near the fire, watching to see that things don't spill over, getting dirty." Another hoarding woman would like to own a little store, "because it is a good business, a clean one, and one gains money."

In general, the hoarding individual has a particular affinity to moralistic maxims and codes, which reflect his concern for order and correctness. More than either the receptive or the exploitative individuals, the hoarder is judgmental and rigid in stating the values which support his mode of assimilation. For him intimacy is a threat, and he strongly defends values which protect him from the demands of others and the world. He has no sympathy for those who threaten his possessions or his privacy, and many villagers with hoarding traits see robbery, taking "what one has not worked for, what belongs to another," as the worst crime of all, worse than murder. Even adultery is considered a crime against property by the hoarder, since it implies taking a woman who belongs to someone else. Similarly murder is described as "taking away a life one has not given."

The unproductive-hoarding character can be distinguished particularly by moralism, rigidity, and often by contempt for those who are weak and self-indulgent. These individuals may stress that man determines his own destiny in order not to feel they owe anything to those who are failures.

4. The Exploitative Orientation. The exploitative individual is most concerned with getting things from others without giving anything in return. The high value he puts on the person who gives and helps sometimes makes him appear similar to the receptive person. But the difference is that, while the receptive individual also values submission, loyalty, and affection, the exploitative individual values either cleverness, "intelligence," and ambition or force as ways of securing what he wants. One moderately productive-exploitative villager states (Question 42), "What I understand by qualities is very extensive, a great deal of science in diverse areas and the virtues follow from that, to be as expert as possible." The qualities desired in others are based in their material usefulness to the exploitative individual. The same villager, speaking of the qualities or virtues a woman should have, says, "She wouldn't have any reason to be educated if this isn't useful to her husband."

The exploitative men generally see love in terms of sex only, as using another person. They are suspicious of love, afraid to be trapped by it, afraid they too will be used. One man, more honest than most, speaks openly of his exploitative motives, which he characteristically generalizes to all men. "I don't believe a man loves a woman just because he loves her. In the first place, we must force her to do the work of the household and in the second place, she is going to serve us and to ease the tensions [sexual] of our nature."

The unproductive exploiter schemes in order to get something from others with a minimum of effort. He is ambitious for success without actually producing anything. In answer to Question 19, a number of unproductive-exploitative men dream of being bureaucrats or lawyers, because they think they could then get rich at the expense of others. Those with more modest ambitions think of small-scale commerce, buying cheap and selling dear, although many lack the interest in maintaining a small shop, which appeals more to the hoarding character. Exploitative individuals often express high ambitions for their children. They may rationalize these unrealistic wishes by saying it would be good for the children or even "useful" for the nation's progress, but they expect to reap benefits from the children's success.

Generally, we found the exploitative tendencies mixed with other orientations. In many cases, a receptive orientation to the mother is combined with an exploitative orientation to other women as in this man: "Who knows? That same affection pulls you. Love for a mother is a sincere affection; one feels loved. For one's wife, it is already to one's advantage to feel affection, not like that affection one has for parents."

In other cases, exploitative tendencies are mixed with the hoarding orientation. One exploitative-hoarding man considers women as property to be guarded and exploited. He described the ideal woman as follows: "She should be honorable, love her husband and not make a fool out of him. She should work hard." He feels the soldiers in Story 3 were wrong to manhandle the woman, "because she was not *their* woman, so they had no right to push her around."

The more productive-exploitative traits are generally shown in the individual's interest in developing new resources and in his initiative. These men characteristically speak of "utilization" of resources and of progress, of using new methods to increase gain. In contrast, unproductive-exploitative men value force and cunning to get what they want from others. For these men, working hard implies letting oneself be used and made into a fool (*pendejo*).

B. THE MODE OF RELATEDNESS

1. Sadism. Sadistic tendencies are so commonly repressed or rationalized that it is often extremely difficult to interpret them. Generally, they are combined with an authoritarian attitude to children. A clear indication of sadism is a parent's enthusiasm about physical punishment, the lustful quality expressed when he or she describes how a child should be punished. In response to Story 1, a sadistic woman stated: "Of course, one must whip him for his carelessness, make him feel the pain and he won't do it again."

Sadistic tendencies are often expressed in the quality of threats to disobedient children. Although the majority of the villagers threaten children, the sadists are likely to tell their children that the crocodile or the wild cat will come and eat them if they don't behave. Those with sadistic tendencies may also describe with pleasure incidents in which they frightened others, or humiliated them.

Sadistic tendencies also may be expressed in descriptions of movies or stories most enjoyed. For example, one villager described his favorite movie as one in which a man "tries to force a woman and overcome her, because she thinks she is the master [*dueña*]. . . . This plot is very interesting. Finally, he convinces her by force and lets her feel who the master really is."

In describing the "worst crime a person can commit" (Question 48) sadistic tendencies are expressed when the individual elaborates on the crime, showing his fascination with the details of violence. Or he may express his need to control his sadistic impulses, as in the case of a man who stated, "It isn't good to shed blood just because one feels like it [*tenga ganas*]." Other responses by the same individual show concern that his sadistic tendencies will get him into trouble.

2. Masochism. The masochistic orientation is traditionally considered the normal one for women in relation to men. For this reason, most of the women expressed a masochistic ideology. They stated that women should obey men, that they should comply with their obligations even if the man betrays them. One woman answered Question 47 saying, "We cannot have the same freedom a man has, for only he is master of himself and of his freedom."

There are differences, however, between women whose masochistic expressions are rooted in their character structures and those who merely repeat formulas. Furthermore, many women express conflict between masochistic tendencies and self-affirmation, and some reject the submissive-masochistic role.

A woman with strong masochistic tendencies said (Question 46a): "The husband should beat the wife. The woman should suffer. She should take it [*aguantarse*]. The man is free to do what he wants, but the woman no!" In response to Story 3, she also expressed destructive tendencies. The husband "should kill those who offend his wife." She admitted in the interview that her husband sometimes beats her, but she interpreted this as proof of his love.

The masochistic mode of relatedness to children was found to be most characteristic of mothers. The masochistic mother bears pain and suffering as a virtue, as long as her children remain attached to her. As is true of the sadist, intimate relationships have the quality of *symbiotic attachments,* but the masochistic mode is to hold others by submitting to them, by suffering indignities, by asking in effect to be used as a door mat.

One masochistic mother described mother love as follows: "The mother, the love that she has for her children, is that the more they do to you always you placate them. Even when your son insults his mother, you don't say anything to him." Some masochists feel others should value them because of their suffering and sacrifices. Here masochism combines with a narcissistic orientation to produce a "martyr complex."

While the sadist threatens with force, the masochist often threatens by playing on the child's guilt and on his fear of losing the parent. Masochists sometimes say that they respond to the child's disobedience by suffering or by becoming ill.

Questions 58 and 59b ask: "What things do you have to sacrifice because of your children?" and "Do your children make you suffer much?" While masochists tended to answer these questions as one would expect, stressing their suffering and sacrifices, it is important that the scorer separate masochism from the real sacrifices and suffering of mothers in a Mexican village. In poor families, loving mothers deny themselves in order to feed their children, and the lack of medical care and food causes extreme suffering. The difference between a loving mother and a masochistic one lies in the motivation for the suffering and the use made of it to maintain a dependent-symbiotic union with children. This can be determined only in the context of total responses; even then, there are a number of Mexican women who combine masochism with real love.

Other statements that indicated masochistic tendencies were in response to questions about movies and stories most enjoyed or historical figures most admired. Religious movies or stories sometimes appeal to masochistic women, especially those dealing with the passion or the suffering and martyrdom of saints. These women are not concerned with the martyrs' convictions but rather with the capacity to suffer as proof of blessedness. When the element of destructiveness is strong, it will be expressed in the intense concern with wounds, dying, and death, and the lack of interest in what is joyful.

Individuals with masochistic tendencies sometimes stated a particular admiration for Cuauhtémoc, who would not give up the hiding place of the Aztec treasure even though he was tortured to death and his feet were burned. Both sadists and masochists showed their special interest in the story by repeating the details with relish.

3. Destructiveness.[2] Like sadism, destructiveness is generally disguised in rationalizations. While the sadist aims at making children feel his power, the destructive parent tries to deaden all impulse life in his or her children for the sake of order. Parents with strong destructive tendencies punish sexual behavior, messiness, or playfulness. In other words, what most displeases these parents (Question 77) is what is most alive about the child. The reason given for this attitude is that one must do everything possible to make sure the child does not become an immoral person.

In relation to children, the destructive orientation is revealed in what is not expressed as well as in what is expressed. Missing from the destructive individual's responses are sympathy and compassion. While the sadist can feel a lustful pleasure in punishing and controlling, the destructive person experiences cold satisfaction, at most. Rather than beat a child, some destructive parents ostracize or coldly cut off relations with the child who displeases them. These threats of punishments are more terrifying than beatings, and a child may be more frightened by an icy look from a destructive parent than by the prospect of a beating.

Some parents with destructive tendencies seem to hold democratic ideals. They may say, for example, that children should be allowed to decide on their own futures. But a careful analysis in the light of other responses shows that such a seemingly democratic attitude reflects indifference, lack of caring about the child, or the certainty that the parent

---

[2] We remind the reader that the analyses were done before Fromm had developed the theory of necrophilia. See Fromm (1964), Maccoby (1969).

has so well succeeded in moulding his child that there is no longer any need to use force. Usually, however, destructiveness combines with authoritarianism and sadism. Such destructive-authoritarian parents are contemptuous of weakness in children. In reply to Questions 61 and 62, they expressed annoyance when their children cry because of punishment or because of fights with other children.

Sometimes destructiveness is expressed in overstrong denial. One woman with repressed destructive impulses tried to give the impression of being a responsible and loving mother. She described in detail how she suffered for her children and sacrificed herself. However, when she stated the worst crime was "killing one's own children," we interpreted the response as one indication that she was guarding against hostile feelings toward her children. The conventional method of scoring might consider this answer another proof of her concern for her children, but psychoanalytically one would ask why the idea of infanticide would come to mind in a woman who supposedly loved her children so dearly, especially when it is a response rarely given in the village. In fact, alerted by these contradictions, we investigated and discovered that this woman often neglected her children, leaving them without food, while she spent her money on jewelry for herself, a most rare occurrence in the village.

In his relations with women, the destructive male seldom shows the need for dependency that one finds in many sadists. If the woman betrays you, one destructive male stated icily, "What you should do is separate her from this world. You should kill her because this betrayal has no pardon." The woman, on the other hand, "should conform herself to her luck."

The destructive person's enjoyment of others' misfortunes usually slips out, even though such satisfaction may be hidden beneath rationalizations stressing rigid morality, order, or economic necessity, e.g., "He got what he deserved," "God punished him," "The fittest should survive." He feels more indignant about "crimes" such as dirtiness, drinking, and robbery (even stealing food to stay alive) than he does about crimes which destroy life, or the crime of calumny which is moral destructiveness. The destructive person's ideal of abstract justice is even more important than his emotional ties to those closest to him. In response to Story 5, destructive parents were the only ones who said they would have handed the child over to the authorities if they had found out that he had stolen from the church. In contrast, the sadist might have beaten the culprit, but he would have wanted to keep his child by his side.

Destructive tendencies also emerged in response to Story 6, which describes how a farmer goes to the city to buy medicine urgently needed by a sick child. He meets a friend and they spend all the money on drink and women. On returning, the farmer finds the child is dead. Practically all of the villagers felt the farmer would feel deeply remorseful and that the mother would feel great sorrow. However, destructive individuals made it clear that since it was not his own child, why should the friend feel anything? After all, *he enjoyed himself*. Cynicism such as this in the face of tragedy implies lack of concern for life and sometimes satisfaction in proving that man in general is destructive. Destructive individuals also said that the tragedy served the farmer right, that it was his just reward for his bad conduct. Similar characteristics are expressed in those who think less about the sadness of the mother in the story than about impulses she might have for revenge against her husband.

4. Narcissism. Low-grade narcissism (narcissism I) generally means indifference, but without destructiveness. As a dominant orientation, narcissism I is more common among those who are unmarried and without children. This orientation often cannot be scored in terms of any one particular statement, but rather by the general lack of deep relatedness and responsiveness. As the factor analysis revealed, there are different types of narcissism I. Young people may express narcissism in their lack of compassion combined with overconcern about their own sensibilities and complaints about parents who do not "understand" them. Often they express a liking for sugary movies, full of sentimentality, and with facile happy endings. Their attraction to sentimentality serves as a shell to protect them from deeper feelings. The individuals they most admire are popular singers and film stars who live glamorous lives.

In older people, low-grade narcissism may be expressed in overconcern about one's illnesses and bodily functioning to the exclusion of more productive interests.

In relation to the other sex the low-grade narcissist is generally more concerned about his image or about public opinion than about losing his wife. What he fears is getting too involved, either in people or in "difficulties."

An example is the following response by a man to question 46: "I believe the man should leave her, because he can't do anything. As the saying goes, 'kill her or leave her,' but better leave her and avoid difficulties."

Extreme narcissism (II). People with this character orientation, in describing their relations with the other sex, generally present a more impressive image of themselves. Simple respect and public approval are not enough for them. They must see themselves as superior and convince others of it. Depending on the other modes combined with extreme narcissism, the image may be of power, destructiveness (the macho), of love, suffering, or saintliness.

In answer to Question 46, the narcissist's preoccupation was in maintaining his image. "One shouldn't hit her, one should take it like a man, but yes, one should leave her, never take her back, so that she sees that one is a man." (Of course, this could be an expression of a sense of weakness rather than strong narcissism.) Women, too, should be concerned about their image, but a very different one. "If she is really a woman [*muy mujer*], she should take it [*aguantar*], resign herself. If she isn't, then she should also leave him." As with narcissism I, there is no concern about the individual relationship itself, about understanding what has caused the rupture and trying to mend it.

Two types of male narcissists are to be found. One is the sadistic-destructive male (the macho) with his image of invulnerability. The second is the type of man who sees himself as morally superior to others.

An example of the latter is a man who responded to Question 46 as follows:

"The man should be prepared to be an adult and be able to confront a difficult situation such as this. He should proceed, arriving at the moment in a judicious manner, serene and as much as possible with nobility. It is crude to kill a woman for infidelity, crude also to beat her and mistreat her, although there is no excuse that apparently justifies betrayal. The most noble would be to separate the woman from the home with all possible care and without even touching her. Her punishment should be to lose her husband and family."

Although few peasants admit to considering themselves better than others, the extreme narcissists make it clear in their responses that others are inferior in their failure to live up to obligations, in their vices, in their lack of honor. In other words, they build themselves up by putting others down. An intelligent narcissist said, "There are very poor people, poorer than I. There are many that find no meaning to their lives and they go off to drink, to drink and pass the time with women and friends. I need nothing of that!" What he says is correct, but his motive in this and other responses is to show his own superiority.

Generally, the extreme narcissist's questionnaire is not difficult to score, since he welcomes the opportunity to lecture the examiner, to expound theories, and relate his life history in an overly detailed fashion.

In response to Story 3, narcissism emerged in moral disapproval of everybody concerned, of the soldiers as well as of the woman who has been attacked. "The husband, if he was a man, strong and with a modicum of culture and a spirit of dignity would put himself at the defense of his companion. The woman should feel shame at putting her husband in that situation." He then implies that it is the woman's fault.

5. Indulgence. As the factor analysis in Chapter 5 shows, indulgence is rooted basically in a receptive-passive orientation, but without

severe pathology, and sometimes it is combined with expressions of real love. Generally, an element of conditional love, of giving in order to be loved, is present. Indulgence, as we scored it, is mainly expressed in the relations of parents to children.

The indulgent parent emphasizes giving and forgiving, without any interest in whether or not indulgence is what the child needs. The "love," or giving, is limited only by the giver's means, but the indulgent parent wants to be loved in return and generally feels sad or depressed if his gifts are not appreciated.

Many indulgent responses reveal an underlying passive-receptiveness and fear of angering the child by not giving him what he wants or by treating him firmly. For example, one indulgent father felt that children should not fear their parents because "The children should be happy with the parents so that one day they don't come to tell their friends in the street that one treated them badly and hit them."

In responding to Story 1, the indulgent parent's response is generally one of giving the child more money. These responses often show a passive and laissez-faire attitude toward the child. The quality of this response becomes clearer if we contrast it with that of the actively loving parents who respond to the ambiguity of the question by distinguishing whether the child is too young to be responsible or old enough to know better. If the child is too young, the loving individual blames the parent in the story for demanding more than the child is able to do. If the child is older, the loving parent considers that he must be made to see his irresponsibility and the consequences of his loss, although he should not be punished. Loving parents do not use force, but they believe parents should educate their children.

Responding to Story 2, the indulgent parent generally sees the boy's action as rebellion or a frivolous impulse (*capricho*) which should be forgiven, while the loving parent is aware of the boy's interest in painting and tries to support the child's attempt to develop his artistic abilities. One loving parent even expressed sadness that the child would lack enough trust in his parents to ask for the paints that he obviously needed. Another says, "Be happy because he paints pictures to color his notebook."

Indulgent parents often idealize children and deny they have any faults. They prefer not to see painful realities in order to avoid unpleasantness with the children.

In describing how a father or a mother should show their love, an indulgent villager says a father expresses his love "by pampering and petting." Another says: "Affection and pity. The father who is good pampers and watches the children and is just like the mother." One more loving-indulgent parent says a good mother "serves her children with pleasure, doesn't scold." Another says that the mother expresses her love by "caressing, giving in occasionally, pampering and giving them what they want." The key to distinguishing these responses from more productive love is the indulgent parent's need, seen throughout the interview, to buy affection, as well as his passiveness and lack of understanding of the child's individual needs.

6. Conditional Love (Material Care). Conditional love is more a behavioral than a dynamic category, but we singled it out because it is so frequently encountered in the village, especially in relations of parents with children. It is generally rooted in a combination of moderate productiveness, traditionalism, and a concern for preserving life (productive hoarding).

Conditional love implies material care and a limited affectionate concern toward children in the sense that the parent is exclusively concerned with the child's material well-being. Negatively, there is no deep interest in the child as an individual nor knowledge of his character or feelings. The responsible parent is not necessarily loving. Responsibility in terms of material care does not imply either productive stimulation, nor understanding. In contrast to loving or indulgent parents, these parents generally make their affection a reward for good behavior.

Conditional love is often combined with one or another mode of relatedness. A parent may show responsibility, care, and affection because his children obey him, because they love him, because they stay with him, or because they are "his."

Responses that indicate this mode of relation are often given to questions about the idea of a good parent or the way in which a parent should show love. Some villagers stress material care and responsibility as equivalent to love. "The father shows his love by working hard with the end in view that the children will live well," one man stated. Another parent said that mothers love children by "taking care of them, giving them food, cleaning them, making them adequate."

Often a responsible father will say something like the following: "I consider myself a good parent because I work hard, bring home food, buy them clothes, and see to it that they do not lack in their needs." Or a responsible mother will say, "I believe that I am a good mother because I watch over them, satisfy their needs, keep them clean, and try to set them in a good path [of life]."

A responsible man, with a more loving attitude than the average, in answering Question 14 described his idea of a good mother as one "who lives well with her children, who gives good advice and spanks when her children don't understand. She is concerned about attending to her children in their meals."

To Question 15, he stated, "I would say that I am a good father.

Because they are my children, I love them, I care for them, I don't mistreat them. I work so they do not lack anything to eat, to wear, nor to cover their feet."

The mode of relation between the sexes characterized by conditional love and material care is often combined with traditionalism. Affection, care, and respect depend on conforming to the traditional roles. A man must provide for his family and protect it, while the woman must comply with the duties of the home and not expect the same freedom as her husband. In answer to Question 42, one traditional-responsible man said, "A man should respect God and authority. He should comply with his obligations. A woman should be respectful and a hard worker." Similarly, another man said, "The man should comply with his obligation, his duties to the home. The woman also should comply with her work. She should be loyal to her husband and children. She should be honorable." But women cannot have the same rights as men, "because they would have no respect for men." The breaking of a relationship is not a matter of indifference or simply of hurt pride for this villager. Conditional love is sometimes accompanied by deeper feelings. For example, a normally cool and responsible husband said, if the woman betrays the male, if she is really a bad woman, "then he should leave her, but with sadness."

Women may also see the relationship between the sexes in rather cold but responsible terms, such as the one who said, "A man should be sober, judicious, a worker, and careful. The woman should be careful, not spend her time in the streets, should see after her house and her family. She should not have vices, and she should see after the well-being of her family."

7. Love. In the beginning of this chapter we quoted examples of love as an expression of the productive orientation in general. We add here some expressions of parents' love for children.

For example, a loving villager was able to describe his children without either idealizing them or belittling them. He stated: "M. was docile when small, with a character that made him manipulable. There is a certain age in children when there are changes that completely transform them, in part because of their age and in part because of a change in their lives when they are away from the village and the family's control. In the contact with other people they suffer changes, a certain pull toward things that are more perverse than proper. M. did not avoid suffering the influence of this pull but he toned down these customs when he became the father of a family. His disorientation wasn't great, but he did not avoid feeling it. Now that he is grown up, his problem is that he is easily carried away by irritations. . . . Outside of that I feel that he is a good son and brother. I see that he is worthy of the esteem and affection, even of those outside his family. He has good friends and he has never given me reason to reproach him either as a son or a citizen. . . . P. is similar to M. He is notable for his sensitivity and he easily cries. He has qualities of nobility, loveableness and affection for his parents. . . . Perhaps he has a predisposition to sentimentality. . . . In my daughter B. we find a certain deference, docility, a greater tendency to be obedient. . . . She is somewhat less able to learn and understand what she is taught. I feel her ability to learn is limited. Her brother L. is a little dark, lazy rogue . . . etc."

The interest and understanding of the child combined with realism is the loving parent's basis for raising the child. He or she respects the child, and unlike the indulgent parent, also respects himself. On using physical punishment, a father says, "I believe that it is bad to hit children in order to educate them because it brutalizes their feelings. The only result is that they just get stubborn and lose respect for their parents. We have mouths in order to make them understand with advice. Only if they don't understand in this way should one spank them, but that would be only a rare exception." Another says, "The important thing is that they do not fear their parents. To the contrary, they should love them and feel affection and confidence."

A loving parent may spank and scold his or her children, but there is no enjoyment in doing this, no wish to make the child fearful and blindly obedient. A mother said, "I believe that hitting and correcting too strongly makes the children worse. . . . There are things which are important that demand spanking children. I hit when there is a reason, without reason, no. I don't like hitting just to hit them. . . . Life teaches and one learns from much experience. They say one's energy diminishes with the years, but I say that the energy doesn't end but rather reflection comes, and before acting one thinks about it carefully." She stated that she considers herself a good mother "because the love that I feel for my family is deep, because even though I scold and punish, I feel at the bottom of my soul I love them and I am not bad with them." This response is contrasted with the conditional loving equation of love with material care. This loving mother is also very responsible in material terms, but her material concern is not what she considers as the proof of her love.

How do the loving parents respond to Stories 1, 2 and 5? Considering the child who loses the money for food because he stops to play, one villager said, "It was the mother's fault for sending such a young child on the errand. She should have found a neighbor to help her."A father said, "If the mother were understanding, it is certain that she would make the child aware of the loss and his carelessness, explain it to him, and if she is not very sick, she will do everything possible to get more money and food for the family." It should be kept in mind that in the village the loss of money for food can be extremely serious, and it is doubtful that a loving person would not feel the importance of making the child aware of the gravity of the loss. Furthermore, we might note that while some of these loving responses might be clichés within progressive circles in the United States, for the village parents they are entirely genuine and un-influenced by prevailing opinions.

In response to Story 5, having to do with the son's robbing the jewels from the church, the loving parents generally considered that the boy's parents would feel ashamed, shocked and/or sad at the crime. Their con-cern, however, is with the son and not with public opinion. In the village culture, stealing is considered one of the worst crimes, and for those who are practicing Catholics, a crime against the church would be especially painful. The unloving villager is not so worried about discovering his child to be a thief as he is about what people will say.

How the loving parents describe their behavior with their children expresses respect for the child's feelings and a wish to stimulate rather than control him. Even so, the loving attitude is modified by cultural pat-terns. Only the most loving parents play with their older children. There is much play and coddling of infants, but parents feel that an older child (older than 5) will lose respect for a parent who is playful. One other-wise loving mother said, "I don't like to play with them because I don't want them to lose respect for me, because then they get very meddlesome and one is not in the mood to put up with it." However, the loving parent is likely to tell his children "stories and simple histories so that they can learn something of life," but the gap between parents and children in a peasant society is large, and the influence of traditional authority is strong.

C. SOCIOPOLITICAL MODES

1. Authoritarianism and Traditionalism. The authoritarian orienta-tion may be expressed in the parent's wish that the child obey without question, and more profoundly in the desire that the child fear him. "Fear is necessary for respect," is mentioned time and again by those with the authoritarian character. They state that respect and obedience are the greatest virtues a child can learn, and the child who disobeys must be punished. The "good" child is described as obedient and the "bad" child as rebellious.

A key to the authoritarian orientation is the description the authori-tarian gives of his children, their virtues, and their faults. Usually, the authoritarian parent describes his children in terms of their obedience or disobedience. Other traits characterizing children are not mentioned.

The authoritarian cannot bear a free child, one who is independent of him. He may rationalize beating as good for the child, "for if you don't beat children, they would do as they like," or "they would not grow up straight." One villager was more aware that corporal punishment is for the parent's benefit, not the child's. He said: "I believe that it is good that the children feel the harshness in order that they do what one tells them and that they have respect for one."

In response to Question 44, authoritarian individuals admired those persons who have had power over others, men who were feared. Although the authoritarian may mouth the ideals of the Mexican revolution he makes no distinction between Pancho Villa, who was a cruel and vain leader of the revolution, and Emiliano Zapata, who fought for the rights of free peasants. The authoritarian admires the fact that both men had power and won battles.

This contrasts with the democratic individual whose admiration is based on the appreciation of qualities other than force, such as the villager who said "Villa differs from Zapata in various ways, the fundamental impulse to rob, violent acts that did not happen with Zapata. . . . Both died tragically, but Zapata died full of an ideal. Villa died in his hacienda in the midst of business transactions . . . with an ideal broken into pieces."

A submissive-authoritarian woman enjoyed the story of Aladdin because "it spoke of many powerful and important men." She admired Cuauhtémoc because he was "the *chief* of the Indians." Another authoritarian woman liked Ben-Hur, because "he was powerful and triumphed."

Villagers also expressed authoritarianism by admiration of the rich and powerful, and justified inequality, attributing greater merit to the strong. There can be no end to poverty, because "if all of us were rich," one authoritarian villager said, "there would be no one to work and not even anyone to ask a favor." This response is also an expression of dependency. It says in effect: it is good to be poor because only then can one enjoy dependency.

The authoritarian orientation characterizes some of the men's relations to women. The authoritarian male feels that women should be subservient to men. "A woman should respect her parents first and then her husband: those who have the right to order her," one villager replied to Question 42. Another said, "She should be respectful and obedient, know her place."

It is important to distinguish between the authoritarian who is contemptuous of women as "weaker," "without capacity," "inferior by birth," in contrast to the man who fears his traditional role will be undermined if women were to have the same rights as men. The authoritarian emphasizes the inherent superiority of the strong and the powerlessness of the weak while the traditional peasant emphasizes customary respect and feels shame if he fails to fulfill his traditional role.

The traditional point of view is patriarchal, and villagers commonly repeat formulas such as, "The man should order and have the respect of the house." "The husband takes over the position of the father and must be at the head of the house." "The Bible tells us God and man, not God and woman." Voicing one of these formulas does not in itself indicate authoritarianism, since the cultural pattern favors an authoritarian-type relationship of man over woman. Three types of responses must be distinguished. One is the conventional acceptance of the patriarchal ideal without personal authoritarianism or sadism. Another is the active rejection of this ideal of male dominance over women, which characterizes the more democratic villagers or more rebellious women. The third is the particular authoritarian-sadistic pleasure in power over women, as well as over other men.

The traditional authoritarian differs from the sadistic authoritarian in that the parent wants respect and obedience but does not want the child to fear him. Rather the parent expects respect and obedience because that is the cultural ideal. For the child to lack this respect and obedience would imply that the parent is less worthy than the average parent, that he does not deserve what is due parents in the village.

In scoring the questionnaires, we found that some individuals combined a traditional orientation with a democratic attitude, while others combined traditionalism with sado-masochistic authoritarianism. An example of the latter, a man with a hoarding-responsible character, stated that a good father should "fulfill his obligations to his children, love them, clean them, care for them. He should correct his wife's conduct from the first day of marriage, with a strong hand. He should guide his sons in a good path, to love them is to discipline them from the time they are children, to work, to learn to earn a living, not to roam the street. He must be vigilant." To Question 16, he stated that "fear serves to make children respect their father. It is desirable that they have it, very little but enough."

In contrast, a traditional-democratic villager stated that a child should respect his father "because he [the father] respects him and cares for him." His answer to how a good father should act was the following:

"If the Architect of the universe sends you a son, tremble. You cannot know if his soul will be good or evil. All you can do is to be a loving father, protecting him until he reaches the age of twelve. From twelve until he is twenty, be his teacher. And from twenty on, be his friend."

2. Submissiveness. In giving an opinion about whether mankind will ever abolish war, poverty, and corruption, most villagers express lack of hope, and fatalism about the future. This traditional peasant submissiveness is based in the feeling of powerlessness to change events. One such villager said, "When there are no wars, it will be because the end of the world has

arrived. Equally poverty. One's poverty ends when one dies. Then everything ends: poverty, vanity, and pride." Another villager commented on corruption: "It will never end. Only God determines it. No one can end it." Individual responses such as these express the peasant's traditional submissiveness to nature and God's will.[3] The usual ideological influence of religious teaching as it comes to the Mexican peasant reinforces this fatalistic attitude.

There is also the traditional submissiveness of young to old, women to men, and the poor to the rich, which does not necessarily indicate masochism or authoritarianism.

A traditionally oriented young man said, "Although I have no reason to feel shame, I feel I am less than the others because I am poorer and younger than the elders, because I cannot contradict what they say."

Sometimes submissiveness reflects a combination of traditionalism and resignation to reality. Women who are not characterologically masochistic may state that they suffer the husband's infidelities out of necessity, but without any satisfaction of suffering, nor because security is found in symbiotic relation to a powerful figure. "Well, the woman here in Mexico, she must let things pass," one wife said. "One must take it, pretend not to see. What is the use of leaving with many children. Afterwards who will support her?"

Another woman gave a similar response to Question 46b. "If the woman is getting along well with her husband and they do not fight, she should not break up the home. She should not leave, for someday at last, he may tire of his mistress and leave her when the drunkenness of his love for her passes."

Another typical response is the following: "Since the man always has had more liberty, I believe the only thing the woman can do is to win the will of the male so that he stops offending her. If the man fulfills his economic obligations, the woman should do everything possible to gain his affection and attract him so that he does not continue betraying her."

Submissiveness may also be rooted in dependency, in the receptive-passive orientation, or in parental fixations (see below). A receptive-submissive man stated (in response to Question 46a), "When a woman betrays him, if he needs her, a man should beg her to change her mind." Another stated, "What is the point of getting angry. Then she will not give him anything to eat."

3. The Democratic Orientation. The ideal of equality which is shared by many villagers is rooted in an authentic democratic orientation, since

---

[3] In response to Question 50, 86 percent of the villagers think that there will always be poverty in the village; and 78 percent believe there will always be corruption.

they do not respond to the cultural pattern. Thus a villager said, "One cannot be either superior or inferior to others. I feel that I am equal to everyone, because all of us are human and we feel in the same way." A woman states, "I don't feel superior to any other person. Yes, I feel what I am, a woman like any other. I believe that even if I had much, I would be the same."

Some villagers express a traditional respect for authorities who have "worked for the good of others," putting Zapata, Benito Juarez, Lázaro Cárdenas, and a few others in this category. However, some villagers repeat the conventional formulas, but add a personal statement which may express their particular sociopolitical mode of relation. One of the democratic villagers expresses his admiration for Zapata in terms that show his distaste for exploitation. "He was a man that did much for the well-being of all the citizens. Because of him we have all our liberty and land. If it had not been for him, we would still be under the whips of the hacendados. Some of the old men have told me that in those days they whipped the peasants who carried the cane in the haciendas."

The democratic orientation may also be expressed in statements about the relationship between men and women, as has been mentioned in the example illustrating love.

D. PARENTAL FIXATIONS

We have defined fixation as the state of being emotionally bound to a mother or father so that the individual continues to seek from the parent solutions to problems that an adult should resolve for himself. The fact of this fixation may be obvious and marked by idealization of the parent, or it may be strongly repressed and there may be a reaction formation of a show of independence.

In analyzing the responses, we found it relatively easy to score fixations when the individuals described their dependent behavior toward parents. But those individuals who believe themselves to be independent remain unaware of the degree to which they seek a substitute mother or father in their wives, husbands, or employers, transferring a dependent attitude from the parents to these substitutes. Psychoanalytic clinical data show that intense fixations, especially to the mother, may be hidden beneath compensatory behavior (reaction formations). Some individuals with deep fixations to the mother may appear to be extremely independent. If this independence is compensatory, the individual may become angry or rebellious whenever he feels anyone is trying to mother him or make him dependent. He is overly fearful of being trapped by motherly domination.

Our method of scoring does not always succeed in uncovering a well-guarded and unconscious fixation to the mother, but a careful examination usually allows us to distinguish compensatory strivings from true independ-

ence; our theory sensitizes us to search for less obvious indications of fixations, such as in responses to projective stories. Intense father fixation is
seldom as repressed as the mother fixation, because the individual does not
feel it to be so irrational and childlike.

Six of the questions proved generally useful in eliciting responses that
indicate underlying fixations. However, in scoring fixations, as in scoring
all other traits, the diagnosis is based on the analysis of the total interview
and not on particular questions.

The first question particularly relevant to parental fixations is #8:
How frequently do you see your mother now (or the person who takes
the place of your mother)? For what reasons, if any, have you consulted
her during the last year? Would you act against her wishes? On what occasions have you done so?

These same questions are then repeated in relation to the father.

The second question is #10: When you are in trouble or have problems, whom do you ask for help? (economic and moral)

The third question is #12: (a) Give a brief description of your
mother (or mother figure) as you see her. (b) Give a brief description of
your father (or father figure) as you see him.

The fourth question is #13: (a) How did your mother treat you
when you were a child? (Did she ever punish you when you did something
bad? Did she ever console you or comfort you?) (b) And your father?
How did he act?

The fifth question is #14: Describe your idea of a good mother.

The sixth question is Story 4 which describes a young man marrying
against his mother's wishes. "His mother becomes sick because of the separation and finally dies." The respondent is asked what he thinks about
this, what he imagines the son to feel, and the wife.

1. Intense fixation to the mother. The individual intensely fixated to
a mother or father will never disobey or go against the parent's wishes.
The responses to Question 8 often express that the intensely fixated person
may rationalize the fixation in terms of trying to please the mother or
father.

"No, doctor," said a woman age 40, "I would not act against either
her wishes or character. I like her to be happy. I try to walk in accord and
harmony with her."

A married man of 27 said that he has never acted against his mother's
wishes, "although I have not satisfied her in the goals she has that one
progresses in life as she wishes. The women understand the world so that
we can progress in life."

In answer to Question 10, the intensely fixated individuals state that
when in trouble they turn to the parent. A bachelor of 28 stated: "Everything that worries me I tell to my mother. She sees how to solve it. She

sees where to find money and to pay, because I don't even ask for a loan without her permission."

Some fixated individuals state that they visit their parents frequently seeking advice, and they mention specific decisions made for them by parents. A bachelor of 29 said, "I often ask my mother advice in things where I don't find myself competent to do them and I have doubt. I have wanted to sell my house. I ask her advice that she tell me if it would be well that I do so or no. She tells me not to sell it and I haven't sold it."

In the case of intense mother fixations, dependence is so extreme that the individual's own will becomes paralyzed. A villager has not seen his mother for five years. He is a married man of almost 40, but in answer to the question whether he would act against his mother's wishes, he said, "No, how can you believe that? I love her still. I haven't been able to go where she is. I would not act against her wishes because in the first place she is my mother and in the second *I couldn't*." While he lived with his mother, he followed her advice about what jobs he should take and what girls he should take out. Now that he has married, this dependence has partly been transferred to his wife, whom he treats as if she were a mother, always fearing that if he displeases her, she will cut off his food and affection.

Some men, especially those who have had no father or who had a very weak one, remain so fixated to the mother that they cannot leave home. A young man of 23 responded to Question 10, "In everything, I ask aid of my mother, because she is the only person of whom I can ask help, and I trust her enough. Since that occasion when I left home, when I came back, I swore to my mother that I would never again separate myself from her. Since then she loves me with much confidence and I her also."

In answer to Questions 12 and 13, the fixated individual idealizes the parent, rationalizing or ignoring aspects of the parent that conflict with the idealized image. One intensely fixated man must justify the fact that his mother is cold and hard (*seca*). He explained that if the mother were not tough, he would have become an angry person (*enojón*), "like everyone else." He stated that "a mother can be good only when her son is good. If the son is bad, she must be bad. It doesn't matter if she is made of sugar. She can't be sweet if the son is a tramp [*vago*]." It is interesting to note that the villager reversed today's psychological concept that children are bad because of the mother. He felt the mother was bad because of the son.

With many fixated individuals the parents' faults are excused, and the individual feels like a naughty child who has provoked the parent. All goodness is projected onto the idealized parent, and all badness is blamed on the self.

In general, the intensely fixated villagers describe parents with vague and laudatory terms such as good, noble, friendly, charitable, and upright. Descriptions of the way the parent treated the respondent as a child often conflict with the idealized picture, but the conflict is glossed over by the individual's putting the blame on himself for the parent's harshness or coldness, thus accepting uncritically the parent's view of self, others, and the world.

In responding to Story 4, the intensely mother-bound individuals justify the mother's right to decide which girl her son should marry, and they blame the son for leaving his mother. "There are many wives," said one man, "but one has only one mother." Another said, "I think the boy did badly to disobey his mother and he was guilty of her death. He felt a very great sadness and repentance for having done what he did. The wife must have felt pleasure since she had no esteem for her mother-in-law."

2. Moderate fixation to the mother. Although the moderately fixated individuals do not express childlike dependence on a parent, they lack the freedom and realism of an individual who has grown up to be independent of his parents. Rather than acting like little children in relation to their parents, the moderately bound often appear more like adolescents who have achieved some independence.

An example is a villager almost 60 years old. His old mother lives with him and his family, and although he can describe her with some realism and make decisions for himself, he still worries about his mother's anger. To Question 8, he said: "Now I don't ask for advice from my mother. To the contrary, I give advice to her. Since she doesn't know how to read, I try to orient her in the way she should act with others and my family. But I would never act against my mother's wishes, because of maternal respect. And I have never done so." Later, in another context, he remarked that he felt worse when his mother got angry with him than when his father did, even though the father was harsher in his punishment. "The father gets rid of his anger when he punishes, but the mother doesn't. She remains with the feelings of anger with one, and at the same time one feels remorse because of the mother's anger." [4]

The conflict between fixation and independence is expressed in a village man's response to Story 4. He first said that the son and his wife "are responsible for the death of the mother because of disobeying." He then expressed a very different feeling: "But I believe that the mother

---

[4] It is of interest that besides indicating fixation, this statement suggests that his mother punished by withdrawing love, by remaining resentful. This form of punishment made her son more unhappy than the father's physical punishment. The statement also reflects a basic difference in the child's *anxiety* in the face of the mother's anger as opposed to his *fear* of the father's wrath. As indicated before, in mother-fixated individuals, anxiety about opposing the mother seems to be much more intense and of a different quality than the feelings brought on by opposing the father.

acted very badly in opposing the son's wish to have a woman, since she should have kept in mind that he was not going to marry for the mother's pleasure. The son must have felt sadness upon realizing that the mother had died. I believe also that the wife must have felt repentant."

Another man also expressed more independence than the intensely fixated individuals, even though he stated that he asks his mother's advice "when I want to make a decision." Yet, he acted against her wishes "on occasions when she did not give her consent, such as when I left the village to work in other parts." He also described his mother with more realism, saying that "she was an angry person [*corajuda*], she always wanted things done rapidly." He feared his mother more than his easy-going father, whom he liked better, yet he justifies the mother's beatings, saying that they were for his benefit and that children should fear their parents. He would seek help first from his mother "because she does more when someone asks for something."

Adolescents sometimes express rebelliousness which appears as an attempt to overcome the tie to the mother. In the following instance, a girl of 16 shows a certain degree of independence. She asks advice of her mother "when I am going badly in my studies or when I have a problem I cannot resolve alone. I also ask her how I should arrange my father's clothes, because when I don't do it well, she pulls my ears. No, I shouldn't act against her wishes. It is not right. Well, at times she tells me not to talk back, but I talk back a lot [*respondona*]. Also sometimes she tells me to arrange the clothes and I don't do it."

3. Intense fixation to the father. The intense fixation to the father seldom reaches the degree of dependence characteristic of the intensely mother-bound, but father-fixated villagers do express fear of the father's displeasure, exaggerated respect for his opinions, and they tend to justify all of father's actions.

A married man with children, in his 30's, said he seeks help from his father "in the first place, and in the second I ask those friends I most trust. My father, because he is the one in whom I feel most confidence. Besides, he gets me out of problems. I go to my friends when I believe they can help me out of trouble I have."

When the child confronts the mother, he feels powerless, since he depends entirely on her; he is also afraid of his anger, because if he destroys the mother, he will destroy his source of life. However, even when an individual is bound to the father, he does not feel the symbiotic unity that a child can experience with the mother. He is more likely to fear the father's power, but it is a fear which can be overcome by opposing the father or by choosing a father substitute whose love one can gain by doing what pleases him. The extremes of regression that can occur in relation to the mother include regression to a state of extreme symbiosis, as is often the case in some psychoses. Regression in relation to the father never approaches such an extreme.

Another man explained away the father's harshness by blaming himself. "He was very severe in correcting us, very hard. *Whenever I gave him reason,* he hit me. But we have always lived in a constant battle for the economic betterment of the family, and we must be obliged to cooperate. When we got *distracted* into play, he punished us." The father appears to be a man who allowed his children little or no freedom, and who exploited them for his own purposes. The son was made to feel that even play was a crime against his father.

4. Moderate fixation to the father. We found not infrequently that moderate fixation to the father had the quality of seeking help from him or from father figures in the process of trying to overcome a deep attachment to the mother. For example, a young man reported that he sees his mother every day, "but asking advice, for what reason? I don't ask advice; one can give oneself advice. I always obey my mother, since she is one's mother, but I only lived with her when I was small. Now, grown-up, I don't live with her. But what the chief [*jefa,* female head refers to the mother] of the house orders is what one does."

He described his mother as a paragon of knowledge and virtue. His father, who died ten years ago, was also described in idealized terms: "He was better than any one of those now here. He defended his honor wherever he was. A good worker, he didn't like drink and never got drunk. When we were children, he taught us to work. He didn't let us go to school in the afternoon, because he took us to the fields."

However, both parents hit him when they got angry, his father beating him with sticks. But he feels it is good to fear your parents, "in order that children are taught to respect the parents."

He has replaced his father with an employer (*patron*) to whom he goes when in trouble. He also seeks out the elders of the village as male support in his struggle to become independent of his mother. To Question 27, he says, "I like the old men to tell me about the Revolution, or Noah's Ark, or how in olden times they lit the fire with stones. That is what I like, because I become aware of things that happened in earlier times, and also afterwards I will be able to tell the same things to my sons when I have them." He expressed respect for the elders which reflects a traditional patriarchal orientation. Although he remains moderately tied to the mother, he consciously rejects the maternal influence and wishes to belong with the men. The saddest experience of his life was his father's death, "since he was my chief." He admires those men who help the village, especially those who take a paternal role and teach children. His answer to Story 4 showed, however, the strength of the attachment to the mother, despite his attempt to be independent of her.

"I believe that the son was guilty of his mother's death, because, knowing that his mother did not love his sweetheart, he married her. He felt bad [*feo*] and he must have repented of having married. She felt bad that the mother-in-law had not loved her and she also felt guilty for the death of her mother-in-law."

Another young man expresses similar need to find support from his father to overcome attachment and fear of his mother. To Question 10, he said: "I turn to my father in search of aid, because I believe that the father [*papa*] can have more power than the mother to help me out of a difficulty." But, he remains mother-bound to the degree that he expects his mother to resolve his life for him. A good mother, he said, "should make her children obey and give them good advice so that they do not become bad."

5. Independence. An example of an independent woman is a villager in her late 30's. Since she was brought up in a fatherless household, she is not bound to her father. But she is also independent of her mother, although she is affectionate with her. She said, "I am rather bull-headed in doing what I want to do, so I don't ask advice. I have acted against her wishes in various occasions." She described her mother realistically. "She is rather violent of nature. Well, she is also rather egoistic, although she has a good heart. She will suddenly decide not to do a favor, but later on she will see her way to doing it." As a child the respondent was treated roughly. "My mother consoled me with blows, yes with pure blows for whatever little thing. Since I was the first, she wanted to control me harder. With the others it was different."

A young man who is independent of his mother responded to Story 4 as follows: "They did go to see her," he said. "They got married, but if they had just gone away and no more, they would have been guilty. But they spoke to her and then were married, and it wasn't their fault. He must have been sad. She also felt sadness, but he more."

The ability to see the parents clearly, neither idealizing nor blaming them for one's own problems, is the mark of independence. For example, a village elder describes his father as follows: "He was a special character. He was illiterate and he liked my mother to read him from histories and novels. He was a long-suffering man [*sufrido*], prudent and silent. I began to feel displeasure at seeing this strong degree of prudence. It influenced my spirit to make my character stronger, because I became angry to see the weak crushed."

As a child, he felt his father "affectionate but severe. But his severity was a result of custom more than character. He wanted to harden us with the old idea of 'spare the rod and spoil the child' [*la letra entra con sangre*]."

Appendix B:

Scoring Agreement
and the Use of the Rorschach
and Thematic Apperception Test

Some diagnoses are relatively easy to make. Evidence and theoretical expectation fit perfectly. In other cases, limited data allow for various interpretations, and the diagnostician with the greater theoretical knowledge, experience, and ability is better able to interpret a particular case or score an interpretative test in terms of character.

In psychological investigation, accuracy of scoring is sometimes confused with agreement between scorers or "reliability" of scoring. This would imply that if two or more trained diagnosticians agreed on their diagnosis, it would be more likely to be accurate. There is no reason to expect that agreement indicates truth. Four out of five psychoanalysts (or surgeons) might agree on a diagnosis, yet the fifth one might be the only one who was right. The idea that majority agreement or even unanimity of scoring "reliability" indicates validity of scoring seems to be a misapplication of the democratic ideal to science, confusing the democratic political process which shows the *will* of the majority with the scientific process which seeks to discover the *truth*. At best, agreement suggests a probability of correctness, but even an overwhelming majority of scientists may in fact be wrong.

Nevertheless, although we consider one very good scorer better than many fairly good scorers in full agreement, we did introduce agreement tests to show the possibility of training students to score the interpretative questionnaire.

Quite different—and much more relevant—is the analysis of the results of different tests comparing the scoring of character from the questionnaire with a character diagnosis based on responses to projective tests, the Rorschach and the Thematic Apperception Test. Our original plan was to administer both the Rorschach and TAT to all of the villagers who responded to the questionnaire, and to base each diagnosis or scoring on information from the three measures. This would have given us more data for the diagnosis, but we had neither the time nor the personnel to achieve this aim, and we therefore decided to use the sample of Rorschachs and TATs as independent measures of character in order to make tests of scoring agreement. Individual character traits can be expressed in many different ways, and we were interested in exploring the usefulness of the Rorschach and the TAT in comparison to standardized questions as a means for studying social character.

TRAINING THE SCORERS

The basic training in scoring was done during the seminars, lasting over a year.[1] For these seminars, one or two questionnaires were chosen, which each participant had scored independently. The scorings were discussed during the seminar, each participant presenting the reasons behind his decision, and the group usually arrived at a consensus based on a consideration of cultural and linguistic considerations as well as psychoanalytic theory.

After the seminar had terminated, the authors continued analyzing questionnaires until we reached the point of basic agreement in 18 of 20 questionnaires chosen at random. The criterion for diagnostic agreement was not that the interview be scored exactly the same in terms of each trait, but that the two scorings did not contradict each other. In other words, one of us might decide that the mode of relatedness was conditional love combined with narcissism I and masochism, while the other scoring was conditional love combined with narcissism I and sadism. Since, theoretically, we expect the sadist to have masochistic tendencies, the two scorings do not contradict each other. There is merely a disagreement on which is more dominant, the sadistic or masochistic element of the sado-masochism. On the other hand, if one scorer had scored love instead of sadism, we would have considered this a basic disagreement between scorings.

In the process of refining scoring, we satisfied ourselves that it is almost always possible to arrive at an optimal scoring of an interview, and that usually disagreements were caused by a scorer's failure to pay sufficient attention to important responses, by his lack of concentration or his misinterpretation of responses. When the scorer concentrates sufficiently on the questionnaire as a whole and on each response, he is likely to arrive at an accurate diagnosis of character. After all, this is not different from what happens in the psychoanalytic interpretation of a dream or in a psychiatric diagnosis.

---

[1] The seminar was led by E. Fromm. The participants included M. Maccoby, F. Sanchez, Dr. T. Schwartz, Dr. L. Romanucci Schwartz, and later Dr. I. Galván.

After satisfying ourselves that a reliable scoring system had been achieved, we set about training new scorers, to see if the methods could be taught to students.[2]

The best way to train a scorer is by going over his scoring and analyzing his errors in the light of theory. We found that scorers at first make characteristic errors. One scorer will consistently interpret indulgence as love, because he has not yet understood the difference between mature, productive love, and giving for the sake of being loved without regard to the real well-being of the other. Another scorer will see all dependent individuals as receptive, failing to distinguish between the exploitative-symbiotic individual and the truly receptive. Some scorers make mistakes because they concentrate on either the negative or positive aspects of a character orientation to the exclusion of the other aspect. For example, a scorer might be able to diagnose an unproductive-hoarding orientation but not a productive-hoarding orientation. A scorer may misinterpret a questionnaire because it expresses dynamic tendencies in himself which he represses. Thus, he may idealize some tendencies or judge harshly and exaggerate traits in himself which he dislikes. Usually the scorers were able to understand their errors when theoretical distinctions were pointed out to them. Sometimes it was necessary for them to become aware of character traits in themselves in order to see them in others.

After a certain level of competency was reached, we began to make statistical agreement measures for the scoring of specific traits. In calculating agreement on specific traits of the modes of assimilation and relatedness, we employed contingency tables. Agreement on paternal fixations and the productivity scale were calculated by product-moment correlations.

During the process of training, agreement between scorers increased. However, we decided to use the final 60 interviews scored independently by two scorers (Maccoby and Galván) as the basis for reporting agreement measures. As Table B:1 shows, the actual percentage of agreement between scorers on the presence or absence of modes of assimilation ranges form a low of 72 percent for the exploitative mode to a high of 83 percent for the receptive mode. Agreement is statistically significant at the 1 percent level for each mode. This agreement is relatively high for scorer reliability measures of projective tests. As noted above, the agreement percentages for Fromm and Maccoby were even higher.

The product-moment correlation of productiveness measures for two scorers was .65, which for 60 cases is also significant at the 1 percent level.

---

[2] The new scorers, Dr. Isidro Galván, a psychologist, and Dr. Raymundo Macías, a psychiatrist, were working with Dr. Guillermo Dávila on a parallel study of industrial workers and their families in Mexico City. It was important for us to train reliable scorers, so that the results of the urban study would be comparable to those of the village study.

TABLE B:1 Questionnaire Scoring

AGREEMENT BETWEEN TWO SCORERS : MODE OF ASSIMILATION
(N=60)

Mode	+ +	+ -	- +	- -	X^2	Percent Agreement
Receptive	38	6	4	12	21.03**	83
Exploitative	13	9	8	30	8.86**	72
Hoarding	29	6	6	19	20.78**	80

** *p* is less than .01

Table B:2 reports the contingency tables for the scoring of the mode of relation. The percentages of agreement between the two scorers on presence or absence of a mode of relation range from the lowest which is 73 percent agreement on conditional love to 100 percent agreement on narcissism II. However, in the case of narcissism II and the loving mode, there were too few cases in which these modes were expressed to allow for meaningful statistical tests. The other modes do lend themselves to meaningful statistical tests, showing significant agreement between the two scorers.

TABLE B:2 Questionnaire Scoring

AGREEMENT BETWEEN TWO SCORERS : MODE OF RELATION
(N=60)

Mode	+ +	+ -	- +	- -	X^2	Percent Agreement
Sadistic	20	5	6	29	23.46*	81
Masochistic	23	3	6	28	29.59*	85
Destructive	8	5	4	43	17.90*	85
Narcissism I	25	9	4	22	19.95*	78
Narcissism II	2	0	0	58	-	100
Indulgent love	9	6	4	41	17.32*	83
Conditional love	33	5	11	11	9.67*	73
Love	3	0	3	54	-	96

* *p* is less than .01

The product-moment coefficient of correlation for scoring of mother fixation is .87, also significant at the 1 percent level. This agreement score is particularly high because the scoring of mother fixation was made easier by basing it in large part on answers to particular questions in the questionnaire.

The product-moment coefficient of correlation for scoring father fixation is .72, which is also significant at the 1 percent level. The product-moment agreement correlation for rebellion against the mother was .41;

rebellion against the father was .35. These correlations, while much lower, are also significant at the 1 percent level.

SCORING CHARACTER FROM RORSCHACH RESPONSES

A note is in order concerning the way in which Mexican peasants respond to projective tests. Compared to those of most people in the United States, the peasant's responses to the Rorschach or TAT seem sparse. Often they are less rich than one would expect from knowing the individual or reading his responses to the questionnaire. The reason for this can only be understood culturally. In a highly industrialized society such as the United States, most individuals are trained to respond to tests. In fact, they are extremely concerned about presenting a favorable impression, since they have learned that a job or admission to college depends on test performance. The individual in an industrial-corporate society responds as fully as he can so that he will be judged well. Usually only the extremely depressed or suspicious individuals, or those hiding an underlying pathology (paranoid schizophrenia, for example), hold back on their responses and give what Rorschach called "coartated" protocols.

The peasant is different. In peasant culture, tests do not determine one's position in society, job, or economic level. Those who have attended the village school are only used to tests where they must repeat the teacher's words verbatim, spell words, or solve simple problems of arithmetic. They are not expected to be creative or to think for themselves. Although many urban people find the inkblots a difficult challenge, testing is a familiar process for them. For the peasant, testing itself is strange and may be unsettling. As others have also observed, some peasants consider the idea of taking a test to be unhealthy and complain that they must "heat up their heads" (*me calienta la cabeza*) for no good purpose.[3] Others are worried they will see something that no one else sees. Still others are ashamed of admitting they see anatomical or sexual images.

As a result, the natural tendency of the peasant is to give as few

---

[3] See, for example, Lewis (1951) who reports the attitudes of children to taking the Rorschach as follows:

"The children did not enjoy being the center of attention in the testing situation. They were shy, ill at ease, and unaccustomed to taking tests involving much talking, and they soon became weary with the effort of expressing themselves. There is a general feeling in the village that it is not good for a person to study or think too much, and the many questions were *molestia* (a bother). One mother objected to the continuation of a test on the grounds that *se calienta la cabeza,* that is, the child's head would get too hot from thinking too much!" (pp. 307-8)

Maccoby found this same reaction when he administered the Rorschach in Tzintzuntzan, where individuals were particularly worried that they would see things that no one else in the village saw.

responses as possible, especially to an individual he does not know well. Rather than making the task an opportunity to show off—or a game— which he might enjoy if he felt confidence in the tester, the peasant may try to finish as fast as he can.

The scoring or diagnosis of character from Rorschach responses is a difficult task, harder to teach than the interpretation of the questionnaire because it demands experience and knowledge of the test beyond theoretical knowledge and clinical experience. Traditionally, Rorschach interpretation is based principally on the analysis of the localizations and the form, color, shading, and movement determinants of the responses. Localizations, determinants and the rating of perceptual accuracy or realism of the response become the variables making up distinct syndromes which are useful for diagnosis of neurosis and psychosis. Rorschach (1942) in his original work also analyzed the patterns of determinants in terms of intelligence level, type of thought process, emotionality, excitability, oppositionism, and other traits. In general, Rorschach did not analyze the symbolic content of responses in terms of dynamic forces, although after Rorschach's death, his analysis of a patient in psychoanalytic treatment was published (Rorschach, 1942). It demonstrated the possibilities for using a combination of formal analysis (localization, determinants, etc.) combined with symbolic analysis of movement and color to uncover unconscious impulses and dynamic character traits. Rorschach considered that types of movement and color responses could provide a view of the individual's unconscious "complexes," but he considered it less likely that the symbolism of pure form responses (without color or movement) would be useful in such depth interpretation. However, he remained open on the point, noting that "there are neurotics whose 'complexes' are related to the form interpretations. . . . An example is found in the towers which were included in the form responses of the politician . . . which probably project narcissistic desires" (page 214).

Of the many investigators who have since worked with Rorschach's test, Ernest G. Schachtel (1966) and Roy Schafer (1954) have made significant contributions to the development of character interpretation in terms of psychoanalytic theory. Their work together with that of Rorschach has served as a basis for our developing methods of character interpretation from the Rorschach responses.

Schachtel's method of analyzing Rorschach responses has much in common with our method of interpreting the questionnaire. The aim is to put oneself into the individual, to feel what has determined his response. This is the same "experiential" method described by Fromm in *The Forgotten Language* for the understanding of dreams and symbolism. Schachtel feels that many of the Rorschach responses, especially those with movement, express the individual's modes of relating and assimilating.

Responding to the unstructured ink blots, the individual projects his own attitudes in the sense that he sees the environment in terms of his own image. Schachtel writes:

"Suppose that two records both show prevailing kinesthetic percepts of 'oral' movements such as receiving, begging, eating, asking for something, but that one shows a predominance of extensor movements and the other of flexor movements, such as people kneeling, inclining their heads, sitting in a hunched-over position; then it is safe to conclude that the person who sees the oral extensor gesture will more actively seek for or demand help, protection, nurturance from others, while the person who sees the flexor movements is likely to sit and wait, perhaps resignedly, for such help. But neither of these two people can be said to have an active attitude. The basic attitude of both is that of dependence on others, they differ only in the way in which they expect to find gratification of their dependent needs. Still another person may see people grabbing things, animals or people trying to eat the same piece of food with each one trying to get the lion's share, people fighting over something in order to get it for themselves or pulling something away from someone else, and so on. This person probably is of the oral-sadistic, aggressive type and, depending on other factors in the record, may also in his overt behavior be quite assertive, competitive, and aggressive. Yet, to think of him only in terms of the dichotomy active-passive, assertive-compliant, and to describe him as an active, assertive person would miss the most essential quality that he, too, is not a truly active person, but that his basic orientation toward the world, according to Fromm's typology of attitudes, is an exploitative one which, 'like the receptive, has as its basic premise the feeling that the source of all good is outside' of one and 'that one cannot produce anything oneself' " (p. 209).

The interpretation of a response as indicating a direct projection of character attitudes is a complicated process. Each response must be understood in terms of the total configuration of responses. A response that means one thing within a particular personality structure will mean quite another in the context of a different personality structure. Not only does the personality structure, including temperament, intelligence, and character, give different meanings to similar responses, but cultural factors also make a difference. To be able to interpret a response experientially, the Rorschach analyst must be able to see through the eyes of the individual and feel the symbolic meaning of his percepts. These meanings vary in different cultures. For example, in Mexico the horns of a bull can refer to the bullfight, to bravery and domination of a fierce animal by grace and artistry. They may also refer, however, to the husband who is betrayed by his wife, made a fool of, and made to wear *cuernos* (horns). Or further, the horns are a sign of defiance which may be expressed against authority by pointing the thumb and pinky at any person. Naturally the horns also symbolize aggressive penetration and danger, the symbolism which is more universal. To understand the meaning of a symbol as expressed in any particular Rorschach protocol, it is necessary to immerse oneself in the individual's world as it appears in the responses to the inkblots.

When responses are not projections of character attitudes, they may be determined by a number of possibilities. Without attempting to exhaust the possible reasons for a response, we can list some of the other meanings or determinations of the content of percepts.

1. It is important to keep in mind that the blots are not totally unstructured perceptually. They do suggest certain popular responses of images which are commonly perceived within a culture. The more conventional an individual, the more he tends to see what everyone else sees. In the case of any particular response, conventional perception of a rather clear-cut, commonly seen figure may determine the response, without the intervention of character forces. However, the individual who sees only or mostly popular responses may be so dependent on others, so lacking conviction and identity, that he is afraid to see anything that others cannot easily see. Some peasants also attempt consciously to report popular images because of a cultural imperative of not being different from others, of anti-individualism. But in most cases, these individuals are capable of seeing in a more original manner when they are stimulated to do so.

2. Some Rorschach responses are projective in the sense not of seeing one's own attitudes in the blots, but rather of perceiving a world which *justifies* one's character attitudes. For example, the individual who is fearful sees frightening images. The individual who is exploitative and cannibalistic sees a jungle in which dog eats dog and the weak are destroyed by the strong. If the world is as he perceives it, then his own behavior no longer feels irrational to him. Often people tend to experience their destructiveness or regressive strivings as rational responses to objective reality rather than irrational drives and emotions. The more the individual distorts the objective configuration of the blots in order to make them fit his needs, the more we can infer that these strivings need to be rationalized and defended. In the psychotic or schizophrenic these distortions are massive, and the individual may take a single detail of the blot and "confabulate" the whole blot, "seeing" it as something that no one else could see. A less disturbed individual will not make such distortions. Rather he will sift and choose what he sees and so interpret his perceptions as to remain within the realm of the possible, but in such a way that his particular solution to life is justified while he closes himself off from experience which would be difficult to assimilate.

3. Some of the configurations in Rorschach's blots often suggest particular "universal" symbols in the sense described in *The Forgotten Language*.[4] The individual's response or percept then represents his deep feelings in regard to that symbol. Various Rorschach analysts have expressed the idea that Card 4 suggests the childhood image of the father, a huge and powerful figure. While this is true in some cases, in others this image will not register or will be interpreted in a totally different way. In our experience, when this configuration does register, it more generally has the significance of power, which may or may not refer to the father. In many cases, it is the mother and not the father who stands for power, and the response is conditioned by unconscious attitudes toward the mother.

Responses to some Rorschach blots will be determined solely by individual factors. However, certain blots suggest a particular theme for many people. For example, the top of Card 6 looks like a phallus and the responses to it often express feelings about male sexuality, including fear, idolatry, belittling, or impotence. In Mexico, we have found that Card 5 is often interpreted in terms of the image of the mother figure. In the United States and Europe, this card is popularly interpreted as a butterfly or bat, but to many Mexicans, the image of a delicate central figure with outspread wings seems to suggest the protecting, enveloping, and sometimes smothering mother figure. Individuals with destructive mothers may perceive a dangerous animal in the figure, as they frequently do in their dreams, even though they consciously idealize the mother. Such a percept may indicate neither a projection of character tendencies nor the wish to see the world in a manner that justifies impulses, but rather, as in many dreams, it expresses a greater acuteness because mental processes have been freed from conventionality.

A basic theoretical problem in the interpretation of both dreams and Rorschach responses is the question of whether an image represents a

---

[4] Fromm (1951) writes that "The *universal* symbol is one in which there is an intrinsic relationship between the symbol and that which it represents. . . . Take, for instance, the symbol of fire. We are fascinated by certain qualities of fire in a fireplace. First of all, by its aliveness. It changes continuously, it moves all the time, and yet there is constancy in it. . . . When we use fire as a symbol, we describe the inner experience characterized by the same elements which we notice in the sensory experience of fire; the mood of energy, lightness, movement, grace, gaiety—sometimes one, sometimes another of these elements being predominant in the feeling.

"Similar in some ways and different in others is the symbol of water—of the ocean or of the stream. Here, too, we find the blending of change and permanence, of constant movement and yet of permanence. We also feel the quality of aliveness, continuity and energy. But there is a difference; where fire is adventurous, quick, exciting, water is quiet, slow and steady. Fire has an element of surprise; water an element of predictability. Water symbolizes the mood of aliveness, too, but one which is 'heavier,' 'slower,' and more comforting than exciting." Pp. 15-17.

subject experience (for example, desires and fears) or a deep perception of reality. Seeing the mother figure as destructive might either express a projection or a perception not conscious to the individual. A mistake many interpreters make is to treat all symbols as projections of impulses. To decide which interpretation is correct, the psychologist must be sensitive to the quality of the percept, to the emotion expressed, and to the relation of the percept to the other responses.

4. Often the individual sees those objects that attract him. He searches for things that satisfy him, towards which he feels a deep and sometimes unconscious affinity. These affinities are expressed not only in the content of responses, but also in the perceptual "determinants," such as location of response and the use of color or shading in describing the percept. For example, Klopfer points out that texture responses, such as seeing many animal skins or materials that look furry, imply a "need" for affection on the level of contact. The concept of need is however more ambiguous than affinity. A need may imply that something is necessary for survival or growth. Or it may imply pathological attraction to things which are not necessary for survival and which neither satisfy one deeply nor enhance life, such as regressive needs or "needs" that are stimulated by propaganda. Rather than use the term "need," it might be better to use "affinity" as a broader term which includes the concept of both types of needs. Furthermore, affinity is a concept less loaded with traditional meanings of instinct or drive.

Deep affinities express character orientations. The receptive individual is attracted to food, a woman's breast, magic wands, wishbones, Santa Claus figures, etc. These symbols of what attract the receptive individual may alternate with the projection of the receptive attitude, in responses such as the open mouth, suckling infants, and passive, reclining figures.

The content of what is seen may express productive affinities as well as unproductive affinities. Indeed, Rorschach considered the main function of content interpretation was to show the quality of the individual's interests. One can often distinguish between interests or affinities which reflect psychopathology and artistic or intellectual interests. In some cases, the content of a percept expresses strivings for self-realization, rebirth, unity with others and with nature, joy, and freedom.

An example of an unproductive affinity expressing a character orientation is the attraction to anatomy concepts of many narcissists whose lives center around their bodies and their illnesses, imagined or real. On the other hand, physicians, physiologists, or nurses may perceive anatomical figures because of their scientific interest. While the content of the Rorschach responses usually indicates what most concerns the individual, the meaning of any particular response can never be separated from the total personality structure.

In diagnosing character from Rorschach protocols, we relied mainly on the dynamic form and movement responses, even though we considered that a more accurate analysis would take into account the other determinants of the responses. However, we limited our analysis to form responses because the quality of the protocols varied considerably. Some were administered by students without sufficient experience to probe for locations and complicated determinants of responses, and we could rely only on the form.

In deciding on the symbolic meaning of content and movement response, we were guided by theoretical understanding and knowledge of the cultural meanings of symbols in the village. We were aided by Schafer's (1954) discussion of thematic analysis and the list of symbols he has compiled to describe various character orientations. Schafer's theoretical basis for choosing symbols is libido theory rather than the concept of psychoanalysis used throughout this book. In most cases, these classifications can be modified in terms of Fromm's characterology which shares with libido theory the expectation that unconscious motivation is revealed by expressive imagery. Furthermore, many of the character orientations we have described correspond clinically to Freudian character orientations.

The following are the types of symbols that were considered as expressing character orientations. These types are based mainly on Schafer's classification with modifications where humanistic psychoanalytic theory sensitizes us to different interpretations. We begin with the Modes of Assimilation.

The Receptive Orientation—An emphasis on perceptions of food, food sources (breasts, udders, nipples), food objects (cups, pots), food providers (cooks, waiters), passive food receivers (birds waiting to be fed), food organs (mouth, lips, stomach), nurturers and protectors (cow, mother, hen, protective angel), givers (Santa Claus, The Three Kings),[5] and oral eroticism (figures kissing, nuzzling).

The Exploitative Orientation—An emphasis on perceptions of devourers (birds and beasts of prey, teeth, claws, vampire, wolf, lion, tiger, shark, crocodile), devouring (animals chasing, clawing, eating each other),[6]

---

[5] Providers, nurturers, and protectors often indicate material care and responsibility.

[6] Schafer also includes the perception of a "carcass" which we would consider more expressive of a necrophilic orientation rather than exploitativeness. He also mentions a category of "engulfing, overwhelming figures and objects," including a woman with an enveloping cloak, witch, spider, etc., which appears to us more expressive of the fear of being trapped by the possessive-destructive mother than an expression of the exploitative mode.

depriving figures and objects (brassieres or breastplates that stand in the way of oral gratification, beggars, scarecrows), impaired oral capacity (mouthless face, toothless face, false teeth), oral or verbal assault (persons or animals arguing, spitting, sticking tongues out).

The Hoarding Orientation—An emphasis on perceptions with direct anal reference, anal content and perspective (figures seen from behind, backs turned, people back to back), dirt (mud, stains), and explosion (erupting lava, flaming tail of rocket). To these categories described by Schafer, we added hoarding animals (rats, squirrels), plants and animals that protect themselves with a hard shell (cactus, snails, turtles).

The following modes of relation were also scored, based principally on Schafer's classifications.

Sadism—oral attack (devouring, stinging, biting, as in the exploitative mode), anal attack (bombs, explosions, as in anal examples), phallic attack (piercing, cutting, shooting objects, arrow, knife, spear, club, charging bull), aggressive primitive men (cavemen, demons, devil, savage), aggressive primitive women (witches). To these categories of Schafer, we added symbols of subjugation (saddles, yoke), people being subjugated—although both of these categories may also refer to masochism, depending on whether the individual identifies with the subjugator or subjugated—powerful figures (charros, king, giant).

Masochism—deprived figures, burdens (ox, yoke, burro weighted by pack), oppression (climbing animal pushed down, person held down, servile positions, trained animal, sheep, dogs—which in the village are usually beaten into a fearful servility), punished (hell, fire and brimstone).[7]

Destructiveness—Schafer does not distinguish between sadism and destructiveness. The symbols we considered expressive of destructiveness included those indicating necrophilia (fascination with dead things, dying, death and decay), mutilation (mangled wings, bleeding leg, squashed animal, headless figures, person torn in half), worn and diseased objects (tattered clothes, infection, pus, withered leaf).

Narcissism I—Schafer only considers the category of body narcissism and sensuality (jewelry, clothing with emphasis on sheen, delicacy, texture, fragility, exotic scenes, chorus girl) which is rarely, if ever, found in a peasant population. We interpreted narcissism I (indifference) when the responses reflected little or no concern for the other people: lack of human content, lack of any movement responses, mild preoccupation with diseases (hypochondriasis), as expressed in anatomy responses, and group narcissism (flags).

---

[7] Schafer also adds symbols of mutilation and of worn, diseased, ruined, or dead things, which we consider in the category of necrophilic destructiveness and not necessarily masochism, although the two are sometimes combined in the same individual.

Narcissism II—This classification is also lacking in Schafer. We constructed it to include grandiosity (kings, powerful figures, crown, Christ, angels), exhibitionism (figures displaying themselves, chorus girl), extreme hypochondriasis, paranoia (eyes looking at the individual, persecution, martyred figures), isolation in one's own world (figures encased in glass or ice, polar bears, person seeing self reflected in lake or mirror, figure standing alone on top of mountain), distance from intimate contact with others (figures seen separated by barriers, masks, small figures distant from each other).

Love—What we looked for in constructing the category for the loving mode of relation were symbols expressing biophilia, or the love of life. These included love of nature and active love of others. Love of nature is expressed by images of flowers, landscapes, sunsets, nondestructive animals, which are often described vividly in terms of color as well as form. Love of others is expressed in human movement responses which show people in acts of cooperation, and enjoyment (dancing, playing instruments).

Scoring the loving mode of relation implies that a depth of feeling is expressed in the biophilic content of the percepts and that the protocol lacks indications of extreme destructiveness, narcissism, or symbiosis.

The more behavioral traits were more difficult to score. We did not find a way of scoring indulgence but we attempted to score conditional love (material care). We constructed the category to include figures that give nurturance (as in food providers, nurturers, and protectors), objects symbolizing protection (tree, flower pot, nest, umbrella), objects of work and the home (pots, pans, broom, agricultural tools), and domestic animals that provide food (cow, chicken).

After some attempts at scoring parental fixations on the basis of the Rorschach, we reached the conclusion that we could not find a reliable system that would correspond to the scoring of the questionnaire. Sometimes, when the mother fixation is expressed in Rorschach responses, it is done so in terms of localizations (enclosed spaces) or determinants (dimension, or texture) rather than by content. Sometimes it does not appear to be present at all, even when there is a deep symbiotic relation with the mother, because the individual does not differentiate himself emotionally from the mother. With further work, however, it may be possible to determine a way of scoring mother fixation.

Finally, we scored each protocol in terms of the scale of productiveness. Both Rorschach and, more recently, Schachtel have concerned themselves with the expression of productiveness in the responses to the inkblots. Schachtel discusses Rorschach's concept of "productive" vs. "reproductive" intelligence as indicating the difference between the active, creative relating to the world and the passive, receptive type of experiencing. Rorschach supposed that the measure of productive intelligence was to be found principally in the number and quality of the human movement responses. Schachtel (1966) comments that "While the factor represented by M is by no means identical with what E. Fromm calls the productive type of relatedness, Fromm's concept of productivity has that in common with the meaning of the M factor that it, too, does not refer to the act of producing something as much as to the way of relating oneself to the world." [8]

Just as the scale of productiveness is based on the activeness, interest, and spontaneity of the individual's relatedness to himself and the world, so in scoring productiveness from Rorschach protocols we look for the degree to which he projects an active attitude into the movement responses, his responsiveness to color, the energy employed in perceiving complex and accurate forms, the interest and pleasure in discovering, and the originality of response. While we were unable to formulate hard and fast rules for scoring productiveness, the experienced Rorschach analyst can soon learn to distinguish between the extremes of the scale: the active, interested, and original individual vs. the passive or rejecting individual. It is not difficult then to set up standards of "moderate interest." This usually includes one or two human movement responses but without originality or deep interest. We found that the passive-inactive individual's responses are determined mainly by the perceptual configurations of the blot; he sees what is easiest to perceive. And the content tends to be what is most conventionally seen, what is "popular" in Rorschach terminology.

AGREEMENT BETWEEN QUESTIONNAIRE AND RORSCHACH

In order to test the agreement between character scoring of the Rorschach and the questionnaire, we took eighty Rorschach protocols from the adult villagers and compared their scoring to that of the questionnaire. The two scorings are not only taken from different tests, but also they were made by two different scorers.

As Table B:3 reports, there is significant (60 to 70 percent) agreement between the questionnaire and the Rorschach on the receptive and hoarding modes. However, more than twice as many respondents are scored as exploitative on the Rorschach as on the questionnaire. What is the reason for this? One possibility is that the Rorschach probes for exploitative tendencies which are deeply repressed and do not emerge on

---

[8] Schachtel (1966), pp. 231-32, f.n. Also see Ernest G. Schachtel, *Metamorphosis, On the Development of Affect, Perception, Attention, and Memory* (New York: Basic Books, Inc., 1959), for a fuller analysis of active vs. passive or embedded perception.

TABLE B:3 Questionnaire – Rorschach Agreement: Mode of Assimilation (N=80)

Mode	+ +	+ -	- +	- -	x^2	Percent Agreement
Receptive	34	22	8	16	5.05*	63
Exploitative	18	8	27	27	2.64	56
Hoarding	21	14	12	33	9.03**	68

*p is less than .05
**p is less than .01

the questionnaire. Another possibility is related to the theoretical problem mentioned above of distinguishing between projections and accurate perceptions of reality. Some of the villagers who are not themselves exploitative may accurately perceive others as exploitative and dangerous. Such perception is not inaccurate, for we have observed (Chapters 5 and 6) that the new entrepreneurs are exploitative and endanger the livelihood of the traditional peasant farmer.[9]

The product-moment correlation between productiveness as scored from the questionnaire and the Rorschach was .56, which is significant at the 1 percent level. (On the final 30 cases scored, the correlation for productiveness reached the level of .69.)

Agreement between questionnaire and Rorschach on the mode of relation (Table B:4) shows significant agreement for sadism, masochism, destructiveness, and conditional love. There is extremely high agreement on scoring narcissism II and love, but the lack of examples of these traits in the sample prohibits the meaningful formulation of chi square tests of significance.

The one mode on which there is low agreement is narcissism I. There are three possible reasons for this. The first is that our criteria for scoring narcissism I from the questionnaire were not accurate. Indeed, the factor analysis implied that there were different kinds of narcissism I (see Chapter 5). The second is that our thematic scoring criteria for the Rorschach are inadequate or do not correspond to the criteria for scoring narcissism I from the questionnaire. A third possibility lies in the circumstances of administering the Rorschachs. When they were first given, some of the villagers decided that the "doctors" giving the test wanted them to see parts of the body in the ink blots. Not only did they oblige by looking for as many anatomical responses as they could find, but they also spread

---

[9] A different possible explanation for the difference in scoring might lie in the Rorschach analyst's tendency to overscore exploitativeness. In order to check on this, both scorers scored exploitativeness on the Rorschachs, and, as Table B:5 reports, there was significant agreement.

TABLE B:4 Questionnaire – Rorschach Agreement: Mode of Relation
(N=80)

Mode	+ +	+ -	- +	- -	x^2	Percent Agreement
Sadistic	15	3	27	35	8.86*	63
Masochistic	11	10	11	48	8.84*	74
Destructive	17	9	11	43	15.63*	75
Narcissism I	36	13	22	9	.06	44
Narcissism II	3	3	8	68	–	89
Conditional love (material care)	48	10	6	16	22.38*	80
Loving	0	5	0	75	–	94

*p is less than .01

the word that others would soon be seeing the pictures of internal organs. Since anatomy responses figure in the scoring of narcissism I, this might explain why more villagers are scored as expressing narcissism I on the Rorschach than on the interview.

Agreement measures were also calculated for the scoring of 30 Rorschach protocols by two independent analysts. Table B:5 reports that the two scorers reached significant agreement on the mode of assimilation. Table B:6 reports significant agreement on all modes of relatedness with the exception of sadism. In analyzing this particular lack of agreement, we found that it was often difficult to determine from the Rorschach content whether the individual was expressing sadism or masochism. For example, the content might include a saddled horse, which would indicate either the desire to dominate or the identification with the dominated horse. Similarly, a bent-over figure could be a symbol of either one's own submission or the wish to make others submit. In the context of the complete protocol, it is often possible to decide whether sadism or masochism predominates. But we would expect that both sadists and masochists have the complementary tendency, which may be repressed. The Rorschach responses may be better than interview responses in uncovering the repressed component. When we considered sadism and masochism as a single mode

TABLE B:5 Rorschach–Rorschach Agreement: Mode of Assimilation
(N=30)

Mode	+ +	+ -	- +	- -	x^2	Percent Agreement
Receptive	14	6	3	7	4.34*	70
Exploitative	13	5	3	9	7.16**	73
Hoarding	11	8	1	10	6.91**	70

*p is less than .05
**p is less than .01

TABLE B:6 Rorschach – Rorschach Agreement: Mode of Relation
(N=30)

Mode	+ +	+ –	– +	– –	χ^2	Percent Agreement
Sadistic	7	3	9	11	1.67	60
Masochistic	5	6	1	18	7.03*	77
Sado-masochism	13	3	3	11	10.74*	80
Destructive	8	2	2	18	14.70*	87
Narcissism I	20	2	3	5	9.35*	83
Narcissism II	2	2	0	26	–	93
Conditional love (material care)	20	0	4	6	15.00*	87
Loving	0	0	0	30	–	100

*p is less than .01

(sado-masochism) for the purpose of Rorschach scoring, there was significant agreement between the two Rorschach analysts (see Table B:6).

The product-moment correlation for productiveness as scored by the two Rorschach analysts was .67, which for 30 cases is significant at the 1 percent level.

SCORING CHARACTER FROM THE THEMATIC APPERCEPTION TEST

A final method of exploring the possibilities of scoring character from different measures was to analyze responses to the Thematic Apperception Test, which was given to 66 villagers.

From ten to twenty cards were administered to each subject. At first the full set was used, but for considerations of economy it was decided to use a minimal number of cards.[10] The subjects were instructed to tell stories in which the figures on the card take part. They were asked to tell a story with a beginning, middle, and end and to describe what the characters were thinking and feeling. As in customary in the administration of the TAT, the villagers were also encouraged to make the stories dramatic, to use their imagination.

Despite these instructions, and even when they were repeated, almost all of the stories told were short and concrete. Unlike TAT subjects in the United States or in urban Mexico, the peasant centers himself in the concrete reality of his senses. He is not comfortable making up an imaginary story. Rather, he describes what he sees, taking account of facial expres-

[10] When the shorter set was used, we included Cards 1, 2, 3BM, 4, 6BM, 6GF (for women), 8BM (for men), 8GF (for women), 10, 11, 12M (for men), 12F (for women), 13MF, 15, and 16.

sions and bodily positions to determine the emotions expressed in the drawings. While imaginative individuals from an industrial society tell stories in which people overcome obstacles to reach goals or in which they experience significant changes in their lives, the productive peasant is one who shows a deep interest in the feelings of the people he sees. This interest is reflected in his TAT responses. In fact, the TAT might be used as a test of "emotional intelligence"—the ability to perceive expressions and feelings of others and to make sense of them in terms of interpersonal relations.

In scoring character from a villager's stories, one must again be aware of the problem of determining how much of what the individual describes is *not* projection, but perceptiveness. Projection may begin when motives are ascribed to the figures or when the future is projected, although even then the peasant may describe real events that have happened to himself and to others, or realistic fears.

When the individual describes a situation which is clearly distorted (when a male figure is seen as female or an ugly face as beautiful) then it is safe to assume that the response is dynamically motivated. As in the case of the Rorschach, such distortion may be determined by the need to see others in one's own image or by the need to see a world which justifies one's own actions. Such distortion is particularly prevalent when a figure is thought to represent the mother. For example, the pregnant woman in Card 2 is a woman who appears hard, disdainful, proud, self-satisfied, or even hostile. As in many of the pictures, there is a range of emotions that the figure could be expressing, but this range is limited. To see the woman as friendly or warm would be a distortion. When the individual does see this figure as a warm mother who is showing loving concern for her family, he expresses his idealization of the mother, implying intense fixation.

Such a distortion would be even clearer in relation to Card 12F, where a witch-like figure is whispering to a younger woman. A common response of mother-fixated villagers is that the old woman is the mother or grandmother giving good advice on how to live well, and that if the young girl heeds the advice, life will go well for her. Some even say that the old woman is very sad because the young girl will not heed her good counsel. The distortion may be motivated by the individual's need to justify his or her dependence by seeing the mother figure always as good, so that the tie to the mother feels rational to him. If he were to see the mother as cruel or evil, he might suddenly become aware of the irrationality of his dependence. The independent villagers are more likely to see the old woman as a witch or a hag making an indecent proposition, one description (and there are other possible ones) that does fit the picture.

Besides distortion, character variables are also revealed by statements about what satisfies the people in the stories, what makes them frightened, what will be the results of their actions, and what is correct and incorrect behavior. Such statements are scored similarly to the questionnaire. The receptive individual states that the boy in Card 1 will learn to play the violin when he finds a good teacher who can give him his knowledge, but that all alone he is helpless and lost. The exploitative individual sees the motives of others as exploitative, as in Card 4, where the woman is said to be trying to get something out of the man and he is justified in getting what he can. The hoarding peasants also may see threats from all sides, but their solution is to follow a correct path and protect themselves from *compromisos* (commitments). One hoarding peasant responds to Card 1 (the boy and the violin), saying, "If he behaves himself [*si se porta bien*] he can be successful in his life, if he has good thoughts. His livelihood depends on that." This same peasant sees the relation between the man and woman in Card 4 as too dangerous. He assumes that the man is in a house of prostitution and that he would be better off elsewhere. "The man is thinking of the future, of getting married, in order to have life more economical and favorable."

The mode of relation may be revealed also in the individual's attitude toward the figures or to the story he tells. The sadist feels excitement in describing violence. The masochist is most interested in describing suffering. The destructive individual shows contempt for the weak, a rigid moralism that allows for no compassion. The indifferent individual may describe conflict or tragedy but without concern for others, unless he can identify himself with the pictures and tell a personal story. The extreme narcissist also puts himself into each story, but in such a way as to present a grandiose image of himself. The responsible individual voices his concern with complying with one's obligations, with providing material care. The loving individual expresses a deep interest in and compassion for the characters. A loving woman projects her concern in response to Card 4:

"I imagine this woman is the wife of this man. I don't know if he is sick or inebriated. She is mortified because he is going away. She considers following him where he goes because he does not want to understand. I don't know if his condition is because of illness or because of poverty, but he is desperate. But at last she tries to convince him and he remains. Because he is not drunk, he is desperate. She can tell him that they are going to work together and continue living."

We have described the distortion motivated by intense mother fixation. Less intense mother fixation may not lead to perceptual distortion, but is commonly expressed by the villagers in their responses to Card 6BM, showing a young man, hat in hand, with an old woman facing away from him. Practically all of the villagers see these two figures as mother and son, with the mother suffering because of her son's troubles, either because he has been unsuccessful or bad, or because he has left her. Here, the picture lends itself to the concept of the suffering, loving mother. The intensity of the mother fixation is expressed in the degree of dependency on the mother. For example, a young man tells a story of a boy who looks unsuccessfully for work and comes back empty-handed. But once with his mother again, he feels fine. "With the blessing of his mother, he should have many friends and the aid of God who will give him what he needs in order to end the suffering of his mama." Such a story shows an intense, irrational dependency on the mother.

Other stories told about Card 6BM may differ in the intensity of feeling expressed. Depending on the individual telling the story, other character attitudes may also be expressed. For example, a masochistic mother told a similar story, but emphasized the mother's suffering.

It is interesting to note that in the United States, Card 6BM frequently suggests the theme of a young man bringing bad news about the death of the woman's husband or son. These stories are generally interpreted as expressing the Freudian version of the Oedipal theme. In the village, stories hardly ever refer to anyone else but mother and son, and rather than the son replacing the father or triumphing over a sibling, the themes of male stories express the conflict between independence and deep fixation on the mother. If the son leaves the mother, he will be able to mature, to become independent, but he loses the mother's unconditional love and the illusion of total security. If he stays with the mother, he feels protected, but at the expense of his own strength and manliness. This conflict is not limited to the village men. Women often express the same conflict between dependence on the mother and independence.

AGREEMENT BETWEEN QUESTIONNAIRE AND TAT

The 66 questionnaires and TATs used for agreement testing were scored by the same person. The TATs were scored a year after the questionnaires. The agreement results for the mode of assimilation (Table B:7) show significant agreement on the scoring of the exploitative and hoarding modes, but not the receptive mode. In 36 percent of the cases, the scorer diagnosed receptiveness from the questionnaire but not from the TAT of the same person. We are unable to explain why this was the case. The

TABLE B:7 Questionnaire – TAT Agreement: Mode of Assimilation (N=66)

Mode	+ +	+ -	- +	- -	X^2	Percent Agreement
Receptive	16	24	6	23	2.03	55
Exploitative	18	8	17	23	4.52*	62
Hoarding	18	9	16	23	4.20*	62

*p is less than .05

best explanation on reviewing the scoring was that the TAT scorer only scored a dominant receptive orientation, considering receptive tendencies as present in practically all cases.

There was high agreement on the scoring of productiveness. The product-moment correlation between questionnaire and TAT scoring was .72, which is significant at the 1 percent level.

There was significant agreement on the scoring of masochism, destructiveness, extreme narcissism (II), indulgence, and love (Table B:8).

TABLE B:8 Questionnaire – TAT Agreement: Mode of Relation

Mode	+ +	+ -	- +	- -	X^2	Percent Agreement
Sadistic	8	3	30	25	1.24	50
Masochistic	18	4	16	28	12.13*	70
Destructive	14	16	5	31	8.58*	68
Narcissism I	10	8	21	27	.73	56
Narcissism II	11	12	4	39	12.67*	76
Narcissism I & II	33	8	12	13	7.56*	70
Indulgence	5	7	5	49	8.02*	82
Conditional love	19	23	9	15	.37	51
Loving	9	3	2	52	35.93*	92

*p is less than .01

Agreement was low on the scoring of sadism, narcissism I (indifference), and conditional love (material care). In the case of sadism, the scorer is more likely to diagnose sadism from the TAT than from the questionnaire. Since the Rorschach scoring also indicated more sadism than the questionnaire scoring, it is likely that the questionnaire is less sensitive than these other projective measures for diagnosing sadism. In the case of narcissism I, we found that the major disagreement was whether narcissism was extreme or not. If we test for the agreement between the scoring of narcissism from the questionnaire and TAT, leaving out distinctions between extreme or lesser narcissism, there is a statistically significant agreement between the two measures. In the case of conditional love, we felt that it was difficult to score from the TAT responses because it is essentially behavioral rather than dynamic.

We did not measure agreement between scoring parental fixations from the TAT and the questionnaire, since we were not able consistently to distinguish intense from moderate fixation on the TAT. The TAT pictures—particularly Cards 2, 6GF, 6BM, and 12—suggested themes of dependence on the mother to practically all of the villagers.

In summary, the significant agreement in scoring character on the basis of questionnaire, Rorschach, and TAT is further evidence on the side of confirming the accuracy of the questionnaire scoring and the power of the theory to interpret projective material from different tests.

Bibliography

ADORNO, T. W., ELSE FRENKEL-BRUNSWIK, DANIEL J. LEVINSON, and R. NEVITT SANFORD, *The Authoritarian Personality*. New York: Harper Brothers, 1950.

ARAMONI, ANICETO, *Psiconanálisis de la Dinámica de un Pueblo*. Mexico, D.F.: UNAM, 1961.

BANFIELD, EDWARD C., *The Moral Basis of a Backward Society*. Glencoe, Illinois: The Free Press, 1958.

BUNZEL, RUTH, "The Role of Alcoholism in Two Central American Cultures." *Psychiatry*, 3: 361-87, 1940.

DIEZ, DOMINGO, *Bosquejo Histórico Geográfico de Morelos*, Cuernavaca, Morelos: Editorial Tiahuica, 1967.

ERIKSON, ERIK H., *Childhood and Society* (2nd ed.). New York: W. W. Norton and Co., Inc., 1963.

FREUD, SIGMUND, "Character and Anal Eroticism" (1908) in *Collected Papers*, Vol. II. London: The Hogarth Press, 1956.

———, *Group Psychology and the Analysis of the Ego*. London: The Hogarth Press, 1922.

———, *An Outline of Psychoanalysis*. New York: W. W. Norton and Co., Inc., 1949.

FROMM, ERICH, *Escape from Freedom*. New York: Rinehart, 1941.

———, *Man for Himself*. New York: Rinehart, 1947.

———, *The Forgotten Language*. New York: Rinehart, 1951.

———, *The Art of Loving*. New York: Harper & Brothers, 1956.

———, *The Dogma of Christ*. New York: Holt, Rinehart & Winston, Inc., 1963.

———, *The Heart of Man*. New York: Harper & Row, Publishers, 1964.

FOSTER, GEORGE, *Tzintzuntzan, Mexican Peasants in a Changing World*. Boston: Little, Brown and Co., 1967.

GONÇALVES DE LIMA, OSWALDO, *El Maguey y El Pulque en los Codices Mexicanos*. Mexico: Fondo de Cultura Económica, 1956.

GONZÁLEZ PINEDA, FRANCISCO, *El Mexicano, Psicología de su Destructividad*. Mexico, D.F.: Editorial Pax-Mexicano, 1961.

HIRSCHMAN, ALBERT O., *Development Projects Observed*. Washington, D.C.: The Brookings Institution, 1967.

HUIZINGA, JOHAN, *The Waning of the Middle Ages*. London: Penguin Books, 1955.

JELLINEK, E. M., *The Disease Concept of Alcoholism*. New Haven: Hill House Press, 1960.

KNIGHT, ROBERT P., "The Psychodynamics of Chronic Alcoholism." *Journal of Nervous and Mental Diseases,* 86: 538-43, 1937.

LEWIS, OSCAR, *Life in a Mexican Village: Tepoztlán Restudied*. Urbana, Ill.: The University of Illinois Press, 1951.

MACCOBY, MICHAEL, "The Psychoanalytic Study of the American Public: Biophilia vs. Necrophilia" (unpublished manuscript, 1969).

————, NANCY MODIANO, and PATRICIA LANDER, "Games and Social Character in a Mexican Village." *Psychiatry,* 26: 150-62, 1964.

————, and NANCY MODIANO, "On Culture and Equivalence," in *Studies in Cognitive Growth*, J. C. Bruner et al. (ed.). New York: John Wiley & Sons, Inc., 1966.

————, and NANCY MODIANO, "Cognitive Style in Rural and Urban Mexico," *Human Development,* 12: 22-33, 1969.

McCLELLAND, DAVID C., *The Achieving Society*. Princeton: D. Van Nostrand Co., Inc., 1961.

McNAMAR, QUINN, *Psychological Statistics* (2nd ed.). New York: John Wiley & Sons, Inc., 1955.

McQUITTY, LOUIS L., "Elementary Factor Analysis." *Psychological Reports,* 9: 71-78, 1961.

————, "Improving the Validity of Crucial Decisions in Pattern Analytic Methods." *Educational and Psychological Measurement,* 28: 9-21, 1968.

MINTZ, SIDNEY W., "The Folk-Urban Continuum and the Rural Proletarian Community." *American Journal of Sociology,* 59: 136-43, 1953-54.

PAZ, OCTAVIO, *El Laberinto de la Soledad*. Mexico, D.F.: Fondo de Cultura Económica, 1959.

PIAGET, JEAN, *The Moral Judgment of the Child*, Glencoe, Ill.: The Free Press, 1955.

————, *Six Psychological Studies*. New York: Random House, 1967.

PITTMAN, DAVID J., and C. WAYNE GORDON, *Revolving Door*. New Haven: Yale Center of Alcohol Studies, 1958.

————, and CHARLES R. SNYDER (eds.), *Society, Culture and Drinking Patterns*. New York: John Wiley & Sons, Inc., 1962.

POTTER, JACK M., MAY N. DÍAZ, and GEORGE M. FOSTER (eds.), *Peasant Society, A Reader*. Boston: Little, Brown and Co., 1967.

RAMIREZ, SANTIAGO, *El Mexicano, Psicología de su Destructividad*. Mexico, D.F.: Editorial Pax-Mexicano, 1961.

REDFIELD, ROBERT, *Peasant Society and Culture, An Anthropological Approach to Civilization*. Chicago: The University of Chicago Press, 1956.

————, *Tepoztlán—a Mexican Village*. Chicago: The University of Chicago Press, 1930.

RORSCHACH, HERMAN, *Psychodiagnostics, A Diagnostic Test Based on Perception,* Berne: Hans Huber, 1942.

SCHACHTEL, ERNEST G., *Experiential Foundations of Rorschach's Test.* New York: Basic Books, Inc., 1966.

SCHAFER, ROY, *Psychoanalytic Interpretation in Rorschach Testing.* New York: Grune & Stratton, Inc., 1954.

SOUSTELLE, JACQUES, *The Daily Life of the Aztecs.* London: Penguin Books, 1964.

TANNENBAUM, FRANK, *The Mexican Agrarian Revolution.* New York: The Macmillan Co., 1929.

TAWNEY, R. H., *Religion and the Rise of Capitalism.* New York: Harcourt, Brace & Co., 1926.

THOMAS, WILLIAM I., and FLORIAN ZNANIECKI, *The Polish Peasant in Europe and America.* New York: Dover Publications, Inc., 1958.

WHETTEN, NATHAN L., *Rural Mexico.* Chicago: The University of Chicago Press, 1948.

WOLF, ERIC R., "Types of Latin American Peasantry: A Preliminary Discussion." *American Anthropologist,* 57: 452-71, 1955.

————, *Sons of the Shaking Earth.* Chicago: The University of Chicago Press, 1959.

WOMACK, JOHN, JR., *Zapata and the Mexican Revolution.* New York: Alfred A. Knopf, Inc., 1969.

Index

Roman Catholicism, *see* Religion
Rorschach tests, 102, 116*n*, 121, 229-30, 271-88
  alcoholics' responses to, 171*n*
  children's responses to, 185, 190, 192, 194-95, 275*n*
  questionnaire agreement with, 284-87, 291
  repression shown in, 227, 284-85
  scoring character from, 275-84
  training scorers of, 227
Rotated loadings, 92, 94*n*, 96-97

Sadism, 17, 88
  anal, 9
  alcoholism related to, 166-67 172
  authoritarian, 80-81, 262
  factor analysis of, 101-3, 105, 108-9
  parental, 21, 186*n*
  repressed, 116, 227
  scoring of, 85, 250, 252-53, 262
  sex-related, 151-52
  as symbiotic phenomenon, 74
  symbols expressing, 282
  test agreement on, 285-87
Salinas, Marta, 141
Schachtel, Ernest G., 276-77, 283-84
Schafer, Roy, 276, 281-83
Schechter, David, 13*n*
Schooling, *see* Education
Schwartz, Lola Romanucci, 150, 152, 272*n*
Schwartz, Theodore, 150, 272*n*
Secondary character traits, 232-33
Self-affirmative democratic syndrome, 195-96
SES, *see* Socioeconomic scale
"Sex and Character" (Fromm), 152*n*, 155*n*
Sex roles, 112*n*, 144-55
  of children, 187-88, 197
  factor analysis of, 98, 108
  productiveness influenced by, 147-48
  traditional, 116, 145
  See also Women
Silva Martínez, Miguel, 156*n*, 158
Smith, B., 24
Social character theory, 7, 16-23, 230-36
  confirmation of, 230-31
  defined, 16
  origin of, 7*n*
  primitive social character, 16-17
Social class, 17-18, 137-39
  of adult offspring, 200, 202
  of alcoholics, 173-78
  community participation related to, 63-65

Social class (*cont.*)
  composition of, 137
  land-based, 32, 53-55; *see also* Ejidatarios; Nonejidatarios
  male dominance and, 153-54
  of parents, 199, 201
  political orientation of, 81
  social character theory and, 230-34, 236
  See also Entrepreneurs
Social selection, 232-35
Socialization process, 14-15, 68-69
  aim of, 15
  character orientations in, 73-76
  defined, 68
Socioeconomic scale (SES), 57-67, 133
  alcoholism related to, 173
  distribution of households on, 59
  for household heads, 138
  product-moment correlations of, 128
  receptiveness correlated with, 135-36
Socioeconomic status, 137, 198-202
Socioeconomic variables, 124-43
  in cane industry, 130-33, 135
  women influenced by, 138-39
Sociopolitical orientations
  democratic vs. authoritarian, 105
  described, 80-82
  scoring of, 260-64
  See also Authoritarianism; Democratic character; Traditionalism
Sociopolitical relations, 85, 89-90
Soustelle, Jacques, 153, 170*n*
Spanish conquest, 31-32, 115, 145
  alcoholism related to, 170-71
Speer, Albert, 235*n*
Spinoza, Baruch, 73
Stavenhagen, Rodolfo, 237*n*
Stimulation, degree of, 215-17
Submissive-ingratiating syndrome, 195
Submissiveness
  attempts to change, 210, 219-20, 222
  of children, 189, 191-92, 194-95
  distribution of, 89-90
  factor analysis of, 93, 99-100, 105-6
  scoring of, 85, 262-63
  sex-related, 145-46, 155
Survival goal, psychic and physical, 14-15
Suspicion, *see* Distrust
Symbiotic mothers, 192, 196, 200
Symbiotic relatedness, 73-74, 251
Symbols, 277-83
  character orientations expressed by, 281-83
  cultural, 277-78
  "universal," 279